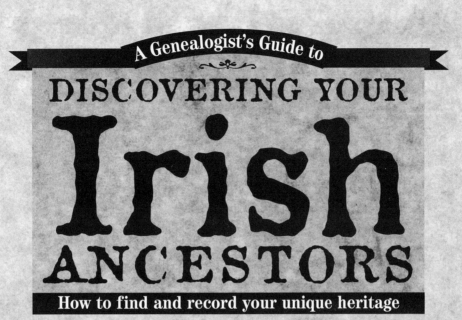

A Genealogist's Guide to

DISCOVERING YOUR
Irish
ANCESTORS

How to find and record your unique heritage

Dwight A. Radford and Kyle J. Betit

BETTERWAY BOOKS
CINCINNATI, OHIO

www.familytreemagazine.com

About the Authors

DWIGHT A. RADFORD is a native of Ooltewah, Tennessee. He resides in Salt Lake City, Utah, with his wife, Cindy, and daughter, Alexandria, where he has been doing genealogy professionally since 1986. He specializes in Irish and Irish immigrant research and travels to the Republic of Ireland and Northern Ireland yearly to conduct on-site research for his clients.

KYLE J. BETIT is a professional genealogist, author, lecturer, and columnist and former coeditor of *The Irish At Home and Abroad* journal. He makes frequent trips to Ireland for research and works in applying genealogy research to medical genetics studies. Kyle is also master of ceremonies and codirector of the Good Samaritan Program at the Cathedral of the Madeleine in Salt Lake City.

05 04 03 02 01   5 4 3 2 1

Library of Congress Cataloging-in-Publication Data

Radford, Dwight A.
    A genealogist's guide to discovering your Irish ancestors / Dwight A. Radford and Kyle J. Betit.
        p.   cm.
    Includes bibliographical references and index.
    ISBN 1-55870-577-5
    1. Ireland—Genealogy—Handbooks, manuals, etc. 2. Irish Americans—Genealogy— Handbooks, manuals, etc. I. Betit, Kyle J. II Title.

CS483 .R33 2001
929′.1′0899162—dc21   00-066690
                                                                                  CIP

Editor: Sharon DeBartolo Carmack, CG
Production editor: Brad Crawford
Production coordinator: Mark Griffin
Interior designer: Sandy Conopeotis Kent
Icon designer: Cindy Beckmeyer
Cover designers: Melissa Wilson and Angela Wilcox

DEDICATION

I dedicate this book to two special people: my wife, Cindy T. Radford, who found out she had breast cancer one month into the writing of this book; and my daughter Alexandria Radford, who grew up and became twelve years old as this book was being finished. They deserve my special mention for their courage. I admire and love them both.

—Dwight A. Radford

I dedicate this book to my four grandparents: Sarah Jane Bonsall Lupro, who first shared with me her love for genealogy when I was nine years old and has continued to share that love with me ever since; Ethel Mae LeTourneau Betit, who during the writing of this book went ahead to join the Lord in heaven, where she no doubt prepares a place for us at His table as she so often did at hers; Lt. Colonel Joseph W. Betit, for whose service to his country and his family I shall always be deeply grateful; and Charles Harrison Lupro, from whom I inherited my Irish Catholicism, which was passed down from his grandmother, Bridget Branniff Butsch, of the County Down Branniff family.

—Kyle J. Betit

We would both like to dedicate this book to James R. Reilly (1921–2000), our good friend and colleague and our strongest critic.

❧

Acknowledgments

We would like to thank the many people who helped make this book possible. Since we strongly believe in the international aspect of Irish genealogy, we have asked key people around the world to preview our manuscript. Among them are Linda Clayton of Dublin, Ireland, a member of the Association of Professional Genealogists in Ireland and the Certified Genealogists Alumni Group, whose efficient research in Dublin records has helped us greatly; Gwen Reiher of the New Zealand Society of Genealogists, who taught us how important are the New Zealand branches of our Irish families; James R. Reilly, CGRS, who blessed us by transplanting himself from his home in Brooklyn, New York, to Salt Lake City, Utah, in his retirement years to seek out a better understanding of Irish genealogy sources; Rosemary Ardolina of Brooklyn, New York; Mary E. Noone of Boston, Massachusetts, who has been our kind host and a true friend over the years; Elizabeth Kelley Kerstens, CGRS, of the National Genealogical Society in Washington, DC, for her support and reviews; and the staff of the British Isles department of the Family History Library in Salt Lake City, Utah, for their encouragement, input, and consistent help, particularly reference consultants Judith Eccles Wight, AG, and Hazel M. Tibbits, AG.

We also would like to thank the following for their mentoring and assistance: David E. Rencher, AG, head of the Family History Library; Steven C. ffeary-Smyrl, probate researcher of Dublin, Ireland; Dr. Bruce S. Elliott of Carleton University, Ottawa, Ontario, Canada; Laura Hanowski of the Saskatchewan Genealogical Society; Perry C. McIntyre of the Society of Australian Genealogists; Patricia Keeney Geyh of the Irish Genealogical Society of Wisconsin; and Suzanne McVetty, CG, a genealogical writer and reseacher of Carle Place, New York. We have learned much from and been helped generously by a list of other colleagues and friends that would go on too long to include here. We are deeply grateful for all of their contributions.

Table of Contents At a Glance

Table of Contents

Introduction

ABOUT US AND ABOUT THIS BOOK

Allow us to introduce ourselves. We are Kyle Betit and Dwight Radford, and we are both professional genealogists and lecturers. Several years ago, we decided to learn all we could about Irish genealogy. The more we delved into it, the more we realized that there was more to it than we had thought. We realized that the biggest problem for most people is getting "over the water," where the use of Irish records then becomes possible. Our experience came partly from tracing the Irish ancestors of our clients. We also published for six years an in-depth Irish genealogy journal, *The Irish At Home and Abroad,* which provided us with an extensive education about Irish and Irish immigrant research. Much of the knowledge we share with you in this book originated in the articles published in *The Irish At Home and Abroad* (1993–1999).

What opportunities do you get from picking up our book and reading about Irish genealogy? You will learn skills to find out about your family generations, the dates and places of important events in their lives, details about how they lived, and what emigrating from Ireland was like. You may be able to find and visit an exact place in Ireland your family came from. We're not just talking about visiting a town or a village. We're talking about setting your foot on the exact spot where your ancestors' house stood. One year, in County Limerick, Ireland, we discovered that the old home of our client's family had been torn down. But we did meet some of her relatives, who said to our astonishment, "We knew someday somebody from America or Australia would come looking for that house, and we've saved some bricks and pieces of the fire grate for you." Was our client happy! This is Irish research at its best. In this book, we want to share the steps that got us to this point.

This book is designed for readers with varying experience in genealogy research. You don't have to know a lot about the subject to use this book to trace your Irish ancestors. Having said this, we must admit that interspersed in this book is some more advanced material. So if you're an experienced researcher, don't be afraid this book will have nothing to offer you. We guarantee you, it will. Because this book is primarily for beginners, though, we have chosen not to cover all possible topics. As if we could! No book on Irish research is complete because of the very nature of the subject. We are constantly learning, just like everyone else, about new sources and strategies. This continual learning is at the heart of Irish research for everyone from the beginner to the seasoned professional. We offer you what we have learned from years of experience, but it may be that the solution to your research lies in your own imagination. We invite you on the journey with us to learn about Irish research and where our imaginations have taken us.

GENERAL GUIDES

There are some standard Irish genealogical works on the market that we are referring to as Grenham's work or Ryan's book. For a list of these standard works, we refer you to the first subsection of chapter twenty-one, "Irish Genealogy and Archives Guides (General)." This will keep us from having to refer to these works in the References and Further Reading section of each chapter.

REPOSITORY CODES

We thought it necessary to provide certain codes for repositories mentioned throughout this book. Here are ones you need to be aware of:

Important

Repository Names	
DFHL:	Dublin Friends Historical Library
FHL:	Family History Library in Salt Lake City, Utah
GO:	Genealogical Office in Dublin
NAI:	National Archives of Ireland in Dublin
NLI:	National Library of Ireland in Dublin
OS:	Ordnance Survey in Dublin
PRO:	Public Record Office at Kew, Surrey, England
PRONI:	Public Record Office of Northern Ireland in Belfast
RCBL:	Representative Church Body Library in Dublin

We realize this can be somewhat cumbersome. To make up for it, we have provided an up-to-date inventory of repositories in the Appendix.

Good luck and happy researching.

Kyle J. Betit
Dwight A. Radford

ONE

What to Do: The Basic Strategies

This section aims to assist you with some important strategies to use in determining your family's origins in Ireland. We begin with a discussion of some issues regarding Irish surnames and given names that may help you to avoid some pitfalls in your research. Then we discuss various strategies for refining what you know about your Irish ancestors. The strategies you use will depend on what you already know about your Irish origins: whether you (1) know only that your ancestors came from Ireland, (2) know the county in Ireland, (3) know the parish, or (4) know the townland of origin. The information you start with may come from your family's oral tradition; a home source such as a Bible, letter, or missal; or a document in your possession, like an obituary.

IRISH NAMES
Given Names

To successfully trace your Irish ancestors, you will need to understand a certain complexity to Irish given names. **Your ancestor may have used several given names during his or her life.** There may have been more than one formal name, including a christening or confirmation name, and nicknames were often used. As a result, you need to be very careful about the assumptions you make based on given names. For Catholics the situation is further complicated because English, Gaelic, and Latin equivalents of given names may have been used in records.

Important

When names are recorded in church records or in civil registrations of births, marriages, and deaths, nicknames may be used instead of formal given names. (For example, Kate for Catherine, Con for Cornelius, or Lackey for Lawrence.) Many nicknames are easy to spot, but others are not, such as Delia for Bridget or Sarah for Cecilia. While undertaking a search, East Galway Heritage Centre identified a death in 1897 registered for Sarah Rhatican. The Heritage Centre noted in its report that Celia and Sarah are often used interchangeably. Indeed, this Sarah was registered as Cecilia when she married, and on registration of her children's births, she was using the name Cecilia or Celia. Two books we recommend that list nicknames are Ronan Coghlan's *Irish Christian Names* and, for Scots-Irish, Leslie Alan Dunkling's *Scottish Christian Names*.

Many of the Irish Catholic parish registers are recorded in Latin, so unless you have a basic understanding of Latin names, you might not recognize your ancestor's baptism or marriage. Some names are fairly easy to translate, such as Maria for Mary or Johannes/Joannes for John; others are not, such as Gulielmus or Guglielmus for William. Some Latin names can have more than one English translation, such as Jacobus, which stands for both Jacob and James.

It is helpful to have a list of Latin names and their English equivalents for reference when reading Latin text. One recommended source is the list in Charles T. Martin's *The Record Interpreter*.

For More Info

SOURCES FOR IRISH GIVEN NAMES AND SURNAMES

Coghlan, Ronan. *Irish Christian Names: An A–Z of First Names.* London: Cassell Ltd., 1979.

Dunkling, Leslie Alan. *Scottish Christian Names: An A–Z of First Names.* London: Cassell Ltd., 1978.

MacLysaght, Edward. *The Surnames of Ireland.* 6th ed. Dublin: Irish Academic Press, 1985.

Maguire, Fidelma. *Irish Names.* Dublin: The Lilliput Press, 1990.

Martin, Charles T. *The Record Interpreter: A Collection of Abbreviations, Latin Words and Names Used in English Historical Manuscripts and Records.* London: Stevens and Sons, Ltd., 1910.

Matheson, Robert E. *Varieties and Synonyms of Surnames and Christian Names in Ireland.* Dublin: Stationery Office, 1901. Reprint, Baltimore: Genealogical Publishing Co., 1968.

O'Dwyer, Riobard. *Who Were My Ancestors?* 4 vols. Astoria, Ill.: K.K. Stevens Publishing, 1976–1989.

Woulfe, Rev. Patrick. *Irish Names and Surnames.* Reprint, Baltimore: Genealogical Publishing Co., 1969.

In some instances names are used interchangeably, such as Eugene and Owen. The Latin or the Irish (Gaelic) name may explain why certain names are used interchangeably. For example, because the Irish (Gaelic) form of Jeremiah or Jerome is Diarmaid, Darby or Dermot is often used in place of Jeremiah or Jerome.

Surnames

Family names, like given names, have variations and peculiarities that can provide some surprising twists. **Variations in both *form* and *spelling* are common problems.** One of the most useful guides available regarding the complexity of Irish surnames is Robert E. Matheson's *Varieties and Synonyms of Surnames and Christian Names in Ireland*. Matheson's 1890 study was based on the family names found in the civil registration of that year. Local variations in spelling, the use of prefixes, and older forms of surnames are some of the helpful topics Matheson discusses. To illustrate this point, we would like to share the story of a fellow researcher (Judith Eccles Wight, AG) who was tracing Delia Holland. When Wight eventually located records of the family in Ireland, the woman's name was found as Bridget Houlihan. As a side note, Hawney, Mulholland, and Wholiham (the older, or Irish, form) are also variations of the Holland surname, and Bedelia and Fidelia are variants of Delia as well.

Particular letters were often substituted for other letters. Some of the more frequent substitutions are *A* and *E* (McAvoy and McEvoy); *C*, *K*, and *G* (Millican, Millikan and Milligan); *C* and *K* (Carney and Kearney); *G* and *K* (Gilhooley and Killooley); and *P* and *W* (Phelan and Whelan).

One of the most common variations you will find is the adding and dropping of *O'* and *Mc* before Irish family names. You may see the family listed as Connor and O'Connor in the same church register. Immigrants from Ireland often dropped or added the *O'* and *Mc* prefixes in their new countries. There's no hard and fast rule about this principle.

One of the most interesting phenomena with Irish names is that sometimes a different surname will be used from the one you are expecting. This happens often with names that are very common in a particular area. For example, we were researching the Briscoe family, which emigrated from Ireland to Australia and then to the United States. When we found them in Kiltoom parish, County Roscommon, the church records appeared to be of no help until we visited the area. We found out from the local people that the Donnelly surname is so common in the area that a branch took the name Briscoe. The local Briscoes all know that historically they're really Donnellys. As you can imagine, this required another search of the church records.

The bottom line is that you must be careful in researching Irish names both at home and abroad. Use available resource books (see page 4), your imagination, and maybe the assistance of a library or heritage centre in Ireland.

What about maiden names? Did Irish Catholic women tend to use their maiden names as their legal names after marriage, as many Italian and French Catholics did? The answer is not clear-cut. Irish women abroad generally used the custom of the culture in which they were living. Thus, in the United States and English-speaking Canada, Irish women went by their husbands' surnames. However, it was the custom among French Canadians in Quebec for women to retain their maiden names throughout life. In many places in Ireland itself, it was customary in casual conversation for married women to be referred to by their maiden names. However, official documents kept by the government usually record a woman by her married name. If you are looking at Catholic parish registers in Ireland, it is often difficult to tell whether a woman is being referred to by her maiden or married name when listed as a godparent or witness. For example, if you see the following three pairs listed as godparents in a baptismal register, are all three the same pair, or are you dealing with more than one Mary?

John and Mary Kelly
John Kelly and Mary Kelly
John Kelly and Mary Sullivan

WHAT TO DO IF YOU KNOW IRELAND ONLY AS YOUR ANCESTOR'S PLACE OF ORIGIN

Technique

If you don't know anything about where your ancestor came from in Ireland, you usually will need to concentrate on sources of the country where your immigrant family settled. There is a wide range of sources in the adoptive country that may hold the key to your family's origins. We do not recommend in most cases that you try to use Irish records if you don't yet know about the family's origins in Ireland. Here are some strategies.

Pursue sources in the adopted land: It is impossible to know in advance which sources will tell you where in Ireland your ancestor was born. You will find many sources useful regardless of whether they state a specific birthplace. As far as listing an Irish place of origin, some of the most useful sources include obituaries, death certificates, and tombstones. These are all records created at a person's death when the family reflects on their loved one's life. For earlier time periods, such as the eighteenth century, you may find family histories and military records useful. Censuses, marriage records, church records, and local histories are also important potential sources. Trace the immigrant ancestor step by step back in time to compile documents from arrival in the adoptive country until death and burial. Besides finding the actual birthplace in Ireland, you will want to look for other important clues, such as the birth date and parents' names, especially the mother's maiden name. It is essential for you not to limit the scope of the sources you use.

Research the extended family: Consider not only records about your immigrant ancestor, but also about other relatives, such as brothers and sisters, who may have come from Ireland. We have found this to be one of the most important principles of Irish research. Trace the lives of these relatives and examine records about them to see where they were born. For example, if you are tracing a Boston Irish family's origins, the answer may lie in records created about a sister or brother who settled in Butte, Montana; Christchurch, New Zealand; or Merthyr-Tydfil, Wales.

Trace associations with friends and neighbors: Immigrants from the same community in Ireland often emigrated together and settled together abroad. If you think about it, it makes sense that people were more likely to go somewhere where they knew someone. For this reason, if an ancestor's origins cannot be found, research might be more successful by focusing on the origins of neighbors and associates. **The three kinds of migration you are likely to encounter are**

Group migration refers to a group of relatives or friends emigrating together at one time from Ireland.

Chain migration refers to a process over a number of years, in which later emigrants follow relatives or friends who emigrated earlier.

Congregational migration refers to a group of members of a particular congregation or surrounding geographical area in Ireland emigrating with a minister.

Both group migration and chain migration were prominent features of the Irish exodus. Some communities were settled largely by immigrants from a particular place in Ireland. In urban areas, Irish from one county often settled in a specific section of a city over the years. An excellent example of chain migration is in Marie Daly's study of Irish immigrants in Boston. She documented settlements from particular Irish counties in Boston neighborhoods in the chapter "Sources of Irish-American Genealogy" in *The Irish in New England*. Another example is Bruce S. Elliott's *Irish Migrants in the Canadas: A New Approach* in which Dr. Elliott meticulously reconstructed the chain migration of 775 Protestant families from County Tipperary to Ontario and Quebec provinces in Canada.

A neighborhood begins to emerge when you can document persons living in the same general area, whether that means on the same watercourse, in the same township, in the same urban parish, or on the same street. For example, the records of a parish may tell you the names of witnesses at marriages and godparents at baptisms. These people are prime candidates to be friends or relatives with common Irish origins.

Trace the immigrant ancestor's descendants: We also advise researching your immigrant ancestor's children and even grandchildren to see if something recorded about their lives gives the family's origins in Ireland. For example, a child's birth or death certificate may give the parents' origins. Irish emigrants of the eighteenth century could have thousands of descendants today, one of whom may have published a book or article preserving the family's origins.

Identify intermediate countries of migration: It is important to remember that your Irish ancestor may have gone to another country prior to settling somewhere permanently. Census records are often the first indication that a family lived in an intermediate country. You may discover that one of your ancestor's children is listed in a census as born not in Ireland or in the country where they settled, but in some country in between. For example, in one Nova Scotia census, we came across the family of Murtoch Callaghan, who had children born in Malta, Corfu, and then Nova Scotia. It's no big surprise that we found that this man was serving in the British Army and can be documented in the records of the 97th Earl of Ulster's Regiment. In particular, many immigrants spent some years in England, Scotland, or Wales prior to going elsewhere.

Rare Irish surnames: If your family has a particularly rare surname, it may be found in only one locality in Ireland. Some books identify the origins of surnames in Ireland, such as Edward MacLysaght's *The Surnames of Ireland*. In most cases Irish surnames are common and can be found just about everywhere. We have cringed more than once when someone has approached us at an Irish gathering convinced that a surname is from a particular county because of one of those popular "surname maps." Unfortunately, it's just not that simple with the vast majority of Irish surnames. But in the case of a very rare surname, MacLysaght's book can help. For example, it shows that the surname Braniff was historically found exclusively on the Ards Peninsula of County Down. You may also use the CD-ROM *Index to Griffith's Primary Valuation*, produced by Brøderbund, to look at the distribution of an uncommon surname in Ireland (see page 269).

Technique

WHAT TO DO IF YOU KNOW THE COUNTY IN IRELAND

If you know the county of origin in Ireland, your goal will be to identify the parish and townland or town of origin. For a full discussion of parishes and townlands, see chapter nine. Knowing a place within a county will be necessary to continue your research in records such as church registers, estate papers, and cemetery transcripts.

More research abroad may be needed: Even if a county has been identified, additional research in records outside Ireland may be necessary to make sure it is the correct county. Don't be alarmed if you find that your ancestor's death certificate lists one county in Ireland as a place of origin, and a brother or sister's lists a different county. Counties such as Cork, Dublin, and Londonderry (Derry) were often the place of departure rather than the actual origin of the family. This accounts for some of the confusion in records abroad. Also, diligent research in records abroad may reward you with the name of the townland or parish within the county.

Researching all branches of the family abroad: There may be historical information available about where emigrants from a county went abroad, for example, County Clare to Australia, counties Longford and Westmeath to Argentina, the Beara Peninsula (Cork) to mining areas such as Montana and Utah in the United States. You can use this information in tracking lost Irish family members. Heritage centres and history books are good sources of information about migrations from particular counties.

Other information known about the ancestors: When a county of origin is known, additional clues about the family, such as religion or occupation, may suggest places of residence within that county. For example, members of minority religions such as Moravians and Quakers lived in specific settlements in Ireland, and miners from Wicklow may be from the copper and sulphur mines of the Avoca area.

Using heritage centres in Ireland: Ireland has a group of heritage centres that have indexed records on a county basis. If you know your family's county of origin and you have enough details about the family, you can search the centre's index to identify a parish. A centre will no doubt find multiple John Murphys, and it will not be possible to know which is your ancestor without more information. Possible additional details include a father's name, mother's maiden name, or siblings' names (see chapter sixteen).

Irish records usable with a known county: Some types of Irish records may be used effectively when a county of residence, but not a parish or townland, is known. Each of these records is discussed in detail elsewhere in this book.

WHAT TO DO IF YOU KNOW A PARISH IN IRELAND

If you have found the name of a parish of origin, you still have to figure out what that really means. **There are two distinct types of parishes in Ireland:** (1) the civil, or government, parish and (2) the ecclesiastical, or church, parish. Both types of parishes comprised surveyed parcels of land known as townlands (see chapter nine). Maps of civil parish boundaries are in Brian Mitchell's *A New Genealogical Atlas of Ireland*. James G. Ryan's *Irish Records: Sources for Family & Local History* lists Catholic parishes located within each civil parish. Approximate Catholic parish boundaries in each county can be found in John Grenham's book.

\di'fin\ *vb*

Definitions

CHURCH AND CIVIL PARISHES

Records may identify a civil or church parish as a place of origin, but in some cases it may be unclear which type of parish a record refers to. In general, a reference to an Irish parish found in church records abroad is a reference to an ecclesiastical parish. A reference in a civil record may refer to a civil parish in Ireland. Religious denominations in Ireland other than the Catholic Church and Church of Ireland did not use a parish system. A parish named for a Presbyterian, Methodist, Moravian, Baptist, Congregational, Mormon, or Quaker ancestor is most likely the civil parish.

With the re-emergence of the Roman Catholic church in the late eighteenth century, the Catholic parish system rapidly expanded. A civil parish can have one or more Catholic parishes within its boundaries; the Catholic and civil parish names may or may not be the same. A Catholic parish is often known by two or three names.

The Church of Ireland parish boundaries generally followed those of the civil parishes. But there may not have been enough members to support a Church of Ireland church in each civil parish. Consequently, parishes joined together as one functional parish. Sometimes more than one Church of Ireland parish existed within a civil parish. This was especially true in Ulster, Dublin city, and Cork city, where there were greater numbers of Church of Ireland members.

For More Info

Once you are clear about the meaning of the parish name you have found, you can find the townland or town of origin. The following are record sources that are discussed in detail elsewhere in this book; however, here we offer some specific strategies:

Church records: Church records of various denominations sometimes list townlands of residence for members. The spellings of townland names may vary from civil records. Sometimes a place name refers to an area *within* a townland or is a historical townland name no longer in use.

If townlands are not given in a church register, you may still find the register useful for determining a townland of residence. For example, Catholic church registers usually list godparents for baptisms and witnesses for marriages. You can determine where the sponsors and witnesses lived by using a source such as Griffith's Primary Valuation, which covers 1847 to 1864. Your ancestral family probably lived in the same or a neighboring townland, since family members and close friends usually acted as godparents and witnesses. Even if your ancestor had emigrated before Griffith's Primary Valuation, the sponsors and witnesses may have remained. Sometimes this is the only way to determine a townland of residence within a parish.

Heritage centres: If you have found a parish of origin, the appropriate centre can search its indexes to confirm the parish by locating the ancestral family in church registers. The centre can focus its search on the parish of interest rather than researching the whole county. This can help sort through families with common surnames and given names. We advise you to specifically request that the centre provide townlands of residence and names of sponsors and witnesses from church registers (see chapter sixteen).

Censuses and census substitutes: Censuses, census fragments, and census substitutes can be used to pinpoint where within a parish a family was living in a given year (see chapter eleven).

Taxation records: Use Griffith's Primary Valuation (for the years 1847 to 1864) and the Tithe Applotment Books (for 1823 to 1837) to determine the townland of residence of an ancestor in the early to mid nineteenth century. If the ancestor left before these records were compiled, you can use these two sources (described in chapter twenty-three) to determine townlands within the civil parish in which the surname appeared. Tax records are among the best means of identifying townlands of residence in nineteenth-century Ireland.

WHAT TO DO IF YOU KNOW A TOWNLAND IN IRELAND

Technique

If you know the townland your ancestor came from, you can access a wide range of sources to finish documenting your family history. Knowing the townland opens up one of the most exciting prospects in Irish research: finding your ancestral home site (or what's left). Even if a townland of origin has been identified in a record or in oral history, you still need to *prove* that this is the right townland by documenting your ancestors in records.

The townland is the smallest official geographical unit in Ireland. Townlands usually consist of a few to several thousand acres and often have Gaelic names. They have specific boundaries, often defined by geographical features such as river valleys, mountains, and hills. The boundaries of townlands were officially surveyed in the 1830s by the Ordnance Survey. Due to their small size, townlands do not usually appear on standard road maps or atlases you would buy in the average bookstore. However, the Ordnance Survey of Ireland and Ordnance Survey of Northern Ireland have published modern road maps, called the "Discovery Series" in the Republic and the "Discoverer Series" in the north, that show townland names but not townland boundaries.

Townland names are often misspelled even in official records. It may take some research to determine the official spelling. A townland name may be so misspelled that you can't identify it in a gazetteer. This often occurs in Irish civil registration records. A quick way to determine the official spelling of the townland is to scan Griffith's Primary Valuation for your civil parish. You can also use George B. Handran's *Townlands in Poor Law Unions: A Reprint of Poor Law Union Pamplets of the General Registrar's Office*. If you don't already know the parish your townland was in, see below for some strategies to determine the parish.

For More Info

GOING FROM TOWNLAND TO PARISH

You may find yourself with the name of a townland and county from records abroad, but no name for the parish it was located in. There are sources to help in this case. Use the 1851, 1871, and 1901 *General Alphabetical Index to the Townlands and Towns, Parishes and Baronies of Ireland* to find the official spelling and location of each townland (with its corresponding civil parish). The 1871 (FHL #476999 item 2) and 1901 (FHL #865092) indexes are available on microfilm. The 1851 edition has been reprinted by Genealogical Publishing Company and is widely available. Ireland's townland names are also being placed in a computerized database on the Internet at the IreAtlas Project web site: <http://www.seanruad.com>. Remember that there may be many townlands of the same name in one county, but each in a different civil parish, so it is important to identify the correct townland. Tax records, land records, and other sources can assist in documenting the ancestral family in the correct townland.

The following are some of the many sources you can use once you know the townland. These can help to flesh out your knowledge of your ancestors' lives and the community in which they lived.

Griffith's Townland Valuation and Tenement Valuation manuscript materials: The compilation of the Townland Valuation in Ireland beginning in 1830 was supervised by commissioner Richard Griffith, after whom the valuations are named. In the course of their work, the valuators compiled manuscript land field books and manuscript house books. The former described what the land and soil in each townland was like, and the latter described the physical dimensions of houses and construction material. All these details can give you an idea as to what kind of environment your ancestor lived in. Was it rich farming land or bog? Were they well-constructed houses or simple mud huts? Some land books recorded names of occupiers. House books listed the name of each person occupying any house that was measured. The manuscript land books and house books are accessible at the National Archives of Ireland (NAI), Valuation Office, and Public Record Office of Northern Ireland (PRONI).

The same type of information is in another survey supervised by Richard Griffith called the Tenement Valuation, which began in 1844 and used the individual tenant's holding as the basis for valuation. Manuscript "perambulation books" and house books were developed in the field prior to the printing of Griffith's Primary Valuation. The perambulation books (sometimes mislabeled as "tenure books") will tell you the situation under which your ancestor held land, such as by a lease, renting from year to year, or squatting (listed as "free" in the records). All of this is valuable information when reconstructing the history of your family. The manuscript books are available at the Valuation Office, NAI and PRONI (see chapter twenty-three).

Estate papers: Most of our ancestors were occupiers rather than owners of land. The private papers of their landlords, commonly called estate papers, may hold valuable details about the tenants on the estate. There may even be comments recorded about the tenants such as "lazy," "industrious," or "does not pay rent on time." Two of the most common types of estate records are rent rolls and leases. Other interesting documents are emigration lists, petitions to the landowner, mortgages, and records of evictions (see chapter fifteen).

Registry of Deeds: The Lands Index or County Index to the Registry of Deeds is arranged geographically. This index is divided by county or city and time period, and groups townland names by first letter. The County Index is an important source because it identifies all registered transactions for a particular townland. This will give you a history of land ownership and occupation in your ancestral townland. The indexes to the Registry of Deeds are available on microfilm at the Family History Library (FHL) (see chapter nineteen).

Locating the home site using Griffith's Valuation maps: Each property listed in Griffith's Primary Valuation (1847–1864) was assigned a map reference number, found in the left-hand column of the record. The numbers correspond to a set of maps where the ancestral lands or home can be located. The Griffith's Primary Valuation maps for Republic of Ireland counties are held at the NAI with electronically scanned copies at the Valuation Office in Dublin. The maps for Northern Ireland are held at the PRONI (see chapter twenty-three).

CONCLUSION

Reminder

- **Be careful in looking for variations in Irish given names and surnames because they may be spelled inconsistently.**
- If you only know Ireland as the place of your ancestor's origin, concentrate on records in the country where he or she settled to find at least a county in Ireland, the names of brothers and sisters, and ideally the mother's maiden name.
- If you know the county of origin, you have a number of options. You can

write to that county's heritage centre to request a search. You can continue your immigrant research to get a more specific place name than the county. Finally, you can search Irish records to see if you can narrow your family's origins further.

- Once you have a parish name, make sure you know what kind of parish it refers to (church or civil). Then you can search church records, tax records, censuses, and census substitutes for your Irish parish to find out what townland your ancestors were living in.
- Knowing your ancestor's townland of residence makes available a myriad of records that can help to reconstruct the lives of your ancestors, even to the point of identifying the exact plot of land they lived on.

REFERENCES AND FURTHER READING

Sources

Daly, Marie E. "Sources of Irish-American Genealogy in New England." In *The Irish in New England,* by Thomas O'Connor, Marie E. Daly, and Edward L Galvin, 10-24. Boston: New England Historic Genealogical Society, 1985.

Elliott, Bruce S. *Irish Migrants in the Canadas: A New Approach.* Kingston and Montreal: McGill-Queen's University Press, 1988.

General Alphabetical Index to the Townlands and Towns, Parishes and Baronies of Ireland. Based on the Census of Ireland for the Year 1851. 1861. Reprint. Baltimore: Genealogical Publishing Co., 1984.

Handran, George B. *Townlands in Poor Law Unions: A Reprint of Poor Law Union Pamphlets of the General Registrar's Office.* Salem, Mass.: Higginson Book Company, 1997.

MacLysaght, Edward. *The Surnames of Ireland.* 6th ed. Dublin: Irish Academic Press, 1985.

Mitchell, Brian. *A Guide to Irish Parish Registers.* Baltimore: Genealogical Publishing Co., 1988.

———. *A New Genealogical Atlas of Ireland.* Baltimore: Genealogical Publishing Co., 1986.

TWO

United States

Tip

I n our search for the Irish in America, we have grown in our awareness of just how complicated the Irish-American experience is. We have also found that historians, for the sake of weaving together this complex history, have sometimes unknowingly contributed to its oversimplification. There are many good books that recount the history of Irish America, and we refer you to a few of these in this chapter. However, **we also have had the chance to see the history in a different light—from the perspective of individual families and communities.** Some of the major points we have observed that have directly affected our genealogical research:

1. During the colonial time period (pre-1776) there were more Roman Catholic Irish in America than anyone can document. The reason for this is that outside Catholic areas, such as Maryland or the Spanish-occupied Gulf Coast, Catholic worship was prohibited. Under British rule, the Church of England (later the Episcopal Church) was the predominant faith. In New England the Congregational Church was the predominant faith. So just because your ancestors were Catholic, don't neglect colonial Protestant records.

2. America is truly a "melting pot." We've all heard this term, but our studies have shown that in the United States the Irish intermarried and had children with Native Americans, African Americans, and just about every other ethnic group imaginable. These mixed-blood families often merged into the larger American society and consequently lost their Irish identity. In fact, we believe you're going to be hard pressed to find an African American or Native American family with roots in the southern United States that does not also have an Irish ancestor. We provide an example of the Scots-Irish in this chapter, and we discuss the Native Americans to illustrate our point (see page 43).

3. With the Irish and religion, people tend to assume that their ancestors always did what they themselves would have done. To be frank, they

didn't. We can't judge our ancestors by our standards. We find all the time that Irish Catholics either left the church or married into non-Catholic families. In reverse, we find that Protestant Irish families married into Catholic families and raised their families as Catholics. The Irish were among the founders or earliest members of nontraditional churches, such as the Latter-day Saints (Mormons), Church of the New Jerusalem (Swedenborg), Shakers, and any number of other experimental or communal groups of the nineteenth century. Also, don't expect your Scots-Irish Presbyterian ancestor to have remained in that church.

4. **We have found that the Irish were members of many fraternal, benevolent, secret, and social societies.** Now this was not unique among the Irish. What is most interesting are the anomalies. For example, Irish Catholics can be documented in the records of the Freemasons, which would have been against the wishes of their church. In places where the Church was less established (e.g., Utah and Nevada), the Lodge became a meeting place where Catholics freely intermingled with their Protestant neighbors.

Research Tip

5. The concept that families spent time elsewhere between Ireland and America is an idea whose time has now arrived. It may be that once you get your ancestors out of the United States, you need to do your Canadian, Australian, or English research before even considering Irish records.

6. We have also noted that the Irish in America were "freewheeling" not only with intermarriage and religious practices but also with their politics. Although large numbers fought for the American side in the Revolutionary War, many others went to Canada and elsewhere because they were Loyalists. During the Mexican-American War, the Irish fought on both sides, just as they did in even greater numbers in the American Civil War. Loyalties were not clean-cut by any means.

7. Not all Irish who came to America were the poor, starving, illiterate peasants that many books would have us believe. Also, not all of them settled in large cities such as New York or Boston. Anyone who has done research in Iowa or Wisconsin knows just how Irish these areas were! The Irish of all social classes settled just about everywhere.

Although none of these factors may be considered unique to America, the sheer numbers are: It is estimated that 250,000 immigrants came to America from 1776 to 1820, and that at least 100,000 were Irish. From 1821 to 1900, 3,884,570 Irish immigrated to America. Although they settled just about everywhere, the largest concentration in 1900 was in New York, Massachusetts, Pennsylvania, Illinois, New Jersey, Connecticut, Ohio, and California.

REFERENCES AND FURTHER READING

Sources

Akenson, Donald Harman. *The Irish Diaspora: A Primer.* Belfast: Queen's University of Belfast, Institute of Irish Studies, 1993.

Blessing, Patrick J. *The Irish in America: A Guide to the Literature and the*

Manuscript Collections. Baltimore: The Catholic University of America Press, 1992.

Gribben, Arthur and Ruth-Ann Harris, eds. *The Great Famine and the Irish Diaspora in America.* Amherst, Mass.: University of Massachusetts Press, 1999.

Keneally, Thomas. *The Great Shame: And the Triumph of the Irish in the English-Speaking World.* Minneapolis, Minn.: Irish Books & Media, 1999.

Laxton, Edward. *The Famine Ships: The Irish Exodus to America.* New York: Henry Holt and Company, 1997.

McCaffrey, Lawrence J. *The Irish Catholic Diaspora in America.* Washington, D.C.: Catholic University of America Press, 1997.

Miller, Kirby. *Emigrants and Exiles: Ireland and the Irish Exodus to North America.* Oxford, England: Oxford University Press, 1985.

O'Sullivan, Patrick, ed. *Patterns of Migration.* Leicester, London, and New York: Leicester University Press, 1992.

———, ed. *The Irish in the New Communities.* Leicester and London: Leicester University Press, 1992.

AMERICAN SOURCES

The most common American records generated that provide Irish immigrant origins are tombstones; death certificates; cemetery records; church marriages and burials; obituaries; citizenship records; and civil recordings of births, marriages, and deaths. Other important sources include passenger arrival lists, land records, fraternal records, and military records.

In this chapter we discuss nine types of record sources: cemeteries, census records, church records, immigration records and passenger arrival lists, land records, military records, naturalization records, society records, and vital records. The list of records that are useful in your Irish research is endless, and we are deliberately limiting ourselves to these nine important sources. This is not, nor is it intended to be, a comprehensive guide to Irish-American research. You may very well need to delve into many other types of American records such as educational, institutional, newspaper, probate, and tax records.

You will also be well served by obtaining a guide to American records, such as any of the following:

Printed Source

Carmack, Sharon DeBartolo. *A Genealogist's Guide to Discovering Your Female Ancestors.* Cincinnati, Ohio: Betterway Books, 1998. A much-welcomed book for the beginner concerning strategies for researching the females in everyone's lineage.

Greenwood, Val D. *The Researcher's Guide to American Genealogy.* 3d ed. Baltimore: Genealogical Publishing Co., 2000. For years, a standard in the genealogical sources and the strategies in how to use them.

Hinckley, Kathleen W. *Locating Lost Family Members & Friends: Modern Genealogical Research Techniques for Locating People of Your Past and Present.* Cincinnati, Ohio: Betterway Books, 1999. If you need to first do modern research before moving back in time, this book will help.

Meyerink, Kory L. *Printed Sources: A Guide to Published Genealogical Records*. Salt Lake City, Utah: Ancestry Inc., 1998. This work discusses records in print and is helpful for those familiar with libraries and books.

Pfeiffer, Laura Szucs. *Hidden Sources: Family History in Unlikely Places*. Orem, Utah: Ancestry Inc., 2000. For a current treatment of American records not listed in this chapter, we recommend this work, which is a good companion to Szucs and Luebking's book.

Szucs, Loretto Dennis and Sandra Hargreaves Luebking, eds. *The Source: A Guidebook of American Genealogy*. Rev. ed. Salt Lake City, Utah: Ancestry Inc., 1997. This could be called the encyclopedia of American research and is for an advanced readership.

We also direct you to some very important Internet resources. **More and more U.S. records and resources are becoming available on the Internet. We recommend you check the following sites frequently:**

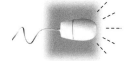

Internet Source

Ancestry.com	http://www.ancestry.com
USGenWeb Project	http://www.usgenweb.org
Cyndi's List	http://www.cyndislist.com

The Ancestry Web site is excellent, with searchable databases including extractions of record sources and books. This is a subscription Web site. The USGenWeb Project is free of charge and staffed by volunteers throughout the United States. You can go directly to a state or county site for information and contacts. Some county and state sites are better than others in their content and quality. Cyndi's List, a site linking you to other genealogy Web sites, is a must for anyone doing U.S. research.

Now a short word about genealogical journals: Each state has a genealogical society that produces journals and operates Web sites. The same is true for county societies. We recommend that you become familiar with the sites for the state and county where you are researching. We would also like to mention two organizations with libraries: the National Genealogical Society and the New England Historic Genealogical Society both publish excellent journals and have Web sites.

Addresses

National Genealogical Society
4527 Seventeenth St. North, Arlington, VA 22207-2399
phone: (703) 525-0050 or (800) 473-0060
Internet: http://www.ngsgenealogy.org/

New England Historic Genealogical Society
99-101 Newbury St., Boston, MA 02116-3084
phone: (617) 536-5740   *fax:* (617) 536-7307
Internet: http://www.newenglandancestors.org

CEMETERIES

Cemeteries in America may hold the key to identifying immigrant origins. Often the immigrant's tombstone or cemetery record indicates the birthplace. Sometimes not only is an Irish county given but also a parish or townland.

Transcripts of tombstones have been compiled and published for some cemeteries. For example, Rosemary Muscarella Ardolina's *Old Calvary Cemetery: New Yorkers Carved in Stone* and Joseph M. Silinonte's *Tombstones of the Irish Born: Cemetery of the Holy Cross, Flatbush, Brooklyn* make special efforts to fully transcribe stones that give Irish origins. An example from Ardolina's book (page 132) is

> Erected by Patrick Hart d 6 June 1883 age 65y native of Sligo. Their daughter Ellen Gilloon d 26 Jan 1879 age 28y. Her husband Patrick Gilloon d 18 July 1883 age 43y. Their daughter Maggie d 17 Nov 1876 age 4y 7mo. His daughter Kate Connor d 18 Nov 1883 age 28y. His daughter Annie Hart d 7 Jan 1898 age 37y. Patrick Hart d 20 Aug 1899 age 81y.

However, it is always advisable to look at the original tombstone when possible because the transcriber may not have listed all the information on the stone.

Some Irish genealogical journals have published abstracts of Irish immigrant tombstones. One example is Paul Martin Doherty's article "Tombstones of Some Irish Emigrants in the Catholic Cemetery at Andover [Massachusetts]," published in *The Irish Ancestor*.

In addition to tombstones, many cemeteries kept records ranging from burial registers to lot cards. Cemetery records may include a birthplace in Ireland; names of next of kin; coordinates of the lot; and name of the lot purchaser. Two examples of extremes are St. Joseph New Cemetery in Cincinnati, Ohio, and St. Patrick Cemetery in New Orleans, Louisiana. Both were the major Irish-Catholic cemeteries for these cities. St. Joseph New Cemetery records list, in the majority of the cases, a county of birth in Ireland, while St. Patrick records only rarely give a place in Ireland.

Reminder

When you examine cemetery records or tombstones you need to consider some basic facts:

1. **Irish Protestants:** Irish Protestants were usually buried in a community cemetery, local Protestant cemetery, or a fraternal or family cemetery. Although there may be separate Episcopal, Presbyterian, Methodist, and other cemeteries in a community, there will be no designated "Irish Protestant Cemetery."

2. **Irish Catholics:** Irish Catholics were usually buried in a Catholic cemetery if the community had a sizable number of Catholics. In some areas Catholic cemeteries were ethnically divided. For example, in Cincinnati friction existed between German Catholics and Irish Catholics. They had separate cemeteries. Catholics may be buried in non-Catholic cemeteries, especially if there was no Catholic cemetery in the area. For example, prior to 1785, Irish Catholics in New York City were usually buried in Trinity and St. Paul's Episcopal churchyards. Also, a community cemetery may have a Catholic section.

3. **Burial Registers:** Don't be surprised that many graves in the United States do not have a tombstone. This makes examining church burial registers or cemetery registers of utmost importance. The burial registers of a local church might also be the only records kept for a church or community cemetery. In larger cities where space was at a premium, cemetery lots held multiple burials. But there may only be tombstones for one or two individuals, even though more people are buried in the lot. In this case use the lot's coordinates to locate all the people buried there. You may find other family members are buried in the same plot.

4. **Removal of Cemeteries:** It is not uncommon for cemeteries, especially in larger cities, to have been removed and unclaimed tombstones destroyed. Such was the case in San Francisco, where most of the city cemeteries were removed and combined with other cemeteries outside the city limits (in Colma, San Mateo County) by 1940. The records of the removals, as well as the original cemetery records, provide an invaluable substitute for the massive record loss during the 1906 earthquake and fire. Removal records may tell who claimed the remains and stone, or where unclaimed remains were reburied. The stones for unclaimed remains in San Francisco were used as landfill in the bay.

In another example, the Tennessee Valley Authority (TVA) removed numerous cemeteries in the valley before building dams that formed lakes. Records were kept of removals and of those who claimed remains. Included in these removals were many of the early Scots-Irish settlers in the Tennessee Valley.

In New Orleans, the Girod Street Cemetery, owned by Christ Church Episcopal was the old Protestant cemetery. Many of the city's early Irish Protestants had tombs there. The tombs were removed when the New Orleans Superdome was developed, but full transcripts of the information from the tombs were made.

To identify the cemetery where your ancestor was buried, look for cemetery information on the death certificate, church burial record, newspaper obituary, or funeral home record. It is not uncommon to find that an individual or society has transcribed and indexed all the cemeteries in a county or town. In this case, you don't need to know an exact cemetery since all the surviving tombstones from a geographical area can be searched under one index or at least in one compilation.

Research Tip

A city or county directory or yellow pages will have a section for cemeteries. Use these to determine the cemeteries in existence when an ancestor died. Also use more modern directories to obtain current information. For example, *Cemeteries of the U.S.: A Guide to Contact Information for U.S. Cemeteries and Their Records*, edited by Deborah M. Burek, lists cemeteries alphabetically by state and county. Burek often states when a given cemetery began operation, the affiliations of the cemetery, and the location of records.

For additional suggestions on using cemetery information, see Rosemary Muscarella Ardolina's article "Cemetery Strategies: Some Lessons Learned at Calvary Cemetery in New York City," in *The Irish At Home and Abroad*.

Sources

REFERENCES AND FURTHER READING

Ardolina, Rosemary Muscarella. "Cemetery Strategies: Some Lessons Learned at Calvary Cemetery in New York City." *The Irish At Home and Abroad* 3 (1995/96): 104–107.

———. *Old Calvary Cemetery: New Yorkers Carved in Stone.* Bowie, Md.: Heritage Books Inc., 1996.

Burek, Deborah M., ed. *Cemeteries of the U.S.: A Guide to Contact Information for U.S. Cemeteries and Their Records.* Detroit, Mich.: Gale Research Inc., 1994.

Doherty, Paul Martin. "Tombstones of Some Irish Emigrants in the Catholic Cemetery at Andover [Massachusetts]." *The Irish Ancestor* 6 (1) (1972): 23–25.

Silinonte, Joseph M. *Tombstones of the Irish Born: Cemetery of the Holy Cross, Flatbush, Brooklyn.* Bowie, Md.: Heritage Books Inc., 1994.

CENSUS RECORDS

Census records are the backbone of U.S. research, providing a picture every ten years (for federal censuses) of the family you are researching. The more complete the picture you have of an immigrant family, the more successful your search for its origins will be. In the census, you may find children or other relatives you didn't know about. Ages, immigration information, relationships, and birthplaces are all important details found in censuses.

The U.S. Constitution mandates that a census be taken every ten years for the purpose of allocating the appropriate number of legislators to the House of Representatives. The first census was taken in 1790. The population schedules for 1790 through 1840 listed the names of the heads of households and the number of other household members, broken down by gender and age. Slaves were also counted. The 1820 and 1830 schedules counted the number of unnaturalized people of foreign birth living in the household. The 1840 census asked for the name and age of each person receiving a federal military pension.

From 1850 on, U.S. censuses listed the names of every member of the household (except slaves in 1850 and 1860) and data such as age, birthplace, and occupation. The census gives the relationship of each individual to the head of house beginning in 1880. Prior to that, you must be careful not to assume relationships. Many of the censuses up to 1870 have either been transcribed and published or have published indexes.

Warning

Ages and given names of members of a family can vary from one census to the next. This kind of discrepancy was extremely common, usually because different people provided the information to the enumerators. Surnames like O'Dwyer and McLoughlin may appear in the census with or without the *O'* or *Mc*. Be sure to look under Dwyer and Loughlin as well.

The laws of privacy mandate that the contents of each decennial census be open to the public only after seventy-two years. The 1920 enumeration, therefore, is the most recent available to researchers. The 1930 census is scheduled to be released in April 2002. (See the 1930 Census Web site at <http://www.nara .gov/genealogy/1930cen.html>.) The 1890 census was almost completely destroyed. The 1900, 1910, 1920, and 1930 censuses list the year of a person's immigration to the United States as well as naturalization status. The unique index to the 1880 to 1930 population schedules is called the Soundex. The Soundex groups surnames that sound similar together in one code. The 1880 Soundex includes only families with children aged ten years or under. The complete population is listed in the 1900 and 1920 Soundexes. The 1910 and 1930 Soundexes do not include all states.

The National Archives, as well as its regional centers throughout the country, has copies of all federal censuses and their indexes. Any local library that has microfilm readers and is on the interlibrary loan network can order the microfilms for you to use in that library for a charge. You can also get the census microfilms from the FHL and its Family History Centers. Major genealogical libraries, many state libraries and county libraries also have copies of the censuses.

Some states enumerated their own censuses in various years. They often fell between the federal censuses, such as 1855, 1875, or 1895. (See Ann S. Lainhart's *State Census Records*.) The state censuses are available on microfilm at the FHL and at state archives.

REFERENCES AND FURTHER READING

Lainhart, Ann S. *State Census Records*. Baltimore: Genealogical Publishing Co., 1992, 2000.

Thorndale, William and William Dollarhide. *Map Guide to the U.S. Federal Censuses 1790–1920*. Baltimore: Genealogical Publishing Co., 1987.

Sources

CHURCH RECORDS

Church records are important research tools for many reasons, although the information varies by denomination, time period, and locality. In some cases, church registers identify specific Irish origins. They may also list birthplaces, parents' names, occupations, residences, and the names of baptismal sponsors and marriage witnesses.

For various reasons, Irish immigrant families may be absent from civil records of birth, marriage, and death. In this case, **church records can serve as a substitute for government records. Church records also may contain details not found on tombstones.** Furthermore, if your Irish immigrants lived only transiently in an area and were not there in a census year, church records and city directories might be used to isolate the place where they resided.

Tip

Denominations

Most of the Irish who came to North America were members of the Church of Ireland, Methodist, Presbyterian, Roman Catholic, or Society of Friends (Quaker) faiths. After coming to North America, many Irish immigrants did not retain their original religion; some switched faiths several times. This includes Irish Catholics, who sometimes joined Protestant or other churches, especially where there were few Catholics. It is also possible that your ancestors attended no church.

It is often helpful to learn something of the history and evolution of a denomination being researched. For example, Scots-Irish immigrants may have belonged to several divisions of Presbyterianism. Then the search for church records is complicated by the question, "Which kind of Presbyterian were they?" Additionally, mergers may affect where records are located. For example, the present-day United Methodist Church is a merger of several denominations. For background information, we recommend Paul K. Conkin's *American Originals: Homemade Varieties of Christianity*, which shows the development of Christianity in America as something different and unique from its European roots; for the Irish, pay attention to the chapters on Unitarians and Universalists, the Restoration Movement, and Mormons. *The Encyclopedia of American Religions*, edited by J. Gordon Melton and Jolen Marya Gedridge, is a very accessible work found in many libraries.

Strategies

You can use church records in a variety of ways to obtain a wide range of information. The following are some strategies to glean the most information:

Technique

1. Search all known church records for your ancestor for information on where in Ireland your ancestor was born. Look for birth/baptism, marriage, and burial/death records as well as church minutes, transfer certificates, and death cards.
2. Search the records for sponsors (godparents) and witnesses to identify friends or family members who came from the same place in Ireland.
3. If a relative of your ancestor (for example, a brother or sister) joined a different religion than that of the rest of the family, search that denomination's records.
4. A family member may have been associated with a religious group for a short time. A short period of involvement with the Quakers, Mormons, Seventh-day Adventists, or Shakers, for example, may have been long enough to be in church records.
5. Always search branches of a denomination to determine which branch your ancestor belonged to. For Presbyterians, this may include the Reformed Presbyterian and the Cumberland Presbyterian congregations, as well as the larger denominations. For Baptists, this could include Free-Will Baptists, "independent" Baptists, American Baptists, and Southern Baptists.
6. Conduct research to see what churches existed in a community or county when your ancestor lived there versus what churches are presently located there. County histories, city directories, and church directories can help.

Baptists

There are many Baptist denominations, all of which baptize adults or mature children rather than infants. The minister may or may not have kept baptismal records. Membership records kept by the local congregations usually do not include ages or parentage. The church minutes may record a member's transfer from Ireland or elsewhere, giving the name of the former Baptist congregation. If a person joined a Baptist church from a denomination that practiced infant baptism, there will not be a record of the former denomination because infant baptism was not recognized by Baptists, especially during and before the nineteenth century.

While there were Baptists in Ireland who emigrated to North America, many other Irish immigrants joined the Baptist church after arriving in the United States, particularly in New England and the South. So the rule of thumb is, if your ancestors were Baptists in the United States, do not assume they were Baptists in Ireland.

In the United States, Baptist records may be deposited just about anywhere or still be with the local congregation. Two noteworthy repositories are the American Baptist Historical Society in Rochester, New York, and the Southern Baptist Historical Library and Archives in Nashville, Tennessee. Both repositories accept genealogical requests; they do not, however, house all Baptist records. If they do not have records for a particular congregation, the staff may be able to provide a contact address. The collections in Nashville concentrate on the states of Georgia, Kentucky, South Carolina, and Tennessee. The FHL also has collections of Baptist records.

Important

Congregationalists

The Irish association with the Congregational Church was mostly in New England, where it was the prominent faith in many states and communities. It was the established church in Massachusetts until 1833. In colonial New England, many Irish, regardless of religious affiliation, were married and had their children christened by a Congregational minister. With the establishment of Church of England (Episcopal) parishes and Presbyterian congregations, the Irish in many New England towns had ministers of their own churches. If you find colonial ancestors in Congregational records in New England, do not automatically assume they belonged to that church in Ireland. Many former Congregational churches are now Unitarian Universalist or United Church of Christ. The records of many current and former Congregational churches have been published in print or on microfilm. The FHL has a large collection of these, and many are also with the Congregational Library and Archives in Boston.

Episcopalians

The Episcopal Church in the United States is part of the Anglican communion, churches which have their roots in the Church of England. In Ireland, the equivalent church is the Church of Ireland. Members of the Anglican tradition brought their religion with them to the American colonies. After the American Revolution, the U.S. congregations of the Church of England were reorganized into the Protestant Episcopal Church in the United States of America. In 1967, the alternate name, the Episcopal Church, came into official use in the United States. The Episcopal Church is organized on a parish and diocesan basis. Each parish has a rector (or priest) and each diocese is administered by a bishop. Because the Church of England was the established religion in many American colonies, members of other denominations are often found in its records. However, early settlers in frontier areas such as Tennessee and Kentucky did not look favorably upon the Episcopal Church.

Sources

The major sources of information for Episcopal churches are the parish registers of baptisms, marriages, burials, confirmations, lists of communicants, and vestry minutes. Marriage and burial records can include important details, such as parents' names, mother's maiden name, occupations, and birthplaces. Communicant rolls and vestry minutes may indicate when and from where a member transferred into the parish, and when and to where a member transferred out.

Many of the original parish records are still at the parishes. Some diocesan archives contain original parish registers or microfilm copies. Some U.S. state libraries and archives also have Episcopal records. Published guides to some U.S. state libraries and archives can help in accessing records on microfilm. The FHL has records of many Episcopal churches on microfilm; in some cases, the records of whole dioceses (such as the Diocese of Massachusetts) have been filmed.

Methodists

Various denominations have identified themselves as Methodists. They all trace their heritage to John Wesley, a Church of England clergyman who started Methodist societies in the 1740s in England and Ireland for members of the Established Church. From the 1760s on, many thousands of Irish Methodists immigrated to America, where they were instrumental in establishing Methodist societies. You can find an excellent historical account of the Irish Methodists in Norman W. Taggart's *The Irish in World Methodism, 1760–1900*. Some of the earliest Methodist societies in America were established in the colonies of New York and Maryland in the 1760s. One of the first two was the John Street Methodist chapel in New York City, built in 1768 to serve a group of Irish Palatines from County Limerick. The Palatines, many of whom became Methodists, were Protestant refugees in Ireland from Germany.

Definitions

The Methodist Episcopal Church (sometimes abbreviated ME) was officially organized in 1784 in Baltimore. The Methodist Protestant Church was established in 1828, and the Methodist Episcopal Church, South separated in 1844 from the Methodist Episcopal Church. The three American branches were united in 1939, and they joined the Evangelical United Brethren Church to form the United Methodist Church in 1968. The governing body of the United Methodist Church is the Annual Conference, within which are individual conferences for different geographical areas.

Local churches generally kept records of membership, baptisms, marriages, and deaths. The membership records were sometimes called "class lists." Churches also kept registers of "probationers," individuals undergoing preparation for membership. The membership or class lists indicate when a member was admitted and from what denomination (if different from Methodist), as well as when a member left. Further detail about research may be found in "Researching Your United Methodist Ancestors: A Brief Guide" on the General

Commission on Archives and History (GCAH) Internet site: <http://www.gcah
.org/Searching.htm>.

Many Methodist church records are still in the custody of individual
churches. Some United Methodist Church conferences have established conference archives. *The United Methodist Church Archives and History Directory*
(Madison, N.J.: General Commission on Archives and History) is published
periodically. It contains addresses of Methodist historical societies and major
repositories of Methodist material. Details about archives may also be found
on the GCAH Web site. The FHL and some state and university archives have
microfilmed Methodist church records.

Moravians

Moravian immigration to America took root in Pennsylvania and North Carolina. Moravian immigrants of all nationalities first located in settlements at
Forsythe County, North Carolina, and the communities of Bethlehem, Naza-
reth, and Lititz, Pennsylvania. Records from these communities may indicate a
member's congregation of origin.

Moravians (also called "United Brethren") established communities where
members immigrated. Most Moravians in America came to America as Moravians, so you will likely be searching Moravian records in Ireland also. Irish
were among the Moravian immigrants, although they were a minority within
the Moravian church.

**Most Moravian Church records of births/baptisms, marriages, and deaths do
not list the birthplace of the member. The record that may provide this information is called a "memoir."** Memoirs are similar to eulogies; before death a person
may have had a memoir written about his or her life and service to the church.
If a memoir was not written before death, the minister may have written one
after the death of the member.

Printed Source

The Moravian Archives in Bethlehem and in Winston-Salem conduct genealogical research for a fee. Both repositories have gathered the births/baptisms,
marriages, burials, minutes, and memoirs for the congregations in their areas.
The memoirs for Forsythe County, North Carolina, for non-Germanic people
have been translated. All of the North Carolina memoirs are indexed at the
Winston-Salem archives. The index is completely cross-referenced in terms of
married women. An example of an Irish-born Moravian's memoir card is

> Mack, Mary (nee Grant). b. 01 Aug 1755, Ballinderry Co., Antrim, Ireland. Called
> to service in W.I. [West Indies], 1799 & to marry Hanan. Trying trip, including
> capture by Irish rebels. m1. J. Hanan; m2. Jacob Mack.

Another source for immigrant origins is the minutes of the North Carolina
congregations; minutes dating 1752 to 1879 have been published in the series
Records of the Moravians in North Carolina. Here is one example:

> November 8, 1826. John Spence, the journeyman tailor who is working for Br.
> Charles Levering, was formerly a Society Brother at Gracehill, Ireland. ("Salem
> Board Minutes," Volume VIII (1823–1837), p. 3777).

Mormons (Latter-day Saints)

The Church of Jesus Christ of Latter-day Saints (Mormons or LDS Church) headquartered in Salt Lake City, Utah, began sending missionaries to Ireland in 1840. Mormonism was a new religious tradition founded in 1830 in New York by Joseph Smith Jr. The LDS Church was of neither the Catholic nor the Protestant tradition, but we discuss it because the Mormons kept detailed genealogical records of their families and ancestors. If your ancestor's brother or sister joined the Mormon Church, you may find a wealth of information about your family. The church's early missionaries were not successful in converting large numbers in Ireland; however, they found greater success in England, Scotland, and Wales. It was in Great Britain that large numbers of Irish-born joined the Mormon Church. It is interesting to note that the oldest Mormon congregation in existence today is in Preston, England—not in Utah.

Unlike other religious organizations, LDS converts were expected to immigrate immediately to Church headquarters (from 1839 to 1846) in Nauvoo, Illinois; after 1848 to the intermountain western states. The average convert to the LDS Church was usually married with young children. Siblings of the couple may have also joined. Not all converts remained Mormon, nor did they all emigrate. Even if an ancestor left, records may list a birthplace and parentage.

Library/Archive Source

Due to Mormon doctrine about keeping genealogies, there are many sources available to document members. **LDS records and resources are available through the FHL**, which has published a guide to LDS research sources in *Research Outline: LDS Records*. Dwight A. Radford also gives details in his article "Irish Immigrants Among Three American Minority Religions" in *The Irish At Home and Abroad*.

Some of the followers of Joseph Smith who did not migrate west to Utah in the 1840s formed the Reorganized Church of Jesus Christ of Latter Day Saints (RLDS Church), now renamed the Community of Christ. These members reorganized the church in 1860 based on doctrinal differences with the Utah LDS Church, particularly concerning church leadership and the doctrine of polygamy. The RLDS Church is now headquartered in Independence, Missouri. Susan Easton Black's six-volume *Early Members of the Reorganized Church of Latter Day Saints* contains biographical sketches. RLDS congregation records are on microfilm at the FHL. The RLDS Church sent missionaries to Utah in the 1860s, and among their converts in the Intermountain West were Irish immigrants who had originally joined the LDS Church in Great Britain. Irish birthplaces may be preserved in the RLDS Church records even if they are not in the LDS Church records. For example, Black's work lists William M. Gibson, born in 1821 (1822) in Wicklow, Down, Ireland. He was baptized into the RLDS Church in Salt Lake City in 1869 and migrated to San Bernardino, California, where he worked with the congregation.

Presbyterians

Various branches of the Presbyterian faith in America have merged and divided through the years. The majority of the Presbyterian congregations in the United States are now part of the Presbyterian Church (USA), but there are a number of smaller groups, such as the Cumberland Presbyterian Church and the Reformed Presbyterian Church. The Scots-Irish immigrants who came in the thousands to the American colonies starting in 1718 were largely Presbyterian in their homeland. When they came to America, however, it was common for Scots-Irish immigrants to join another denomination or not attend any church at all. On the other hand, during times of revival, many families were brought into the Presbyterian church; church registers list the names of those who were admitted by the session. The session is the governmental body for the local congregation.

Presbyterian registers vary in their content depending on the congregation. The registers may include records of birth/baptism, marriage, death/burial, session minutes, and communion rolls. If immigrant origins are recorded, it is usually in the session minutes or the communion rolls. In order to be accepted into a congregation, there was an interview between the prospective communicant and the session. The session minutes recorded the acceptance or rejection of the communicant and noted transfers from other congregations (such as in Ireland). Major repositories with registers are the Presbyterian Church (USA) Department of History in Philadelphia; the Presbyterian Church (USA) Department of History in Montreat, North Carolina; and the FHL. The Philadelphia and Montreat repositories collect records from all branches of Presbyterianism. The "National Directory of Congregations of the Presbyterian Church (USA)," listing all churches and addresses, is available on the Internet: <http://www.pff.net/pc-list.html>.

Religious Society of Friends (Quakers)

The Religious Society of Friends was formed in England in 1652 under the leadership of George Fox. The society spread to Ireland shortly thereafter. Quakers from Ireland immigrated to a number of American colonies such as Maryland, New Jersey, Pennsylvania, Rhode Island, and Virginia. The largest migration was to the colony of Pennsylvania in the years from 1682 to 1750. Remember, this colony was founded by William Penn, himself a Quaker. The Friends gathered in "meetings," which were grouped together into "monthly meetings." **You will find the minutes of monthly meetings are generally the most useful source for tracing Quaker families.** Various splits have occurred in American Quakerism since 1828.

Research Tip

Albert Cook Myers, in his *Immigration of the Irish Quakers*, undertook a detailed study of the approximately fifteen hundred to two thousand Irish Quaker immigrants who settled in Pennsylvania between 1682 and 1750. He identified the Irish origins of many of these immigrants. Genealogical data from this book were published separately as Myers's *Irish Quaker Arrivals to Pennsylvania 1682–1750*. Another book by Myers, *Quaker Arrivals at Philadelphia 1682–1750*, includes certificates of removal received at the Philadelphia Monthly Meeting from meetings in America, England, and Ireland.

For Irish immigrant research, records of births, deaths, marriages, and minutes recording members received by certificate are particularly useful. Berry and Berry's *Our Quaker Ancestors: Finding Them in Quaker Records* is a genealogical guide to tracing members of the Society of Friends. Thomas C. Hill's *Monthly Meetings in North America: An Index* includes historical descriptions of each yearly and monthly meeting and indicates where you can find records of each meeting. The FHL has microfilm copies of records from numerous monthly meetings. William Wade Hinshaw's six-volume work *Encyclopedia of American Quaker Genealogy* includes extracts from the minutes of monthly meetings in Georgia, Michigan, New Jersey, New York, North Carolina, Ohio, Pennsylvania, South Carolina, Tennessee, and Virginia. *Genealogical Records: The Encyclopedia of Quaker Genealogy, 1740–1930* is a CD-ROM version of Hinshaw's six volumes produced by Family Tree Maker.

Roman Catholics

Reminder

The largest group of Irish immigrants who came to the United States were Roman Catholics. In places where the Catholic Church was well established, it was often the center of many Irish Catholics' lives. The records created in relation to church membership and participation are essential tools for tracing Irish immigrants in America and identifying their origins in Ireland. For additional reading, we recommend Duane L.C.M. Galles' article "Roman Catholic Church Records and the Genealogist" in *National Genealogical Society Quarterly*. On the Internet you can find the Catholic Information Center <http://www.catholic.net/rcc/diocese/index3.html> and Local Catholic Church History and Genealogy Research Guide <http://home.att.net/~local_catholic/>.

The records of primary interest in Irish immigrant research are registers of baptism, marriage, and death or burial. Each of these types of registers sometimes indicates a family's origins in Ireland. Baptismal records may state parents' birthplaces, particularly in the twentieth century. It was customary for a child to be baptized as soon as possible after birth. Catholic parish records may be in Latin or in the language of the parish, such as English, French, or Spanish. In 1868, the Second Plenary Council of Baltimore required that all sacramental registers in the United States be kept in Latin. From 1907 it was required that the parish of baptism be notified when a person married, and in some cases, a priest in the United States would record the parish of baptism in Ireland. The 1918 Code of Canon Law required information about confirmations, ordinations, and religious professions to also be recorded with a person's baptismal record.

Most parish records in the United States are held by individual parishes. Some diocesan archives, such as the Archdiocese of Boston Archives, have records centrally available. The FHL has microfilm copies of registers from many parishes. Virginia Humling's *U.S. Catholic Sources: A Diocesan Research Guide* gives contact information for each diocesan archives.

Other types of Catholic records may be useful in tracing an Irish immigrant ancestor, including the following:

Marriage dispensations: If a couple seeking marriage was unable to fulfill all the requirements of church law for marriage, a dispensation could be obtained from the bishop to allow the marriage to occur within the church anyway. Couples sought dispensations for many reasons; for example, because the bride and groom were related (consanguinity), because one of them was not a Roman Catholic (mixed marriage), or because the marriage banns were not read in church prior to the ceremony as required. Dispensation records were kept at the diocesan level, but a dispensation is usually noted in the marriage record itself. The content and availability of the records varies by diocese.

Parish histories: Fortunately, you will find that histories have been written of many Catholic parishes and dioceses, especially when celebrating their anniversaries. Some parish histories contain biographical information about parishioners, or an indication of the predominant origins of Irish immigrants in the parish. *Parish History Collection: A Directory of Works at the University of Notre Dame*, compiled by Sowinski, Cawley, and Ames, inventories the large number of parish histories contained in this collection. *Parish History Collection* is also available on the Internet at <http://archives1.archives.nd.edu/parishes.htm>. The Catholic University of America's Mullen Library holds some three thousand parish histories arranged geographically.

Directories: Consult the current edition of *The Official Catholic Directory* (for the United States) to determine what parish(es) now exist where the family lived. Earlier Catholic directories for the United States were produced beginning in 1817. Microfilm copies of pre-1900 directories are available at the Catholic University of America. Directories from 1900 on are available on microfilm at the University of Notre Dame archives. For details about the various directories see Mark G. Thiel's *Index to the Catholic Directories for the United States With Appended Countries, 1817, 1822, 1833–.*

Records of priests and religious Orders: Irish Catholic families commonly had one or more members who became a priest, religious brother, or nun. **We are truly believers in researching these family members.** You might ask, "Why? They didn't leave any descendants!" In fact, records of these family members may provide the clue you are looking for to the whole family's Irish origins. Very detailed biographical information was often kept about priests and men and women in religious orders. For example, in the old days, a man couldn't become a priest if he was born out of wedlock. Thus, a seminarian had to prove that his parents were legitimately married before his birth and that he was baptized.

Research Tip

Nuns, religious brothers, and religious order priests all belong to religious orders headed by a superior. This would include Dominican and Franciscan priests, for example. Another group of priests (called "secular" or "diocesan" priests) are attached to a diocese headed by a bishop and do not belong to an order. Both types of priests could serve in parishes.

Religious sisters (nuns) generally took on religious names (usually derived from saints' names or pious terms) when they joined their order. For example, Teresa Doherty (born in County Tyrone in 1825) came from Boston in 1859 to join the Sisters of the Holy Cross in Indiana, and changed her name to Sister Mary Hortense. It is under the religious name (Sister Mary Hortense) rather than birth name (Teresa Doherty) that you will usually find nuns listed in census records.

Individual dioceses and seminaries keep biographical information about diocesan priests, while information about nuns and religious brothers and priests is kept by the order to which they belonged. Further detail about accessing these records is in Kyle J. Betit's article "Researching Catholic Nuns, Brothers and Priests in the U.S. for Place of Origin" in *The Irish At Home and Abroad*.

REFERENCES AND FURTHER READING

Sources

General

Conkin, Paul K. *American Originals: Homemade Varieties of Christianity*. Chapel Hill, N.C.: University of North Carolina Press, 1997.

Mead, Frank S. *Handbook of Denominations in the United States*. 10th ed., revised by Samuel S. Hill. Nashville, Tenn.: Abingdon Press, 1995.

Melton, J. Gordon and Jolen Marya Gedridge. *The Encyclopedia of American Religions*. Detroit, Mich.: Gale Research Co., 1998.

Melton, J. Gordon and John Krol, eds. *The National Directory of Churches, Synagogues, and Other Houses of Worship*. 4 vols. Detroit, Mich.: Gale Research Co., 1994.

Piepkorn, Arthur C. *Profiles in Belief: The Religious Bodies of the United States and Canada*. 4 vols. San Francisco: Harper and Row, 1978.

Radford, Dwight A. "Irish Immigrants Among Three American Minority Religions." *The Irish At Home and Abroad* 5 (2) (2d Quarter 1998): 77–83. This article discusses records of Mormons, Moravians, and Shakers.

Baptists

Helmbold, F. Wilbur. "Baptist Records for Genealogy and History." *National Genealogical Society Quarterly* 61 (Sept. 1973): 168–178.

McBeth, H. Leon. *The Baptist Heritage*. Nashville, Tenn.: Broadman Press, 1986.

Congregationalists

Walker, Willeston. *The History of the Congregational Churches in the United States*. New York: A.C.H.S., 1894.

Episcopalians

Bellamy, V. Nelle. "Church Records of the United States, Part B. Part IV: Protestant Episcopal." World Conference on Records and Genealogical Seminar, Salt Lake City, Utah, 5–8 August 1969.

Methodists

Taggart, Norman W. *The Irish in World Methodism, 1760–1900*. Westminster, England: Epworth Press, 1986.

Moravians

Hamilton, John Taylor. *A History of the Church Known as the Moravian Church*. Bethlehem, Pa.: Times Publishing Co., 1900. Reprint, New York: A.M.S. Press, 1971.

Records of the Moravians in North Carolina. Raleigh: Edwards and Broughton Printers, 1922–1969. 11 vols. Volumes 6–7 were reprinted by the North Carolina Department of Archives and History.

Mormons (Latter-day Saints)

Black, Susan Easton. *Membership of the Church of Jesus Christ of Latter-day Saints, 1830–1848.* 50 vols. Provo, Utah: BYU Religious Studies Center, 1984–1988.

———. *Early Members of the Reorganized Church of Jesus Christ of Latter Day Saints.* 6 vols. Provo, Utah: BYU Religious Studies Center, 1993.

Daughters of Utah Pioneers. "The Mormons from Ireland." *Our Pioneer Heritage* 13 (1970): 313–372.

Research Outline: LDS Records. Salt Lake City, Utah: The Church of Jesus Christ of Latter-day Saints, 1992.

Presbyterians

Betit, Kyle J. "Scotch-Irish in Colonial America." *The Irish At Home and Abroad* 2 (1994/95): 1–8.

Smith, Dean Crawford. *The Ancestry of Emily Jane Angell, 1844–1910.* Boston: New England Historic Genealogical Society, 1992.

Stewart, Reid W. "Scotch-Irish Emigrations from Scotland to Ireland and Ireland to America and SW Pennsylvania." *Western Pennsylvania Genealogical Society Quarterly* 10 (Spring 1990): 4–14.

Thompson, Ernest Trice. *Presbyterianism in the South.* 3 vols. Richmond, Va.: John Knox Press, 1963–1972.

Religious Society of Friends (Quakers)

Berry, Ellen Thomas and David Allen Berry. *Our Quaker Ancestors: Finding Them in Quaker Records.* Baltimore: Genealogical Publishing Co., 1987.

Hill, Thomas C. *Monthly Meetings in North America: A Quaker Index.* 1992 Formal Edition. Cincinnati, Ohio: the author, 1992.

Hinshaw, William Wade. *Encyclopedia of American Quaker Genealogy.* 6 vols. Ann Arbor, Mich.: Edward Brothers Inc., 1938–1950.

Myers, Albert Cook. *Immigration of the Irish Quakers into Pennsylvania 1682–1750.* 1902. Reprint, Baltimore: Genealogical Publishing Co., 1969.

———. *Irish Quaker Arrivals to Pennsylvania 1682–1750.* Baltimore: Genealogical Publishing Co., 1964.

———. *Quaker Arrivals at Philadelphia 1682–1750.* 1902. Reprint, Baltimore: Genealogical Publishing Co., 1978.

Roman Catholics

Betit, Kyle J. "Researching Catholic Nuns, Brothers and Priests in the U.S. for Place of Origin." *The Irish At Home and Abroad* 4 (3) (3d Quarter): 121–125.

Galles, Duane L.C.M. "Roman Catholic Church Records and the Genealogist." *National Genealogical Society Quarterly* 74 (Dec. 1986): 271–278.

Humling, Virginia. *U.S. Catholic Sources: A Diocesan Research Guide.* Salt Lake City, Utah: Ancestry Inc., 1995.

O'Toole, James M. "Reconstructing Catholic Family History." *New York Irish History* 5 (1990–91): 43–48.

Sowinski, Carolyn Mankell, William Kevin Cawley, and Charlotte Ames, comps. *Parish History Collection: A Directory of Works at The University of Notre Dame.* 2d ed. Notre Dame, Ind: University Archives, 1988.

Thiel, Mark G. *Index to the Catholic Directories for the United States With Appended Countries, 1817, 1822, 1833–.* Milwaukee, Wis.: Marquette University, 1995.

Addresses

American Baptist Historical Society
1106 S. Goodman St., Rochester, NY 14620-2532
phone/fax: (716) 473-1740
Internet: http://www.crds.edu/abhs.htm

Archives of the University of Notre Dame
Notre Dame, IN 46556
Internet: http://www.nd.edu/~archives/

Catholic University of America, Mullen Library
Washington, DC 20064
Internet: http://libraries.cua.edu/rarecoll.html

Congregational Library and Archives
14 Beacon St., Boston, MA 02108
phone: (617) 523-0470.

Friends Historical Library
Swarthmore College, 500 College Ave., Swarthmore, PA 19081
phone: (610) 328-8497   *fax:* (610) 328-7329
Internet: http://www.swarthmore.edu/library/friends/

General Commission on Archives and History United Methodist Church
P.O. Box 127, Madison, NJ 07940
phone: (201) 822-2787
Internet: http://www.gcah.org/

Presbyterian Church (USA) Department of History
425 Lombard St., Philadelphia, PA 19147-1516
phone: (215) 627-1852   *fax:* (215) 627-0509
Internet: http://www.libertynet.org/pacscl/phs/index.html

Presbyterian Church (USA) Department of History (Montreat)
318 Georgia Terr., P.O. Box 849, Montreat, NC 28757
phone: (704) 669-7061   *fax:* (704) 669-5369

Southern Baptist Historical Library and Archives
901 Commerce St., #400, Nashville, TN 37203-3630
phone: (615) 244-0344 #270   *fax:* (615) 782-4821
Internet: http://www.sbhla.org/

IMMIGRATION RECORDS

Irish immigrants came to America through all ports of entry, most often Baltimore, Boston, New Orleans, New York City, and Philadelphia. However, often ignored are the lesser known ports such as Galveston, San Francisco, Mobile, and any number of smaller ports along the Atlantic coast. Other immigrants arrived at Canadian ports and crossed the border into the United States. **The U.S. government generally began keeping arrival lists of immigrants about 1820.** Various other lists of arrivals prior to this time are available. However, these other sources are not as complete as the government lists beginning in 1820. Some of the U.S. and colonial arrival lists are available in published form or are indexed on CD-ROM.

Notes

In the American colonial time period, you can use sources such as British public records, colonial land records, and New England town records to document emigrants. As early as 1649, political prisoners were sent from Ireland to the British colonies during Cromwell's suppression of the Irish Rebellion. Irish men and women who were convicted of crimes were also sent to the colonies. For details about some published colonial sources by Peter Wilson Coldham, see chapter fourteen, "Emigration Lists," and chapter seven, "The British West Indies," including the ideas of bondage and "white slavery." In some cases land records can serve as a substitute passenger list during the colonial time period by giving the names of immigrants. For example, in the 1760s and 1770s in South Carolina, groups of immigrants from Ireland were listed together, sometimes with the name of their ship, in the Council Journals as they were granted land. For extracts from the Council Journals, see Janie Revill's *A Compilation of the Original Lists of Protestant Immigrants to South Carolina, 1763–1773.* Town records from New England in the colonial time period sometimes list the arriving immigrants. Many immigrants as identified from Massachusetts town records are listed in George F. Donovan's *The Pre-Revolutionary Irish in Massachusetts, 1620–1775.*

U.S. Passenger Arrival Records

Often the port records of arrivals indicate only that a person or family was from Ireland, or even broader, Great Britain. As frustrating as this may be, you must still check port records for data such as the names of persons accompanying an ancestor, ages, and any number of other valuable clues. These can open up other opportunities, such as tracing the life of a sibling in American records to find clues to the family's Irish origins.

It is essential to look at passenger lists for the arrival of an ancestor, an ancestor's siblings, or parents. Port records, especially those from the late nineteenth century and twentieth century, do sometimes provide a place of origin in Ireland for a person or family.

Passenger arrival lists are available on microfilm from the National Archives, in many libraries, and at the FHL. Card indexes to arrival records for many ports are also available on microfilm. One exception is that there is no complete index to New York City arrival records between 1846 and 1897. Irish arrivals in New York City have been indexed on CD-ROM for the period 1846 to 1865 (see CD-ROM listing on page 35). In some cases two indexes exist for ports. For example, there is a general Atlantic Ports Index that encompasses many minor ports, and there are separate indexes for individual ports. If an ancestor is not found in one index, always check the other one.

Published Passenger Lists

Passenger and Immigration Lists Index, edited by P. William Filby and Mary K. Meyer, is an extensive series indexing published passenger and immigration lists. Supplements to the original 1981 edition of this work have been published regularly. In some cases, the names of Irish immigrants found in passenger lists have been specifically transcribed and published. An example is John Finn's *New Orleans Irish: Arrivals, Departures*, which includes lists of passengers arriving at New Orleans between 1815 to 1847.

The Famine Immigrants: Lists of Irish Immigrants Arriving at the Port of New York, edited by Glazier and Tepper, includes Irish immigrants arriving at the port of New York City between 1846 and 1851. This work helps fill the gap for part of the period in which New York City passenger lists are not indexed. It can be difficult to find an ancestor in this work because so many Irish names are common. *The Famine Immigrants* series does not include all arriving Irish passengers, but rather Irish on ships that carried predominantly Irish passengers.

Arrival lists may also be found in newspapers. For example, the *Shamrock* or *Hibernian Chronicle* newspaper was published in New York between 1811 and 1817 and contained information on the arrival of passengers from Ireland. Information on 7,308 immigrants is included in the abstracts in Donald M. Schlegel's *Passengers from Ireland: Lists of Passengers Arriving at American Ports Between 1811 and 1817*.

Printed Source

Although they are not passenger lists, **the notices published in the series *The Search for Missing Friends: Irish Immigrant Advertisements Placed in the Boston Pilot*, edited by Harris, Jacobs, and O'Keeffe, can serve as an important source for Irish immigrants.** The series consists of extracts of advertisements in the "Missing Friends" column in the *Boston Pilot* Catholic newspaper between 1831 and 1916. The advertisements provide information on relationships between members of Irish immigrant families who were looking for each other, as well as their Irish origins and places of settlement. People from all over the United States and Canada, as well as other countries, placed ads. Here is an example from 9 October 1858:

OF DENNIS WALSH, of parish Crookstown, Redgap [co. Kildare], who came to this country in 1846. Any person giving information will receive the above reward [$20] by addressing his mother, Mary Walsh, or his brother Edward, Johnstown, Cambria county, Pa.

CD Source

Many passenger and emigration lists are available on CD-ROM by Family Tree Maker <http://www.FamilyTreeMaker.com> and you can purchase them from Genealogical Publishing Co. <http://www.genealogybookshop.com>. **Three CD-ROMs particularly important for Irish immigrant research are**

1. *Passenger and Immigration Lists Index: 2000 Edition, 1500s–1900s,* edited by P. William Filby, published by Gale Research (CD #354). Includes about 3,280,000 individuals, listed in published sources, who arrived in United States and Canadian ports.

2. *Passenger and Immigration Lists: Irish to America, 1846–1865* (CD#357). Includes 1.5 million Irish immigrants arriving in Boston from 1846 to 1851, and New York from 1846 to 1865.

3. *Passenger and Immigration Lists: Irish Immigrants to North America, 1803-1871* (CD #257). Contains twelve volumes of compiled passenger lists with about forty-six thousand Irish who arrived in the United States and Canada. This combines on one CD-ROM many of the scattered surviving passenger lists for Irish immigrants. Don't be fooled by the title since one source is for the period 1735 to 1743. The passenger lists compiled by Brian Mitchell for the years 1803 to 1806, 1833 to 1839, and 1847 to 1871 are also on this CD-ROM.

USA/Canada Border Crossings

The United States began in 1895 to keep extensive records of border crossings from Canada (sometimes called "St. Albans Border Crossings" after the principal crossing point at St. Albans, Vermont). The border crossing records give birthplaces, including those in Ireland. They also identify the person (such as a relative) whom the person crossing the border would join in the United States. Even if the ancestor arrived in the United States much earlier than 1895, these records may still hold important information. For example, many people went back and forth across the border for various reasons, such as to work or to visit family members. In addition, a relative of your ancestor may have come from Ireland through Canada on the way to the United States in the post-1894 period.

If your immigrant ancestor crossed the border into the United States after 1894, the border crossing records may help locate a passenger list from a Canadian port. Many of the border crossing records give details regarding the immigrant's original arrival in Canada, even if it was decades earlier. You may find the date of arrival, place of arrival, and name of the ship. The United States/Canada border crossing records are at the National Archives and on microfilm at the FHL.

REFERENCES AND FURTHER READING

Colletta, John Philip. *They Came in Ships: A Guide to Finding Your Immigrant Ancestor's Arrival Record.* Salt Lake City, Utah: Ancestry Inc., 1997.

Donovan, George F. *The Pre-Revolutionary Irish in Massachusetts, 1620–1775.* Thesis (Ph.D.), Saint Louis University, 1931.

Filby, P. William and Mary K. Meyer, eds. *Passenger and Immigration Lists Index.* Detroit: Gale Research Co., 1981 and supplements.

Sources

Finn, John. *New Orleans Irish: Arrivals, Departures.* Jefferson, La.: the author, 1983.

Glazier, Ira A. and Michael Tepper, eds. *Famine Immigrants: Lists of Irish Immigrants Arriving at the Port of New York.* 7 vols. Baltimore: Genealogical Publishing Co., 1983–1986.

Harris, Ruth-Ann M., Donald M. Jacobs, and B. Emer O'Keeffe, eds. *The Search for Missing Friends: Irish Immigrant Advertisements Placed in the Boston Pilot.* 8 vols. Boston: New England Historic Genealogical Society, 1989–2000.

Revill, Janie. *A Compilation of the Original Lists of Protestant Immigrants to South Carolina, 1763–1773.* 1939. Reprint, Baltimore: Clearfield, Co., 1999.

Schlegal, Donald M. *Passengers From Ireland: Lists of Passengers Arriving at American Ports Between 1811 and 1817.* Baltimore: Clearfield, Co., 1990.

Szucs, Loretto Dennis. *They Became Americans: Finding Naturalization Records and Ethnic Origins.* Salt Lake City, Utah: Ancestry Inc., 1998.

Tepper, Michael *American Passenger Arrival Records.* Updated ed. Baltimore: Genealogical Publishing Co., 1993.

LAND RECORDS

Land records in the United States will be one of the basic foundations of your research, but be warned that they tend to be complicated. Land records probably will not tell you where in Ireland your ancestor was born. However, applying the right strategies and understanding why you are using them may be one of the important steps to lead you to a birthplace. For example, some land records predate censuses and can be used to document when your ancestor immigrated and first received land. There are some types of land records that provide birthplaces or name of last residence, which may have been in Ireland.

\di'fin\ *vb*

Definitions

You might encounter the term "colonial lands." To understand what this means, you cannot picture the United States as it is today. Colonial land belonged to British, French, and Spanish colonies prior to its incorporation into the United States. Land records generated under these colonial governments are an important resource for documenting your Irish immigrant ancestor if he or she arrived in the colonial time period. For example, much of the land in the western United States was previously part of Mexico, and part of Spain before that, so there is a paper trail in several countries. Many colonial and Mexican land records are on microfilm at the FHL, with originals at various U.S. state archives and university libraries.

As the United States developed, it was divided into state land states and federal land states. Most state land states are east of the Mississippi River. In these states, the state had primary control over granting land to applicants, which, of course, generated records. State land states were mostly divided into metes and bounds. Federal land states were divided into townships, sections, and ranges, and land sale was supervised by federal land offices in each state or territory. Thus, in these states you can use a map to tell exactly where a piece of land was, which is not so easy with the state land states.

There are a couple of published works to help you with the wide scope of this topic. The first is E. Wade Hone's monumental work *Land & Property Research in the United States*, covering the records of colonial lands, state land states, federal land states, and Native American lands. As good as this book is, though 517 pages long, it still could not possibly treat every land topic. That is literally how immense this topic is. The second source is Sandra Hargreaves Luebking's chapter "Research in Land and Tax Records" in *The Source: A Guidebook of American Genealogy*, edited by Szucs and Luebking. This chapter discusses resources for each state.

You will find land records are such important legal and historical documents that unless there has been a courthouse fire, records generally survive and can be found in a number of places including county courthouses, state archives and libraries, the National Archives, and town halls. Large collections are also available on microfilm at the FHL.

Printed Source

Initial Questions

It's important to keep in mind that for many Irish immigrants, coming to America and obtaining land was tied together. In the computer age, which has allowed so many excellent indexing projects to happen, land records that were once relegated to dusty courthouse books or a sterile roll of microfilm now can be used in many new and creative ways. When considering land records to document your Irish ancestor, **we hope that the several questions we propose here might help direct you in your search.**

Did the ancestor own or lease land? This is the first question. An immigrant in Brooklyn or Chicago probably rented an apartment. By contrast the chances of an immigrant owning land in Iowa, Kansas, or Montana is much higher. If your ancestor was a merchant or blacksmith, he may have owned, rented, or leased a shop. If the ancestor was a small farmer or large rancher, land ownership would have been more important for livelihood.

Technique

Have the county or town deeds of the ancestor's place of residence been indexed? You can be creative with a published index, especially if the index isn't limited to the buyers and sellers of land. Of course, indexes and abstracts are no substitute for the original records. However, you can search a good published index or set of abstracts for details such as property descriptions, names of neighbors, witnesses to the transaction, and of course any place names mentioned within the text of the deed.

What types of land records were generated about the ancestor's land? Land records include leases, homesteads, grants, general conveyances of land, warrants, the sale of former Native American lands, and land granted for military service. Find out what type of record best suits your needs and then proceed.

Strategies for Using Land Records

In our constant use of American land records, we have found some valuable clues that may help in your search for immigrant origins. We suggest that you look at a land record with some particular strategies in mind:

Place name identification: You will find that in some parts of the country farms are named. An immigrant family may have named a tract of land after its town, townland, or county in Ireland. This is common in Maryland and Pennsylvania. Now, be warned that even though your ancestor's land may carry an Irish place name, you need to make sure that it was your ancestor who obtained the original ground and gave that name to it. Otherwise it may be that someone unrelated received and named the farm, and the name was just passed down.

There is another way of looking at this. If your ancestor's property was located in a community or township with an Irish name, you will need to determine by whom the township or community was named. If your ancestor was with a group of people from the same area of Ireland settling together in America, you might have an important clue about where the entire group came from.

Searching the neighborhood: In researching land records, it is so important to remember that emigrants from the same community in Ireland often emigrated together and settled together. So if an ancestor's origins cannot be found, you may have success focusing on the origins of neighbors. Neighbors can often be identified in deeds, where they may be listed as witnesses to transactions.

Sorting through common surnames: Use land records to sort through the many families in an area with the same surname. For example, researching a Brown family from Northern Ireland in the 1700s may be complicated because the county or township was also populated by unrelated Brown families from England and elsewhere. To circumvent this problem, use land descriptions, including acreage and geographical features shown in an ancestral deed, to sort through the families. For an example of this strategy, see Ge Lee Corley Hendrix's article "John Bond vs John Bond: Sorting Identities via Neighborhood Reconstruction," in *National Genealogical Society Quarterly*.

Land Grants

In general, the records of initial land grants for state land states are filed with the state, and when the land was subsequently sold in a private land sale, the record would be with a county or town. The sale of lands in the federal land states began with the grant from the U.S. government, usually through a local land office, and then when that land was sold in a private sale, records would be found on the county level.

In saying this, we need to point out that some states generated unique land records that are often overlooked by family historians. We provide two examples that often give birthplaces in Ireland: the registration of alien landowners in New York state and the granting of "donation lands" in Washington and Oregon. The records have been discussed in articles in *The Irish At Home and Abroad*: E. Wade Hone's article "Oregon and Washington Donation Lands" and Gordon Lewis Remington's article "Alien Landowners in New York State, 1790–1913."

The grant process for state land states varied from state to state. As these grants are usually indexed, it is possible to find family members who settled in the same area, thus expanding the search for all of their origins. Keep in mind that if ancestors bought grant lands from land speculators, a county deed index can help determine if other family members settled in the same area.

In lands controlled and sold by the United States government in federal land states, the grant process was more uniform and generated more valuable genealogical information. This is because the government placed restrictions on the sale. For most types of grants an immigrant had to be naturalized or in the process of naturalization to purchase land. **The Bureau of Land Management has an incredible online database of those claims that actually went to patent for many states in their jurisdiction: <http://www.glorecords.blm.gov/>.** This Internet site, "The Official Land Patent Records Site," contains an index, and you can call up a scanned image of the patent. When doing this remember that the patent is only one document in a file of documents that may have been created about that piece of land. Other papers are at the National Archives.

Internet Source

REFERENCES AND FURTHER READING

Sources

Carter, Fran. *Searching American Land and Deed Records.* Orting, Wash.: Heritage Quest, 1991.

Hendrix, Ge Lee Corley. "John Bond vs John Bond: Sorting Identities via Neighborhood Reconstruction." *National Genealogical Society Quarterly* 79 (Dec 1991): 268–282.

Hibbard, Benjamin Horace. *A History of the Public Land Policies.* New York: The MacMillan Company, 1924.

Hone, E. Wade. ". . . By the Company They Keep: Using Land Records to Form Associations of Your Ancestor." *Genealogical Journal* (Utah Genealogical Association) 25 (1) (1997): 3–14.

———. *Land & Property Research in the United States.* Salt Lake City, Utah: Ancestry Inc., 1997.

———. "Homestead Records for Tracing Irish Immigrants." *The Irish At Home and Abroad* 3 (1995/96): 23–26.

———. "Oregon and Washington Donation Lands." *The Irish at Home and Abroad* 2 (1994/95): 69–72.

Neill, Michael John. "Homestead Records: An Important Source." *Heritage Quest* 15 (March/April 1988): 8–10.

Radford, Dwight A. and Kyle J. Betit. "Identifying Immigrant Origins Using U.S. Land Records." *The Irish At Home and Abroad* 5 (3) (3d Quarter 1998): 114–120.

Remington, Gordon Lewis. "Alien Landowners in New York State, 1790–1913." *The Irish At Home and Abroad* 1 (4) (Spring 1994): 8–9.

United States Congress. *The American State Papers: Public Lands.* Washington D.C.: Gales and Seaton, 1832–1861.

White, Albert C. *A History of the Rectangular Survey System.* Washington, D.C.: U.S. Government Printing Office, 1991.

Addresses

U.S. Department of the Interior, Bureau of Land Management
Eastern States Office, 7450 Boston Blvd.
Springfield, VA 22153-3121
phone: (703) 440-1600   *fax:* (703) 440-1609

MILITARY RECORDS

You can use a variety of United States military records and organizations in tracing an Irish immigrant soldier or officer and determining where in Ireland he was born. Among these are pension and service records. Lesser-known military records, discussed below, may also be of benefit. Sometimes research must turn to obscure sources when an ancestor did not receive a pension, or you cannot find military records to document enlistments. Military records are at the National Archives, state archives, and on microfilm at the FHL. The major American conflicts whose records are useful for tracing Irish immigrants include:

Colonial Wars (e.g., King Philip's War, Queen Anne's War)
French and Indian War (1754–1763)
Revolutionary War (1775–1783)
War of 1812 (1812–1815)
Indian Wars (1816–1858)
Mexican War (1846–1848)
Civil War (1861–1865)
Spanish-American War (1898–1899)
Phillipine Insurrection (1899–1902)
World War I (1917–1918)

Both regular U.S. forces—Army, Navy, or Marines—and state volunteer regiments may have been involved in wars. An ancestor may have served in any of these ways. The regular forces of the Army, Navy, or Marines also operated during peacetime, and detailed records of the servicemen are available. For details about particular military records and conflicts, see James C. Neagles's *U.S. Military Records: A Guide to Federal and State Sources, Colonial America to the Present.* Neagles's book lists published works on military records by state and war.

Technique

Following we discuss some helpful hints for using military records and some examples of the records you can find.

1. Familiarize yourself with the records that pertain to the wars or branches of the military in which your ancestors may have participated. Examine all records possible, but concentrate on those records that may provide Irish immigrant origins.

2. Consider relatives of the ancestor and whether they may also have served in the American military. As with many types of records, use military records to document not only the ancestor but the ancestor's brothers, cousins, relatives, and close associates. Information on these individuals may provide Irish origins if information on the ancestor does not.

3. In some cases records generated by a military conflict may provide information on Irish immigrants who were not soldiers participating in the war. For example, the Revolutionary War produced records of colonists loyal to the British Crown who fled to Canada, as well as records of citizens who gave supplies or suffered losses for the cause of the Revolution. The "Revolutionary War public service claims recorded in county court booklets, lists & index (Virginia)" are at the state library in Richmond and on microfilm at the FHL. There is a general index for the whole

state of Virginia, which is especially helpful because Virginia's 1790 census was destroyed. Another example is the nationwide World War I draft registration cards compiled with detailed information about millions of American men who were never called to serve in the war.

4. Remember that records relating to the military may have been created both at the time of military service, as in the case of muster rolls, and later, as in the case of pension records or soldiers' home records. Consider both categories of records, since both may be useful in tracing Irish origins. From the time of the Civil War, federal soldiers' homes have been operated throughout the United States. Each of the federal homes (ten of which were founded prior to 1910) kept records of the veterans who were admitted. Homes for disabled Confederate soldiers were operated in each of the eleven states of the former Confederacy, as well as Missouri, Maryland, Kentucky, Oklahoma, and California.

5. Descendants of military veterans joined various lineage societies based on the service records of their ancestors. The application papers, lineage books, and other records of these lineage societies may reveal additional information regarding ancestors who served in the military.

Some Types of Military Records

Muster Rolls

Muster rolls are lists of soldiers assigned to each military unit that give varying amounts of information about the soldiers, such as birthplaces and ages. Rolls were made at the time the unit (company or regiment) was created and were used as the basis for pay due to soldiers. **The Web site Ancestry.com has published three CD-ROMs with millions of names of soldiers from muster rolls.** These are a major, highly recommended source for documenting an ancestor who served in one of three American conflicts from 1775 to 1865:

1. *Military Records: Civil War Muster Rolls* (5.3 million records)
2. *Military Records: War of 1812 Muster Rolls* (580,000 records)
3. *Military Records: Revolutionary War Muster Rolls* (more than 400,000 records)

CD Source

Although the muster rolls of the French and Indian War can be difficult to access, they often contain birthplaces for Irish-born soldiers in an early time period. The relevant state archives, which may have some manuscript collections, are a good place to start. Many records are published. "Officers and Soldiers in the Services of the Province of Pennsylvania 1744–1764," in *Pennsylvania Archives* (Second Series, Vol. 2, Part 2, pp. 417–528) contains muster rolls and lists of soldiers, often giving age, birthplace, date of enlistment, and occupation. The following examples are from the list "Recruits Inlisted By Captain John Mather, Jun'r—15th June 1759." [page 504]:

Bresland, James, 50, Templemore, Ir., May 22, mason.
Campbell, George, 24, Antrim, Ir., June 13, lab.
Connor, Thomas, 45, Cork, Ir., May 23, shoemaker.

Likewise, *Muster Rolls of New York Provincial Troops, 1755–1764* (published in the 1892 *Collections of the New York Historical Society*) gives in most cases the soldier's name, birthplace, trade, and date of enlistment. While many of the birthplaces are only given as "Ireland," for some of the soldiers the muster rolls were more specific. For example, "A Muster Roll of the Men Rais'd and Pass'd Muster in Queens County For Captn Daniel Wright's Company 12 April 1759" (pp. 148–149) indicates that William McCord, age 38, turner, was born in County Longford, Ireland, while Edward King, "marriner," was born in County Waterford, Ireland. This information was also included in *New York Colonial Muster Rolls, 1664–1775 (Report of the State Historian of the State of New York)*, which contains transcriptions of all colonial muster rolls on deposit in the state capital at Albany for the years 1664 to 1775.

Enlistment Records

Many Irish immigrants enlisted in regular Army regiments during and between conflicts. *Registers of Enlistments in the United States Army, 1798–1914* (National Archives Microfilm Publication M233) includes information about men who enlisted in U.S. Army regiments in wartime or peacetime. This only pertains to regular federal regiments, rather than volunteer state regiments, which were raised during wartime. These enlistment registers are also available on microfilm through the FHL. They indicate the soldier's age, place of birth, occupation, date and place of enlistment, unit, period of enlistment, and physical description.

Pension Records

Pension records of the Revolutionary War, War of 1812, and Civil War are at the National Archives, and the Revolutionary War pension records are also on microfilm at the FHL. Indexes of all are available in print and on microfilm at the National Archives and the FHL. Sometimes exact birthplaces in Ireland are given in these records, or a widow's pension may state where she married a veteran in Ireland. For information about pension records of a particular war, see Neagles's work.

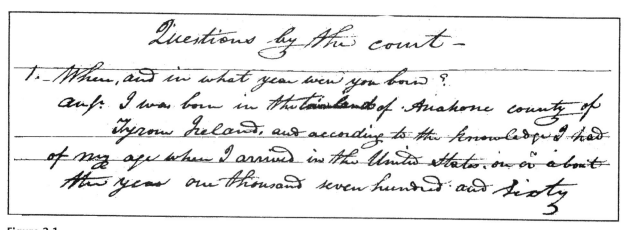

Figure 2-1
Excerpt from Revolutionary War Pension Application File of Thomas McMillen, S13897, Pa. Line. From the National Archives, Washington, D.C.

For More Info

TRACING THE ORIGINS OF SCOTS-IRISH IMMIGRANTS TO AMERICA

The Scots-Irish (sometimes called Scotch-Irish or Ulster Scots) were those people who went to the northern Ireland province of Ulster, mainly during the 1600s, as plantation workers from Scotland. Most of these families were Presbyterian. James I, the English monarch, sought to solidify control by transferring land ownership to Protestants and settling their lands with Scottish and English Protestant tenants. It was these Scottish families or their descendants who came *en masse* to settle in colonial America.

A broader view of the term Scots-Irish is drawn from history and the records. Many Scots-Irish families were in Ulster for several generations during the 1600s and 1700s prior to immigrating to colonial America. During this time, much intermarriage and even conversion took place. Scottish Protestant families intermarried with English families and joined the Church of Ireland. The same holds true for the native Roman Catholic Gaelic families. So it is possible after a few generations to have Scots-Irish families who were Roman Catholic or Church of Ireland. Scots-Irish families in Ulster are documented as converts to various minority faiths, most noteworthy the Society of Friends (Quakers) and the United Brethren (Moravian).

In Scots-Irish research the historical background is an important tool. You can find clues to the details of a group migration or the origin of a community in local histories. One noteworthy book is Patrick J. Blessing's *The Irish in America: A Guide to the Literature and the Manuscript Collections.* Use chapter thirteen, "Scotch-Irish," and chapter fourteen, "Irish in Places," to access more historical material.

There are many historical works available on the general market that, although not necessarily genealogical in nature, are useful in learning about migration patterns and the historical context from which to begin the research process. Some of the more valuable works on the Scots-Irish are

Blessing, Patrick J. *The Irish in America: A Guide to the Literature and the Manuscript Collections.* Washington, D.C.: The Catholic University of America Press, 1992.

Blethen, H. Tyler and Curtis Wood, eds. *Ulster and North America: Transatlantic Perspectives on the Scotch-Irish.* Tuscaloosa, Ala.: University of Alabama Press, 1997.

Bolton, C.K. *Scotch-Irish Pioneers in Ulster and America.* Boston, Mass.: Bacon and Brown, 1910.

Chepesiuk, Ron. *The Scotch-Irish: From the North of Ireland to the Making of America.* Jefferson, N.C.: McFarland and Co. Inc., 2000.

Dickson, R.J. *Ulster Emigration to Colonial America 1718–1775.* London: Routledge and Kegan Paul, 1966.

Falley, Margaret Dickson. *Irish and Scotch-Irish Ancestral Research: A Guide to the Genealogical Records, Methods and Sources in Ireland.* 2 vols. Reprint Baltimore, Md.: Genealogical Publishing Co., 1988. Originally published Strasburg, Va., 1962.

Ford, Henry J. *The Scotch-Irish in America.* Princeton, N.J.: University Press, 1915.

Hanna, Charles A. *The Scotch-Irish.* New York: G.P. Putnam's Sons, 1902. Reprint, Baltimore: Genealogical Publishing Co., 1995.

Leyburn, James G. *The Scotch-Irish: A Social History.* Chapel Hill, N.C.: The University of North Carolina Press, 1962.

Marshall, William F. *Ulster Sails West: The Story of the Great Immigration from Ulster to North America.* Baltimore: Genealogical Publishing Co., 1977.

McWhiney, Grady. *Cracker Culture: Celtic Ways in the Old South.* Tuscaloosa, Ala.: University of Alabama Press, 1988.

Technique

General Research Strategies

You will need to concentrate on American records first to trace the origins of your Scots-Irish ancestor before you start looking at Irish records. It is in American, not Irish, records that you are probably going to find the answer to your immigration question. Remember, if you cannot find Ulster origins by researching the direct line, then switch your efforts to locating your ancestors' other family members who may have also immigrated. This is based on the assumption that they were all born in the same place in Ulster. Research their lives. Other strategies we recommend to you are

Determine if the ancestor settled among other Scots-Irish: If historical research reveals that an ancestor's town or even neighbors were other Scots-Irish, there is a chance that a group of families immigrated together. It was common for families or friends to travel together during the eighteenth century. If you do find a pattern, this opens up numerous research avenues. Searching the neighbors is an important strategy. You can identify neighbors listed as witnesses in the deed transactions of your ancestor, in church records, and in tax records.

Identify the immigrant's religion: It was common for Scots-Irish immigrants to be nominal Presbyterians, if Presbyterian at all. This means you should pursue a paper trail of an ancestor's religious affiliation. On the American frontier, where the Scots-Irish may have been among the pioneers, it was common for families to join a Baptist, Methodist and later the Disciples (or Christian) movements. A transfer record into the new denomination probably will not exist until the nineteenth century; however, minister's diaries or even denominational newspapers may shed some light on immigrant origins. This is especially true if an ancestor became a minister or missionary.

Presbyterian Congregational Migrations: Many members from a particular Presbyterian congregation (or surrounding geographical area) in Northern Ireland often came to North America with a minister. This type of congregational migration makes finding immigrant origins easier. To determine where the pastor came from in Northern Ireland may be to find where his followers came from as well. Presbyterian repositories have compiled sources you can use to trace a minister's life and possibly his origins (see the church records section of this chapter).

Identify the Legends Associated With the Immigrant: Often legends exist about an immigrant or an immigrant's family. A legend that an ancestor is related to some earl, baron, or other gentry usually can be quickly checked into and often disproved. A more reasonable legend is that an ancestor may have been in the Siege of Londonderry in 1689. This is a well-known and important part of Irish history about which many works exist. One excellent and noteworthy work is William R. Young's *Fighters of Derry, Their Deeds and Descendants* (London: Eyre and Spottiswoode, 1932).

Check Nineteenth-Century Published Histories: One of the major sources for documenting the Irish origins of a Scots-Irish family are published family and county histories. Numerous such histories date from the nineteenth century, when many of the immigrants themselves were elderly or their children and grandchildren were still living. Scots-Irish families were among the first families in many counties and were considered among the founders of local communities, which often generated a degree of pride for several generations.

Genealogies of Native American Descendants

Tip

One overlooked source for locating Scots-Irish origins are the genealogies generated by Native Americans who are descendants of these immigrants. During the eighteenth and early nineteenth centuries Scots-Irish commonly intermarried with local Native American tribes. In fact, today families throughout the American South have legends of this connection still fresh in their family lore. These early immigrants served as interpreters for tribes, lived within the native nations, acted as traders, and served as missionaries. Genealogical material was generated from two perspectives: (1) from families who were removed westward by the U.S. government and (2) from families who remained in their ancestral lands and may have either "passed for white" or intermarried with African-American families.

Although there are numerous tribes with historical mixed-blood connections in the Americas, some noteworthy ones for the purpose of finding Scots-Irish immigrant origins are

    Catawba (North Carolina and South Carolina)

    Cherokee (Alabama, Georgia, North Carolina, and Tennessee)

Chickasaw (Alabama, Mississippi, and Tennessee)
Choctaw (Mississippi)
Muscogee (Creek) (Alabama, Florida, and Georgia)
Shawnee (Kentucky and Ohio)

See the series of articles concerning Native American genealogies and the search for Irish origins, written by Pat Smith (White Buffalo Woman) and Dwight A. Radford, in *The Irish At Home and Abroad.* These articles provide strategies and suggestions regarding special difficulties in researching the tribes:

"The Scots-Irish as Catawba," 6 (2) (1999): 112–119.
"The Scots-Irish as Cherokee," 2 (1994/95): 37–42.
"The Scots-Irish as Chickasaw," 3 (1995/96): 96–101.
"The Scots-Irish as Choctaw," 4 (2) (1996/97): 83–88.
"The Scots-Irish as Muscogee (Creek)," 3 (1995/96): 14–19.

This aspect of American history has not been entirely overlooked by family historians. Books such as George Morrison Bell Sr.'s *Genealogy of Old & New Cherokee Indian Families* (Bartlesville, Okla.: the author, 1978) and Don Martini's *Southeastern Indian Notebook: A Biographical and Genealogical Guide to the Five Civilized Tribes, 1685–1865* (Ripley, Miss.: Ripley Printing Co., 1986) can provide a wealth of information not only on the native ancestors but on the Scots-Irish ancestors as well. Immigrant origins for tribal members in the midwestern United States are also in books such as Richard L. Pangburn's *Indian Blood: Finding Your Native American Ancestor* (Louisville, Ky.: Butler Books, 1993). Pangburn's work documents the early families of the Cherokee, Delaware, Miami, Seneca, Shawnee, and Wyandot.

World War I Draft Registration

The United States declared war on Germany in April 1917, although the war had begun in Europe in 1914. Germany surrendered to the Allied forces in November 1918. World War I draft registration took place in three stages in 1917 and 1918. This source is important because altogether about twenty-four million men—nearly all of them born between 1873 and 1900—completed draft registration cards. This included men up to the age of forty-five in the final stage of registration. About half of the cards list a place of birth, while the other half do not give birth location but list an address of next of kin. This address may provide clues to the Irish origin of the person registering by identifying the residence of a relative in Ireland or a relative living elsewhere in America. The draft cards for about one million men born in 1896 and 1897 also list the father's place of birth. World War I selective service draft registration cards are kept at the National Archives' Southeast Regional Archives in Atlanta, Georgia (RG 163). **The FHL has microfilm copies of the draft registration cards.** You will find a growing database of these records on the Web at <http://www.Ancestry.com>.

Microfilm Source

REFERENCES AND FURTHER READING

Neagles, James C. *U.S. Military Records: A Guide to Federal and State Sources, Colonial America to the Present.* Salt Lake City, Utah: Ancestry Inc., 1994.

New York Colonial Muster Rolls, 1664–1775 (Report of the State Historian of the State of New York). 2 vols. 1897, 1898. Reprint, Baltimore: Genealogical Publishing Co., 2000.

Sources

NATURALIZATION RECORDS

An immigrant ancestor's citizenship and naturalization records may provide vitally important information for tracking the family back to its origin in Ireland. Some naturalization papers will divulge a county, town, or parish of origin, but most of the time they will not state anything more specific than "Ireland." Nineteenth-century naturalization records from the Boston, Massachusetts, area often gave at least a county of origin for Irish immigrants. But even if no specific origin is given, use the other information contained in the naturalization records to access additional records and generate new research strategies. For example, such information may include the birth date or age of the immigrant, the date and place of departure from Ireland and/or arrival in the United States, the name of the ship on which sailed, the number of years resided in the country, residence at the time of petitioning, previous residences in the United States, or the name of a U.S. resident who sponsored the citizenship application.

Some Irish immigrants to the United States never became citizens; some never began the process, and others only partly completed it. Even if an ancestor remained an alien until death, some citizenship records may still have been created because some immigrants filed declarations of intention that were never carried out. The 1900 U.S. census was the first to note whether foreign-born persons were aliens, citizens, or in the process of gaining citizenship. The abbreviations you find in the twentieth century censuses referring to citizenship status are Al = Alien; Pa = Applied but not completed; and Na = Naturalized.

Reminder

The United States' naturalization process generated several different kinds of records corresponding to steps in the process of becoming a citizen. The two most common records were the declaration of intention and the petition for naturalization, both of which have generally been required to gain U.S. citizenship since 1795. The alien usually filed a declaration of intention (also known as "first papers") to become a citizen, then after waiting at least the required number of years for residency, would make the petition ("second" or "final" papers). Other naturalization records include the report and registry of aliens, court orders, and certificates of naturalization.

Free white males had to be twenty-one years old to be naturalized. Between 1790 and 1940 a child (defined as under twenty-one between 1790 and 1906 and under eighteen between 1906 and 1940) automatically became a citizen when his or her father was naturalized. Likewise, between 1790 and 1922 married women became citizens when their husbands gained citizenship. In addition, a woman could lose her American citizenship by marrying an alien. From 1795, on single women age twenty-one or older could also be naturalized.

The declaration of intention and the petition for naturalization may be filed in the same court. Many immigrants, however, filed them in separate courts in the same locality or different localities. The petition will sometimes indicate when and where the declaration was filed, which may help in tracing the whereabouts of an immigrant ancestor. The information found in declarations and petitions varies depending on the court and time period. Sometimes a place of birth is stated, but this is the exception rather than the rule. An additional affidavit from a United States citizen who knows the immigrant—and who may be a relative or an acquaintance from the same place in Ireland—may also be included.

Courts from the county courts of common pleas to the state supreme courts to the federal district and circuit courts naturalized aliens. It was only required that the court have a clerk, a seal, and jurisdiction (which it would have for those aliens residing in its judicial district). Some courts had divided jurisdictions for different proceedings (for example, probate cases versus civil cases), and each jurisdiction could have included naturalization records. Court jurisdictions overlapped geographically so a county court, a state court, a federal district court, and a federal circuit court could all naturalize aliens living in the same area. Consequently, finding the court in which an ancestor was naturalized can be a challenge, especially for urban areas. It is necessary to consider courts at each level (local, state, federal). Fortunately, some areas have comprehensive indexes to naturalization records from many courts.

Some naturalization record indexes are for just one court, while others cover a number of courts in a city or area. A multi-court index can save you much time spent searching for the court in which an ancestor was naturalized. For example, a comprehensive Soundex to naturalization petitions in the New England states (Connecticut, Maine, Massachusetts, New Hampshire, Rhode Island, and Vermont), dating 1791 to 1906, is available on microfilm through the National Archives or the FHL. An example from this index concerns the Fogerty family of Providence, Rhode Island. This card index shows several Fogertys with petitions in Providence courts, listing that they were born in County Tipperary, Ireland. Even if you didn't know any of these Fogertys were related to your ancestors, this would be your first clue that there was a group of Fogertys from County Tipperary who came to the Providence area. Beware, however, that indexes of naturalization records may omit important information from the original records (such as the county of origin in Ireland), so always check the original records.

Tip

Other record sources, such as voter's registers, may identify the date and court of naturalization for an immigrant ancestor. For example, the Great Registers of California list all of the voters in a locality and give information about a naturalized citizen's date and court of naturalization. Another example is from the 1924 voter registrations of Providence, Rhode Island. They show that John Hayes was born in 1865 in England (we already knew his parents were from Ireland) and that he had received his naturalization through his father, also named John Hayes, in 1873 in the U.S. Circuit Court in Boston.

A new federal naturalization procedure went into effect 27 September 1906. The new process required that all naturalizing courts use standard forms for the declaration of intention, petition for naturalization, and certificate of naturalization. These forms, which were produced and controlled by the newly created Bureau of Immigration and Naturalization, were much more detailed than the previous forms and their content of the forms was updated throughout the twentieth century. For example, the declaration of intention form used between 1906 and 1929 included blanks for birth date, birthplace, date of emigration, and last foreign residence; information about spouse and children was also included. The forms from 1906 and afterward are now held by the Immigration and Naturalization Service (INS).

Most state, county, and local naturalization records remain in the custody of the court that produced them, although some may have been transferred to other repositories. The naturalization records of many federal district and circuit courts have been transferred to the National Archives branches serving the area where the court had jurisdiction. The FHL has microfilm copies of many federal, state, county, and local naturalization records. For further reading, see Loretto Dennis Szucs's *They Became Americans: Finding Naturalization Records and Ethnic Origins.*

REFERENCES AND FURTHER READING

Szucs, Loretto Dennis. *They Became Americans: Finding Naturalization Records and Ethnic Origins.* Salt Lake City, Utah: Ancestry Inc., 1998.

Sources

SOCIETY RECORDS

Membership in societies and associations was a common feature in the lives of Irish immigrants. Irish immigrants belonged to a myriad of societies: religious, political, ethnic, charitable, fraternal. While this may not have been necessarily unique to the Irish, some of the societies were specifically Irish, such as the Ancient Order of Hibernians. The Irish also belonged to local chapters of national or international organizations that were not specifically Irish, such as the Freemasons. Other organizations to which Irish immigrants belonged were strictly local in nature. The records for Irish societies may have preserved where in Ireland an immigrant came from.

Michael Funchion's *Irish-American Voluntary Organizations* distills much of the historical research that has been done into Irish societies, but comparatively little has been studied about the genealogical use of the societies' records. Here we offer some of the findings from our own investigations:

Ancient Order of Hibernians: The AOH has its roots in Ireland and reached America in 1836 in New York City. Requirements for membership in the AOH include being a man at least sixteen years of age, of Irish descent or birth, and a practicing Catholic. The AOH has over the years given insurance benefits to its members, operated newspapers, and funded many Catholic causes and cultural activities throughout America. Local units of the AOH are called divisions.

Records generated include division records (membership applications, minute books), directories (including a modern computerized directory), histories, and newspapers. The records of individual divisions are generally still with the division if it is active. The Balch Institute for Ethnic Studies has collected some AOH division records. For further details, see Dwight A. Radford's article "Records of the Ancient Order of Hibernians in the United States" in *The Irish At Home and Abroad.*

Important

Freemasons: Freemasonry has existed in the United States since colonial times, and many of the fathers of the nation were Freemasons. Many Irish immigrants belonged to local lodges. Each state in America has its own grand lodge. **While the Catholic Church did not approve of lodge membership, Catholics tended to belong to the lodge in areas where the church was less established** such as Nevada, Utah, and Idaho. Masonic records may provide vital information such as birthplace or death data and may document transfers between lodges. Local lodges sent copies of their membership records to the grand lodge, and it is the grand lodge copies that we suggest you seek. Find the addresses for the various grand lodges in the *List of Lodges—Masonic*, published annually. The directory includes only active lodges.

Irish county associations: In the larger American cities of the nineteenth century, such as New York, Philadelphia, and Boston, associations of Irish immigrants from the same county in Ireland organized for mutual aid. Some of these organizations were known simply by their county names, while others had different titles (such as the Knights and Ladies of St. Finbar, which was the County Cork association in Boston). The county associations were generally composed of Catholic immigrants. The Balch Institute for Ethnic Studies in Philadelphia has collected various items relating to the county associations, and they are the place to start your search. The records of the county associations are often limited to meeting minutes and lists of members. However, simply finding your ancestor or other relative as a member of one of these county associations pinpoints the county of origin in Ireland.

Knights of Columbus: The Knights of Columbus (KOC) is a fraternal organization for Catholic men at least eighteen years of age. Founded in New Haven, Connecticut, in 1882, KOC provided insurance for its members. Copies of records from individual local councils are forwarded to the Supreme Council in New Haven. The Supreme Council archives has nine of the early insurance record books; all other insurance books and records are with the Supreme Council's director of membership. The KOC insurance and membership records are in order of council number, then by initiation date. Thus you would have to know the number or name of the council (just the city, if only one council existed in that city) to locate a member. Information given sometimes includes the occupation, the date initiated, the age at initiation, the beneficiary for insurance, and the date and place of birth.

Loyal Orange Institution: The Orange Order originated in 1795 in Ireland with Protestant members only. Although Orangemen arrived in America perhaps as early as 1820, they were not fully organized until 1870, when the Supreme Grand Lodge was established in New York City. Around the turn of the twentieth century, the center of American Orangeism was Pittsburgh and Philadelphia, where many Irish Protestants settled. For most of its history American Orangeism was not readily passed down from the immigrant generation to the second generation. Membership was sustained through new immigration from Ireland and transfers from Canadian lodges, where it was passed down to the second generation. Records of genealogical value for the Loyal Orange Institution in the United States include Orange newspapers, directories, lodge records, and cemetery records. Look for further detail, as well as a listing of all the lodges as of 1911, in Dwight A. Radford's article "The Loyal Orange Institution in the United States" in *The Irish At Home and Abroad*. Use this list of lodges to start the search for Orange records. The Balch Institute is the official repository for records of defunct Orange lodges.

Repeal societies: The Act of Union in 1801 united Great Britain and Ireland as the United Kingdom. Societies organized to oppose the union existed in both Ireland and North America. They were most often known as repeal societies or Friends of Ireland. The movement was particularly strong from 1841 to 1845. Societies were especially active in U.S. cities such as Boston, New York, and Philadelphia. The records left behind by repeal societies are primarily in the form of lists published in newspapers in the early 1840s, such as the *Boston Pilot* of meeting attendees. These lists sometimes give only the names of the attendees and/or what they contributed to the collection of funds for the movement. However, often these newspaper lists gave the origins of Irish immigrants who belonged to the societies and attended meetings. A table in the *Boston Pilot* of "Repeal Society Meeting Reports" in which members' origins are listed from January 1842 to December 1845 was included in Marie E. Daly's article, "Sources of Irish-American Genealogy in New England" in *The Irish in New England*. Many cities and towns in the New England states as well as locations in Maryland, Virginia, Missouri, Louisiana, and New Brunswick are covered. For further information see Kyle J. Betit's article "Irish Repeal Societies in North America" in *The Irish At Home and Abroad*.

REFERENCES AND FURTHER READING

Betit, Kyle J. "Irish Repeal Societies in North America." *The Irish At Home and Abroad* 5 (1) (1st Quarter 1998): 23–25.

Daly, Marie E. "Sources of Irish-American Genealogy in New England" in *The Irish in New England,* 10–24. Boston: New England Historic Genealogical Society, 1985.

Funchion, Michael F., ed. *Irish American Voluntary Organizations.* Westport, Conn.: Greenwood Press, 1983.

Radford, Dwight A. "The Loyal Orange Institution in the United States." *The Irish At Home and Abroad* 3 (2) (1995/96): 69–77.

———. "Records of the Ancient Order of Hibernians in the United States." *The Irish At Home and Abroad* 4 (4) (4th Quarter 1997): 162–164.

Sources

VITAL RECORDS

Some areas, such as the New England states, kept vital records (records of births, marriages, and deaths) from the early 1600s. Other places, such as Pennsylvania, did not keep vital records until the late 1800s. In the southern United States, counties began keeping marriage records from their creation, while births and deaths may not have been recorded until the twentieth century. Policies regarding privacy and the availability of later records vary by state. In most localities the local or county government kept earlier vital records, but states kept later vital records. Vital records vary in terms of their usefulness for tracing Irish immigrants. For example, nineteenth-century Massachusetts death records give the deceased person's father's name and mother's maiden name.

Tip

Vital records were often kept earlier in a city than in rural areas. For example, Brooklyn and New York established boards of health in 1866 to keep vital records, and some records were kept even earlier for these cities. New York state, though, began in 1880 to require all towns and cities to record births, marriages, and deaths.

In one example, we were trying to find the birthplace of Edward McQuaid in Ireland, so we were researching the birth records of his children in Chicago. We found the births of several children, including his son Edward, born 7 May 1886, whose birth record states that his father was born in County Limerick and that his mother, Adelia, was born in Madison, Wisconsin.

You can consult published and Internet reference sources to determine when vital records were kept in a particular state, at what government levels, and where to access the records. We recommend the Internet Web sites of USGenWeb and Cyndi's List. The FHL has extensive collections of vital records.

THREE

Canada

C anada has a rather complicated history, and to better understand the records and how to use them, here is a brief overview of Canadian history. One of the most important facts is that both the French and English colonized areas of Canada. France lost nearly all of its possessions to the British in 1763. Soon after, thousands of families traveled to the Canadian colonies from what was to become the United States. This group of refugees arrived during the American Revolution and after U.S. independence was formally recognized in 1783; these settlers were known as Loyalists. In other words, they sided with the British and not the Americans during the war. The Loyalist aspect of Canadian history is important, and there are entire Web sites, lineage societies, and books about the subject. One Web site for Loyalists is the United Empire Loyalists' Association of Canada at <http://www.npiec.on.ca/~uela/uela1.htm>.

What we know today as Canada developed over many decades from British colonies into an independent nation that is now part of the British Commonwealth of Nations. The year 1867 is a key year in the history of Canada. That year the colonies of New Brunswick, Nova Scotia, Canada East (now called Quebec) and Canada West (now called Ontario) were united to form the Dominion of Canada. Quebec was a French colony until 1763, so it has a different history, set of laws, and way of keeping records than the British colonies. Many of Quebec's legal records were kept by notaries and are thus called notary records. While Quebec research has its challenges, the Irish presence there was just as strong as in the English-speaking parts of Canada.

To help you more completely understand Canadian history, we recommend a few Internet sites: Canadian Genealogy and History Links <http://www.islandnet.com/~jveinot/cghl/cghl.html>, a highly organized system of links for provinces and sources, including searchable databases and history sites; **and The History of Canada and Canadians** <http://www.linksnorth.com/canada-history>.

We are fortunate that there are many guides to help sort through research in

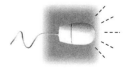

Internet Source

the provinces. We are also fortunate that there is a keen interest in studying the Irish presence in Canada, so there is no lack of reference material from the genealogical and the historical perspective. **Here are only a few of the historical references to the Irish in Canada:**

Printed Source

Grace, Robert J. *The Irish in Quebec: An Introduction to the Historiography, Followed by An Annotated Bibliography on the Irish in Quebec.* Quebec, PQ: Institut québécois de recherche sur la culture, 1993.

Houston, Cecil J. and William J. Smyth. *Irish Emigration and Canadian Settlement: Patterns, Links and Letters.* Toronto and Buffalo: University of Toronto Press, 1990.

MacKay, Donald. *Flight From Famine: The Coming of the Irish to Canada.* Toronto: McClelland and Stewart Inc., 1990.

Toner, P.M., ed. *New Ireland Remembered: Historical Essays on the Irish in New Brunswick.* Fredericton, NB: New Ireland Press, 1988.

If you're going to do Canadian research, arm yourself with some of the following material, each having a different and important focus. All of these are for general Canadian research:

Printed Source

Barclay-Lapointe, Elizabeth. *Sourcing Canada: Genealogy Addresses–Ed., 1997.* Buckingham, PQ: Buckingham Press, 1997. (For each province, this book lists genealogical societies, public archives, church archives, libraries, historical societies, and museums. Addresses, telephone and fax numbers, e-mail and Web site addresses, and hours of operation are given, in addition to a brief description of holdings. Details regarding the National Archives of Canada and the National Library of Canada are at the front of the book. Publisher's address: Buckingham Press, 10 des Castors, Buckingham, PQ J8L 2W7, Canada; Phone: (819) 281-7575; Fax: (819) 281-9322.

Baxter, Angus. *In Search Of Your Canadian Roots, Tracing Family Tree In Canada.* 3d ed. Baltimore: Genealogical Publishing Co., 1999. (This is the most widely available introduction to Canadian research and serves the beginner well in getting started with Canadian records and repositories.)

Douglas, Althea. *Here Be Dragons! Navigating the Hazards Found in Canadian Family Research: A Guide for Genealogists with Some Uncommon Useful Knowledge.* Toronto: Ontario Genealogical Society, 1996. (This work focuses primarily on strategies for successful research, and we highly recommend reading it prior to delving into record sources.) Publisher's address: Ontario Genealogical Society, 40 Orchard View Blvd., Suite 102, Toronto, ON M4R 1B9, Canada.)

Jonasson, Eric. *The Canadian Genealogical Handbook: A Comprehensive Guide to Finding Your Ancestors in Canada.* 2d ed. Winnipeg: Wheatfield Press, 1978. (Though outdated, this book contains excellent descriptions of Canadian source material.)

National Archives of Canada. *Tracing your Ancestors in Canada.* 12th ed. Ottawa: National Archives of Canada, 1997.

When researching in a particular province, use the following provincial research guides. You would also do well to join a provincial genealogical society and subscribe to its journal to keep current. Some of the Canadian genealogical societies are among the best in the world.

There is such an interest in genealogy in Canada that you have the benefit of many online databases and quality Web sites. **There are two free reference sources on the Internet that may prove valuable in your Irish immigrant research.**

Internet Source

- A Canadian genealogy newsletter, the *Global Gazette*, is published regularly at <http://globalgazette.net>. Search the back issue list of *Global Gazette* by topic or keyword at <http://globalgazette.net/backtop.htm>. This list contains many freely accessible articles about Canada in general and about individual provinces.

- You can find and print out for free the research outlines for each of the Canadian provinces primarily detailing sources at the FHL in Salt Lake City, on the LDS Family Search Web site <http://www.familysearch.org> under "Custom Search."

WHERE TO FIND CANADIAN RECORDS

Library/Archive Source

Many of the important Canadian records are accessible at the National Archives of Canada, the National Library of Canada, and provincial archives. Many of these archives have Web sites describing their holdings, and some allow interlibrary loan of materials. A large body of Canadian records, including many censuses, church records, and land records, is on microfilm at the FHL. To keep current on what is available for Canadian research, watch for the latest on Cyndi's List <http://www.cyndislist.com> and the Canada GenWeb Project <http://www.rootsweb.com/~canwgw/>. Another interesting listing of electronic and printed material is "Genealogical Research in Canada" <http://www.king.igs.net/~bdmilhm/cangenealogy.html>.

Below we have divided our discussion by province. This list is not by any means complete, but it provides a solid foundation.

Alberta: This province actually benefits from two genealogical societies: the Alberta Family Histories Society in Calgary and the Alberta Genealogical Society in Edmonton. Many of the province's records are housed at the Provincial Archives of Alberta, also in Edmonton. The Glenbow Archives is one of Canada's largest non-governmental repositories. A fine guide to research in the province is Victoria Lemieux and David Leonard's *Tracing Your Ancestors in Alberta: A Guide to Sources of Genealogical Interest in Alberta's Archives and Research Centres.* We also recommend Laura Hanowski's article "The Irish in Alberta" in *The Irish At Home and Abroad.* The Alberta GenWeb Project <http://users.rootsweb.com/~canab/index.htm/> hosts two noteworthy databases for the 1891 census and for cemetery transcriptions from throughout Alberta.

British Columbia: For handbooks, see the British Columbia Vital Statistics Agency's *Genealogical Resources For British Columbians* and Barbara Monasch's *Genealogical Sources in British Columbia.* Many of the records of the province are at the British Columbia Archives. The Archives' Web site <http://www2.bcarchi

ves.gov.bc.ca/textual/governmt/vstats/v_events.htm> includes extracts of vital records from the province. The British Columbia Genealogical Society is also an excellent place to start your search. The British Columbia GenWeb Project <http://www.rootsweb.com/~canbc/> is divided into sections of the province where you can find volunteers extracting just about every kind of record imaginable. One major database is for cemeteries in British Columbia Cemetery Finding Aid <http://www.islandnet.co/bccfa>.

Manitoba: The primary focus of Elizabeth Briggs' book *Access to Ancestry: A Genealogical Resource Manual for Canadians Tracing Their Heritage* is resources in the province of Manitoba. Friesen and Potyondi's *A Guide to the Study of Manitoba Local History* is also useful. See also Linda White's article "The Irish in Manitoba" in *The Irish At Home and Abroad*. Many of the province's records are kept at the Provincial Archives of Manitoba. The Manitoba Genealogical Society is a major resource because it has ongoing projects extracting and indexing cemetery inscriptions, the 1901 census, and Anglican and United Church of Canada registers. The Manitoba GenWeb Project <http://www.rootsweb.com/~canmb/index.htm> also has ongoing indexing projects, one important online resource being the 1827 census of the Red River.

New Brunswick: For guides to records of this province, see Robert F. Fellows's *Researching Your Ancestors in New Brunswick* and Terrence M. Punch's *Genealogist's Handbook for Atlantic Canada Research*. You can find extensive records at the Public Archives of New Brunswick. The Archives Web site hosts a grant book database concerning land grants from 1765 to 1900. Another important organization is the New Brunswick Genealogical Society. The NB GenWeb Project <http://www.rootsweb.com/~cannb/nbgenweb> is divided by county and includes many resources, indexes, and historical materials.

Newfoundland: For a guide to research, see the Newfoundland chapter in *Genealogist's Handbook for Atlantic Canada Research*, edited by Terrence M. Punch. An important organization is the Newfoundland and Labrador Genealogical Society, which produces a quarterly journal. The Provincial Archives of Newfoundland and Labrador is the principal repository for this area. The Newfoundland & Labrador GenWeb Project <http://www.huronweb.com/genweb/nf.htm> is divided into region; here you have access to the ongoing projects indexing church records, vital records, and cemetery inscriptions.

Northwest Territories: The NWT Archives holds numerous records for the territories. The NWT Genealogical Society has an obituary index at its Web site. Some issues of the society's newsletter *Under the Jack Pine* are also on its Web site. The NWT and Nunavut GenWeb Project <http://www.rootsweb.com/~cannt/> has links and addresses.

Nova Scotia: Two guides to research in this province are Julie Morris's *Tracing Your Ancestors in Nova Scotia* and Terrence M. Punch's *Genealogical Research in Nova Scotia*. Many records are held at the Public Archives of Nova Scotia, and its Web site has databases of marriage bonds and licenses, as well as Cape Breton land petitions. The Nova Scotia GenWeb Project <http://www.rootsweb.com/~canns/index.html> is an excellent source.

Nunavut: This territory was created in 1999 from the Northwest Territories;

most of its genealogical material, however, is still linked with the NWT.

Ontario: The amount of material published in print and on the Internet for Ontario is truly staggering. To fully understand the records of the province in all their complexity, we recommend Brenda Dougall Merriman's *Genealogy in Ontario: Searching the Records*. Merriman's guide can be supplemented with Ryan Taylor's bibliography, *Books You Need to do Genealogy in Ontario: An Annotated Bibliography*. The Archives of Ontario is a major repository that holds many of the province's records. Then there is the essential Ontario Genealogical Society. The Ontario GenWeb Project <http://www.multiboard.com/~spettit/ongenweb/> has pages for each county and district in the province with many extractions and indexes. Three other important Web sites are

1. Ontario Genealogy Resources <http://wwnet.com/~treesrch/ontario.html>.
2. Ontario Cemetery Finding Aid <http://www.islandnet.com/ocfa/home page.html>, an index to more than two million tombstone transcripts made by the Ontario Genealogical Society.
3. 1871 Census Index to Heads of Households and Strays <http://xcat.stauffer.queenssu.ca/census/>.

Prince Edward Island: The chapter on Prince Edward Island in *Genealogist's Handbook for Atlantic Canada Research*, edited by Terrence M. Punch, includes background on records and where they are located. Many records are available at the Public Archives and Records Office of Prince Edward Island, which is the major repository for the province. The Prince Edward Island Genealogical Society, Inc., is based in Charlottetown. The PEI GenWeb Project <http://www.islandregister.com/> is simply an excellent resource. It includes several databases concerning censuses, land, wills, directories, and shipping lists.

Quebec: Probably the most detailed guide to Quebec research in English is Douglas Miller's *Miller's Manual, A Research Guide to the Major French-Canadian Genealogical Resources, What They Are and How to Use Them*. A guide that discusses some of the more basic sources is John P. DuLong's *French-Canadian Genealogical Research*. If you can read French, a large work on Quebec research by René Jetté is *Traité de Généalogie*. The National Archives of Quebec (Archives Nationales de Québec) holds many records for the province. The Project GenWeb du Quebec <http://www.rootsweb.com/~canqc/index.htm> is an excellent source for articles concerning Quebec sources and research. There is a major online database indexing some of the province's notarial records at <http://www.cdnq.org/cnq/origines/origines.html>.

Saskatchewan: The major repositories in the province are the Saskatchewan Archives Board and the Glenbow Archives. The main genealogical organization, the Saskatchewan Genealogical Society, is a professional institution with an excellent library. The guide *Exploring Family History in Saskatchewan* by Hande and Pittendrigh is published by the Saskatchewan Archives. Also see Laura Hanowski's article "The Irish in Saskatchewan" in *The Irish At Home and Abroad*. The Saskatchewan GenWeb Project <http://www.rootsweb.com/~cansk/saskatchewan/> has a general links section including an important database of cemetery transcriptions.

Yukon: The Yukon Archives is the major record repository for the territory. The Yukon GenWeb Project <http://www.rootsweb.com/~canyk/> is an excellent resource. Use it along with another Web site, Ghosts of the Klondike Gold Rush <http://www.gold-rush.org/ghost-01.htm> to access vital links and databases for the area, especially concerning those who were in the gold rush and crossed from Alaska into the Yukon.

SOME SOURCES TO GET YOU STARTED

Sources

In this section we discuss selected Canadian sources that will be important to researching your Irish immigrant ancestor: censuses, church records, civil registration, immigration records, Internet sites, and land records. We have purposely limited ourselves to these six important sources, since we have already referred you to some of the best books on Canadian research. We want to remind you that your Canadian research by no means ends with the sources we are discussing; there are many more to look at. Here's a taste of some Canadian records.

CENSUS RECORDS

Censuses of what is now Canada were taken in 1841, 1851, 1861, 1871, 1881, 1891, and 1901 (the latest released to the public). Some areas are not covered by the surviving 1841 and 1851 census returns, while other areas have census records from even earlier dates. These records are available at the National Archives of Canada and at the FHL on microfilm. The censuses from 1851 and later list each member of the household, the ethnic origin, and religion. For the most part Canadian censuses are unindexed. One notable exception is the 1871 census of Ontario, which was indexed by county. The 1901 census of Canada lists each person's date of birth and year of immigration. The <http://www.ingeneas.com> Web site contains an index to foreign-born persons in the 1901 census of Quebec as well as parts of other provinces.

Tip

Prior to searching the microfilm copies of the censuses, look at the Web sites of the provincial archives, the GenWeb Project, and the genealogical society for the area you're interested in. You would be surprised at the indexes being placed on the Internet. When you examine the original census manuscript, make sure you jot down any possible relatives or neighbors from Ireland, as these could be friends or family from the same place in Ireland as your ancestors.

Now a word about religion in the censuses. Don't be surprised if a Protestant family's religious affiliation changes with every census report. This is actually a positive, since it gives you a reason to look at more than one denomination's records, and it also might increase the odds that your ancestors' birthplace was noted when they joined a new church. We were tracing a McDonald family in Ontario, and to say the least, the township seemed to be flooded with McDonalds. So how did we discover which ones we were interested in? We were looking for a Catholic McDonald family from Ireland, so we could disregard the Scottish McDonalds who were Protestants. This left a manageable core of families from which to continue our search!

CHURCH RECORDS

Church records can be one of the most important tools for identifying immigrant origins in Ireland. We have seen many times a marriage or burial record that lists the county in Ireland where the person was born. We do need to point out that the quality and even the quantity of the records varies by denomination, time period, locality, and congregation. You may be able to find birthplaces, parents' names, occupations, residences, and the names of baptismal sponsors (godparents) and marriage witnesses. The major sources of information for most churches are registers of baptisms/births, marriages, and burials/deaths. If your ancestors lived only transiently in an area and were not there in a census year, use church records to isolate the specific place they resided. For example, many immigrants lived briefly in Ontario or Quebec before going to the United States. Finding a baptismal record for a child born in Ontario or Quebec can identify where the family lived and reveal other records to be searched.

In some denominations congregation or parish meeting minutes document transfers in and out. This is good especially if the transfer is from an Irish church. These minutes are just as useful in tracing migrations within Canada or between denominations, so do not neglect them.

There are (and were) many religious denominations in Canada. You will find that some denominations have merged over time, such as the United Church of Canada, and this will affect where you find records deposited now. Also, don't close your mind to the possible range of your ancestors' church affiliations. Keep in mind that if your ancestors were Catholic and settled in an area only occasionally visited by a priest, you may find baptisms, marriages, and burials in another denomination. Yes, although they lived and died as Roman Catholics, this is more common than you might think. Many church records are available on microfilm from the National Archives of Canada and you can order them through your local public library. Church registers are also available at the FHL. Now let's focus on the records of the Anglican Church of Canada, the Presbyterian Church in Canada, the Roman Catholic Church, the United Church of Canada (which includes Methodists, Congregationalists, and many Presbyterians), the Baptist Church, and the Church of Jesus Christ of Latter-day Saints (Mormons).

Anglican Church of Canada: The Anglican Church of Canada is part of the Anglican communion, whose churches have their roots in the Church of England. In Ireland, the equivalent church is the Church of Ireland, and many members immigrated to Canada. The denomination was originally known as the Church of England in Canada and is now called the Anglican Church of Canada. The church is organized on a parish and diocesan basis. Each parish has a rector (or parish priest), and each diocese is administered by a bishop. This is a major faith in Canadian history, and its records should not be ignored for persons of all denominations.

Reminder

Each of the Anglican dioceses in Canada has an archives with material about local parishes. The Anglican Church of Canada Archives also has records from a few local parishes. The *Records of the Anglican Church of Canada* series lists the holdings of Anglican dioceses. Each book in the series covers a group of diocese (known as an ecclesiastical province). These incredible books show where parish records are located and the dates for which registers are available. For example, the book on the Province of Ontario includes maps showing the townships in each of the seven dioceses [*Guide to the Holdings of the Ecclesiastical Province of Ontario*, by the Archivists of the Ecclesiastical Province of Ontario (Agincourt, ON: Generation Press, Inc., 1990)].

Presbyterians: Many Presbyterian congregations were part of the union of churches that became the United Church of Canada; however, about half of them did not join the merger. For congregations that are now a United Church, you will need to contact that denomination. Congregations that did not join the merger became part of the Presbyterian Church in Canada, and you can find records at the Presbyterian Church in Canada Archives. So if you only know that your ancestor was a Presbyterian, you may need to check both denominations.

Presbyterian registers vary in their content depending on the congregation. The registers may include records of birth/baptism, marriage, death/burial, session minutes, and communion rolls. If immigrant origins are preserved, it is usually in the session minutes or the communion rolls. The session is the governmental body for the local congregation. In order to be accepted into a congregation, the session had to interview the prospective communicant. The session minutes recorded the acceptance or rejection of the communicant and, perhaps transfers from other congregations (such as in Ireland). The minutes of a Presbyterian congregation are of the utmost importance. When looking at Presbyterian records, make sure that you also gain access to the minutes, which may be in a separate register from the typical births/baptisms, marriages, and deaths/burials. The Presbyterian Church in Canada Archives also holds an index to ministers and students at Knox College in Toronto.

Roman Catholic Church: Many Catholic parish registers are available on microfilm at the FHL, particularly for Quebec and Ontario. If you are tracing French Canadian ancestors, the Quebec marriage registers will form the backbone of your research. These registers give great detail including the names and residences of the bride's and groom's parents. There are several indexes to Quebec Catholic marriages, the most commonly used probably being the Loiselle Index, which you can get on microfilm from the FHL. A more comprehensive index for the period from 1760 to 1935 was compiled by the Drouin Institute [*Répertoire alphabétique des mariages des Canadiens Francais 1760–1935*. (Longueuil, Québec: Institut Généalogique Drouin)]. Copies of the Drouin Index from 1760 to 1935 are at the Salle Gagnon, Montreal Public Library, and some libraries in the United States such as the American-French Genealogical Society in Woonsocket, Rhode Island, and the New England Historic Genealogical Society in Boston, Massachusetts.

Microfilm Source

The typical Catholic register will consist of baptisms, marriages, and sometimes burials. Remember, burial is not a sacrament in the Catholic faith, so whether these records were kept varies from parish to parish. Another type of record that most researchers don't think about are marriage dispensations. If there was some question or concern about a couple being married, the matter went before the bishop, who could grant a dispensation to allow the marriage by a Catholic priest. Causes for receiving a dispensation range from the couple being related, a Catholic marrying a non-Catholic, and, most often, the banns not being properly read in church. Dispensation records are usually kept at the diocese and a notation in the local parish register was made at the time of the marriage.

For finding Irish origins in the records, we recommend the marriages and burials. However, dispensations have been known to not only provide birthplaces but also birth dates and parents' names. If the parish you're looking at does not contain birthplaces, then use the godparents' names at a baptism and the witnesses' names at a marriage to indirectly lead you to the same information. You would assume that these were trusted friends and possibly family. If they were from the same area of Ireland, then researching the godparents and witnesses may uncover your own family's origins.

Another important historical aspect of Canadian Catholicism is that it was common for a parish to comprise families from the same area in Ireland. Some of these parishes were surrounded by a sea of Protestants, so the chances of all the Kellys in a parish being related may actually be quite good. Also, in chain migrations or government schemes, many people would emigrate from the same area of Ireland and settle together in Canada.

Research Tip

When you seek parish registers, always check the FHL or the National Archives of Canada first to see if a microfilm is available. If not, contact individual dioceses for information on parish registers by using the Web site Local Catholic Church History and Genealogy—Canada, <http://home.att.net/~Local_Catholic/Catholic-Canada.htm>.

United Church of Canada: The largest denomination in Canada today dates back to only 1925. That year the United Church of Canada was formed by a union of the Methodist Church (Canada), over half of the Presbyterian Church in Canada congregations, and the Congregational Churches of Canada. Then the Canada Conference of the Evangelical United Brethren Church joined the United Church of Canada in 1968. Local church records of the uniting denominations are being collected by the United Church of Canada archives network, but many local church records are still kept by the churches. However, the appropriate archives is the place to start the search for old records. Regional archives with their contact information are described in the Committee on Archives and History; the United Church of Canada's book, *Guide to Family History Research in the Archival Repositories of the United Church of Canada*; and on the United Church of Canada Archives Network's Internet site: <http://www.uccan.org/archives/home.htm>.

The Methodist Episcopal Church (sometimes abbreviated ME) was officially organized in 1784 in Baltimore and included Methodist churches in the United

States and Canada. In 1828, the Canadian churches became independent. Various branches of Methodism then developed in Canada, including the Wesleyan Methodist Church, the Methodist Episcopal Church, the New Connexion Methodists, and the Primitive Methodists. The branches were united in 1884 to form the Methodist Church, Canada.

Local Methodist congregations generally kept records of membership, baptisms, marriages, and deaths. Marriage records sometimes indicate birthplaces, including specific places in Ireland, as well as parents' names and witnesses. The records of membership were sometimes called class lists. The churches also kept registers of probationers, individuals undergoing preparation for admission to membership. The membership or class lists indicate when a member was admitted and from what denomination (if different from Methodist), as well as when a member left. Class and probationer lists may give addresses an urban area.

Microfilm Source

So the places to start the search for a Methodist register would be with one of the United Church of Canada conference archives, the microfilm at the National Archives of Canada, or the microfilm at the FHL.

Methodism provides an interesting historical twist when it comes to the Irish. Large numbers of Irish people of German descent, called the Palatines, immigrated to Ontario. This makes them a noteworthy group not only because of their German origins but also because they can be traced back to the same areas of Ireland. Many of the Irish Palatines converted to the Methodist Church in Ireland. For a discussion of sources, see Carolyn A. Heald's article "Researching Irish Palatines in Ireland and Ontario" in *The Irish At Home and Abroad*. For Canadian Methodist ministers, an excellent resource, "Irish-Born Methodist Ministers and Probationers in Canada," is in the appendix of Taggart's *The Irish in World Methodism, 1760–1900*.

Baptist: The Baptist Church provides an interesting case study of how emigrating families changed churches. There are many branches of the Baptist faith, none of which could be called good record keepers. Baptists differ from the other Protestant faiths discussed in this section in that they baptized adults upon a confession of faith, not infants, so the only way you will find a birth record is if the minister just happened to keep one. While there were Baptists in Ireland, it remained a small denomination until the late nineteenth and early twentieth centuries. However, if you're glancing through the censuses of the maritime provinces (i.e., New Brunswick, Prince Edward Island, and Nova Scotia), you will notice a large number of Irish listed as Baptists. This means that most of them were of another faith in Ireland and joined the Baptist Church upon arriving in Canada. We mention the maritime provinces because this was a stronghold for Baptist faith among Irish immigrants. Baptists of Irish descent served as ministers and missionaries in Canada. An example of a work documenting many of these is Ingraham E. Bill's *Fifty Years with the Baptist Ministers and Churches of the Maritime Provinces of Canada* (1880).

Although Baptist records may be of limited genealogical value, do not assume there is nothing in them for you. Certainly don't totally ignore them. Baptist records may be in the form of minutes, which report transfers in and out of the congregation, new members, believers' baptisms, sometimes marriages, and deaths or burials. Records are located in two main repositories: the Canadian Baptist Archives at McMaster University Divinity College in Hamilton, Ontario, and the Atlantic Baptist Archives of the Acadia University in Wolfville, Nova Scotia.

Latter-day Saints (Mormons): The Church of Jesus Christ of Latter-day Saints (called Mormons or LDS Church) has had missionary activity in Canada since the church's founding in 1830. From 1830 to 1845, missionaries were sent from the United States to what is now Ontario and the maritime provinces. Many converts came from these two areas; the strength of the faith was around Kingston, Earnestown, Toronto, Brantford, Mount Pleasant, and North and South Crosby, all in Ontario. This early Mormon influence is somewhat masked in Canadian history because most early converts emigrated to Mormon settlements in the United States. The second phase of influence, which still has a legacy today, is the group of Mormon colonies in southern Alberta. In 1887, colonists from Mormon communities in the western United States fled to Canada after anti-plural marriage laws were enacted. After 1890, when the plural marriage issue died down in both America and Canada, these Alberta colonies served as a base for other Americans to settle lands opened by the Canadian government.

The importance of Mormonism is that the church records may list where in Ireland a person was born. Also because of the faith's emphasis on genealogy and family history, a large collection of journals, family histories, and pedigrees has been compiled on nineteenth-century converts. It is among such records that you can find information on several generations of family members who never joined the faith (see chapter two).

CIVIL REGISTRATION

Government registration of births, marriages, and deaths is termed civil registration in Canada. The dates the records begin vary by province and territory. You will also find that the information on the certificates varies over time. **These are important records in the search for Irish origins, as an Irish birthplace may be preserved in a marriage or death record.** Remember that the person who died does not give the information on the death certificate, so it may be suspect to some degree. Also remember that these records are not complete. An excellent guide to the topic of civil registration is George Emery's *Facts of Life: The Social Construction of Vital Statistics*. Emery points out that for the time from 1875 to 1895, only two-thirds of the people were registered, and that it was no more than 85 percent from 1896 to 1919.

Since each province or territory kept its own records, you will need to know where to write to request a certificate. Some civil registration is on microfilm in Canada or at the FHL while others, such as that for British Columbia, are on the Internet. You will find that the older records are open to the public; there are right-of-privacy rules, however, so depending on what your needs are, you

Important

may encounter some problems. When seeking information from civil registration, make sure that you branch out to your ancestor's siblings and anyone with whom you think they may have been associated in Ireland. This will increase your odds of finding one certificate that will tell where the entire group of family and friends was from.

Use the following information by province and territory as a place to start your search. **Always be aware that the status of older records may change, as do the prices for obtaining certificates.** Keep current on this subject and do not assume that the ordering information today is the same as when you ordered something five years ago. One last word about ordering certificates: Make sure you say it is for genealogical purposes and you need all the information on the record.

Reminder

Alberta: These records predate the formation of the province, when Alberta was part of the Northwest Territories. The older records start in 1898. The records from 1898 to 1905 are at the Provincial Archives of Alberta. Obtain records from 1906 on via mail from Alberta Municipal Affairs, Alberta Registries, Vital Statistics, P.O. Box 2023, Edmonton, Alberta T5J 4W7, Canada; *(location)* 3d Floor—10365-97 Street, Edmonton, Alberta; Phone: (780) 427-7013; Internet: <http://www.gov.ab.ca/gs>.

British Columbia: The government began recording births, marriages, and deaths in 1872. You can search these indexes on the Web site of the British Columbia Archives: Births (1872–1899), Marriages (1872–1824), Deaths (1872–1979). Records for these years are also on microfilm at several libraries in British Columbia as well as the FHL. Order certificates from these and later years from: Vital Statistics, British Columbia Ministry of Health, 818 Fort Street, Victoria, British Columbia V8W 1H8, Canada; Phone: (604) 952-2681; Fax: (250) 952-1829; Internet: <http://www.hlth.gov.bc.ca/vs/>.

Manitoba: The government began recording statistics from 1882. They are located at the Division of Vital Statistics, Community Services, 254 Portage Avenue, Winnipeg, Manitoba R3C 0B6, Canada; Phone: (204) 945-3701; Fax: (204) 948-3128; Internet: <http://www.gov.mb.ca/cca/vital.html>.

New Brunswick: The Provincial Archives of New Brunswick holds Births (1888–1902), Marriages (1888–1921), and Deaths (1888–1948). The archives also has numerous searchable databases on its Web site for vital statistics. For more modern certificates contact: Vital Statistics Office, Health and Community Services, Suite 203, 435 King Street, Fredericton, New Brunswick E3B 1E5, Canada; Mailing: P.O. Box 6000, Fredericton, New Brunswick E3B 5H1, Canada; Phone: (506) 453-2385; Fax: (506) 444-4139; Internet: <http://www.gov.nb.ca/0379/en/>.

Newfoundland: Newfoundland did not join Canada until the twentieth century; however, its civil registration began in 1892. Order certificates from Vital Statistics, Government Service Centre, Department of Government Services & Lands, 5 Mews Place, P.O. Box 8700, St. John's, Newfoundland A1B 4J6, Canada; Phone: (709) 729-3308; Fax: (709) 729-0946; Internet: <http://www.gov.nf.ca/gsl/gslvfaq.htm>.

Northwest Territories: Incomplete records begin in 1925. Make requests at

Registrar General, Vital Statistics, Department of Health and Social Services, Government of NWT, Bag 9, Inuvik, Northwest Territories X0E 0T0, Canada; Phone: (867) 777-7420; Fax: (867) 777-3197; Internet: <http://www.gov.nt.ca/>.

Nova Scotia: The government began registration in 1908; Obtain records at Vital Statistics, Department of Business and Consumer Services, 1723 Hollis Street, P.O. Box 157, Halifax, Nova Scotia B3J 2M9, Canada; Phone: (902) 424-4381; Fax: (902) 424-0678; Internet: <http://www.gov.ns.ca/bacs/vstat/>.

Nunavut: In 1999 Nunavut became Canada's newest territory. For additional information see the Web site <http://www.nunavut.com/home.html>.

Ontario: Province-wide civil registration began in 1869. The early records are at the Archives of Ontario with microfilm copies at the FHL: Births (1869–1903), Marriages (1869–1918), and Deaths (1869–1928). For more modern records contact: Office of the Registrar General, P.O. Box 4600, 189 Red River Road, Thunder Bay, Ontario P7B 6L8, Canada; Phone: (416) 325-8305; Fax: (807) 343-7459; Internet: <http://www.ccr.gov.on.ca/mccr/orgindex.htm>. There are earlier civil registers of marriage based on the county and district levels.

Prince Edward Island: Registration began in 1906. Earlier records are at the Public Archives and Records Office of Prince Edward Island, and its Web site has some searchable databases. Order certificates from Director of Vital Statistics, Office of Vital Statistics, Department of Health and Social Services, 35 Douses Road, Box 3000, Montague, Prince Edward Island C0A 1R0, Canada; Phone: (902) 838-0880; Fax: (902) 838-0883; Internet: <http://www.gov.pe.ca/vitalstatistics/index.php3>.

Quebec: This province provides some of its own unique situations that you will need to be aware of. Although church registration of events extends into the early seventeenth century, the government took the responsibility of registering events in 1926 for those who did not belong to a church. All marriages were still expected to occur in a church until 1969. So the church registers became the civil registers; one copy was kept with the church, and another was forwarded to a district protonotary. Not until 1994 did Quebec as a government begin to centrally keep civil registration. Most pre-1900 records are in the custody of the nine regional offices of the Archives nationales du Quebec, and a vast majority of them are also on microfilm at the FHL. For more information on vital statistics in Quebec, visit the Web site of the Quebec Family History Society. Obtain other records at Direction de l'état civil, Ministère des Relations avec les citoyens et de l'Immigration, 205, rue Montmagny, Quebec, PQ G1N 2Z9, Canada; Phone: (418) 643-3900.

Saskatchewan: Civil registration began in 1905 when Saskatchewan entered Canada; however, some marriages records date back to 1895. Obtain records at Division of Vital Statistics, Department of Health, 1942 Hamilton Street, Regina, Saskatchewan S4P 3V7, Canada; Phone: (306) 787-3092; Fax: (306) 787-2288; Internet: <http://www.gov.sk.ca/>.

Yukon Territory: Civil registration began in 1898 and remained incomplete until the 1940s. Records are at Vital Statistics Department of Health and Human Resources, P.O. Box 2703, Whitehorse, Yukon Y1A 2C6, Canada; Phone:

(403) 667-5207; Fax: (403) 393-6486; Internet: <http://www.hss.gov.yk.ca/vsa frame.html>.

IMMIGRATION RECORDS

The three primary ports of entry into Canada were Quebec City, Quebec; Saint John, New Brunswick; and Halifax, Nova Scotia. From these three ports, immigrants often moved inland to other areas of Canada, such as Ontario. **More Irish immigrants landed in Canada than in the United States in the early decades of the nineteenth century.** Many of the immigrants who landed in Canada throughout the 1800s subsequently settled in the United States, perhaps after staying for a period of time in Canada. It may have been cheaper to travel from Ireland or Britain to Canada than directly to the United States.

Only in 1865 did the government begin keeping regular lists of passengers arriving at Quebec City. For other Canadian ports, passenger lists start even later; for example, Halifax, Nova Scotia, lists commence in 1881.

The general lack of passenger lists prior to 1865 makes it necessary to consider a variety of other immigration records as substitutes, such as almshouse records, assisted immigration records, and newspaper notices. Two useful references for substitutes are Bruce Elliott's chapter, "Canadian Sources of Irish Genealogy," in *Aspects of Irish Genealogy: Proceedings of the 1st Irish Genealogical Congress* and Eric Jonasson's chapter, "Immigration and Citizenship Records," in *The Canadian Genealogical Handbook.* Also, for some provinces, you can use the land and township records to document a person arriving in Canada.

The problem with the pre-1865 Canadian immigration material is that it is scattered. Fortunately, today we have an Internet index combining many of the sources: the inGeneas passenger and immigration list index <http://www.inGeneas .com>. This index is an incredible source that can save you a lot of time. It also includes post-1865 records such as extracts from the official passenger lists and extracts of foreign-born people in the 1901 census of Canada. Surviving passenger lists show who immigrated with an ancestor, and some also identify the prior residence of the immigrant and the destination in Canada or the United States.

Below are some of the major collections of arrival records.

Quebec and Halifax Arrival Lists, 1865–1900

Records of passenger arrivals at Quebec from 1865 to 1900 are available on microfilm at the National Archives of Canada (NAL) and the FHL. An incomplete index to passengers covering 1865 to 1869 is available from the NAC and the FHL. Halifax, Nova Scotia, passenger lists are available from 1881. Those dated 1881 to 1899 are available on microfilm from the National Archives of Canada, the FHL, or the Public Archives of Nova Scotia.

The Quebec and Halifax passenger lists do not usually identify specific origins in Ireland; however, they do sometimes list destinations in Canada or the United States. There is an index to ships available for Halifax and Quebec passenger lists from 1865 to 1900. Thus, if you know the name of the ship on which your immigrant ancestor arrived, use the index to access passenger lists. This index is available through the FHL.

When attempting to locate an ancestor in the unindexed arrivals at Quebec or Halifax, using the 1901 census of Canada or the 1900 through 1920 censuses of the United States can help. Many immigrants who came to Canada from 1865 on were still living by the time these censuses were enumerated. Each of these censuses gives the year that the immigrant arrived in the country of residence.

Twentieth-Century Arrival Lists

Canadian passenger lists from 1900 to 1918 are available from the National Archives of Canada, and you can obtain them through interlibrary loan at public libraries. These records are not available at the FHL. For arrivals after 1918, contact the Records of Entry Unit, Canada Employment and Immigration Commission. *Ships' Passenger Lists and Boarder Entry Lists in PAC, RG 76 (Records of the Immigration Branch): Microfilm Finding Aid* lists ships' passenger lists, 1865 to 1918 by port and by date. It includes National Archives of Canada microfilm reel numbers, which you can then use to order the microfilm through interlibrary loan at a public library. This guide does not index passengers' names. Find those by searching the indicated films.

National Archives of Canada
Miscellaneous Immigration Index

The National Archives of Canada has a nominal card index, "Miscellaneous Immigration Index," to lists of immigrants taken from a variety of sources who arrived in Canada prior to 1865. Compiling this index is an ongoing project at the archives. This index includes only a small percentage of the total number of Irish immigrants who came to Canada prior to 1865.

The card index is available in the archives reference room in twenty card file drawers. The cards generally indicate the source of data, name of immigrant, age, country of origin, date of arrival, and sometimes the name of the ship, occupation, number of family members, and intended place of residence. The card index is not available on microfilm, but it is now available as a search on the inGeneas.com Web site.

Some Selected Pre-1865 Immigration Sources

Canada Company: The Canada Company was formed in 1824 to sell and settle land in Upper Canada (now Ontario). The company purchased the unleased Crown reserves (one seventh of the land in Upper Canada, scattered throughout the province) plus the one million acre Huron Tract in the southwestern part of Upper Canada. The company ceased operation in 1951, and the Archives of Ontario acquired its records. Among the records were four volumes reporting a service of the company whereby it sent money to family back home as support payments or to pay passage to Canada. These volumes are extracted in Holt and Williams's *Genealogical Extraction and Index of the Canada Company Remittance Books, 1843–1847*. The books list the residences of the sender and the recipient, and

Sources

sometimes a relationship. More than half the recipients lived in Ireland.

Assisted or Subsidized Emigration Records: There are some surviving pre-Confederation lists of immigrants to Canada who participated in subsidized British immigration schemes. In these cases, groups of immigrants went to Canada to settle land with the help of the government. Surviving lists of subsidized British immigrants, dating between the years 1817 and 1831, are available at the National Archives of Canada, indexed in Manuscript Group eleven, on microfilm reel C-4252. The immigrants in these lists are *not* included in the National Archives of Canada Miscellaneous Immigration Index. The lists come from Colonial Office 384 (of the British government documents). Colonial Office 384 includes other immigration records as well.

The lists themselves provide names, former residence, occupations, and dates of entry. Some of the lists are returns of families preparing to emigrate. For example, a pair of November 1817 lists includes Catholics and Protestants, primarily from counties Carlow and Wexford (but also including families from counties Kilkenny and Wicklow). This pair of lists was published as an appendix to Bruce S. Elliott's chapter, "Immigration from South Leinster to Eastern Upper Canada," in *Wexford: History and Society*.

Peter Robinson Settlers: Peter Robinson brought two separate groups of Irish emigrants, which he selected, to Canada. The first group of 568 people embarked in 1823 and settled in the Bathurst District (Ottawa Valley); the second group of 2,024 people embarked in 1825 and settled in the Newcastle District (Peterborough area). Many of the 1823 and 1825 families were linked by blood and marriage. The complete lists of Peter Robinson settlers are included in the National Archives of Canada Miscellaneous Immigration Index and in Carol Bennett's *Peter Robinson's Settlers*. Bennett's work examines many of the Robinson families, giving their origins in Ireland, where they settled in Ontario, and details about descendants.

Peter Robinson settlers' places of origin as listed in the government records were often where the interview occurred or the nearest market or post town named by the individual, rather than the townland of residence. Bennett's listings in many cases supplement the government records with information from family Bibles, old correspondence, and other family records.

McCabe List: In February 1829, a petition was circulated, largely among Irish working on construction of the Rideau Canal near Bytown (Ottawa), advocating government assistance for bringing impoverished relatives to Canada. Some of the petitioners had been in Canada for a decade. Although the scheme was never approved, the documents were collected in Colonial Office series 384/22, with copies available at the National Archives of Canada. They provide the signature or mark of each petitioner, place of origin in Ireland (usually including the townland), family size and gender of members, the names and residences of relatives in Ireland, and a named reference in Ireland who knew the family. A copy of the petition was discovered by John McCabe, a Belfast genealogist, and it was published in Bruce S. Elliott's *The McCabe List: Early Irish in the Ottawa Valley*.

Chain Migration Studies

Irish immigration to Canada commonly took the form of "chain migration." Successive members of a family or community would follow one another from Ireland to Canada, often settling together in Canada. The following are some published examples of studies of Ireland-to-Canada chain migrations from:

County Cork: Joseph A. King's *Ireland to North America: Emigrants from West Cork* focuses on a chain migration of Irish immigrants from Schull civil parish, County Cork, to Miramichi, New Brunswick; and then along the "Northern Migration Route" into Wisconsin, Minnesota, and Washington state.

About sixteen Methodist families from Bandon, County Cork, emigrated to New Brunswick in 1817 and established New Bandon. Further details are contained in Donald F. Parrott and Nora M. Hickey's article "New Bandon, New Brunswick," *Bandon Historical Journal* 7 (1991): 45–49.

County Down: Catharine Anne Wilson's *A New Lease on Life: Landlords, Tenants, and Immigrants in Ireland and Canada* contains chapters concerning more than one hundred families from the Ards Peninsula of County Down, who settled on Amherst Island, near Kingston, Ontario, in the nineteenth century.

County Kilkenny: Many Irish from southern and southwestern Ireland went to Newfoundland in the maritime trade. John J. Mannion, in his chapter, "Old World Antecedents, New World Adaptations: Inistioge (Co. Kilkenny) Immigrants in Newfoundland," in *The Irish in Atlantic Canada, 1780–1900* examined the migration of immigrants from one parish to Newfoundland.

County Limerick: Carolyn A. Heald's *The Irish Palatines in Ontario: Religion, Ethnicity, and Rural Migration* concerns Protestants from Germany who settled in Ireland in the early 1700s, mostly in County Limerick. In the early 1800s, many Irish Palatine descendants immigrated to Ontario. In particular, Irish Palatines settled in Brock Township, Ontario County; Ramsay and Pakenham townships, Lanark County; Emily Township, Victoria County; and Blanshard Township, Perth County.

County Louth: Peter Murphy's *Together in Exile* is a history and genealogy of Catholic families who emigrated from Carlingford parish, County Louth, to the Lower Cove district of Saint John, New Brunswick, where many worked in the harbor fishery.

County Tipperary: In *Irish Migrants in the Canadas: A New Approach*, Bruce S. Elliott studied the chain migration of 775 Protestant families from North Tipperary to Canada, mostly to Carleton and Middlesex Counties, Ontario.

Yukon Border Crossings

During the gold rush in Alaska and the Yukon in the 1890s, the North West Mounted Police were concerned about the passage of many people across their borders. Their records include the name of the person who crossed and the last place of residence, which may have been in Ireland or the United States. These records are available at the Yukon Archives in Whitehorse. **Filson's Pan for Gold Database <http://www.gold-rush.org/ghost-07.htm> includes the North West Mounted Police checkpoint lists and a wide variety of other sources,** such as censuses, placer mining claims, and society records, that contain information

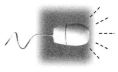

on individuals who were in the Yukon during the gold rush years. The records start in 1898 and extend into the early twentieth century. Microfilm copies are available at many Canadian repositories, including the Glenbow Archives.

We cannot underestimate this source, although most people have never heard of it. Consider this: many men went to the gold fields of Alaska and the Yukon and were never heard from again. Some found fame and fortune, though most did not.

LAND RECORDS

Tip

In your search for Irish birthplaces in Canadian records, land records should be at the top of your list. Canada is such a huge country that many schemes and programs enticed settlement. Even if land records do not provide your ancestor's birthplace, they are still one of the most important sources you can use. **You will find that land records often predate censuses, and they can help date an immigrant's arrival.** Sometimes a land record will provide the place of last residence, which, even if not Ireland, is still important in your search. Of course, pinpointing just where your ancestors lived in Canada may be the first information you need to continue your search in other records. Because of the sheer size of Canada, this is really more important and difficult than it sounds.

You can find land records in a number of places. Fortunately, many are on microfilm at provincial archives, the National Archives of Canada, the Public Record Office in England, and the FHL. The Internet is changing the face of land record research in Canada as indexes continue to appear on genealogical and archival Web sites. So it is wise to stay current with the Web site of a provincial archives or genealogical society.

Technique

In considering what types of land records may have been generated concerning your ancestor's land, think about what happened when an ancestor received land. Think of the records leading to transfer of land from the government or Crown to the first patentees; subsequent transactions involving the land; official indexes or files listing land transactions and changes of ownership for particular plots of land; maps showing the boundaries of land holdings and the names of their owners or occupiers; and of course tax records. **If you believe that your ancestors had land, we suggest some general principles to use when looking for their birthplaces.**

Place name identification: If your ancestor's property was located in a community or township with an Irish name, it is important to determine when and by whom the township or community was named, and if a group of immigrants arrived together during this time. Use deeds to determine how early the ancestor was in this locality and with whom the ancestor was associated. You may just find that the families who initially settled the township may be from the same area in Ireland. Even if your ancestral family arrived in later migrations, they may still be from the same place in Ireland, coming to join relatives or friends.

Searching the neighborhood: You will see that the Irish are notorious for immigrating together from the same community in Ireland. So if you cannot find your ancestor's birthplace, by all means direct your search to the origins of neighbors. Identify the names of neighbors in records such as deeds, maps, and censuses.

Sorting through common surnames: As you are probably aware, Irish names can be so common (we call it the Mary Kelly syndrome) that you will have to sort through many families to find the one you are looking for. For example, the search for a Wilson family from Northern Ireland may be complicated by the county or township being populated by unrelated Wilson families from England or elsewhere. Land descriptions, including acreage and geographical features, can be vital to sorting through families.

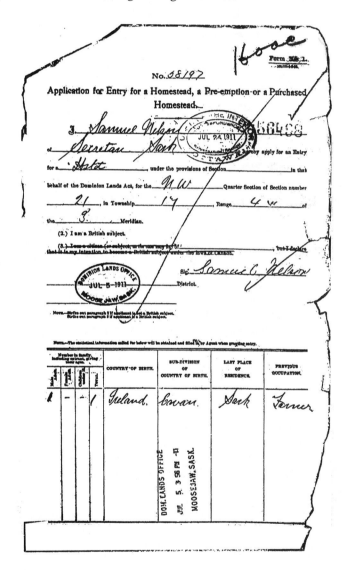

Figure 3-1
Application for Saskatchewan Homestead for Samuel Nelson, dated 1911, #2456498. Used with permission of the Saskatchewan Archives Board.

The Types of Records

Now that we have discussed some important strategies for using land records, let's discuss some of the types of land records that apply to more than one province. These extended explanations will help you as you refer to the province and territorial sections on land that we will be presenting later. We cannot, of course, exhaust all record types, since this is a vast topic worthy of a book in its own right. We will be discussing homesteads, landownership maps and atlases, and British Loyalist claims.

Homesteads were generated regarding land in Alberta, Manitoba, and Saskatchewan. These are the three prairie provinces, and a huge piece of real estate! It is the process of applying for land that your ancestors may have left clues to a birthplace in Ireland. Beginning in 1870, to encourage settlement in the West, the Canadian government offered potential settlers 160 acres of land for a $10 fee. Settlers could purchase provisions to receive an additional 160 acres near the first patented land. Interestingly enough, many settlers migrated from the United States into the Canadian homestead areas. To receive the patent, the applicant had to meet certain criteria. The homestead records ask questions such as country of birth, subdivision of country of birth, last place of residence, and previous occupation. These records are being indexed on the Internet site of the National Archives of Canada as "Dominion Land Grants" and include grants issued in Manitoba, Saskatchewan, Alberta, and the railway belt of British Columbia (ca. 1870–1930).

In our opinion some of the most interesting and essential tools in land research are the old maps and atlases that show landownership. In the nineteenth century, historical atlases were published for some Canadian provinces showing a township divided into farms with the names of those living on the property. Although these atlases were mostly published in the 1870s and after, many original immigrants were still alive and on their land. These types of historical atlases are a quick way to become acquainted with your ancestor's neighborhood. This is also a good way to trace your ancestor's neighbors if you cannot find origins on your ancestor. Microfilm copies of many of these atlases are at the FHL. **For further information on these important sources and where in Canada they may be located, see the following reference material:**

Printed Source

Eric Jonasson's section "County Maps and Atlases of Canada" in *The Canadian Genealogical Handbook* (pp. 126–127) provides a list of atlases by county and the year of publication.

Eric Jonasson. "Oliver F. Cummins' Directory Maps." *Canadian Genealogist* 3 (3) (1981): 140–156.

Betty H. Kidd. *Using Maps in Tracing Your Family History* (Ottawa: Ontario Genealogical Society, 1974). This work is on microfilm at the FHL (#1036817 item 5).

Heather Maddick. *County Maps: Land Ownership Maps of Canada in the 19th Century* (Ottawa: Public Archives of Canada, 1976).

Betty May. *County Atlases of Canada: A Descriptive Catalogue.* (Ottawa: Public Archives of Canada, 1970).

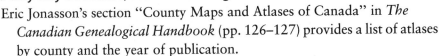

Definitions

You will also come across the term "Cadastral Maps." These are maps produced for the maritime provinces for landowners to use in approving lease agreements and collecting rents. These are an important series of maps. The government in New Brunswick has a series of 167 half-mile-to-the-inch maps showing the boundaries of original land patents throughout the province with names of grantees. Purchase blueprints of the maps from the New Brunswick Department of Natural Resources and Energy.

Land Records by Province

Alberta: The major land records for what is now Alberta are the homestead papers, available for the years 1885 to 1930. These records are arranged by the property description; there is an alphabetical index. If the person being researched is not found in the index, the homestead files can be accessed by the description of the land. The records are available on microfilm at the Provincial Archives of Alberta. Also, don't neglect the online index at the Web site of the NAC.

British Columbia: Many of the early grants are at the British Columbia Archives, and the original Crown grants are at the Lands Branch Department in Victoria. Copies of Crown Land Grants are with the land title offices. To access information about property ownership, you must know a legal description of the property. The British Columbia Archives has the F.W. Laing manuscript "Colonial Farm Settlers on the Mainland of British Columbia 1858–1871," which indexes early settlers and their landholdings. For other information about early British Columbia, see Brian Porter's article "B.C. Land Registration Until 1870" in *The British Columbia Genealogist* and Wendy Teece's article "Land Records and Maps for Genealogists in British Columbia" in *Association of Canadian Map Libraries Bulletin*.

Manitoba: The area that was originally called the Red River settlement came into the Canadian confederacy in 1870 as Manitoba. Because of its historical importance and its unique record-keeping system, we need to spend a little time here. The major land records of use in Irish immigrant research are the Hudson's Bay Company records (1811 to 1871) and the land grants (1871 to 1930). For background information about Manitoba land records see C.A. Evans's article "Land Records and Registration in Manitoba" in *Generations: The Journal of the Manitoba Genealogical Society*.

Hudson's Bay Company controlled land in Manitoba prior to 1870. The land records associated with the company consist of Land Register A (1811 to 1830) and Land Register B (1830 to 1871). The Hudson's Bay Company records also include some land registration and sales volumes for 1823 to 1862. The Hudson's Bay Company Archives is held at the Provincial Archives of Manitoba. Internet pages for Hudson's Bay Archives include general information about the collection, a description of holdings, and information about accessing records through interlibrary loan: <http://www.gov.mb.ca/chc/archives/hbca/index.html>.

Prior to 1870 the lands in Manitoba were surveyed into numbered lots, mostly along the Red and Assiniboine rivers. Manitoba land grants began in 1870 when the jurisdiction over Crown lands was transferred from the Hudson's Bay Company to the Dominion of Canada. The lands were then surveyed and sold to homesteaders until 1930. The survey assigned the old lots new numbers. The land grants in Manitoba are on microfilm through 1930 at the Crown Lands Registry (Manitoba Department of the Natural Resources) and the NAC.

New Brunswick: Land in New Brunswick was granted by the Crown. People petitioned the provincial officials, and these petitions often included biographical information. In the search for immigrant origins, the petitions are helpful. The original Crown Land Petitions are at the Provincial Archives of New Brunswick with microfilm copies from 1784 to 1918 at the FHL. Indexes for the petitions exist.

The Crown Land Grants themselves usually do not provide much detailed information. They may provide clues such as military regiment and precise location of the tract of land. The Crown Land Grants are at the Provincial Archives of New Brunswick, and microfilm copies from 1763 to 1868 are at the FHL. The Provincial Archives of New Brunswick Grantbook Database on the Internet at <http://degaulle.hil.unb.ca/library/data/panb/panbweb.html> includes records of land settlement in New Brunswick in the period 1765 to 1900.

Newfoundland and Labrador: Until 1820 there were restrictions on settlement in this area. Permission was needed to erect a building, and land ownership was generally restricted to people in the fishing trade. The restrictions were difficult to enforce, and a resident squatter population took root despite the British government's efforts. Leases for twenty-one years were given beginning in 1803. In 1820, when all restrictions were eased, people were permitted to own land and build houses. The two major types of land records for Newfoundland and Labrador are Crown Land Grants and the Registry of Deeds.

The Crown Land Grants are the records for the original land owners. These records usually tell the residence and occupation of the person receiving the grant. The Crown Land records are on microfilm at the FHL from 1803 to 1926. A description and drawing of the lands received are also given in the grant. The maps of the grants often provide the names of the neighbors. The description of the land, such as the bay or cove it was located on, can also be helpful when searching for other records such as from a church or cemetery. For background material and information about accessing these records, see Leslie A. Winsor's article "Crown Lands Records" in *Newfoundland and Labrador Genealogical Society Newsletter.*

The Registry of Deeds dates from 1825; the deeds are indexed by year and by the names of the grantors and the grantees. These records are at the Government of Newfoundland and Labrador, Registry of Deeds, Companies and Securities.

For further information about Newfoundland land records, see Don Hutchens's articles "Tracing Your Roots Through Land Ownership" and "English Land Ownership in Newfoundland," both in *Newfoundland Ancestor.*

Northwest Territories: All land transactions including the original Crown Grants for the Northwest Territories are with the Registrar of Land Titles in Yellowknife. The records, which start in 1911, are indexed by the description of land.

Nova Scotia and Cape Breton: Land grant records and the Registry of Deeds documents are at the Public Archives of Nova Scotia with microfilm copies at the FHL. You will also find information about Loyalist settlement in Nova Scotia in Marion Gilroy's *Loyalists and Land Settlement in Nova Scotia.* This work was reprinted and indexed by the Genealogical Committee of the Royal Nova Scotia Historical Society in 1980.

Crown Land Grants in Nova Scotia began as early as 1787. This indexed collection includes grants, petitions (which may provide information on the petitioner's family and immigrant origins), survey warrants, survey descriptions, and certificates from the Surveyor General of the King's Woods. You can find the grants on microfilm at the FHL, with an index from 1784 to 1877.

The Registry of Deeds for each county may predate the Crown Land Grants. These records include deeds for land transactions as well as leases and mortgages.

Cape Breton was a separate colony until 1821, when it became part of Nova Scotia, and there is a separate series of Cape Breton land grants and petitions available at PANS. Most of the settlers in Cape Breton were Scots, but the counties of origin of the Irish minority are often stated in the land petitions.

Nunavut: Land title records for Nunavut, which was created in 1999, are currently held at the Yellowknife office in the Northwest Territories.

Ontario: Ontario has a variety of land records, and they are one of the most important sources to use in identifying immigrant origins. The land records that may provide immigrant origins range from Crown Grants to correspondence found in the Township Papers. You can find these records and indexes to them at the Archives of Ontario and the National Archives of Canada.

One of the major steps in locating pertinent land records in Ontario is to identify where the ancestor's land was located. Large parts of Ontario were surveyed into townships, concessions, and lot numbers. The counties (earlier they were called districts) were divided into townships, and each township was divided into strips of land known as concessions. Each concession was divided into lots. If you know a concession and lot, you can then determine in what part of the township the ancestor's land was located.

Research Tip

Starting in 1797, after land had been patented (granted to the initial settler), subsequent land transactions were the concern of the county land registry offices. You can find information about the records of the land registries in *A Guide to Ontario Land Registry Records*, published by the Ontario Genealogical Society. Included in this work are registry addresses and a helpful glossary of terms found in deeds. The Abstract Index Books index land transactions after patenting and are arranged by lot and concession.

A source for further reading is R.W. Widdis's chapter "Tracing Property Ownership in Nineteenth-Century Ontario: A Guide to Archival Sources" in *Canadian Papers in Rural History*. For detailed historical background, see L.F. Gates's *Land Policies of Upper Canada*.

Some selected Ontario land record sources especially useful for Irish immigrant research are as follows:

Sources

- Upper Canada Land Petitions were submitted as the beginning of the Crown land grant process. Some petitions give such details as birthplace or arrival date in Canada. There are several series of these at the Archives of Ontario and the National Archives of Canada. The three National Archives series deal mostly with petitions for Crown leases and free grants prior to the initiation of a Crown land sale policy in 1827. The main Archives of Ontario series consists of petitions to the commissioner of Crown lands after the policy of granting lands to ordinary settlers changed to one of sales in 1827. There is a second Archives of Ontario series consisting of petitions extracted from the Township Papers (RG1, C-IV series). Many petitions are also available on microfilm through the FHL.

- Crown Grants document the initial transfer of land from the Crown to the first private owner. Up to 1826, land in Upper Canada could be obtained from the Crown by free grant; from 1827 on the Crown sold land in Upper Canada. Crown Grants are accessed using the Ontario Archives Land Record Index. J. Mezaks's *Preliminary Inventory of the Records of . . . Record Group 1* describes the Archives of Ontario collection in which each record group 1 reference number is found. The records of the Crown Lands Department are at the Archives of Ontario. Some of the records dating from 1792 to 1876 are available on microfilm at the FHL. For background, as well as an example of how to use the records, see John Mezaks's article "Crown Grants in the Home District: The System and the Existing Records" published in *Families*.

- The *Ontario Archives Land Records Index* is a microfiche research tool compiled by the Archives of Ontario in Toronto. It indexes by name the settlers who received land grants or leases in Ontario as found in three groups of records: Crown Lands Papers (denoted "RG1" for Record Group 1 at the Archives of Ontario), Canada Company Papers (CC), and the Peter Robinson Papers (MS-12). The *Ontario Archives Land Records Index* does not index the land petitions, which are among the most useful land records; many people who were not given land grants nevertheless petitioned for them.

  This index may provide the township, concession and lot on which the land was located. There is also a separate index by township so you can examine the grants for each township. Use this index to find the residence of an ancestor when all you know is an Ontario origin. This index is widely available on microfiche in libraries and archives across North America. Brenda Dougall Merriman's article "An Interpretation of The Ontario Land Records Index" in *Families* shows how to use this index and provides a listing of what the various codes used in the index mean.

- Township Papers from 1783 to the 1870s may be used to identify if an ancestor came with a particular colonization scheme or possibly to tell where in Ireland the immigrant came from. The Township Papers are records concerning land occupation prior to patenting. Thus, you can find letters requesting land, location certificates, land grants, wills, probate documents, or particulars of family or neighbor disputes in Township Papers. Also, some of the papers may help to identify a particular regiment in which a soldier served. They are filed by township, then numerically by lot and concession. There is no name index. The Township Papers are at the Archives of Ontario in Toronto (RG1, C-IV series) with microfilm copies at the FHL.

- The Canada Company was formed in 1824 to sell and settle land in Upper Canada (now Ontario). The company purchased the unleased Crown reserves (amounting to one-seventh of the land in Upper Canada, scattered throughout the province) and the one million acre Huron Tract in southwestern Upper Canada. The company ceased operation in 1951, and the Archives of Ontario obtained its records, including registers of sales and leases. Coleman and Anderson's *The Canada Company* contains information from some early sales records of the Canada Company. Canada Company sales and leases are indexed in the *Ontario Archives Land Records Index*.
- The Abstract Index Books for Ontario index post-patent transactions at the county land registry offices, arranged in each township by lot and concession. If you know in which lot and concession an ancestor lived, then you can access the history of not only that lot and concession but also neighboring ones. The Abstract Index Books are at the county registry offices with microfilm copies available at the FHL. The original books are to be transferred to local heritage societies after computerization of the data.

Prince Edward Island: The island was divided into three counties and sixty-seven lots in 1764 and 1765. Lots are similar to townships and comprise about twenty thousand acres each. These lots were distributed in 1767 to about one hundred individuals. The rest of the population leased or rented from the landowners. The Land Purchase Acts of 1853 and 1875 took the lands away from the large land owners and provided the lands as Crown Grants to the former tenants. The new landowners had up to ten years to pay off their grants but were allowed to sell prior to that time.

When considering land research for Irish immigrants, consider some facts about the land system:

- Land could be passed from one individual to another in a will without a registered deed until 1939.
- If an ancestor was living on the estate of a large land owner, you might find the ancestor in the owner's lease agreements and rent books rather than in the deeds. For an example of how land records and estate records are used for genealogical purposes, see James P. Lawson's article "Montgomery's Land 1833: Land Records and Genealogy" in *The Island Magazine* (Prince Edward Island Museum and Heritage Foundation).
- To locate an ancestor in the land records or the estate records of a landowner, the lot number is the identifier designating the correct parcel of ground. Determine the lot number from historical maps, the deed indexes (by surname), the censuses, a history book or biographical sketch, or a mention in a will.
- Cadastral maps were prepared for land on Prince Edward Island for the use of the landowner in approving lease agreements and collecting rents.

In Prince Edward Island deeds, the address of the lessee or purchaser is usually his or her former residence; it is here that you might find immigrant origins. The deeds are in the land registry records at the Public Archives and

Notes

Records Office of Prince Edward Island (PARO) with microfilm copies at the FHL from 1769 to 1872. For background information and a detailed treatment of land records from a genealogical perspective, see Ann Coles's article "A Beginner's Guide to Island Land Records" in *The Island Magazine* (Prince Edward Island Museum and Heritage Foundation).

There are two provincial atlases that include maps with residents' names:

Printed Source

J.H. Meacham & Co. *Illustrated Historical Atlas of the Province of Prince Edward Island.* 1880. Reprint, Belleville, Ontario: Mika Publishing Co., 1977.

Cummins Map Co. *Atlas of Province of Prince Edward Island, Canada.* Toronto: Cummins Map Co., 1928.

The Cummins Map Co. atlas includes rural directory pages for each lot, listing the names of all members of rural families, often with details of occupation and military service and sometimes specifying agricultural specialization and wives' maiden names. PARO holds a large collection of manuscript maps for the island as a whole and for individual lots. Many are cadastral maps.

Quebec: Because Quebec is different than the other provinces in its history and record keeping, we need to spend time helping you sort through it. The French seigneurial system was in operation in New France (Quebec) from the early seventeenth century. All land belonged to the King of France, who granted it in large tracts (each called a *seigneury*) to the *seigneurs* who populated the land with tenant farmers (known as *habitants*). The *habitants* did not own their land but held the "right of occupancy" to occupy specific parcels of land; these rights could be sold and inherited.

Britain took control of Quebec in 1760. The British continued the seigneurial system in many places. The British also gave land grants in Quebec after 1763, for example, to Loyalists of the American Revolution. Consequently, two systems were operating in Quebec after 1763 in which some residents were *habitants* living under the seigneurial system and other residents actually owned their land. Irish immigrants in Quebec, whether Catholic or Protestant, might have lived in either situation. The seigneurial system was completely abolished in 1854.

You can use **two indexed sources, one of land grants and the other of land grant petitions, to trace land ownership and to determine the specific residence of an Irish immigrant in Quebec:**

Sources

- *List of Lands Granted by the Crown in the Province of Quebec From 1763 to 31st December 1890* is arranged by township within each county, listing persons to whom land was granted by the British Crown between 1763 and 1890. The names of the grantees, the numbers of the lots granted, ranges, acres, date of letters-patent, book, and page number are all given. The grants are in chronological order within the township. There is a semi-alphabetical index to this work; within the first letter of the surname the index is arranged geographically. The introduction gives extensive historical background regarding the granting of land in Quebec.

  The original land grant records to which this book is an index are at the National Archives of Quebec at Sainte-Foy. Microfilm copies of grant books from 1788 to 1851 (vols. A–Z) and sales books from 1831 to 1863 (vols. A–Z) are available through the FHL.

- The Lower Canada Land Index for the Land Petitions (RG 1, L 3 L, at the NAC) indexes petitions for land grants submitted to the Land Committee of the Executive Council in Quebec and Lower Canada between 1764 and 1841, with related documents dating from 1637 to 1842. The petitions are now in alphabetical order by the name of the petitioner, or the group leader in the case of group petitions. The index gives the name of the petitioner; year of the petition; and pages of the petition. Use the page numbers to access the microfilmed petitions available at the NAC. Only volumes 29 to 36 (covering surnames Ackley through Baby) of the petitions are available on microfilm through the FHL. Land grant petitions might give such information as place of origin and date of arrival in Canada.

Many types of land records for Quebec, including seigneurial records and land transaction records, are among the notarial records. These records were kept by local notaries and in addition to land records include marriage contracts, wills, and other legal documents. See John P. DuLong's article "The Notarial Acts of Québec: Their Genealogical Value and Use" in *National Genealogical Society Quarterly*.

Saskatchewan: Saskatchewan homestead records are the province's major land documents useful for locating immigrant origins. The index provides the name of the applicant, the location, and file number for each homestead. The original records are at the Saskatoon Office of the Saskatchewan Archives Board with microfilm copies from 1870 to 1930 at the FHL. For further information about Saskatchewan homestead records, see Lloyd Rodwell's article "Saskatchewan Homestead Records" in *Saskatchewan History*. Also don't neglect the Internet index to these grants on the National Archives of Canada Web site.

Yukon: You will find that most land records for the Yukon concern the mining industry. It was not until 1906 that Yukon land was opened for homesteads. Even after that, a miner could work a claim regardless of the homestead entry.

The Yukon Archives has records of original locators of placer claims from 1896 to 1908. These include those miners who were the first to obtain the Crown grant of a particular claim. Other Records of Placer Documents are arranged by grantor and grantee, and include bills of sales from 1896 to 1907. The Archives also has records of persons applying for hydraulic leases from 1898 to 1900. Free Miner's Certificates from 1897 to 1907 are also at the Archives. All persons and companies involved in mining had to purchase a Free Miner's Certificate, which authorized its owner to engage in mining.

Sources

REFERENCES AND FURTHER READING

Antliff, W. Bruce. *Loyalist Settlements 1783–1789: New Evidence of Canadian Loyalist Claims*. Toronto: Archives of Ontario, 1985.

Bennett, Carol. *Peter Robinson's Settlers*. Renfrew, ON: Juniper Press, 1987.

Bill, Ingraham E. *Fifty Years with the Baptist Ministers and Churches of the*

Maritime Provinces of Canada. Saint John, NB: Barnes and Co., 1880.

Briggs, Elizabeth. *Access to ancestry: a genealogical resource manual for Canadians tracing their heritage.* Winnipeg, MB: Westgarth, 1995.

British Columbia Vital Statistics Agency. *Genealogical Resources For British Columbians.* Victoria, BC: BC Vital Statistics Agency, 1997.

Coldham, Peter Wilson. *American Loyalist Claims Vol. 1, Abstracted from the Public Record Office Audit Office Series 13, Bundles 1–35 & 37.* Washington, D.C.: National Genealogical Society, 1980.

Coles, Ann. "A Beginner's Guide to Island Land Records." *The Island Magazine* 25 (Spring/Summer 1989): 35–41.

Coleman, Thelma and James Anderson. *The Canada Company.* Stratford, ON: County of Perth and Cumming Pub., 1978.

Cornish, George H. *Hand-Book of Canadian Methodism.* Toronto: The Wesleyan Printing Establishment, 1867.

DuLong, John P. *French-Canadian Genealogical Research.* Palm Harbor, Fla: The LISI Press, 1995.

———. "The Notarial Acts of Québec: Their Genealogical Value and Use." *National Genealogical Society Quarterly* 82 (March 1994): 5–16.

Elliott, Bruce S. "Canadian Sources of Irish Immigration." In *Aspects of Irish Genealogy: Proceedings of the 1st Irish Genealogical Congress*, edited by M.D. Evans and Eileen O' Duill, 105–122. [Dublin]: 1st Irish Genealogical Congress Committee, 1993.

———. *The McCabe List: Early Irish in the Ottawa Valley.* Toronto: Ontario Genealogical Society, 1991.

———. "Immigration from South Leinster to Eastern Upper Canada." In *Wexford: History and Society*, edited by Kevin Whelan. Dublin: Geography Publications, 1987.

———. *Irish Migrants in the Canadas: A New Approach.* Kingston and Montreal: McGill-Queen's University Press, 1988.

Evans, C.A. "Land Records and Registration in Manitoba." *Generations: The Journal of the Manitoba Genealogical Society* 9 (2) (Summer 1984): 11–16.

Fellows, Robert F. *Researching Your Ancestors in New Brunswick.* Fredericton, 1979.

Fraser, Alexander. *United Empire Loyalists: Enquiry into the Losses and Services in Consequence of Their Loyalty: Evidence in the Canadian Claims. Facsimile of the Second Report of the Bureau of Archives for the Province of Ontario.* 1904. Reprint, Baltimore: Genealogical Publishing Co., 1994.

Friesen, Gerald and Barry Potyondi. *A Guide to the Study of Manitoba Local History.* Winnipeg: University of Manitoba Press, 1981.

Gates, Lilliam F. *Land Policies of Upper Canada.* Toronto: University of Toronto Press, 1968.

A Guide to Ontario Land Registry Records. Toronto: The Ontario Genealogical Society, 1994.

Hande, D'Arcy and Robert L. Pittendrigh. *Exploring Family History in Saskatchewan.* Regina and Saskatoon: Saskatchewan Archives Board, 1983.

Hanowski, Laura. "The Irish in Alberta." *The Irish At Home and Abroad* 6 (1) (1st Quarter 1999): 19–25.

———. "The Irish in Saskatchewan." *The Irish At Home and Abroad* 3 (1) (1995/96): 27–31.

Heald, Carolyn A. *The Irish Palatines in Ontario: Religion, Ethnicity and Rural Migration.* Gananoque, ON: Langdale Press, 1994.

———. "Researching Irish Palatines in Ireland and Ontario." *The Irish At Home and Abroad* 4 (2) (1997): 64–71.

Holt, Ruth and Margaret Williams, comp. *Genealogical Extraction and Index of the Canada Company Remittance Books, 1843–1847.* 3 vols. Weston, ON: the authors, 1990.

Houston, Cecil J. and William J. Smyth. *Irish Emigration and Canadian Settlement: Patterns, Links, and Letters.* Toronto: University of Toronto Press, 1990.

Hutchens, Don. "Tracing Your Roots Through Land Ownership." *Newfoundland Ancestor* 13 (1) (Spring 1997): 43–44.

———. "Early History of English Land Ownership in Newfoundland." *Newfoundland Ancestor* 13 (1) (Spring 1997): 45–47.

Irish Research Group (Ottawa Branch, Ontario Genealogical Society). *Names of Emigrants: From the 1845–1847 Records of James Allison, Emigrant Agent at Montreal.* Ottawa, ON: Ottawa Branch OGS, 1994.

Jetté, René. *Traité de Généalogie.* Montréal, Canada: Les Presses de l'Université de Montréal, 1991.

Johnson, D.F. *St. John County Alms and Work House Records.* Saint John, NB: the author, 1985.

Johnson, Daniel F. and Kenneth Kanner, eds. *Passengers to New Brunswick: The Custom House Records, 1833, 34, 37 & 38.* St. John, NB: New Brunswick Genealogical Society, 1987.

Jonasson, Eric. "Sources for Family History in Western Canada." *Alberta Family Histories Society Quarterly: A Publication of the Alberta Family Histories Society* 1 (Winter 1980): 52–55.

Kennedy, Patricia. "Records of the Land Settlement Process in Pre-Confederation Canada." *Families* 16 (4) (1977): 193–198.

Lafortune, Hélène, Norman Robert and Serge Goudreau. *Parchemin s'explique . . . Guide de dépouillement des actes notariés du Québec ancien.* Montréal: Société de recherche historique ArchivHisto, 1989.

Laing, F.W. "Colonial Farm Settlers on the Mainland of British Columbia 1858–1871." Victoria, BC, 1939.

Lambrecht, Kirk N. *The Administration of Dominion Lands 1870–1930.* Regina, SK: Canadian Plains Research Center, University of Regina, 1991.

Lawson, James P. "Montgomery's Lands 1833: Land Records and Genealogy." *The Island Magazine* 11 (1) (Autumn 1981): 33–39.

Lemieux, Victoria and David Leonard. *Tracing Your Ancestors in Alberta: A Guide to Sources of Genealogical Interest in Alberta's Archives and Research Centres.* Edmonton, AB: Lemieux/Leonard Research Associates, 1992.

List of Lands Granted By the Crown in the Province of Quebec From 1763 to 31st December 1890. Quebec: Charles-François Langlois, 1891.

Martin, Chester. *"Dominion Lands" Policy*. Toronto, ON: McClelland and Stewart Limited, 1973.

McKercher, Robert B. and Bertram Wolfe. *Understanding Western Canada's Dominion Land Survey System*. Saskatoon, SK: Division of Extension and Community Relations, University of Saskatchewan, 1986.

Merriman, Brenda Dougall. *Genealogy in Ontario: Searching the Records*. 3d ed. Toronto: Ontario Genealogical Society, 1996.

———. "An Interpretation of The Ontario Land Records Index." *Families* 25 (2) (May 1986): 77–83.

Mezaks, John. "Crown Grants in the Home District: The System and the Existing Records." *Families* 14 (4) (Fall 1975): 126–134.

———. *Preliminary Inventory of the Records of . . . Record Group 1*. Toronto: Archives of Ontario, 1988.

———. "Records of the Heir and Devisee Commissions." *Families* 16 (4) (1977): 199–206.

Miller, Douglas. *Miller's Manual, A Research Guide to the Major French-Canadian Genealogical Resources, What They Are and How to Use Them*. Pawtucket, R.I.: Quintin Publications, 1997.

Monasch, Barbara. *Genealogical Sources in British Columbia*. Surrey, BC: B. Monasch, 1996.

Morris, Julie. *Tracing Your Ancestors in Nova Scotia*. 2d ed. Halifax: Public Archives of Nova Scotia, 1981.

O'Gallagher, Marianna. *Grosse Île: Gateway to Canada, 1832–1937*. Quebec: Carraig Books, 1984.

Porter, Brian. "B.C. Land Registration Until 1870." *The British Columbia Genealogist* 12 (3) (September 1983): 82–84.

Power, Thomas P., ed. *The Irish in Atlantic Canada, 1780–1900*. Fredericton, NB: New Ireland Press, 1991.

Punch, Terrence M. *Genealogical Research in Nova Scotia*. 3d ed. Halifax: Petheric Press Ltd., 1983.

Punch, Terrence M., ed., with George F. Sanborn Jr. *Genealogist's Handbook for Atlantic Canada Research*. Rev. ed. Boston, Mass.: New England Historic Genealogical Society, 1997.

Rodwell, Lloyd. "Saskatchewan Homestead Records." *Saskatchewan History* 18 (1) (1965): 10–29.

Sanderson, J.E. *The First Century of Methodism in Canada*. 2 vols. Toronto: William Briggs, 1908.

Stratford-Devai, Fawne and Bruce S. Elliott. "Upper Canada Land Settlement Records: The Second District Land Boards, 1819–1825." *Families* (Ontario Genealogical Society) 34 (3) (August 1995): 132–137.

Taggart, Norman W. *The Irish in World Methodism, 1760–1900*. Westminster, England: Epworth Press, 1986.

Taylor, Ryan. *Books You Need to do Genealogy in Ontario: An Annotated Bibliography*. Ft. Wayne, Ind.: Round Tower Books, 1996.

Teece, Wendy. "Land Records and Maps for Genealogists in British Columbia."

Association of Canadian Map Libraries Bulletin 19 (1975): 16–19.

United Church of Canada. *Guide to Family History Research in the Archival Repositories of the United Church of Canada.* Toronto, ON: Ontario Genealogical Society, 1996.

White, Linda. "The Irish in Manitoba." *The Irish At Home and Abroad* 4 (1) (1997): 19–25.

Widdis, R.W. "Tracing Property Ownership in Nineteenth-Century Ontario: A Guide to Archival Sources." In *Canadian Papers in Rural History*, edited by D.H. Akenson, vol. 2. Gananoque, ON: Langdale Press, 1980.

Wilson, Catharine. *A New Lease on Life: Landlords, Tenants, and Immigrants in Ireland and Canada.* Montreal and Kingston: McGill-Queen's University Press, 1994.

Winsor, Leslie A. "Crown Land Records." *Newfoundland and Labrador Genealogical Society Newsletter* 3 (4) (Fall 1987): 8–9.

Addresses
Provincial and National Archives

Archives nationales de Québec (National Archives of Quebec)
Pavillon Louis-Jacques-Casault, Cité universitaire,1210 avenue du Séminaire, Case postale 10450, Sainte-Foy, Québec G1V 4N1, Canada
phone: (418) 643-8904   *fax:* (418) 646-0868
Internet (in French): http://www.anq.gouv.qc.ca/

Archives of Ontario
77 Grenville St., Unit 300, Toronto, ON M5S 1B3, Canada
phone: (416) 327-1583   *fax:* (416) 327-1999
Internet: http://www.gov.on.ca/mczcr/archives/

British Columbia Archives
(Location) 655 Belleville St., Victoria, BC V8V 1X4, Canada
(Mailing) P.O. Box 9419 Stn. PROV GOVT, V8W 9V1, Canada
phone: (250) 387-1952   *fax:* (250) 387-2072
Internet: http://www.bcarchives.gov.bc.ca/index.htm

National Archives of Canada
Genealogy Unit, Researcher Services Division
395 Wellington St., Ottawa, ON K1A 0N3, Canada
fax: (613) 995-6274
Internet: http://www.archives.ca/

National Library of Canada
395 Wellington Street, Ottawa, ON K1A 0N4, Canada
Internet: http://www.nlc-bnc.ca/

Northwest Territories Archives
Government of the Northwest Territories, Yellowknife, NT X1A 2L9, Canada
phone: (403) 873-7698   *fax:* (403) 873-0205
Internet: http://www.pwnhc.learnnet.nt.ca/programs/archive.htm

Provincial Archives of Alberta
12845-102 Ave., Edmonton, AB T5N 0M6, Canada

phone: (403) 427-1750
Internet: http://www.gov.ab.ca/~mcd/mhs/paa/paa.htm
Provincial Archives of Manitoba
200 Vaughan St., Winnipeg, MB R3C 1T5, Canada
phone: (204) 945-3971
Internet: http://www.gov.mb.ca/chc/archives/
Provincial Archives of New Brunswick
(Location) Bonar Law-Bennett Building, Dineen Dr., University of New
Brunswick Campus, Fredericton, NB, Canada
(Mailing) P.O. Box 6000, Fredericton, NB E3B 5H1, Canada
phone: (506) 453-2122   *fax:* (506) 453-3288
Internet: http://www.gnb.ca/Archives/Index.htm
Provincial Archives of Newfoundland and Labrador
Colonial Building, Military Rd., St. John's, NF A1C 2C9, Canada
phone: (709) 729-0475   *fax:* (709) 729-0578
Internet: http://www.gov.nf.ca/panl/
Public Archives and Records Office of Prince Edward Island
(Location) Hon. George Coles Building, Richmond St., Charlottetown, PE
(Mailing) P.O. Box 1000, Charlottetown, PE C1A 7M4, Canada
phone: (902) 368-4290
Internet: http://www2.gov.pe.ca/educ/archives/archives_index.asp
Public Archives of Nova Scotia
6016 University Ave., Halifax, NS B3H 1W4, Canada
phone: (902) 424-6060   *fax:* (902) 424-0628
Saskatchewan Archives Board
Saskatoon Office, Murray Memorial Building, 3 Campus Dr., University
of Saskatchewan, Saskatoon, SK S7N 5A4, Canada
phone: (306) 933-5832
Internet: http://www.gov.sk.ca/
Yukon Archives
P.O. Box 2703, Whitehorse, YT Y1A 2C6, Canada
phone: (867) 667-5321   *fax:* (867) 393-6253
Internet: http://yukoncollege.yk.ca/archives/yarch.html

Provincial Genealogical Societies
Alberta Family Histories Society
P.O. Box 30270, Station B, Calgary, AB T2M 4P1, Canada
phone: (403) 214-1447
Internet: http://www.calcna.ab.ca/afhs/
Alberta Genealogical Society
Prince of Wales Armouries Heritage Centre, #116, 10440—108 Ave.,
Edmonton, AB T5H 3Z9, Canada
phone: (780) 424-4429   *fax:* (780) 423-8980
Internet: http://www.compusmart.ab.ca/abgensoc/
British Columbia Genealogical Society
P.O. Box 88054, Lansdowne Mall, Richmond, BC V6X 3T6, Canada

phone: (604) 502-9119   *fax:* (604) 263-4952
Internet: http://www.npsnet.com/bcgs/
Manitoba Genealogical Society
 Unit E—1045 St. James St., Winnipeg, MB R3H 1B1, Canada
 Internet: http://www.mbnet.mb.ca/~mgs/
New Brunswick Genealogical Society
 P.O. Box 3235, Station B, Fredericton, NB E3A 5G9, Canada
 Internet: http://www.bitheads.com/nbgs/
Newfoundland and Labrador Genealogical Society
 Colonial Building, Military Rd., St. John's, NF A1C 2C9, Canada
 phone/fax: (709) 754-9525
 Internet: http://www3.nf.sympatico.ca/nlgs/
The NWT Genealogical Society
 P.O. Box 1715, Yellowknife, NT X1A 2P3, Canada
 Internet: http://www.ssimicro.com/nonprofit/nwtgs
Genealogical Association of Nova Scotia
 P.O.Box 641, Station "Central," Halifax, NS B3J 2T3, Canada
 phone: (902) 454-0322
 Internet: http://www.chebucto.ns.ca/recreation/gans/
Ontario Genealogical Society
 40 Orchard View Blvd., Suite 102, Toronto, ON M4R 1B9, Canada
 phone: (416) 489-0734   *fax:* (416) 489-9803
 Internet: http://www.ogs.on.ca/
The Prince Edward Island Genealogical Society Inc.
 P.O. Box 2744, Charlottetown, PE C1A 8C4, Canada
 Internet: http://www.isn.net/~dhunter/peigs.html
Société de généalogie de Québec
 Salle 4266, Pavillon Louis-Jacques-Casault, Cité Universaire
 Case Postale 9066, Sainte-Foy, Québec G1V 4A8, Canada
 phone: (418) 651-9127   *fax:* (418) 651-2643
 Internet: http://www.genealogie.org/club/sgq/index.htm
Québec Family History Society
 P.O. Box 1026, Pointe Claire, PQ H9S 4H9, Canada
 phone: (514) 695-1502
 Internet: http://www.cam.org/~qfhs/index.html
Saskatchewan Genealogical Society
 2d Floor, 1870 Lorne St.,
 P.O. Box 1894, Regina, SK S4P 3E1, Canada
 phone: (306) 780-9207   *fax:* (306) 781-6021
 Internet: http://www.saskgenealogy.com/

Other Archives
 Anglican Church of Canada Archives
  600 Jarvis St., Toronto, ON M4Y 2J6, Canada
  phone: (416) 924-9192
  Internet: http://anglican.ca/

Atlantic Baptist Archives: Acadia University Esther Clark Wright Archives
Vaughan Memorial Library, Wolfville, NS B0P 1X0, Canada
phone: (902) 585-1731   *fax:* (902) 585-1748
Internet: http://www.acadiau.ca/vaughan/archives/genresearch.html
British Columbia Lands Branch
Department of Lands, Forest and Water Resources, Parliament Bldgs.
Victoria, BC V8V 1X5, Canada
Canadian Baptist Archives
McMaster Divinity College, 1280 Main St. West
Hamilton, ON L8S 4K1, Canada
phone: (905) 525-9140 ext. 23511   *fax:* (905) 577-4782
Internet: http://www.mcmaster.ca/divinity/archives.html
Crown Lands Registry, Manitoba Department of the Natural Resources
1495 St. James St., Winnipeg, MB R3H OW9, Canada
Glenbow Archives
130 Ninth Ave. S.E., Calgary, AB T2G 0P3, Canada
phone: (402) 268-4204   *fax:* (402) 232-6569
Internet: http://www.glenbow.org/archives.htm
Government of Newfoundland and Labrador Registry of Deeds,
Companies and Securities
P.O. Box 4750, Confederation Bldg.,
St. John's, NF A1C 517, Canada
phone: (709) 576-3317
New Brunswick Department of Natural Resources and Energy
P.O. Box 6000 Hugh John Flemming Forestry Complex
Fredericton, NB E3B 5H1, Canada
phone: (506) 453-2614   *fax:* (506) 457-4881
Presbyterian Church in Canada Archives
50 Wynford Dr., Toronto, ON M3C 1J7, Canada
phone: (416) 441-1111   *fax:* (416) 441-2825
Internet: http://www.presbyterian.ca/archives/index.html
Registrar of Land Titles
Land Titles Office, Department of Justice, Government of the Northwest
Territories, P.O. Box 1320, Yellowknife, NT X1A 2L9, Canada
phone: (405) 873-7491   *fax:* (405) 873-0243
United Church of Canada/Victoria University Archives
Birge-Carnegie Bldg., Victoria University, 73 Queen's Park, Crescent East,
Toronto, ON M5S 1K7, Canada
phone: (416) 585-4563   *fax:* (416) 585-4584
Internet: http://www.vicu.utoronto.ca/archives/archives.htm
United Empire Loyalists' Association of Canada
50 Baldwin St., Suite 202, Toronto, ON M5T 1L4, Canada
phone: (416) 591-1783   *fax:* (416) 591-7506
Internet: http://www.npiec.on.ca/~uela/uela1.htm

FOUR

Australia

Important

A ustralia can be described as one of the most important links in determining immigrant origins. This is because of Australia's complex history involving Irish immigration and the legacy it left behind in the
written word. Australia is a huge country geographically; however, it has always
had a small population. There was a tradition from early on of documenting
the people going into the continent. Remember, after the American Revolution,
what became the United States was closed down as a dumping ground for
prisoners; thus the idea of Australia was born.

Prisoners sent to Australia can be documented from their lives in Britain and
Ireland to their transportation and subsequent release. Therefore, **chances of a
birthplace or place of residence in Ireland for prisoners being preserved in Australian and Irish records are excellent**. In fact, in the case of convicts, the records
generated in Ireland and in Australia are linked and must be used in unison.

Australia's history as a penal colony paved the way for others to come: the
military, merchants, families of the convicts, and of course typical immigrants
like those who settled everywhere else throughout the British Empire.

The records generated about this small population, whether arriving as convicts or as free persons, are extraordinary in their attention to detail. It is not
uncommon to find birthplace information preserved, and we don't just mean
county either—we mean parish and townland in Ireland. Also, genealogy is so
popular in Australia now that indexes are constantly created documenting large
segments of the population.

So, why is this subject important to those outside of Australia? Let's put it this
way: If we had to choose between digging records of an immigrant out of New
York City to try to find origins or tracing the brother or sister who went to Australia, there is just no contest. The Australian records will most likely give us the
place of birth in Ireland, and the New York City records most likely will not!

So, how do you know if your ancestor had a relative in Australia? The answer

Oral History

is actually easier than you think. If your direct line did not go to Australia, chances are good that they had a family member who did.

Keep in mind that many families have preserved the lore of someone who immigrated either as a convict or free. These are the types of stories that stick with families. To say the least, the shipping off of a convict never to be seen again is a traumatic event in any family's history. Even if no one remembers the name of the relative, with so many indexes available, it is not difficult to identify those with your surname who went to Australia. So, there is no problem starting the search; the next task is narrowing the search to find the correct person.

To start the search, learn about the vast amount of material available on the Internet. There are genealogical societies scattered throughout the continent that have banded together under the umbrella organization of the Australasian Federation of Family History Organisations. You will find you can obtain some help from local societies with research problems or even make connections with distant family members. The societies who are members of the Federation can be reached at <http://carmen.murdoch.edu.au/~affho/>.

In fact, you will find that there are so many Web sites for Australia that the trouble will not be finding a site, but sorting through the sites to find the one that applies to you. To keep current on the Internet sites, we stress that you look at Cyndi's List at <http://www.cyndislist.com>. Also check the Internet site of the AustraliaGenWeb for updates <http://www.rootsweb.com/~auswgw/>.

There is one organization to which we must pay special recognition: the Society of Australian Genealogists in Sydney. Chapters of the society are scattered throughout Australia, and they are actively engaged in transcribing and indexing just about any kind of record imaginable. Their Web site, <http://www.sag.org.au/>, offers books as well as a research service. The society houses a major genealogical library of more than one hundred thousand microfilm, forty thousand books, five hundred thousand index cards and twenty-eight thousand manuscripts. Their collections for Australia include family histories and biographies; local and school histories; birth, marriage, and death indexes; shipping records; probates; cemetery transcriptions; and parish registers. They also publish the quarterly journal *Descent.* This society certainly should be on your list of resources in your search for Irish origins.

In your research you will also encounter the National Archives of Australia and state archives and libraries. These are important repositories for records. Some of their collections are on microfilm at the FHL; however, much is still deposited locally in Australia.

The National Archives of Australia published a guide to their collections, *Finding Families: The Guide to the National Archives of Australia for Genealogists,* compiled by M. Chambers. The National Archives of Australia is an archive of the commonwealth government, so most of its collections date from federation in 1901 and afterward.

For a general overview of major Australian records, the standard work is Nick Vine Hall's *Tracing Your Family History in Australia: A Guide to Sources,* which discusses where various records are deposited. The major libraries and archives in Australia can be reached through Archives of Australia Web site at <http://www.archivenet.gov.au/archives.html>.

RESOURCES FOR THE AUSTRALIAN STATES

The major state libraries, archives, and research guides you need to be aware of as a foundation for your Australian research are

Library/Archive Source

Australian Capital Territory: Aside from the National Archives of Australia, the National Library of Australia is located in Canberra. The Heraldry and Genealogical Society of Canberra houses a library of interest for this area.

New South Wales: The Archives of the State of New South Wales and the State Library of New South Wales are the major repositories. The guide *Family and Local History Sources in the Sydney Area*, by Jennie Fairs and Dom Meadley, focuses on Sydney repositories and their holdings.

Northern Territory: The Genealogical Society of the Northern Territory has a library, located in Darwin, that houses many indexes and records for the territory.

Queensland: The State Library of Queensland and the Queensland State Archives are the major repositories. Also check the Web site Research Tips for Queensland at <http://www.judywebster.gil.com.au/tips-qld.html>.

South Australia: The State Library of South Australia and the State Records of South Australia are the major repositories. Several guides have been published: *Ancestors in Archives: A Guide to Family History Sources in the Official Records of South Australia*; Burrows, Mildred, Moore, and Talbot's *Kith and Kin: Sources for Family History*; and an older work by Andrew Peake, *Sources for South Australian Family History*. The South Australian Genealogical and Heraldry Society in Unley has extensive collections and publications.

Tasmania: The two main resources in Tasmania are the Archives Office of Tasmania, which has a "Tasmanian Family Links" online database of more than five hundred thousand birth, marriage, and death entries from records at the archive; and the State Library of Tasmania. Anne M. Bartlett's book *Local and Family History Sources in Tasmania* provides information on the major repositories and record sources.

Victoria: The Public Record Office Victoria is a major archives of the state of Victoria, and the State Library of Victoria has a Genealogy Centre. The Centre has a research archive called the Melbourne Archives Centre, operated in conjunction with the Australian Archives State Office. The Melbourne Archives Centre houses microfilm copies of records frequently used by genealogists. Dom Meadley and Frances Brown's book *Family and Local History Sources in Victoria* is a valuable guide to the main repositories in the state.

Western Australia: The State Reference Library at the Alexander Library Building has a Genealogy Centre.

THE RECORDS

When approaching the subject of Australian records, some history will come in handy. White settlement began in Australia in 1788, when Captain Arthur

Phillip established a penal colony on the East Coast at Port Jackson (now Sydney Harbour). This first colony was called New South Wales. Other colonies were later separated from New South Wales, and they attained statehood on 1 January 1901. There are now six states and two territories in Australia. Since so much Australian history began in New South Wales, you might find records there of your ancestor even if he or she lived elsewhere in Australia. Although there are so many records we could discuss in our search for Irish origins, we have decided to limit the focus to the following: the Australasian Genealogical Computer Index, civil registration, free settlement records, and convict transportation records. You can certainly obtain any other records you need by using the Web sites and guides mentioned in this chapter.

AUSTRALASIAN GENEALOGICAL COMPUTER INDEX (AGCI)

Although there are many databases essential to your Australian research, we need to make special mention of the Australasian Genealogical Computer Index (AGCI). This is an index of records submitted by some twenty-four societies throughout Australia and New Zealand. The project is overseen by the Society of Australian Genealogists, and the index's purpose is to make records more accessible by providing a quick and easy index to genealogical material held throughout Australasia. AGCI is updated on microfiche every few years, and the third edition (1996) includes some 1.9 million entries.

What is actually indexed in AGCI? Major record types include cemetery transcriptions, especially from New South Wales, Victoria, Western Australia, and New Zealand; newspaper cuttings; *New South Wales Government Gazette* (1832–1840); Irish Transportation Records (1788–1868); and shipping into New South Wales and South Australia. Because the AGCI is a growing index and its coverage is wide, microfiche copies are held in many Australian libraries, and at the FHL. However, due to copyright, the FHL copies do not circulate outside Salt Lake City.

CIVIL REGISTRATION

Australian birth, marriage, and death records contain an extraordinary amount of information and rank among the most important sources for identifying where in Ireland an ancestor was from. However, before we discuss exactly what is in a civil registration certificate of birth, marriage, or death, note that these records go far beyond the record keeping of the individual states and territories. In fact, to generate records not kept on citizens, the government extracted church registers, thus generating certificates using church information. This is not to say that all church registers were extracted, nor that the various states were even able to make the churches send them in, only that what was extracted complements existing civil registration well. So the line between what is a church record and what is a civil record in many cases can be thin indeed.

Australian birth certificates may contain the ages and birthplaces of the parents as well as names of previous children of the marriage. Marriage certificates may provide the names of the parents of both parties as well as the father's occupation and the age, marital status, birthplace, and residence of the bride and groom. Death certificates can supply age, parents, spouse and children, and birthplace. In the listing of birthplaces, it was common for an Irish townland or parish as well as the county to be given.

You will find that there is no centralization of births, marriages, and deaths outside of each individual state and territory. Therefore, each had its own civil registration and accompanying indexes. In fact, speaking of indexes, the ones covering these records are astounding. There are two versions on the market that you can purchase. One is produced by the Genealogical Society of Utah as "Australian Vital Records Index, 1788–1905," on four CDs, indexing 4.8 million births, christenings, marriages, and deaths from New South Wales (1788–1888), Tasmania (1803–1899), Victoria (1837–1888), and Western Australia (1841–1905). This set of CDs by copyright is not allowed to be sold in Australia or its territories, but it is available everywhere else. Order it through the Web site of the FHL <http://www.familysearch.org>. The second set of indexes, produced in Australia, lists more information and includes more recent coverage than the Utah version does. Obtain this series of CDs, produced by Informit, RMIT Libraries in Melbourne, from any number of genealogical societies or software distributors in Australia.

The index for New South Wales is on the Internet site of the New South Wales Registry of Births, Deaths, and Marriages. The searchable database includes births (1788–1905), marriages (1788–1945), and deaths (1788–1945) and is at <http://www.bdm.nsw.gov.au/>.

You can obtain certificates in two ways. If you have access to one of the CD or online databases, order the certificate from the state office. You can also have the state office conduct a search on your behalf. There is a general Web site with links to all the registries at Australasian Registries of Births, Deaths, and Marriages, <http://www.ke.com.au/bdmaus/index.html>. There are forms on these sites that you can fill in to order the certificate directly. Otherwise, orders are taken through the mail. The registries are as follows:

Australian Capital Territory (Records from 1930): The Registrar, Births, Deaths, and Marriages, GPO Box 788, Canberra, ACT 2601, Australia; Phone: (02) 6207 6444; Internet: <http://www.act.gov.au/NewServices/law/births.html>.

New South Wales (Records from 1856): Registry of Births, Deaths and Marriages, GPO Box 30, Sydney, NSW 2001, Australia; Phone: (02) 9243 8585; Internet: <http://www.bdm.nsw.gov.au/>.

Northern Territory (Records from 1870): Registrar General, Registry of Births, Deaths and Marriages, GPO Box 3021, Darwin, NT 0801, Australia; Phone: (08) 8999 6119; Internet: <http://www.ke.com.au/bdmaus/bdmnt/index .html/>.

Queensland (Records from 1856): For pre-1890 certificates contact the Queensland State Archives. For post-1889 certificates: The Registrar-General, Births, Deaths, and Marriages, P.O. Box 188, Albert Street, North Quay QLD

Sources

4002, Australia; Phone: (07) 3247 9203; Fax: (07) 3247 5803; Internet: <http://www.ke.com.au/bdmaus/bdmqld/index.html/>.

South Australia (Records from 1842): The Principal Registrar, Births, Deaths and Marriage Division, GPO 1351, Adelaide, SA 5001, Australia; Phone: (08) 8204 9605; Internet: <http://www.ocba.sa.gov.au/births.htm>.

Tasmania (Records from 1838): For records before 1899 contact the Office of Archives Tasmania; for records after 1899 contact The Registrar General, Registry of Births, Deaths, and Marriages, GPO Box 875J, Hobart TAS 7001, Australia; Phone: (03) 6233 3793; Internet: <http://www.justice.tas.gov.au/bdm/>.

Victoria (Records from 1853): Registry of Births, Deaths & Marriages, GPO Box 4332, Melbourne VIC 3001, Australia; Phone: (03) 9603 5888.

Western Australia (Records from 1841): The Registrar General, Registrar Generals Office, P.O. Box 7720, Cloisters Sq., Perth WA 6850, Australia; Phone: (08) 9264 1555; Fax: (08) 9264 1599; Internet: <http://www.moj.wa.go v.au/>.

Reminder

RECORDS OF FREE SETTLEMENT

Although the popular image of Australia is one of a penal colony, not everybody who immigrated to this vast continent was a convict; many were free settlers. During the period of convict transportation, 1788 to1868, approximately 161,000 convicts were sent to the Australian colonies. Consider that these convicts, when freed, could encourage Irish friends and family members to emigrate. Others chose to immigrate to Australia without ever knowing a convict.

Now, we would like you to consider that in the early years of free settlement few people actually paid their own way; most were assisted by other means. Various schemes began to pay passage for potential settlers. Initially, there was no provision for free immigration to eastern Australia, except for wives and servants accompanying those who came in the service of the government. These, along with members of the military, made up the major section of the non-government population. Only a few lists of passengers on ships prior to 1826 have survived.

Before 1831, authorities granted land in New South Wales and Van Diemen's Land (now Tasmania) in proportion to the amount of capital a settler possessed. A few emigrants to New South Wales were granted free passage, usually in one of the convict ships, and were given land on their arrival in the colony. These schemes generated some excellent documentation on the emigrants and where they were from.

One particularly interesting scheme related to bringing over the families of convicts. The theory behind these was that freed convicts could apply through the governor in the colony to have their families brought out; these were some of the first free assisted immigrants to Australia. One example is of a petition from the 1826 papers of James Brien (alias Brady) who had arrived on the transport *Prince Regent* some years previously, and applied for his wife, Julia Brien (alias Brady), to join him in the colony. Julia was in the care of Catherine Taylor at Bishop Murray's Orphan School in Cork City, and the papers show that she was known to Sir Henry Browne Hayes and Dr. Hewitt of Cork.

Until the end of transportation to New South Wales in 1840, small groups of these assisted immigrants traveled to Australia on female convict ships. When transportation ceased, this scheme was suspended for some time. As a result of the distress caused by the famine in Ireland in the late 1840s, this scheme was reintroduced in 1847 and continued until at least the end of 1855. One historian in Australia, Dr. Richard Reid, found that of the 845 convicts in his sample who applied for their families to go to Australia between 1849 and 1855, the families of 57 percent actually went.

Another example is from 1849. On 22 September, the ship *William Jardine* arrived in Sydney with wives and children of convicts on board. Among the passengers was William Roache, age thirty-three, a Catholic farm laborer from Fenagh who could read and write. With him on the ship was his wife, Mary Roache (age twenty-five), born in County Limerick. Also with William and Mary Roache were their two children, Mary (age four) and John (an infant). Who had applied for this family to go to Australia under the wives and families of convicts scheme? The answer is interesting. The manifest of the *William Jardine* shows that Mrs. Mary Roache was the daughter of Patrick and Johanna Doniher, and that Patrick was the applicant. He had no relatives in the colony when he applied for his daughter and her family to emigrate. He had been transported as a convict on the *Eliza* in 1827, twenty-two years earlier and he was living with Mr. Smith, presumably his employer, at Wentworthville, New South Wales. Imagine the reunion after twenty-two years! His daughter, who was three years old when he left, was now married with two children of her own. This is just one example of the rich and valuable documents that relate to the arrival of assisted Irish immigrants in nineteenth-century Australia. These documents resulted from government intervention through immigration schemes.

There were other assisted immigration schemes that did not involve convicts or their families. Schemes developed as early as 1823, when state-sponsored emigration from County Cork began with the departure of single girls who were perceived as distressed but virtuous. Ships such as the *Borodino*, the *Cleopatra*, and the *Sir Joseph Banks* left Cork Harbour for Australia in 1828. It was the departure of single females on the *Red Rover* in 1832, however, that heralded the adoption of Edward Gibbon Wakefield's principles of systematic assisted emigration in Ireland. Many of these single women came from institutions such as the Cork Foundling Hospital, and the government made the decision to emigrate for them.

Notes

There were, of course, exceptions to this rule. More than four thousand single women went to Australia between October 1848 and August 1850 under the female orphan scheme, which aimed to solve problems in both Australia and Ireland. Remember that in the Australian colonies there were more men than women, while in Ireland the workhouses were overflowing with women. So the scheme of bringing poor single girls into the colonies worked to solve problems for both governments. Girls from these schemes went to Sydney, Port Phillip, and Adelaide. These girls were some of the few assisted emigrants who left Ireland at no cost to themselves. For the most part, even assisted emigration was not absolutely free, and large families in particular needed some money before they could consider an assisted passage.

A run of the numbers will help drive home the importance of assisted emigration schemes in Australian history. Between 1840 and 1914 these schemes had added at least 300,000 Irish to the Australian population.

The records of free immigrants are at state archives and libraries, including the FHL. Some are even being indexed and placed on the Internet. For example, the Public Record Office of Victoria has an index to inward passengers called Immigration to Victoria 1852–1879 on its Web site <http://www.prov.vic.gov.au>.

IRISH RECORDS OF AUSTRALIAN CONVICTS

Not long ago having a convict ancestor was something Australians were somewhat ashamed of. That changed with the Australian Bicentennial in 1988. This aspect of Australian social history has come into its own and is more understood now than it has ever been. As mentioned, Australia was settled as a penal colony in 1788, and the earliest arrivals were either convicts or the military guarding them. You will see the term "transportation" in reference to the shipping of convicts to Australia. In fact, the transportation of convicts continued from Britain, Ireland, and British colonies until 1840 in New South Wales and 1853 in Tasmania (then called Van Dieman's Land). A few convicts continued to arrive after these dates to New South Wales, Port Philip in Victoria, and Moreton Bay in Queensland, with the last going to Western Australia in 1863. So from 1788 to 1863 the Australian colonies received almost 161,000 transportees. While some Irish convicts arrived before 1791, in that year the ship *Queen* was the first to transport convicts directly from Ireland to Australia.

Reminder

Historians have calculated that approximately 50,000 transportees out of the 161,000 were Irish. Think about it: this is about one-third of the convicts. Remember, **not all the Irish came directly from Ireland. Many were actually convicted in England or at military outposts in British India or in another colony.** Many of these Irish were in the British Army. For those soldiers who were convicted while in the British Army, it is possible to find records of their trials and trace their careers through army records held at the PRO in England. David T. Hawkings' *Bound for Australia* discusses this aspect of transportation. For the Irish convicted in English county courts, seek records at local County Record Offices, which usually hold trial transcripts. Neither of these aspects of transportation, however, is our main focus.

Records in Ireland

Unfortunately, for Irish tried and transported from Ireland, the record situation is not very encouraging. The vast majority of eighteenth and nineteenth century Irish court archives, together with other convict records, were destroyed by fire in Dublin during the Civil War in 1922. However, it is still possible to piece together the story of a convict ancestor transported to Australia. Keith Johnson

The National Archives of Ireland

Search results

Found **117** records matching **Brennan**.
Printing first **10** of **117** records.

The document reference in each entry below is the National Archives of Ireland reference to the original document in the archives. The microfilm reference number refers to the set of microfilms presented to Australia in 1988.

Record 1 of 117

SURNAME: BRENNAN   OTHER NAMES: ANDREW
     AGE: 40   SEX: M   ALIAS: Brerman, Andrew.

PLACE OF TRIAL: Co. Donegal   TRIAL DATE: 20/07/1837
PLACE OF IMPRISONMENT: DOCUMENT DATE:

    CRIME DESCRIPTION: LARCENY
    SENTENCE: Transportation life.
    SHIP:

PETITIONER: RELATIONSHIP:

DOCUMENT REFERENCES: TR 2 p 33
MICROFILM REFERENCES:
COMMENTS:

Record 2 of 117

SURNAME: BRENNAN   OTHER NAMES: ANDREW
     AGE: 0   SEX: M   ALIAS:

PLACE OF TRIAL: TRIAL DATE: 13/01/1849
PLACE OF IMPRISONMENT: Co. Limerick.   DOCUMENT DATE:

    CRIME DESCRIPTION: LARCENY
    SENTENCE: Transportation 7 years
    SHIP: LORD AUCKLAND, SEPT 1852

PETITIONER: RELATIONSHIP:

DOCUMENT REFERENCES: TR 8 p 109
MICROFILM REFERENCES:
COMMENTS:

Record 3 of 117

SURNAME: BRENNAN   OTHER NAMES: ANNE
     AGE: 20   SEX: F   ALIAS:

PLACE OF TRIAL: TRIAL DATE: 18/03/1842
PLACE OF IMPRISONMENT: Co. Kildare.   DOCUMENT DATE:

    CRIME DESCRIPTION: LARCENY
    SENTENCE: Transportation 7 years
    SHIP:

PETITIONER: RELATIONSHIP:

Figure 4-1
Sample from Ireland-Australia Transportation Index 1791–1868, National Archives of Ireland Web site <http://www.national archives.ie>. Used with permission of the NAI.

and Michael Flynn, when researching the 155 male convicts transported on the *Queen* in 1791, found details of the crimes of more than half from contemporary Irish newspaper reports. For this time period they found the *Hibernian Journal* a particularly helpful paper. The results of their study were published in *Exiles from Erin: Convicts' Lives in Ireland and Australia,* edited by Bob Reece. For any convict ancestor you are researching, search local Irish county newspapers for crime and conviction details. Irish newspapers are held at the National Library of Ireland (NLI) in Dublin and at the British Library Newspaper Library in London.

Internet Source

We must point out that there are scores of other records you can use to trace a convict to a trial in Ireland, thus likely giving you the residence of the family. In fact, **there are so many records you can use that the National Archives of Ireland (NAI) has two online research guides to these records.** One is Transportation to Australia at <http://www.nationalarchives.ie/transportation.html> and the other, Sources in the National Archives for Research into the Transportation of Irish Convicts to Australia (1791–1853) at <http://www.nationalarchives.ie/transp1.html>. Among the Irish records you can use are the following:

Convict Indents: These are among the main sources for tracing a convict transported to Australia. The originals are at the Public Records Office (PRO) in England with microfiche copies available from the Archives Office of New South Wales. The indents cover the complete period of transportation to Australia and include date and place of trial and, beginning in the early 1820s, other details such as age, marital status, number of children, occupation, crime, native place, complexion, height, color of eyes, and distinguishing marks such as scars or tattoos. Using the Convict Indents, you should be able to identify the time of a prisoner's transportation from Ireland, a major step leading you into records such as the Chief Secretary's Office Correspondence.

Chief Secretary's Office Correspondence: Until 1922, the power of British administration in Ireland resided in the lord lieutenant, who was assisted by a chief secretary. In the absence of court records, you can search for details about your convict ancestor in these categories of the Chief Secretary's Office Correspondence: Convict Reference Files (CRF), Prisoners Petitions and Cases, and Rebellion Papers and Outrage Papers.

A Transportation Database is hosted on the Web site of the NAI and is an index to the CRF, Prisoner's Petitions and Cases, and the accompanying transportation registers: <http://www.nationalarchives.ie/search01.html>. This is one of the most important databases you will use in your convict research; however, there is a clincher you need to be aware of: While the database does include surviving transportation registers from Ireland to Australia, as well as petitions to the government for pardon or commutation of sentence (in an incomplete form), remember that all transportation registers prior to 1836 were destroyed. This means that if your ancestor was convicted prior to 1836, he or she will not appear in the database unless there was a petition for pardon filed. The petitions begin as early as 1791.

Convict Reference Files

The CRF in the years 1836 to 1853 include a number of files for convicts sentenced to banishment to Australia. The usual run of files concerning a transportee has a petition from a relative and a letter from the trial judge giving an outline of the charge, the evidence, his observations, the sentence passed, and the character and general conduct of the person charged. In addition to the CRF, there are sixteen convict reference books (from 1836 to 1924) in which the names of all convicts are recorded alphabetically.

Prisoners' Petitions and Cases

There is a series among the state papers titled *Prisoners Petitions and Cases* (twenty cartons), which contains 4,251 files. This is the only pre-1836 archive source surviving in Ireland for those sentenced to transportation, mainly to New South Wales, and in later years also to Van Dieman's Land (Tasmania). There are also four cartons of petitions from state prisoners for the period 1796 to 1799 for men accused of involvement in the 1798 rebellion.

Rebellion Papers and Outrage Papers

This series of records is interesting in that it deals with law and order. Thus, from these papers you might actually find an investigation of an ancestor's life and activities prior to transportation. The first class of these papers is the Rebellion Papers, covering the years 1790 to 1807 (sixty-seven cartons) and the events and participants of the 1798 and 1803 rebellions. A second class of papers is the State of the Country Papers, covering 1790 to 1831 (107 cartons), which contain reports of local violations and transgressions of the law and order. From 1832 until almost the end of the transportation period, these papers are known as the Outrage Papers.

Thus, while trial records of convicts transported directly from Ireland to Australia do not survive, it is possible to find other sources such as the Chief Secretary's Papers and newspapers, which combined with documents in Australia, give a clearer picture of the situation before transportation.

REFERENCES AND FURTHER READING

Sources

Ancestors in Archives: A Guide to Family History Sources in the Official Records of South Australia. Adelaide, South Australia: Research and Access Services of State Records, 1994.

Bartlett, Anne M. *Local and Family History Sources in Tasmania.* Hobart: Genealogical Society of Tasmania, 1994.

Burrows, Anne, Susan Mildred, Patricia Moore, and Michael Talbot. *Kith and Kin: Sources for Family History.* Adelaide, South Australia: Libraries Board of South Australia, 1994.

Chambers, M. *Finding Families: The Guide to the National Archives of Australia for Genealogists.* Alexandria, New South Wales, Australia: National Archives of Australia, 1998.

Fairs, Jennie and Dom Meadley. *Family and Local Sources in the Sydney*

Area. Nunawading, Victoria, Australia: Custodians of Records, 1995.

Hall, Nick Vine. *Tracing Your Family History in Australia: A Guide to Sources.* Albert Park, Victoria, Australia: N.V. Hall, 1994.

Hawkings, David T., *Bound for Australia*, Phillimore, Sussex, 1987.

Henry, Brian. *Dublin Hanged: Crime, Law Enforcement and Punishment in Late Eighteenth-Century Dublin.* Dublin: Irish Academic Press, 1994.

McClaughlin, Trevor. *Barefoot and Pregnant? Irish Famine Orphans in Australia: Documents and Register.* Melbourne: The Genealogical Society of Victoria, 1991.

McIntyre, Perry C. "Transportation Registers Ireland to Australia: An International Research Tool." *The Irish At Home and Abroad* 1 (Fall 1993): 9–11.

Meadley, Dom and Frances Brown. *Family and Local History Sources in Victoria.* Nunawading, Victoria, Australia: Custodians of Records, 1996.

O'Farrell, Patrick. *The Irish in Australia.* Kensington: University of New South Wales, 1987.

Peake, Andrew. *Sources for South Australian Family History.* Adelaide, South Australia: A.G. Peake and South Australia Genealogical and Heraldic Society, 1977.

Reid, Richard. "Aspects of Assisted Emigration to New South Wales, 1848–1870." Ph.D. Thesis, Australian National University (Canberra), 1992.

Reid, Richard and Keith Johnson, eds. *The Irish Australians: Selected Articles for Australian and Irish Family Historians.* Jointly published by the Society of Australian Genealogists and Ulster Historical Foundation, 1984.

Reece, Bob, ed. *Irish Convict Lives.* Darlinghurst, Sydney: Crossing Press, 1993.

———. *Exiles from Erin: Convict Lives in Ireland and Australia.* Hampshire: Macmillan, 1991.

Sherington, Geoffrey. *Australia's Immigrants, 1788–1978.* Sydney, London, Boston: George Allen and Unwin, 1980.

Waldersee, James. *Catholic Society in New South Wales, 1788–1860.* Sydney: University Press, 1974.

Woolcock, Helen R. *Rights of Passage: Emigration to Australia in the Nineteenth Century.* London: Travistock Publications, 1986.

Addresses

Archives Office of Tasmania
    77 Murray St., Hobart TAS 7000, Australia
    phone: (03) 6233 7488/7490   *fax:* (03) 6233 7471
    Internet: http://www.tased.edu.au/archives/
Archives of the State of New South Wales
    City Search Room, 2 Globe St., The Rocks, Sydney, NSW 2000, Australia
    phone: (02) 9237 0254   *fax:* (02) 9237 0142
    Western Sydney Search Room, 143 O'Connell St.
    Kingswood NSW 2747, Australia

phone: (02) 9673 1788   *fax:* (02) 9833 4518
Internet: http://www.records.nsw.gov.au/

Genealogical Society of the Northern Territory
   P.O. Box 37212, Winnellie, NT 0821, Australia
   Library: 25 Cavenagh St., Dawrin NT, Australia
   phone: (08) 8981 7363
   Internet: http://sites.archivenet.gov.au/gsnt/

Heraldry and Genealogical Society of Canberra
   G.P.O. Box 585, Canberra, ACT 2601, Australia
   phone: (02) 6282 9356
   Internet: http://www.hagsoc.org .au/

Melbourne Archives Centre
   Level 2, Casselden Pl., 2 Lonsdale St., Melbourne, VIC 3000, Australia
   phone: (03) 9285 7999

National Archives of Australia
   (Location) Queen Victoria Terrace, Parkes, ACT 2600, Australia
   (Mailing) P.O. Box 7425, Canberra Mail Centre, ACT 2610, Australia
   phone: (02) 6212 3900   *fax:* (02) 6212 3999
   Internet: http://www.naa.gov.au/index.htm

National Library of Australia
   Canberra, ACT 2600, Australia
   phone: (02) 6262 1111   *fax:* (02) 6257 1703
   Internet: http://www.nla.gov.au/library/

Public Record Office Victoria
   P.O. Box 2100, North Melbourne, VIC 3051, Australia
   phone: (03) 9360 9665
   Internet: http://www.prov.vic.gov.au

Queensland State Archives
   (Location) 435 Compton Rd., Runcord QLD 4113, Australia
   (Mailing) P.O. Box 1397, Sunnybank Hills, QLD 4109, Australia
   phone: (07) 3875 8755   *fax:* (07) 3875 8764
   Internet: http://www.archives.qld.gov.au/

Society of Australian Genealogists
   Richmond Villa, 120 Kent St., Sydney, NSW 2000, Australia
   phone: (02) 9247 3953   *fax:* (02) 9241 4872
   Internet: http://www.sag.org.au/

South Australian Genealogical and Heraldry Society
   (Location) 201 Unley Rd., Unley, SA 5001, Australia
   (Mailing) G.P.O. Box 592, Adelaide, SA 5001, Australia
   phone: (08) 8272 4222   *fax:* (08) 8272 4910
   Internet: http://dove.net.au/~saghs/

State Library of New South Wales
   Macquarie St., Sydney, NSW 2000, Australia
   phone: (02) 9273 1414   *fax:* (02) 9273 1255
   Internet: http://www.slnsw.gov.au/

State Library of Queensland
    Family History Unit, P.O. Box 3488
    South Brisbane, QLD 4101, Australia
    phone: (07) 3840 7775   *fax:* (07) 3840 7840
    Internet: http://www.slq.qld.gov.au/scd/famhist/index.htm

State Library of South Australia
    (Location) North Terrace, corner of Kintore Ave., Adelaide, SA, Australia
    (Mailing) G.P.O. Box 419, Adelaide, SA 5001, Australia
    phone: (08) 8207 7200   *fax:* (08) 8207 7247
    Internet: http://www.slsa.sa.gov.au/

State Library of Tasmania
    91 Murray St., Hobart, TAS 7000, Australia
    phone: (03) 6233 7939
    Internet: http://www.tased.edu.au/library/

State Library of Victoria
    328 Swanton St., Melbourne, VIC 3000, Australia
    phone: (03) 9669 9888   *fax:* (03) 9669 9645
    Internet: http://www.slv.vic.gov.au/

State Records of South Australia
    (Location) 222 Marion Rd., Netley, Australia
    (Mailing) P.O. Box 1056, Blair Athol West, SA 5084, Australia
    phone: (08) 8343 6800   *fax:* (08) 8226 8002
    Internet: http://www.archives.sa.gov.au/

State Reference Library
    Alexander Library Bldg., Perth Cultural Centre Bldg.
    Perth, WA 6000, Australia
    phone: (08) 9427 3111   *fax:* (08) 9427 3256
    Internet: http://www.liswa.wa.gov.au/

FIVE

New Zealand

Technique

Many thousands of Irish immigrants went to New Zealand in the nineteenth century. If your ancestors immigrated to the United States or Canada, chances are they also had a relative immigrate to New Zealand. **So, if you can't find immigrant origins by tracing your ancestor, then branch off to the brother or sister who went to New Zealand since the New Zealand records are so good about giving exact birthplaces in Ireland.** This principle applies even when you have identified a county in Ireland, only to find that either the church records in Ireland do not start early enough or record destruction has been especially bad. Use the New Zealand branch of the family to get around this problem. Commonly you'll find not only the county of birth for a New Zealand immigrant but also the parish and townland.

Keep in mind that because of the geography of New Zealand, it was on the trade routes to and from just about everywhere. For this reason, you will not only find the Irish coming directly to these islands but also families who had spent time in the United States, South Africa, and Gibraltar. On the other hand, you'll also find New Zealand families going to far-flung places such as the United States, Chile, and closer to home, Australia.

There are logical reasons for New Zealand records being so good. Geographically, it is a small country with a relatively small population that was easy to document. It wasn't until 1840 that New Zealand was annexed by Great Britain and its residents became British citizens; then immigration began in full force. So with a small geography and a small population, it is realistically possible to index records covering the population.

Anne Bromell has written two books that discuss New Zealand genealogy from two perspectives. Her *Tracing Family History in New Zealand* discusses the major record types and where they are located. Her second book, *Tracing Family History Overseas From New Zealand*, takes the approach of "getting them over the water." We recommend both books for grounding yourself in methodology and source material. To complement Bromell's books, we recommend the New Zealand Society of Genealogists. This is a professional organization well versed in research methods, and it has a Web site: <http://www.genealogy.org.n2>.

The New Zealand Society of Genealogists has indexed many records from throughout the country. The indexes include church, civil, vital, immigration, land, probate, school, and tombstone records.

Other repositories important to your research are the system of National Archives of New Zealand and the National Library of New Zealand. Both have Web sites. The Auckland City Library, Research Centre has the largest family history collection of any New Zealand public library, and it has a Web site and online catalog. Check the New Zealand Libraries Web site at <http://tepuna.natl ib.govt.nz/web_directory/nz/libraries.htm> for how to contact libraries and archives throughout the country. Also see the microfilm collections at the FHL. They hold copies of the many wonderful microfiche indexes produced by the New Zealand Society of Genealogists.

To stay up to date on the world of New Zealand genealogy, see <http://www.cyndislist.com>. Also, the New ZealandGenWeb Project is continually updated: <http://www.rootsweb.com/~nzlwgw/>.

In this chapter we will discuss the major record sources for New Zealand. We have chosen to include civil registration, church records, old age pensions, and immigration records, with a special section on Maori research. These native people of New Zealand both fought and intermarried with the incoming Europeans. Today they are a mixed-blood people with strong Irish roots (see pages 107–108).

CIVIL REGISTRATION

The government in New Zealand began recording births and deaths from 1848 and marriages from 1855. These records by themselves are an incredible source for identifying not only birthplaces in Ireland but also information on relatives who never emigrated.

There were registration districts throughout New Zealand from the earliest days, and the registrars were responsible for registering the births and deaths in that district. The local registrars sent copies to the Registrar General Office each quarter. Ministers who officiated at marriages sent this information directly to the Registrar General Office. For periods prior to civil registration, church records are the source from which to document births/baptisms, marriages, and deaths/burials. One overlooked aspect about the registration of family events in New Zealand is that before it became a British Sovereignty in 1840, New Zealand was governed from New South Wales, Australia, so you may find early records registered there.

To begin the search in New Zealand civil registration, there are a few facts handy to know. Among these are

Births: Birth certificates prior to 1876 may record the date, place of birth, child's name, parents' names, maiden name of mother, and father's occupation. From January 1876, the age and birthplace of each parent, the date and place of the parents' marriage, and the signature of the informant are included. From

Notes

1912, the sex and age of other living children, and the number and gender of any deceased children, is registered.

Marriages: Marriage certificates prior to 1881 state the date, marriage place, names, ages, marital status, and bridegroom's occupation. From January 1881 added details include the birthplace and residence of the bride and groom, parents' names, mother's maiden name, and father's occupation. If either party was under twenty-one, the name, address, and signature of the father or mother was required. Don't neglect the "Notices of intention to marry" card index of all New Zealand marriages, which is generated by the Registrar General and deposited at the National Archives of New Zealand. This index includes each bride and groom in New Zealand from 1855 to 1880. If either party was under twenty-one, a parent's name, address, and signature is registered.

Deaths: Death certificates prior to 1876 state only the date and place of death, usual residence, age, occupation, and cause of death. From January 1876, other details required included the birthplace of the deceased, parents' names, father's occupation, mother's maiden name, name of spouse, age when married, marriage place, gender and age of surviving children, place of burial, length of residence in colony, minister or witness, and undertaker.

Civil registration is relatively easy to use because there are annual indexes to the births and deaths (1848 to 1990) and marriages (1855 to 1990). These have been published on microfiche by the Registrar General Office. The indexes list the surname, given name, and reference number to the original district of registration. Since the indexes are microfiched, they are widely available at major New Zealand libraries and even internationally in such major libraries as the Society of Genealogists in London and the FHL. All New Zealand certificates are available from the Central Registry in Lower Hutt, New Zealand, and you can order either a certified copy or a photocopy.

CHURCH RECORDS

The earliest church registers start about 1815. These early records will document seamen, mainly sealers, whalers, and adventurers. You would be surprised how many Americans are in the New Zealand church records. Americans going to New Zealand is a migration most people have never thought about. Think about it this way: When gold was discovered in Otago, the news spread to the gold fields of California and Australia, and the Irish and Irish-Americans flocked to find their fortunes. Fortunately, many church records are being indexed by the New Zealand Society of Genealogists. Unfortunately, there is no master index to these extractions, so you have to know a geographic location to begin the search. **If you're unsure where to begin the search, we suggest the "Intention to marry" notices described under civil registration.**

Church of England (Anglican)
Province of Auckland

The Church of England, or Anglican Church, is an important denomination in New Zealand. The Anglican Diocesan Archives in Auckland holds records for

Tip

more than fifteen hundred parish registers deposited by local churches within the Auckland Province (which includes several dioceses). For example, they hold records for the earliest parish registers in the country, including the Bay of Islands churches of Waimate North (1815), Paihia (1823), and Kaitaia (1835). Another important collection you will find is the parishes of the Irish soldiers in the Imperial regiments stationed at the Auckland Army Barracks. These registers include St. Paul's (1841), St. Stephen (1844), St. Thomas (1844), and St. Mary's (1844), as well as other Auckland churches. The archives holds journals of traveling ministers who visited rural areas.

There were some interesting if not unique records generated by the Church of England in New Zealand. For example, the Chelsea Hospital pensioners (The Fencibles) from the British Army arrived from Great Britain with their families in Auckland in 1847. They settled in "Fencible villages." Their parish churches are at Onehunga, Howick, Otahuhu, and Panmure. Onehunga and Howick churches kept an 1855 census of church members, noting overseas birth/baptism place and date, marriage place and date, and confirmations. St. Mark's, Remuera, kept a similar census. If your ancestor lived in the Fencible villages, the archives of the Auckland Province would be the place to start.

Other Anglican Provinces

Similar records have been entrusted to other Anglican Provincial Archives. The churches of Nelson and Westland Provinces house their registers at the Anglican Centre in Nelson. Anglican Church House in Hamilton cares for the archives of the Waikato Diocese, while the Anglican records for Hawke's Bay are deposited at the Diocese of Waiapu, Napier. Research Anglican parish registers of Wellington Province are in the Manuscript Department of Alexander Turnball Library, Wellington. Canterbury Public Library has transcribed the baptism, marriage, and burial entries from the registers in their care of the Diocese of Christchurch. This information was added to its large biographical card index.

Otago/Southland New Zealand Anglican Marriages, 1852–1920, an index of brides, grooms, dates, and reference numbers, is available on microfiche from the Anglican Diocesan Office in Dunedin at <http://www.dn.anglican.org.nz>. In addition to Anglican marriages, this index includes marriage entries extracted from Congregational Churches from 1864 to 1920, Associated Church of Christ from 1873 to 1920, Wesleyan Waikouaiti Mission from 1841 to 1857, Ruapuke Fouveaux Strait Mission from 1845 to 1882, and Bishop Selwyn marriages in 1844 and 1851. Registers from the Diocese of Dunedin have been deposited at the Hocken Library. The Anglican Diocesan Offices at Christchurch, Dunedin, and Wellington also have deposited Anglican records there.

Roman Catholic

Although there have been Roman Catholics in New Zealand since the earliest days of European settlement, it wasn't until 1838 that the first Mass was celebrated. For searches prior to this time, the Church of England records would be the prime source to look at for Catholic families. Some Catholic parish registers have been indexed by the New Zealand Society of Genealogists. *Otago/Southland Catholic Marriages, 1855–1920* was published on microfiche by the Catholic Diocese of Dunedin. Registers from churches were built for the Catholic Chelsea Pensioners living in the Fencible villages of Onehunga (1848), Howick (1847), Panmure (1852), and Otahuhu (1848) are indexed to 1885.

Catholic registers are also deposited at the Catholic Diocesan Centres in Christchurch, Hamilton, and Wellington. Registers from some Catholic parishes of the Diocese of Christchurch are housed at the Canterbury Public Library, where entries have been transcribed and included in the extensive biographical card index. The Catholic Diocese of Auckland retains the church records for the Auckland and Hamilton Dioceses.

Presbyterian

The archivist of the Presbyterian Church of Aotearoa, New Zealand Archives, Dunedin, is compiling *A National Register of Presbyterian Archives*, held in its library and repositories. A microfiche edition of *Otago/Southland Presbyterian Marriages 1848–1920* is available. Auckland City Library holds *Register of Families in Connection with the Free Presbyterian Church, Auckland 1849 St. Andrew's Presbyterian Church, Register of Births and Baptisms*. The Auckland Institute and Museum Library has a catalog of Presbyterian registers deposited by churches in the Auckland district, and local Presbyterian records are deposited at regional libraries and museums.

Methodist

Samuel Leigh opened the first mission station in Whangaroa, Northland, in 1822. The registers of the Wesleyan Mission in Hokianga (1830), and Auckland Wesleyan Chapel (1844) are housed with Auckland Provincial records at the Methodist Church Archives in Auckland. The Methodist Church of New Zealand Connexional Office in Christchurch cares for the Methodist church records of New Zealand. The earliest records at this repository are for Wellington (1840), Waikouaiti Mission (1840), Taranaki Wesleyan, William Kirk (1841), and Auckland High Street (1844).

Congregational

Original books of Beresford Street Congregational Church in Auckland (indexed from 1851 to 1918) are at the Auckland City Library. Minute books and registers of the Auckland High Street Church (1851), Onehunga (1861), the church book of Kororareka (1840), and other Congregational registers are cataloged at the Auckland Institute and Museum Library. Hocken Library in Dunedin has some records deposited, and the Canterbury Public Library at Christchurch has a card index of entries from Presbyterian and Congregational records entrusted to it.

IMMIGRATION RECORDS

The New Zealand Company brought the first assisted immigrants to New Zealand from 1839 to 1850. There were two additional periods of assisted immigration, which included schemes initiated by the Provincial Councils of New Zealand (1853 to 1870) and General Government Assisted Immigration (1871 to 1888). Between the years 1870 and 1880 there were 100,000 assisted immigrants in New Zealand. During this time period there were forty thousand unassisted immigrants. **So if you don't find your ancestor arriving as an assisted immigrant, make sure you expand your search to include those who were unassisted.** All of these records are indexed at the National Archives of New Zealand with microfilm copies at the FHL.

Research Tip

Two interesting indexes transcribed by the Auckland New Zealand Society of Genealogists are of passenger lists (1845 to 1895) and of the names of immigrants published in Auckland newspapers. The Wellington New Zealand Society of Genealogists published an index of immigrants reported from Wellington newspapers.

From 1871, under the Julius Vogel Immigration Scheme, settlers could nominate friends and family as suitable immigrants to New Zealand. You can imagine how beneficial for Irish research the records generated under this scheme are. The nomination registers listing Passage Orders for Nominated Immigrants (1871 to 1874 and 1878 to 1891) are at the National Archives (reference IM 10/1-13). The records show chain migrations in which Irish families emigrated from the same areas of Ireland to the same areas of New Zealand. These nomination registers are not indexed; however, you can accesses them by using the nomination numbers given on the passenger lists themselves, which are indexed as Assisted Immigration Index (1871 to 1888). You will also find nominations under other programs prior to the Vogel Scheme. For example, Auckland settlers nominated members of their families and friends from 1859 to 1872. These lists have been indexed in the immigration indexes at the National Archives of New Zealand.

There are other even more intriguing schemes generated to bring settlers into New Zealand. These include the Waikato Settlement Scheme and the Royal New Zealand Fencibles settlement. The Waikato Settlement Scheme (1864 to 1865) brought settlers from Great Britain and Ireland as well as South Africa. The records provide details on each passenger and the land he was allocated in the Bombay District of Auckland. There were similar immigration schemes at Puhoi, Bay of Islands, and Port Albert. All the immigration scheme records are at the National Archives in Auckland, where they are indexed.

OLD-AGE PENSIONS

You will also find information concerning the personal lives and origins of Irish immigrants in old-age pension records. In 1896 the government began a nationwide program whereby individuals could apply for pensions. Under the Registration of Peoples Claims Act (1896), seventy-three Old-Age Pension Districts were established where people could apply for an old-age pension. Information in the records of these districts included applicant's name, occupation, address, birthplace, date of birth, age at next birthday, date of arrival in the

For More Info

THE IRISH-MAORI CONNECTION

The Maori are the native people of New Zealand, and they have a long and interesting historical connection with the Irish. Unlike other native peoples who came into contact with the Europeans, there was no genocide of the Maori, nor were they forcibly removed. In fact what makes the Maori so important to Irish studies is that they intermarried with so many Irish immigrant families that today there are entire family histories written about both the Irish and the Maori sides of families. There are few pure-blood Maori today. The tribe itself composes about 12 percent of New Zealand's population. It is common for many an unsuspecting New Zealander to discover a Maori ancestor through genealogical research. Whether their descendants chose to remain culturally Maori or to assimilate into the dominant European society varies from family to family.

The Maori-Irish connection has been explored from a genealogical perspective by New Zealander Verna E. Mossong in her article "The Irish as Maori" in *The Irish At Home and Abroad*. In this article she discusses sources to trace Maori pedigrees and includes a list of important Maori words as found in the records. You can find an Internet introduction to Maori genealogy at Whakapapa Maori (Maori Genealogy), <http://www.ourworld.compuserve.com/home pages/ rhimona/whakapap.htm>.

So how did the Maori come to be intermarried so strongly with the Irish? First, we must state that by "marriage" we mean legal church weddings as well as common-law unions. Both were common in early New Zealand history. Some of the earliest written records of mixed-blood Maori-Irish families are church records that document European traders and whalers, and sometimes Americans, in Maori lands. Keep in mind these early marriages were before the massive immigration of Irish to New Zealand, so they represent the older mixed-blood families.

Under the Treaty of Waitangi signed on 6 February 1840, New Zealand was annexed by Great Britain and the Maori became British subjects. The treaty between the Maori and the British meant the Maori gave up their independence in exchange for retaining their lands. This allowed for frequent contact between the incoming Irish and Maori from this time forward.

You will also see that many Irish men came to New Zealand as discharged soldiers of the British Army and many found wives among the Maori. In fact a number of officers (as opposed to soldiers) of the British Army had common-law marriages with Maori women during the decade 1840 to 1850. Another wave of contact came not from Ireland but from Australia. In 1860 the gold mines in Australia were closing, so when gold was discovered in the Otago area of New Zealand (1860) and in Hokitika (1864), large numbers of Irish-Australians arrived and married Maori women.

continued on page 108

There are Maori pedigrees, some from the European perspective and some from the oral and ancient Maori perspective. It is common to find oral Maori genealogies preserved in written form. In fact, some libraries in New Zealand have their own Maori studies sections. The FHL has a large collection of microfilmed Maori genealogies. If records are in Maori, a Maori-English dictionary will be helpful (yes, there is one on the Internet at <http://www.nzcer.org.nz/kimikupu/>). During the twentieth century, large numbers of Maori converted to the Church of Jesus Christ of Latter-day Saints (Mormons). The conversions to Mormonism prompted more family record keeping due to the faith's emphasis on family history and genealogy, so there is no lack of Maori-related records. Our advice before starting in the search for Maori-Irish roots is to become familiar with the source material and be aware of the special strategies associated with this type of rewarding research.

Sources

References and Further Reading

Austin, W. Rex. "Early Settlement of Riverton by Maori and Pakeha." In *The Gateway to Scenic Southland: Proceedings of the 1996 Conference, New Zealand Society of Genealogists, Inc.* Invercargill, N.Z.: New Zealand Society of Genealogists, Inc., 1996.

Bromell, Anne. "Maori Genealogy or Whakapapa." In *Tracing Family History in New Zealand*, 60–64. Birkenhead, Auckland, N.Z.: Godwit Publishing, Ltd., 1996.

Butchers, A.G. "The Maori Schools." *The Education System.* Auckland, N.Z.: The National Printing Co., 1932.

Cherry, Stella. *Te Ao Maori-The Maori World.* Dublin: The National Museum of Ireland, 1990.

Dancey, Harry. *Maori Custom Today.* Auckland, N.Z.: New Zealand Newspapers, Ltd, 1971.

Griffith, Keith C. "Maori Adoptions," *Adoption—Procedure, Documentation, Statistics, New Zealand, 1881–1981.* n.p.: K.S.G., 1981.

Herlihy, Brian. "The Maori Land Court as a Source of Information." *Archifacts* (June 1985): 45–48.

Metge, Joan. *The Maoris of New Zealand.* London: Routledge and Kegan Paul, 1967.

Mossong, Verna E. "The Irish as Maori." *The Irish At Home and Abroad* 6 (1) (1st Quarter 1999): 6–13.

Stevens, M. *Location Guide to Maori Schools, 1879–1969.* Auckland: National Archives of New Zealand, Auckland Regional Office.

colony, and the name of the ship. This act was in force until the passage of the Social Security Act in 1938.

Again and again the problem of proving a potential pensioner's age was the most difficult part of the application process. Sworn evidence from a friend or someone who had traveled on the same boat and knew the age of the applicant was accepted. To give you an example of this, the entry for Margaret Gault reads: "Michael McKenna sworn—I live in Well'n St.—tailor—I and claimant lived in Newtowngore, Leitrim, Ire.—about 50 yrs ago—I am . . . about 65 myself. I believe she is my senior because we were brought . . . together—I knew her as long as I can remember."

Records used in court investigations to prove income included land transfer and deeds registration; records of chattels at the Supreme Court; the district valuation roll; and personal property, including any documents relating to the property or income of the applicant. Investigations were extended to the Registrar General of Births, Deaths, and Marriages in 1900. Passenger and shipping lists were also considered. As you can see, the investigations of applications for old-age pensions were quite thorough and can provide a virtual biography.

Some District Courts still retain their old-age pension records and may answer queries. The best way to access any pension records still held by a court would be having the New Zealand Society of Genealogists conduct the research on your behalf. Other court records are now at the National Archives in Auckland and Dunedin. Some have been indexed. The Auckland Old-Age Pension registers from 1899 to 1906 are available through the FHL.

REFERENCES AND FURTHER READING

Borrie, Wilfred David. *Immigration to New Zealand, 1854–1938.* Demography Programme, Research School of Social Sciences. Canberra: Australian National University, 1991.

Family History at National Archives. Wellington, New Zealand: Allen and Unwin, New Zealand, Ltd., and National Archives of New Zealand, 1990.

King, Michael. *God's Farthest Outpost: A History of Catholics in New Zealand.* Auckland, New Zealand: Penguin Books (N.Z.), Ltd., 1997.

Neill, Mary, Meryl Lowrie and Aileen Wood. *District Keys to the New Zealand Registration Indexes, Births and Deaths, 1840–1920.* 4 vols. Auckland: New Zealand Society of Genealogists Inc., 1990.

Reiher, Gwen. "Old Age Pensions in New Zealand." *The Irish At Home and Abroad* 4 (1) (1997): 42–45.

Sources

Addresses

Alexander Turnbull Library (at the National Library of New Zealand)
(*Location*) Corner of Molesworth and Aitken streets
(*Mailing*) P.O. Box 12-349, Wellington, New Zealand
phone: (64-4) 474 3120   *fax:* (64-4) 474 3063
Internet: http://www.natlib.govt.nz/docher/atl.htm

Auckland City Libraries
Family Historian Librarian, Auckland Research Centre
P.O. Box 4138, Auckland, New Zealand
fax: (09) 377 0209
Internet: http://akcity.govt.nz/library/
Central Registry, Births, Deaths and Marriages
(*Location*) 191 High St., Lower Hutt, New Zealand
(*Mailing*) P.O. Box 31 115, Lower Hutt, New Zealand
fax: (4) 566 5311
Internet: http://www.bdm.govt.nz/

National Archives of New Zealand
Internet: http://www.archives.dia.govt.nz/index.html
1. National Archives of New Zealand: (*Location*) Auckland Regional Office, 525 Mt. Wellington Highway, Auckland, New Zealand; (*Mailing*) P.O. Box 91-220, Auckland, New Zealand; Phone: (64-9) 270 1100; Fax: (64-9) 276 4472.
2. National Archives of New Zealand: (*Location*) Christchurch Regional Office: 90 Peterborough St., Christchurch, New Zealand; (*Mailing*) P.O. Box 642, Christchurch, New Zealand; Phone: (64-3) 377 0760; Fax: (64-3) 365 2662.
3. National Archives of New Zealand: (*Location*) Dunedin Regional Office: 556 George St., Dunedin, New Zealand; (*Mailing*) P.O. Box 6183, Dunedin North, Dunedin, New Zealand; Phone: (64-3) 477 0404; Fax: (64-3) 477 0422.
4. National Archives of New Zealand: (*Location*) Wellington Head Office: 10 Mulgrave St., Thorndon, Wellington, New Zealand; (*Mailing*) P.O. Box 12-050, Wellington, New Zealand; Phone: (64-4) 499 5595; Fax: (64-4) 495 6210.

National Library of New Zealand
(*Location*) Corner Molesworth and Aitken streets
(*Mailing*) P.O. Box 1467, Wellington, New Zealand
phone: (64-4) 474 3000   *fax:* (64-4) 474 3035
Internet: http://www.natlib.govt.nz/
New Zealand Society of Genealogists Inc.
P.O. Box 8795, Symonds St., Auckland 1035, New Zealand
phone: (64 9) 525 0625   *fax:* (64 9) 525 0620
Internet: http://www.genealogy.org.nz
Registrar General Office
P.O. Box 31-115, Lower Hutt, New Zealand
phone: (04) 569 4489   *fax:* (04) 566-5311

Addresses: Churches
Anglican Repositories
Archivist, Anglican Diocesan Office

P.O. Box 37-242, Auckland 1003, New Zealand
phone: (09) 377-1989   *fax:* (09) 366-0703
Diocesan Manager, Anglican Church House
P.O. Box 21, Hamilton, New Zealand
phone: (07) 838-2309   *fax:* (07) 838-0052
Anglican Diocesan Centre, Diocese of Waiapu
P.O. Box 227, Napier, New Zealand
phone: (06) 835-8230   *fax:* (06) 835-0680
The Anglican Centre
P.O. Box 100, Nelson, New Zealand
phone: (03) 548-3124   *fax:* (03) 548-2125
Anglican Diocesan Office
P.O. Box 12-046, Wellington, New Zealand
phone: (04) 472-1057   *fax:* (04) 499-1360
Anglican Diocesan Office
P.O. Box 8471, Riccarton, Christchurch 4, New Zealand
phone: (03) 343-0519   *fax:* (03) 348-3827
Anglican Diocesan Office
P.O. Box 5445, Dunedin, New Zealand
phone: (03) 477-4931   *fax:* (03) 477-4932

Roman Catholic Repositories

Catholic Diocesan Archives
Private Bag 47-904, Ponsonby, Auckland, New Zealand
phone: (09) 378-4380   *fax:* (09) 376-2829
Archivist, Bishop's House
277 Rattray St., Dunedin, New Zealand
phone: (03) 477-6030   *fax:* (03) 477-2528 (Education Department)
Catholic Diocesan Centre
P.O. Box 4353, Hamilton, New Zealand
phone: (07) 856-6989   *fax:* (07) 856-7035
Catholic Diocesan Centre
P.O. Box 1937, Wellington, New Zealand
phone: (04) 496-1777   *fax:* (04) 499-2512
Catholic Diocesan Centre
P.O. Box 10069, Christchurch, New Zealand
phone: (03) 366-9869   *fax:* (03) 366-9451

Presbyterian Repositories

Presbyterian Church of Aotearoa New Zealand
Presbyterian Church Archives: Knox College, Arden St.,
Dunedin, New Zealand
phone: (03) 473 0107, ext. 7851, 7857   *fax:* (03) 473 8466
Internet: http://www.freeyellow.com/members6/pcanz/

Presbyterian Repositories (Regional)

Tauranga Public Library
   Private Bag, Tauranga, New Zealand
   phone: (07) 577-7177   *fax:* (07) 578-6787

Gisborne Museum and Arts Centre
   P.O. Box 716, Gisborne, New Zealand
   phone: (06) 867-3832

Hawke's Bay Gallery and Museum Library
   P.O. Box 429, Napier, New Zealand
   phone: (06) 835-7781   *fax:* (06) 835-3984

Taranaki Museum
   P.O. Box 315, New Plymouth, New Zealand
   phone: (06) 758-9583   *fax:* (06) 758-5485

Wanganui Regional Museum
   P.O. Box 352, Wanganui, New Zealand
   phone: (06) 345-7443   *fax:* (06) 347-6512

Palmerston North Public Library
   P.O. Box 1948, Palmerston North, New Zealand
   phone: (06) 358-3076   *fax:* (06) 356-8869

Nelson Provincial Museum
   P.O. Box 2069, Stoke, Nelson, New Zealand
   phone/fax: (03) 547-9740

Methodist Repositories

Archivist, Methodist Church of New Zealand
   P.O. Box 9573, Newmarket, Auckland, New Zealand
   phone: (09) 525-4179   *fax:* (09) 525-4346

Archivist, Methodist Church of New Zealand Connexional Office
   P.O. Box 931, Christchurch, New Zealand
   phone: (03) 366-6049   *fax:* (03) 366-6009

SIX

Great Britain (England, Scotland, and Wales)

I n this chapter we will discuss some of the major British sources you can use to trace an Irish immigrant. We will be discussing only England, Scotland, and south Wales. Keep in mind the Irish also settled in other parts of Great Britain such as the Isle of Man and the Channel Islands, and these areas may come into play in your research.

Many Irish immigrated to cities such as Liverpool, England; Merthyr-Tydfil, Wales; and Dundee, Scotland, and Irish neighborhoods were formed in these cities. Irish in these communities commonly continued their immigration to other countries, where they took up permanent settlement.

One important book used to explore communities of Irish in Britain is *The Irish in Victorian Britain*, edited by Roger Swift and Sheridan Gilley, which consists of essays focused on the Irish experience in towns including Birmingham, Camborne, Hull, London, and Stafford. Another example comes from Greenhill in Swansea, Wales, in R.T. Prices's *Little Ireland: Aspects of the Irish and Greenhill, Swansea.*

You can document the Irish in British records of the sixteenth and seventeenth centuries. The Irish would go to cities in England and Scotland where the army was recruiting or where passenger ships were leaving for the American and Caribbean colonies in the sixteenth century. During the famine years and long afterward, both Catholic and Protestant Irish flooded into cities such as Liverpool.

In 1974, the counties of England, Scotland, and Wales were resurveyed and often renamed. So we will be using the names of the pre-1974 counties, except in our address section. In this chapter we will refer to many repositories as County Record Office, which, of course, refers to the new counties. These localized archives hold vast amounts of material for their areas. **To help you find addresses and Internet sites for localized record offices, and often what is deposited at them, see these Web sites:**

Open.gov.uk lists council and borough governments and their Web sites from throughout the UK: http://www.open.gov.uk/

Reminder

Internet Source

Familia: The UK and Ireland's Guide to Genealogical Resources in Public Libraries: http://www.earl.org.uk/familia/

Historical Manuscript Commission: ARCHON—information gateway for UK archivist and users of manuscripts sources for British history: http://www.hmc.gov.uk/archon/archon.htm

The listing of repositories on Mark Howell's Web site, English Record Offices and Archives on the Web: http://www.oz.net/~markhow/english ros.htm

Scottish Record Offices and Archives on the Web: http://www.oz.net/~mar khow/scotsros.htm

Welsh Record Offices and Archives on the Web: http://www.oz.net/~mark how/welshros.htm

Gibson and Peskett's booklet *Record Offices: How to Find Them*, published by the Federation of Family History Societies, not only lists more than one hundred record offices throughout Great Britain but also has maps showing how to get to them.

Genealogy is popular in Great Britain. To keep current, constantly refer to the GENUKI Web site, UK and Ireland Genealogy, at <http://www.genuki.org.uk>, and Cyndi's List <http://www.cyndislist.com>. Both have sections for each county in Britain (the old county names are often used as a reference). The FHL has a tremendous microfilm and book collection for Great Britain, and we recommend that you regularly refer to its FHL catalog, available online at <http://www.familysearch.org>. In its cataloging system, the FHL uses the pre-1974 county names to make your research easier.

To supplement and to keep current with regard to our further reading list for genealogy in Great Britain, see the guides published by the Federation of Family History Societies (Birmingham, England) and the Society of Genealogists (London). Both list just about every conceivable record type you could possibly use in British genealogy.

ENGLAND

Important

There has always been an association between England and Ireland. Due to English colonization plans in Ireland and elsewhere, the two nations have been tied even to this day by migration between them. Also, due to England's effort to redistribute its population over the centuries, the Irish have been dispersed worldwide and have contributed to just about every culture on the planet.

The massive Irish influx into England in the famine years and afterward included both Catholics and Protestants. The difference here is that Protestants became absorbed into the English Protestant culture, while the Irish Catholics established their own places of worship and kept their culture alive.

Interest in genealogy has grown so much in England that many records have now become available through microfiche, CD-ROM, the Internet, and published by family history societies throughout England. The Public Records Office (PRO) in London has to be one of most organized and outstanding archives in the world. The FHL also has microfilm copies of records from many different types of repositories in England, thus making its collection especially valuable. The Society of Genealogists in London has gathered books and transcripts from throughout England, bringing together a large and varied collection under one roof. The Family Records Centre in London houses the nation's censuses and civil records.

This section on England cannot address every record source available. We have chosen what we consider the most important in the search for Irish origins. To fill in any gaps we have intentionally left, we recommend Mark D. Herber's *Ancestral Trails*, written in association with the Society of Genealogists; Sherry Irvine's *Your English Ancestry: A Guide for North Americans*, written by a Canadian; Paul Milner and Linda Jonas's *A Genealogist's Guide to Discovering Your English Ancestors*, published in America; and the *England Research Outline* by the Genealogical Society of Utah, available online at <http://www.family search.org>.

Cemeteries

Records of English graveyards come in three forms: tombstones, burial records of the church or parish, and records kept by the cemetery itself. It is important to remember that not everybody had a tombstone. It is common for genealogical societies and individuals in England to have transcribed and published tombstone inscriptions. The Federation of Family History Societies in Birmingham is transcribing all British tombstones in a National Burial Index.

The Society of Genealogists in London has an excellent collection of published and manuscript transcripts in their library. It publishes a guide to its collections, *Monumental Inscriptions in the Library of the Society of Genealogists*, by Lydia Collins and Mabel Morton. The term *monumental inscriptions*, or *MI*, used in the title of this book, is common in British publications and means the same thing as tombstone inscriptions.

In the early days persons of all faiths would be buried in Church of England graveyards. Around the beginning of the nineteenth century, the older parish graveyards were being filled up and, to say the least, sanitation was a matter of public concern. For this reason, private companies were formed to establish and operate public cemeteries. Between 1852 and 1857 the government set up Burial Boards run by public officials across the country. These public cemeteries, which date from the mid-nineteenth century, have registers of burials. Sometimes they are indexed and sometimes they are not. Today these cemeteries are part of the local county council. Originally each cemetery was divided along the lines of Church of England, Non-Conformists, and Roman Catholic.

Important

Since there is no national register of cemeteries in England, you can contact the local government board, often by Internet, for the area, and place an inquiry. Also, we recommend using the wonderful system of family history societies in England. Contact them through the Federation of Family History Societies. Of course, sometimes finding the right cemetery is as easy as using a phone book. Large cities can be a problem. Fortunately, the Society of Genealogists published a guide to cemeteries in London in Patricia Wolfston's *Greater London Cemeteries and Crematoria* (revised by Cliff Webb).

Censuses

There are census enumerations open to the public for 1841, 1851, 1861, 1871, 1881, and 1891. The PRO is currently scanning the 1901 Census in a database format. Censuses are at the Family Records Centre and on microfilm at the FHL. Censuses are important from the immigrant perspective for two purposes: After the 1841 enumeration, censuses began to record the parish and county of birth for families. Unfortunately, the census takers often did not apply the parish and county questions to the Irish. So Ireland will be listed as a birthplace. However, it's always that one census you don't check that gives the parish or a county in Ireland. So make sure to search every census for your family if you're looking for a birthplace in Ireland. The 1841 enumeration will state "I" for an Irish birth, but always compare that with the later census schedules.

English censuses provide the geography and the approximate dates necessary to look at other records, such as civil registration and church records. It is fortunate for all of us that some indexes do exist for English censuses. Some regional censuses have been published by genealogical societies, and these are usually available through the society, sometimes on the Internet, in published format or on CD-ROM. You can find a listing of these local indexes in Jeremy Gibson and Elizabeth Hampson's *Marriage and Census Indexes for Family Historians* published by the Federation of Family History Societies. The most notable one on CD is the 1881 census, which covers all English counties as well as Scotland, Wales, the Channel Islands, the Isle of Man, and the Royal Navy. See the FHL Web site for more information at <http://www.familysearch.org>. It was produced by the LDS Church's Genealogical Society of Utah in cooperation with the PRO and the Federation of Family History Societies.

Church Records

Research Tip

Church records are one of the prime sources for tracing a family who lived in England. Fortunately, an excellent collection of church registers, mainly from Protestant denominations, is on microfilm at the FHL. What has not yet been microfilmed might be at a county record office. The Society of Genealogists publishes the series *National Index of Parish Registers*, which lists by county when records of all denominations start and where they are deposited. The PRO holds many church registers, summarized in David Shorney's *Protestant Nonconformity and Roman Catholicism: A Guide to Sources in the Public Record Office*. In this section we will address four topics: Church of England; Roman Catholic church; the explosion of non-conformity throughout England; and the Mormons.

Church of England

The state religion in England historically has been the Church of England, which is part of the worldwide Anglican communion. Because it was the state religion, all other churches were classified as "non-conformists" (see page 119).

THE IMPORTANCE OF CHURCH OF ENGLAND REGISTERS

The early Church of England and Church in Wales records will list persons of all faiths to some degree. So you should not underestimate their importance, even for Roman Catholic families. The government placed restrictions on persons of other faiths, such as voting and legal recognition of marriages, which would affect the probating of estates. Thus it was convenient for persons of all faiths to have their births, marriages, and even burials performed in the Church of England.

The passage of Lord Hardwick's Act in 1753 was designed to put an end to clandestine marriages. This act provided the first standard forms for recording events in the parish register, and marriages had to be by banns or license. The banns were engagement announcements made in public at the church on three Sundays. Also under this act only three types of marriages were recognized as legal: Anglican (Church of England), Quaker, and Jewish.

Complying with this law was important because any child born of a marriage not considered legal was illegitimate, and that affected inheritances. It is common to find Catholics, Methodists, Congregationalists, and Presbyterians in the records of the Church of England. This act was in effect until civil registration was instituted in 1837.

The Church of England considers itself a "reformed" Catholic church. King Henry VIII broke with the Pope in Rome in 1538, and it was about this time that the new Church of England began keeping records of baptisms, marriages, and burials. It took another sixty or more years for record keeping to become commonplace. Although most parish registers do not record a birthplace in Ireland, they do help open up other sources such as burial records, civil registration, and wills and administrations.

The Church of England is organized into parishes, each with its own priest, and parishes are gathered into dioceses governed by a bishop. Cecil Humphery-Smith's *The Phillimore Atlas and Index of Parish Registers* has maps showing parish locations as well as when records begin and where they are deposited.

There were copies of parish registers made and sent to the local bishop. These are known as "Bishops' Transcripts" or "BT's." When you are doing your research, make sure you know if you're looking at the originals or the BT's, as they can contain different information. Sometimes the BT's are the only remaining copy. The Federation of Family History Societies has published a guide to BT's in Jeremy Gibson's *Bishops' Transcripts and Marriage Licences, Bonds & Allegations*, which shows where they have been deposited.

The FHL has made it a goal to obtain as many parish registers and BT's as possible. In some English counties nearly all parishes have records represented

Notes

at the FHL. The LDS Church had a program in which it extracted parish registers and placed the information on the computer database International Genealogical Index (IGI), and it is on the IGI that most people find their Church of England ancestors. If baptisms and marriages are not on the IGI (it does not extract burials), it will be necessary to identify which parishes have not been extracted and look at the records. The maps found in Cecil Humphery-Smith's work can help with this task. See Milner and Jonas's book for how to use these records.

Roman Catholic Church

The history of Catholicism in England is a difficult one indeed. With the creation of the Church of England in 1532, power struggles began between the two faiths for the political and spiritual control of the population. To place some perspective on this, in 1536, which was the twenty-seventh year of the reign of Henry VIII, there were more than eight hundred Catholic monasteries, nunneries, and friaries in Britain. By 1541 there were none. Henry VIII's dissolution of the Catholic Church left huge religious buildings in ruins and dispersed more than ten thousand monks and nuns. Former religious buildings were seized and sold off by the Crown, and other great buildings went to the Protestants. However, not all Roman Catholic families converted to the Church of England during this time. Small groups continued to meet quietly, keeping few records, and it was into these small groups that the Irish came and provided the basis for what was to emerge as a once again strong Roman Catholic presence in England.

If your ancestors were Catholic, registers of baptisms, marriages, and burials (if burials were kept) are of the utmost importance. Catholicism was a minority religion in a predominantly Protestant country, so the chances of not only finding your ancestor but also other relatives or family members from the same place in Ireland are good. Sometimes records of marriages and burials will tell birthplaces in Ireland. Using the rule of thumb of an immigrant minority faith within a larger society, we have extracted all entries for a given time period for a specific surname, and compared the godparents' and witnesses' names. Then armed with this information, we go to records such as the censuses and graveyards to see if we can identify birthplaces.

Notes

You may be surprised to learn that there were no Roman Catholic parishes in England until the end of World War I. The first diocese was founded in 1850, and the various chapels functioned under the Catholic dioceses as missions. This somewhat complicates research for where an ancestor may have gone to church. Under this mission system, priests would serve anyone they could reach, which meant that large areas were left untouched. Thus, if a priest could not reach a family, you must look for their baptisms, marriages, and burials in denominations other than Roman Catholic. A "riding" priest may have kept notes of baptisms in personal notebooks or in the registers of his home chapel. So where events occurred and where you find them recorded may be different. Also, without parish boundaries a family may attend any number of chapels in a larger town or city, so you may have to have check them all to find a baptism or marriage. **It was not until 1791 that Catholics could register their chapels for public worship, so if you're looking for information prior to this time, remember that everything was private.**

Michael Gandy of the Catholic Family History Society in London published a series of booklets on identifying these chapels, where they were located, and if residents will be found in an earlier church record due to traveling priests. This series *Catholic Missions and Registers, 1700–1880* is a must for anyone seeking early Roman Catholic registers. Gandy also published other helpful books on the Catholic Church in England such as *Catholic Family History: A Bibliography of Local Sources* and *Catholic Family History: A Bibliography of General Sources.*

You can also contact the individual diocese by e-mail to inquire about records. The Web site for the Catholic Church in England and Wales with links to dioceseses is at <http://www.tasc.ac.uk/cc/>.

Non-Conformity

From the Reformation of King Henry VIII until the nineteenth century, most people in England belonged to the official Church of England. However, there were groups that operated independently and were termed "non-conformists" by the established church. This included Protestant dissenters, such as Baptists and Methodists; new traditions, such as the Society of Friends (Quakers); and the English Presbyterians/Unitarians. Other faiths such as Catholic, Moravians, Mormons, and the many independent chapels scattered across the landscape of nineteenth-century England could also be included in this list. This section on non-conformity will include some of the Protestant non-conformists.

Protestant non-conformist research after 1837 is rather straightforward because family births, marriages, and deaths will usually be recorded in civil registration as well as in the home chapel. Research before 1837 does provide its own set of challenges. **Usually the first clue that a family belonged to or joined any of the mushrooming number of non-conformist churches is that it fails to appear in the Church of England parish registers.** The next steps are to determine what non-conformist chapels were in the area where your ancestor lived and where the records are located. Another clue would be if you are missing a few baptisms from a family unit. Due to the nature of non-conformity, some families would hop from church to church or be members only for a short while. Due to Hardwick's Marriage Act (enforced from 1754 to 1837) the only marriages recognized by the government were those performed by the Church of England, Jews, and Quakers. So it will be common to see a couple's marriage occur in a Church of England parish, but all baptisms and burials in a non-conformist church.

Methodist societies were established in England in 1740. In 1818 a Methodist General Registry (known as the Metropolitan Wesleyan Registry) was established in London to centrally record births and baptisms. Some entries were recorded retrospectively back to 1773. About ten thousand entries were recorded up to 1838, when the registry was closed. The registry is now at the PRO (RG 4) and on microfilm at the FHL; it has been also added to the IGI.

If you are looking for an entry that cannot be found in this registry, contact the local county record office or see if the congregation's records have since been microfilmed and deposited at the FHL. The Society of Genealogists published a book on Methodist research, *My Ancestors Were Methodists: How Can I Find Out More About Them?* by William Leary.

English Presbyterianism, while originally Calvinist became more Unitarian in belief than did Calvinists elsewhere in Europe. However, the chapels either kept the name Presbyterian or went with the name "Free" to denote that they were "free Christians." Other independent congregations, all with Calvinist roots, began to call themselves Congregational.

You may also find that your ancestor retained the faith as found in Scotland or in Ulster. These congregations are mainly in the northern part of England, in Durham and Northumberland, and will be labeled "United Presbyterian" or "Scotch Church." So be creative when tracing an Irish Presbyterian family in England, and be aware of just how complex the history of Calvinism in that country really is. Also see Alan Ruston's booklet *My Ancestors Were English Presbyterians/Unitarians: How Can I Find Out More About Them?* and D.J.H. Clifford's *My Ancestors Were Congregationalists in England and Wales: How Can I Find Out More About Them?* Both booklets are well researched and published by the Society of Genealogists in London.

Microfilm Source

The first place to look for non-conformist registers is on microfilm at the FHL. Under the Non-Parochial Register Act of 1840, all non-conformist groups were to surrender to the Register General any registers that contained entries for the period before 1837. The surrendered registers are now part of the PRO collection. As not all registers were surrendered, a second attempt to gather them was made in 1857. These have been microfilmed and are at the FHL, where they have been extracted and added to the IGI. If records are not at the FHL on microfilm, check the County Record Offices and the local congregation in the area your ancestors lived.

Latter-day Saints (Mormons)

The Church of Jesus Christ of Latter-day Saints (Mormon or LDS Church) provides a unique historical twist in the search for Irish origins. Mormons, along with Catholics and other groups, were among non-Protestants to be classified non-conformists in England. The LDS Church found some of its earliest European converts in England. Among these converts were Irish families living in England. Even today the world's oldest Mormon congregation is in Preston, England.

The importance of this part of the English religious landscape is that if your ancestors were Protestant in England from the 1840s, it really was not that uncommon for a family member to have joined the Mormons and immigrated. Due to the LDS doctrine concerning the keeping of genealogies, there may be a family history written by these early Mormons documenting the family not only in England but also in Ireland. See the "Church Records" section in chapter two.

Civil Registration

Civil registration of births, marriages, and deaths began on 1 July 1837 in England and Wales, and continues to the present. The indexes always include both England and Wales. The registration of these events continues today. **Civil Registration is one of the most important sources in English research, as it will supplement church registers and censuses.**

Research Tip

Indexes to births, marriages, and deaths in England and Wales from 1837 to 1983 are available at the FHL and the Family Records Centre in London. The indexes provide the name of the person, the registration district, the volume, and the page number. In 1866, the death indexes included age at death; in 1911, the birth indexes added mother's maiden name; and in 1912, the marriage indexes included spouse's name. With common Irish names this can really be troublesome unless you know an exact event date and place. Each registration district covers a large geographical area, so it is helpful to know in which registration district your ancestor lived. Use the *Imperial Gazetteer of England and Wales*, which shows in which registration district a town or village was located. The Society of Genealogists publishes a guide to these districts, *Registration Districts* by Ray Wiggins.

Although the FHL makes the indexes readily available, the original records are still under royal copyright and are only available in England. You can get the corresponding certificate by visiting the Family Records Centre in London or by writing to the General Register Office in Merseyside. For details about the specific content of English and Welsh civil registration certificates, see Milner and Jonas's *A Genealogist's Guide to Discovering Your English Ancestors*.

Now, having said all this, there is one big ugly fact that you need to be aware of. From 1837 through 1874 the superintendent registrar was responsible to see that each birth, marriage, and death was registered; and **it was not until 1874 that civil registration became mandatory.** In theory, coverage was still good pre-1874; after all, marriages were to be recorded at the time of the event, and deaths had to be registered before the burial could be performed. Births, on the other hand, could be easily left unregistered since the registrar might not be aware of each one. You will find that Catholics and Mormons did not register births and even marriages as often as the rest of the population.

Reminder

Poor Law Records

The responsibility of the poor was with the Church of England parish until 1834, when the government created Poor Law unions that existed until 1948, when the modern welfare state was created. This topic is so important to finding immigrant origins because there were many Irish who found themselves no better off in England than they were in their homeland. Their care was a matter of local concern, and it became part of the written record. Often their birthplaces were mentioned in the records.

Pre-1834 Poor Law Records

You will see that the Poor Law records that exist prior to 1834 are mainly the day-to-day records of caring for the poor generated by the local Church of

England parish. Most parishes kept these records, along with the registers of baptisms, marriages, and burials, in a large chest known as the "parish chest." You might also find information about the poor from records such as Quarter Session Records.

The theory behind caring for the poor in a given parish was simple: the funds were collected from the parishioners, and as expected, funds were usually in short supply. This raised the question of whether a poor family or individual really belonged to the parish or if they should be shipped back to their "home" parish. Keep in mind that the "home" parish may have been in Ireland. This investigation process generated many records.

By definition, a person gained a "legal settlement" by being born in the parish of a legally settled father, by paying taxes on property in the parish, serving as a parish officer, being apprenticed to a settled man for seven full years, or being hired to work for a settled man for 365 continuous days. The wife and children, including illegitimate children, took the husband or father's place of settlement. One caution: A man could have more than one place of settlement, and often the place of settlement listed in the parish chest records was not his actual birthplace.

As far back as 1697, a poor family could move into a parish that was not its "legal" parish if there was a Settlement Certificate. This certificate would have been obtained from the officers of the legal parish, attested that the man of the family belonged to the parish and, in effect, accepting responsibility for him if he needed help. You will find that these certificates might contain the names and ages of family members, the occupation of the husband, and the legal place of settlement. Of course, not all certificates give all this information. Now, if help became necessary, the pauper and the family were to be returned to the legal parish. One example is from a transcription of a Settlement Paper from Chelsea, England:

Notes

> Julia Haggerty now residing at 2 Queen's Yard in the Parish of Saint Luke, Chelsea in the County of Middlesex on her oath saith that she was lawfully married to her present husband James Haggerty at Balleshannan in the county of Donegal in that part of the United Kingdom called Ireland about 15 years ago and by whom she has 4 children (viz) Richard 13 years of age, Ellen 7 years, Mary Ann 4 years and John 16 months and further saith that her said husband is an Irishman and never gained any settlement in England or Wales and that he was born in Balleshannan aforesaid where she this deponent was also born and that she hath not gained any settlement in England or Wales and otherwise says that she is deserted by her said husband and is now chargeable to the said parish of Chelsea.
>
> Julia (her X mark) Haggerty
>
> Sworn before me Dec'r 18th 1832

If a person went to the parish for help and did not possess a Settlement Certificate, the parish officers would conduct an investigation, which included questions regarding to which parish the pauper belonged. Notes were taken and a decision made about the legal parish. The examination papers can contain some useful information about the pauper, especially the previous residence, the birthplace, if apprenticed and to whom, the person's travels and work, wife, children, and sometimes the person's father.

Concerning the pre-1837 records, see Anne Coles's booklet *An Introduction to Poor Law Documents Before 1834* and Jeremy Gibson's *Quarter Sessions Records for Family Historians*. Also Hazel M. Tibbitts's article "The Poor and Their Records in England Before 1834," in *The Irish At Home and Abroad*, provides some excellent insights. The classic work on this topic is W.E. Tate's *The Parish Chest: A Study of the Records of Parochial Administration in England*.

Find the pre-1834 parish chest and related poor records at local diocesan record offices or county record offices throughout England. Some are on microfilm at the FHL. Local English genealogical or historical societies also index records of the poor.

Post-1834 Poor Law Records

By the nineteenth century, poor relief had become expensive. The parish relief system was seen as encouraging people to avoid work by living off the parish, and employers to pay lower wages. Under the Poor Law Amendment Act of 1834, parishes were combined into unions, each of which elected a Board of Guardians to administer poor relief. Each union was divided into districts in which an officer would consider poor requests. Under this system the poor could be admitted to a workhouse, which could range from excellent to nearly prisonlike.

If you think an ancestor might have received help from the Poor Law Union, first determine in which union he or she lived. This will be based on the parish of residence. The records are part of the guardians' records, usually in the County Record Offices or at the PRO in the Poor Law Commission records. To help with the task of identifying unions and records, read Jeremy Gibson, Colin Rogers, and Cliff Webb's four-volume work *Poor Law Union Records*, published by the Federation of Family History Societies in Birmingham.

REFERENCES AND FURTHER READING

Sources

Bevan, Amanda. *Tracing Your Ancestors in The Public Record Office*. Kew, Richmond, Surrey: Public Record Office, 1999.

Clifford, D.J.H. *My Ancestors Were Congregationalists in England and Wales: How Can I Find Out More About Them?* London: Society of Genealogists, 1992.

Collins, Lydia and Mabel Morton. *Monumental Inscriptions in the Library of the Society of Genealogists*. London: Society of Genealogists, 1987.

Coles, Anne. *An Introduction to Poor Law Documents Before 1834*. Birmingham, England: Federation of Family History Societies, 1993.

Gandy, Michael. *Catholic Family History: A Bibliography of General Sources*. London: the author, 1996.

———. *Catholic Family History: A Bibliography of Local Sources*. London: the author, 1996.

———. *Catholic Missions and Registers, 1700–1880*. London: the author, 1993.

Gibson, Jeremy. *Bishops' Transcripts and Marriage Licences, Bonds & Allegations: A guide to their location and indexes.* Birmingham, England: Federation of Family History Societies, 1998.

———. *Quarter Sessions Records for Family Historians: a Select List.* Birmingham, England: Federation of Family History Societies, 1992.

Gibson, Jeremy and Elizabeth Hampson. *Marriage and Census Indexes for Family Historians.* Birmingham, England: Federation of Family History Societies, 1998.

Gibson, Jeremy, Colin Rogers and Cliff Webb. *Poor Law Union Records.* 4 vols. Birmingham, England: Federation of Family History Societies, 1993.

Gibson, Jeremy and Pamela Peskett. *Record Offices: How to Find Them.* Birmingham, England: Federation of Family History Societies, 1998.

Herber, Mark D. *Ancestral Trails: The Complete Guide to British Genealogy and Family History.* Baltimore: Genealogical Publishing Co., 1997.

Humphery-Smith, Cecil. *The Phillimore Atlas and Index of Parish Registers.* Chichester, Sussex, England, 1995, 1999.

Leary, William. *My Ancestors Were Methodists: How Can I Find Out More About Them?* London: Society of Genealogists, 1999.

Mayhew, Henry. *London Labour and the London Poor.* London: Frank Cass and Co., 1851 (1st ed.), 1861–62 (enlarged ed.).

Milner, Paul and Linda Jonas. *A Genealogist's Guide to Discovering Your English Ancestors.* Cincinnati, Ohio: Betterway Books, 2000.

Morris, Andrew J. *The Poor in England: 3800 Names from the Poor Law: British Parliamentary Papers 1834–1847.* Ft. Collins, Colo: the author, 1985.

Ruston, Alan. *My Ancestors Were English Presbyterians/Unitarians: How Can I Find Out More About Them?* London: Society of Genealogists, 1993.

Shorney, David. *Protestant Nonconformity and Roman Catholicism: A Guide to Sources in the Public Record Office.* London: Public Record Office, 1996.

Swift, Roger and Sheridan Gilley. *The Irish in Victorian Britain: The Local Dimension.* Dublin: Four Courts Press, 1999.

Tate, W.E. *The Parish Chest: A Study of the Records of Parochial Administration in England.* Cambridge, England: Cambridge University Press, 1969.

Tibbitts, Hazel M. "The Poor and Their Records in England Before 1834." *The Irish At Home and Abroad* 3 (4) (1995/6): 158–161.

Wiggins, Ray. *Registration Districts.* London: Society of Genealogists, 1998.

Wolfston, Patricia, rev. by Cliff Webb. *Greater London Cemeteries and Crematoria.* London: Society of Genealogists, 1999.

Addresses

Catholic Family History Society
2 Winscombe Crescent, Ealing, London W5 1AZ, England

Family Records Centre

1 Myddelton St., London EC1R 1UW, England

phone: (020) 8392 5300   *fax:* (020) 8392 5307

Internet: http://www.pro.gov.uk/about/frc/

Federation of Family History Societies

The Benson Room, Birmingham and Midland Institute

Margaret St., Birmingham B3 3BS, England

Internet: http://www.ffhs.org .uk/

General Register Office

P.O. Box 2, Southport, Merseyside PR8 2JD, England

phone: (0151) 471 4816   *fax:* (0170) 455 0013

Internet: http://www.statistics.gov.uk/nsbase/registration/other_certificat e_obtain.asp

Society of Genealogists

14 Charterhouse Buildings, Goswell Rd., London EC1 7BA, England

phone: (020) 7251 8799   *fax:* (020) 7250 1800

Internet: http://www.sog.org.uk/

SCOTLAND

If you look on a map, you will see just how close the coast of Scotland is to northern Ireland. For this reason, there is a long tradition of emigration between Scotland and Ireland. **The massive transplanting of Scottish colonists to Ulster created the group historically dubbed the Scots-Irish (Scotch-Irish) or Ulster-Scots.** Some of the original colonists and their descendants immigrated en masse to America beginning in 1718. (See chapter two.) Other descendants went back to Scotland, where they lost their Irish identity. These Irish are often hard to identify in the records because their names matched those of local Scots.

The potato famine in Ireland resulted in a mass exodus from Ireland to Scotland. In 1841, before the famine, there were around 126,000 Irish-born in Scotland. By 1851, just after the famine, that number had increased to 207,366. The counties with the greatest number of Irish-born in 1851 were Lanarkshire, which is the Glasgow area (roughly 89,000); Renfrewshire (about 25,000); Ayrshire (about 21,000); Forfar or the Dundee area (roughly 16,000); and the Edinburgh area (about 15,000).

In this section we will discuss the major records we feel have the best chance of either identifying immigrant origins in Ireland or leading to other records that will. Some books you can use to elaborate on what we have presented are *Tracing Your Scottish Ancestors: Scottish Record Office* published by the Record Office (now the National Archives of Scotland); *Tracing Your Scottish Ancestry* by Kathleen B. Cory, a resident Scot; *Your Scottish Ancestry: A Guide for North Americans* by Sherry Irvine; and the *Scotland Research Outline* by the Genealogical Society of Utah (available online at <http://www.familysearch.org>).

You can also find a large collection of Scottish material at the Society of Genealogists in London. The guide to its collection is Marjorie Moore's *Sources for Scottish Genealogy in the Library of the Society of Genealogists.* The PRO

\di'fin\ *vb*

Definitions

in London also has records relating to Scotland. For a published list of repositories, see Michael Cox's *Exploring Scottish History*. See the following Web site to find archives, especially local ones throughout Scotland: Libraries and Archives Sources in Scotland <http://www.ifb.co.uk/~kinman/arcnlib.htm/>.

In Scottish research you will at some point come across some major repositories. The National Archives of Scotland (formerly the Scottish Record Office) and the New Register House (the main building of the General Register Office for Scotland) are the two major ones. Be aware that large collections from both of these repositories have been microfilmed and are at the FHL, so access to major collections is easy. But keep in mind that not all records are microfilmed, so your search will at some point need to consult records only found in Scotland.

Also the Internet site Scots Origins, which indexes Church of Scotland parish registers, 1881 and 1891 census indexes and civil registration indexes at New Register House, will be a vital tool in your research: <http://www.origins.net/ GRO/>.

Cemeteries

There has been an effort throughout Scotland to transcribe and publish tombstone inscriptions (called monumental inscriptions or MIs). You can find transcripts of monumental inscriptions at the Scottish Genealogical Society in Edinburgh with copies at New Register House. The Scottish Genealogical Society also publishes transcripts, and you can purchase or view these at major libraries such as the FHL. There are unpublished monumental inscriptions at the Scottish Genealogical Society, as well as other transcripts at local family history societies. So finding a transcript of a cemetery, especially for the pre-1855 time period, is not necessarily a problem. More about what you can find in a Scottish graveyard is described in Willsher's book *Understanding Scottish Graveyards*.

Censuses

You will find that the Scottish censuses have been released to the public for 1841, 1851, 1861, 1871, 1881, and 1891. The 1841 enumeration provides the least amount of information, but it does list an "I" if someone was born in Ireland.

Important

A word about ages is vital to understanding the 1841 census. The listed ages are not exact—that's just the way they took the census. The rule of thumb for the logic is that the ages are correct for anyone fifteen years old and younger, and for everyone else the actual age was rounded down to the nearest five years. However, even though the census takers were armed with the instructions, you will see that some actually rounded up five years. So when you use this particular census, just be aware of its odd nature and hope you can find the same family in the 1851 census or in the church registers!

Beginning with the 1851 census, you will find that birthplaces listed range from simply "Ireland" to a parish and county in Ireland. Again, it is so important to look at all enumerations and not just one or two. The censuses have been microfilmed and are at the FHL and the National Archives of Scotland.

The 1881 census of Scotland has been transcribed and indexed on CD-ROM, and we refer you to the previous section on the English for further detail. The enumeration of 1891 has also been indexed. Search the index online for a fee at Scots Origins. The Scottish Association of Family History Societies published a booklet concerning other locally produced indexes. This booklet by Peter Ruthven-Murray, *Scottish Census Indexes, 1841–1871*, is available from the association.

Church Records

Scottish church records are certainly one of the major resources you will encounter in your research. The state religion or "main" church was the Church of Scotland. This is Presbyterian, not Anglican as found in Ireland, England, and Wales. Not only was Presbyterian the state religion, but it was the main Presbyterian faith, keeping in mind there were numerous offshoots and smaller denominations of this Calvinist tradition. For the purpose of this section we will use the term Church of Scotland to refer only to the main family of Calvinists. **All others we will refer to as non-conformists—those who chose not to conform to the state religion.** Church of Scotland records are so important that you may find persons of all faiths, including Roman Catholics, in them.

\di'fin\ *vb*

Definitions

That the Church of Scotland was the state religion is interesting because the Episcopal Church of Scotland (in the Anglican tradition) was a non-conformist faith, while over the border in England its sister Church of England was the state religion.

So many families belonged to non-conformist faiths by the nineteenth century that it is just as common to see a Congregational, Baptist, Independent, Methodist, Mormon, or Catholic family as it is to see an established Church of Scotland family. In this section we will discuss religious non-conformity in Scotland since it affects so many Scottish and immigrant families. We will, however, divide out the Episcopal Church, the Latter-day Saints (Mormons) and the Roman Catholics for additional details.

Church of Scotland (Presbyterian)

The Calvinist tradition (Church of Scotland) and the Anglican tradition (Church of England or the Episcopal Church of Scotland) have struggled for the heart and soul of Scotland. Remember, it was the Protestant faith that swept through Scotland during the Reformation, replacing the Catholic Church, which was abolished in 1560.

In the political carnage that followed, the Church of Scotland replaced the Church of England and the 1707 Act of Union between England and Scotland guaranteed that Presbyterianism would remain the established faith in Scotland. Internal conflict in the early eighteenth century and onward caused the Church of Scotland to divide, forming several non-conformist branches. These often used the term "Free" to denote their difference.

Records generated by the Church of Scotland are known as the Old Parochial Registers (OPR). These have all been microfilmed through 1855, which is when civil registration began, and are on microfilm at New Register House. The births/baptisms and marriages have been indexed by the Genealogical Society of Utah, and many are on the FHL Web site under the International Genealogical Index (IGI) <http://www.familysearch.org>. All births/baptisms and marriages from the Old Parochial Registers are indexed in the Old Parochial Register Index, available at the FHL and at family history centers worldwide. They are also on the Scots Origins Web site, where you can view the index for a fee, so searching the indexes is not a problem. **What is important in searching for the Irish is the following:**

1. You will find Roman Catholics in the records. This is not just limited to Scottish families who survived the Reformation; it also includes Irish Catholic families. So if you're missing an odd child or two from a family unit, always check the OPR.

2. Not all the parishes kept burial records, which are important when you are trying to sort through common names and decide who lived and who died.

3. Not all people are recorded. There are gaps, and some families just didn't have a child baptized. Another interesting Scottish tradition was "hand festing" which would be equivalent to "jumping the broom" in America. This practice is also referred to as an "irregular" marriage. A couple held hands before their peers and were counted as married in the eyes of the community, without the aid of a clergyman. This drove the strict Calvinist ministers nuts!

4. Although you will find many non-conformists in the OPR, do not assume that they always will be there. Often they are not.

5. The OPR can be the key to identifying Irish origins as sometimes birthplaces are preserved in them, most likely in the marriages and burials.

6. The minutes of a parish are called Kirk Session Minutes, and they might contain information on your ancestor, so don't neglect them. Many of these are on microfilm at the FHL, and they are also at New Register House.

Roman Catholics

The Catholic faith is an interesting thread in the religious fabric of Scotland. Although pockets of Catholic families survived through the Reformation, it was the en masse arrival of the Irish that established a firm foundation for the church. Dioceses were not created in Scotland until 1878, although there were numerous Catholics in Scotland at the time. There were no Catholic parishes in Scotland until the end of World War I, so think in terms of "missions." Each mission had a chapel, and the priest or priests would work in the general area. This can complicate matters somewhat, in that without boundaries you might find your ancestor registered in more than one chapel. Even worse, without a regular priest, you might not find your ancestors at all in a Catholic register.

Photocopies of pre-1855 Catholic registers are at New Register House with copies and the originals now back at the parishes. You will also see that in some cases copies were made after the 1855 cutoff date. As wonderful as having records at New Register House might be, keep in mind that since the majority of Irish immigration to Scotland occurred from the 1840s onward, there is a good chance you will need to contact the parish itself and have post-1855 records examined. Volume 6 of Michael Gandy's series *Catholic Missions and*

Registers, 1700–1880 is dedicated to Scotland and tells when records begin. We discussed Gandy's monumental work in the England section. Gandy also published, with the Scottish Association of Family History Societies, *Catholic Family History: A Bibliography for Scotland*. Some Catholic records are at the FHL, but the majority of them are not.

Non-Conformists

Non-conformity in Scotland is an important concept when researching your Protestant ancestors. You may come across the non-conformist records if you can't find your ancestors in Church of Scotland records. Although there were various denominations in Scotland from the eighteenth century, most had their roots in the Calvinist tradition and the Church of Scotland.

As we previously stated and want to reiterate, the great source of Scottish non-conformity were those congregations who separated from the Church of Scotland while keeping their Calvinist leanings and teachings. These smaller Calvinist churches also existed in Ulster, so it may be that an ancestor from Ireland transferred to a non-conformist congregation upon immigrating to Scotland. The first major non-conformist Presbyterian division occurred in 1733 and was known as the Secession Church. This church splintered into Burgher and Anti-Burgher factions. In 1847, some non-conformist Presbyterian churches joined to form the United Presbyterian Church. In 1843 the Free Church withdrew from the Church of Scotland. Thus by the time the government instituted civil registration in 1855, there were more non-conformist Presbyterians than there were members of the Church of Scotland. Thus, the records of these non-conformist Presbyterians are important in your research prior to civil registration.

There was more non-conformity in Scotland than there was in Ireland. Although a family may have been Presbyterian in Ulster or elsewhere in Ireland, this does not guarantee you will find them in the main Church of Scotland records. The Methodist church was the fifth largest denomination in Ireland, so finding your relatives in a Methodist church in Scotland might be your first clue that you should be looking at Irish Methodist records also. For background on non-conformity, see the two-part Internet article by Sherry Irvine, "Protestant Nonconformity in Scotland—An Introduction" at <http://www.genuki.org .uk/big/sct/noncon1.html>. Non-conformist records are at New Register House, and some are on microfilm at the FHL.

Notes

Episcopal Church of Scotland

The Episcopal Church is certainly noteworthy in our discussion on non-conformity. This denomination did not have a large following in Scotland; in fact there were penal laws against it from 1746 to 1792. After the Church of Scotland replaced it as the established religion, it lost its power base and became a minority in a Calvinist majority. The Episcopal Church was the state religion from 1661 to 1690. Episcopal records are at the New Register House with some on microfilm at the FHL. They do not begin as early as the Church of Scotland, so it is still necessary to look at the OPR indexes for earlier records. If an immigrant Church of Ireland family remained with

Anglicanism, you should find it in the Episcopal Church of Scotland records. There is also the chance that the church records you need are not at New Register House. If this is the case, check with the local parish or diocese. Contact these through the Web site of the Scottish Episcopal Church at <http://www.scotland.anglican.org/>.

Latter-day Saints (Mormons)

Like in England and Wales, the Mormon faith swept through Scotland providing some of the earliest converts to the church. The Church of Jesus Christ of Latter-day Saints (Mormons or LDS Church) is neither of the Catholic nor Protestant tradition. It was founded in America in 1830, and by the 1840s had missionaries in Scotland. Many Scots joined, and Irish immigrants from Ulster joined the new faith in Scotland. We cannot underestimate the value of looking at records concerning early Mormon converts from Scotland.

Church policy was that upon conversion new members were to join the main body of Mormons in America. In America many of them left accounts of their lives in Scotland and even in Ireland. Even if your ancestor never met a Mormon in Scotland, a sibling or cousin might have found the message appealing. In these side branches of the family, you might find the origin in Ireland preserved. For additional details see the Church Records section of chapter two.

Civil Registration

The registration of births, marriages, and deaths in Scotland began on 1 January 1855, and these are some of the first records we recommend using in Irish immigrant research. The vast majority of Scottish births and marriages from 1855–1875 are included in the IGI. The indexes are on the Web, where you can view them for a fee at Scots Origins. The first year of marriage record keeping gave additional information such as birthplace, so if you have a family member (regardless of who it was) who married in 1855, this might be the easiest way of determining the Irish origins of the entire family! After 1860, birth records list parents' dates and places of marriage, including ones that took place in Ireland.

Remember that the big cities of Scotland were industrialized (unlike Ireland, which was mostly rural); thus many single young Irish people immigrated to the large cities to find work. A civil registration certificate for a marriage or death might be the first clue you get to the next generation back, who may or may not have remained in Ireland. **Look for the following information in birth, marriage, or death records:**

Birth: a street address in the city, which will allow you to correctly locate and view censuses and other records.

Marriage: the names of the fathers and the mothers of the couple and the name of the church, which allows you to examine church records.

Death: the names of the parents of the deceased. Be careful with this information because the deceased did *not* give the information and depending on the state of mind of the informant, the information could be fuzzy at best.

The records and indexes are housed at the General Register Office with a partial collection at the FHL. The FHL collection is not as current as that of

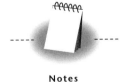

Notes

the General Register Office; however, it is especially noteworthy in that the certificates for births and marriages (1855–1875) have been extracted and are on the International Genealogical Index (IGI), which you can view on the Internet, <http://www.familysearch.org>.

Poor Law Records

You will find that the care of the poor can be thought of in two time frames. The first period is before 1845, when the Church of Scotland was primarily responsible; after 1845, when the Poor Law Act was passed, care was the government's responsibility. Each of these periods saw different records produced documenting those receiving care. See Judith Eccles Wight's article " 'And Be It Enacted': Scottish Poor Law and Its Records" in *The Irish At Home and Abroad* in which she treats both time periods. She uses Irish examples to show that records concerning the care of the poor can be a major resource for identifying Irish birthplaces.

Pre-1845 Records

Prior to 1845 each Church of Scotland parish's kirk session administered poor relief. The kirk session included the parish minister and elected elders and was the lowest ecclesiastical court in the church. Poor relief took the form of monetary payments, and the main source of income for this relief was the weekly collections. The kirk also distributed assistance in the form of shelter, food, clothing, fuel, medical care, funeral expenses, and education for children.

You will find in the session minutes information on poor relief prior to 1845. **Some of the clues you need to look for in these records are reports concerning where a destitute person or family had obtained a "legal settlement."** This meant that their parish of residence was responsible for them rather than another parish where they might apply for poor relief. So a destitute person or family could be sent back to the parish that agreed to be responsible. Maybe that parish was in Ireland or elsewhere in Scotland, thus giving you valuable clues to former residences and birthplaces.

Tip

Post-1844 Records

The government's Poor Law Act of 1845 created an organized system for the relief of the poor. You will find the poor law records from 1845 informative and, if you're dealing with a poor family, an essential part of your research. Among the most valuable part of these Poor Law records are the applications for poor relief. A major collection of them from the Glasgow City Archives, including more than 310,000 applications for Glasgow, has been computerized. The applications can include such valuable information as the name of the applicant, the maiden name if the applicant was a married woman, age or date of birth, birthplace, name of spouse, date and place of marriage, information on the children of the applicant, and history of the individual's or family's moves.

Locating Records

Kirk session records as well as poor law records are in several locations. Certainly start the search with the National Archives of Scotland in Edinburgh, then expand it to the district archives in the area where your ancestor lived.

With the many Internet resources available, the task of determining in which repository records are located is much easier.

REFERENCES AND FURTHER READING

Sources

Cox, Michael. *Exploring Scottish History: With a Directory of Resource Centres for Scottish Local and National History in Scotland.* Glasgow: Scottish Library Association, Scottish Local History Forum, and Scottish Records Association, 1999.

Gandy, Michael. *Catholic Family History: A Bibliography for Scotland.* London: Michael Gandy and the Scottish Association of Family History Societies, 1996.

Irvine, Sherry. *Your Scottish Ancestry: A Guide for North Americans.* Salt Lake City: Ancestry Inc., 1997.

Lindsay, Jean. *The Scottish Poor Law: Its Operation in the North-East from 1745–1845.* Ilfracombe, Devon, England: Stockwell, 1975.

Moore, Marjorie. *Sources for Scottish Genealogy in the Library of the Society of Genealogists.* London: Society of Genealogists, 1999.

Sinclair, Cecil. *Tracing Your Scottish Ancestors: A Guide to Ancestry Research in the Scottish Record Office.* Edinburgh: HMSO, 1990.

Wight, Judith Eccles. " 'And Be It Enacted': Scottish Poor Law and Its Records." *The Irish At Home and Abroad.*

Willsher, Betty. *Understanding Scottish Graveyards: An Interpretive Approach.* Reprint, Edinburgh: Council for Scottish Archaeology, 1995.

Addresses

New Register House
   3 West Register St., Edinburgh EH1 3YT, Scotland
   phone: (0131) 314 4433   *fax:* (0131) 314 4400
   Internet: http://wood.ccta.gov.uk/grosweb/grosweb.nsf

Scottish Association of Family History Societies
   5 1/3 Mortonhall Rd., Edinburgh EH9 2HN, Scotland
   Internet: http://www.safhs.org.uk/

The Scottish Genealogy Society
   Library and Family History Centre, 15 Victoria Terr., Edinburgh EH1 2JL, Scotland
   phone/fax: (0131) 220 3677
   Internet: http://www.sol.co.uk/s/scotgensoc/

Scottish Record Office
   HM General Register House, Princes St., Edinburgh EH1 3YY, Scotland
   phone: (0131) 556 6585   *fax:* (0131) 557 9569

WALES

In this section we will be discussing the huge Irish community dating back to the earliest years of the nineteenth century in the industrial areas of south Wales. In southern Wales the Irish flooded cities and factories seeking work, especially during the Great Famine years (1845–1852). The industrial cities of Cardiff, Merthyr-Tydfil, and Swansea, along with the industrial Rhondda Valley (between Cardiff and Merthyr-Tydfil)—all in old Glamorgan County were the major settlement areas. Significant numbers of Irish were also in the adjacent areas of old Monmouth County, mainly the iron and coal districts in the northwest part of the county. The Irish did not necessarily stay put upon arriving in Wales; they tended to go where the jobs were. Thus, the Irish who were migrants in Cardiff and the Rhondda Valley commonly had earlier roots in the Merthyr-Tydfil area. Researching the Irish immigrant in south Wales is by no means straightforward.

As far as identifying where in Ireland these immigrants came from, we are fortunate. The geography of Ireland and of Wales itself can help solve the puzzle of origins. For example, the Irish port of Rosslare, County Wexford, was connected directly to the port of Fishguard, Pembrokeshire, in south Wales. There is another port in Wales, Holyhead in Anglesey, but it served as a gateway into northern Wales by way of the port of Dublin. A mountain range through the center of Wales separated the two ports, resulting in two distinct immigration patterns from Ireland. So if your ancestors immigrated to industrial south Wales, you can be fairly certain that they came from one of the southern Ireland counties of Cork, Kerry, Kilkenny, Tipperary, Waterford, or Wexford. Of these counties, studies have shown that the greatest numbers came from counties Cork and Tipperary.

The type of work available in southern Wales actually prepared Irish immigrants to go elsewhere to seek similar types of employment. This helps to reconstruct a family history even further and provides much-needed clues along the way. For example, numerous Irish went to the newly opened coal fields in northern England and to industrial cities such as Scranton and Pittsburgh in Pennsylvania. **If you find your family in northern England or in Pennsylvania working in heavy industry, then you might want to consider that they had earlier roots in southern Wales.** Also consider that if you are seeking immigrant origins, the answer might lie in Wales. We must point out that researching Irish Catholic and Irish Protestant families in Wales is not as bad as, for comparison, Scotland, because native Welsh surnames are so distinct that you should be able to sift through who is who in a community.

Research Tip

We have selected a few record types from which to reconstruct an immigrant's life in southern Wales. We are not going to treat the civil registration of births, marriages, and deaths or poor law records; instead we refer you to the section on England, since the records are basically the same. At some point in your research, you will need to see what is available locally in Wales, at the National Library of Wales, and the Family Records Centre in London. The FHL collection for Wales is good but not as extensive as needed to fully document an Irish family in southern Wales. For this area of Wales, check into what is being produced by the Glamorgan Family History Society. All the family history societies in Wales can be reached through the Web site of the Association of Family History Societies of Wales <http://www.rootsweb.com/~wlsafhs/>. If you need other archives or libraries in Wales, see the Web site of the Archives Council Wales <http://www.llgc.org.uk/cac/>.

Don't be fooled by the term "Welsh" in books and guides about Welsh research as you will find them full of resources for tracing your Irish ancestors. Among some of the ones we recommend are *Guide to the Department of Manuscripts and Records* by the National Library of Wales (1996); the two works *Welsh Family History: A Guide to Research* and *Second Stages in Researching Welsh Ancestry*, edited by John Rowlands and Sheila Rowlands from the Welsh perspective; and *Wales Research Outline* by the Genealogical Society of Utah, available online at <http://www.familysearch.org>.

Cemetery Records

Prior to 1853, Irish Catholics in Wales were usually buried in the local Church in Wales (Anglican) parish cemeteries. Records of burials are in parish registers. The Glamorgan Family History Society and the Glamorgan Record Office have transcribed headstones of many parish and chapel cemeteries. After 1853 most Irish were buried in the municipal cemeteries (many of which had Catholic sections). The cemeteries of some parish churches and non-conformist chapels were still used under the new system, although much less often than the municipal cemeteries. The addresses for the various municipal authorities are on the Internet.

Census Records

Census enumerations for Wales begin in 1841 and were taken every ten years. Schedules through 1891 are released to the public and available at the Family Records Centre and at the FHL. The 1901 census will be released in 2001. Beginning in 1841, you will see an "I" for Ireland as a birthplace, so always make sure that you compare this with later censuses that will spell the birthplace. Some of the enumerations for industrial south Wales beginning in 1851 list places of birth in Ireland. An index to the 1851 census of Glamorgan County, including 240,000 residents, was compiled by the Glamorgan Family History Society. R.T. Price's *Little Ireland: Aspects of the Irish and Greenhill, Swansea* lists all the Irish enumerated in Swansea in the 1841, 1851, and 1861 censuses. The 1881 census, as we have already discussed in the England section, has been extracted, indexed and is available on CD-ROM.

Church Records

The Church in Wales, a member of the Anglican Communion, was the established Church until 1920. As the state religion, it required that everyone (except Quakers and Jews) be married in the Church. This requirement was in effect until 1837, and we have discussed it in more detail under the England section. The Glamorgan Family History Society compiled an index to all recorded pre-1837 marriages from 125 Church in Wales parishes in Glamorgan County, with 60,000 marriages. Many Catholics, however, were married clandestinely by Catholic priests, and you might not find a record of such a marriage. After 1837 it became possible to marry in Catholic and non-conformist chapels as long as they were registered for that purpose.

Anybody who didn't belong to the established Church in Wales was considered non-conformist. The interesting thing about Wales is that by the mid nineteenth century more than half the population could have been considered non-conformist. In Wales non-conformity did not necessarily develop out of the main church as it did in Scotland; it came from the outside, e.g. the Catholics from Ireland, the Mormons from America, and the Methodists and Baptists from England. Let us divide our discussion of church records into sections for the Church in Wales, the Catholic Church, non-conformists, and Latter-day Saints (Mormons).

Church in Wales

As the Church in Wales was the state religion, look for persons of all faiths in its records, especially prior to 1837. Although some Welsh parish registers begin in the 1500s, the majority begin after 1660. Most parish registers are deposited at the National Library of Wales or at one of the county record offices. **When seeking the parish registers, keep in mind that there were also Bishop's Transcripts (called BT's).** These were annual returns submitted from the parish churches to the local bishops containing all the entries recorded from the previous year. Most BT's in Wales date after 1723, so if you have access to both the originals and the BT's, make sure to check them both for accuracy. They do not necessarily say the same thing.

Reminder

The place to start in the search for parish registers is the FHL, as its microfilm is readily available and might even be indexed on the IGI at <http://www.family search.org>. The next place would be the National Library of Wales in Aberystwyth, and then the county record offices. If you need more recent records, they are probably still with the local parishes.

Another source the Church in Wales generated from 1661 to 1930 are the "Marriage Bonds and Allegations." These are marriage licences that were obtained without having banns read in church. They are kept with the diocesan offices and might contain information that has not survived in the parish registers. The pre-1837 bonds are indexed and are at the National Library of Wales. The licenses account for about 10 percent of marriages.

Roman Catholics

There was no Catholic parish system in Great Britain until the end of World War I. Up to that point, there were Catholic chapels or missions rather than parishes. There was one old Welsh Catholic chapel in Abergavenny (founded in 1687), which served the Irish community of the early nineteenth century. The Abergavenny chapel records included Catholics living in the Merthyr-Tydfil area until 1836. The Abergavenny Catholics were families that did not become Protestants during the Reformation. The influx of Irish Catholics escaping the Great Famine resulted in rapid formation of Catholic churches in south Wales. The industrial area of Wales is divided between the Catholic Archdiocese of Cardiff (including Cardiff and Merthyr-Tydfil) and the Diocese of Menevia (including Swansea). An excellent listing of Catholic registers in Wales is in Michael Gandy's invaluable resource *Catholic Missions and Registers, 1700–1880, Volume 3, Wales and the West of England*. Gandy also wrote *Catholic Family History: A Bibliography for Wales*.

Non-Conformists

Wales underwent a rapid movement into non-conformity by the mid nineteenth century and later. As a result, numerous non-conformist churches developed. By the time the Irish were immigrating into the area, nonconformists were in the majority, including Baptists, Independents (Congregationalists), Methodists, Presbyterians, and Unitarians. We have discussed in some detail nonconformity under the England section. Microfilm copies for many of these Protestant non-conformists are at the FHL. Pre-1837 records were sent to the PRO in London; others are at local county record offices.

If you're wondering how to know what churches were in a parish or county, let us suggest an unusual yet intriguing source. There was a religious census taken to accompany the 1851 census, and it shows where places of worship were located. Published as *The Religious Census of 1851: A Calendar of the Returns Relating to Wales*, it is available at the FHL. Once you identify possible chapels an ancestor might have attended, sources such as D.J. Steel's *National Index of Parish Registers, II: Sources for Nonconformist Genealogy and Family History* can be very helpful. Dafydd Ifans's book *Cofrestri anghydffurfiol Cymru/Nonconformist Registers of Wales* written in Welsh and English tells where non-conformist registers are deposited in Wales and in England.

Latter-day Saints (Mormons)

Non-conformity also took the form of a strong presence of the Church of Jesus Christ of Latter-day Saints (Mormons or LDS Church). The historical presence of the LDS Church in Wales is often overlooked because members were expected to immigrate to the western United States, thus diluting their presence in the religious tapestry of Welsh non-conformity. Along with Catholics, the Mormons are the second non-Protestant group to be classified as non-conformists in Wales. LDS missionaries began arriving in 1840, and persons joining the Mormon faith would most likely have been native Welsh, although it is possible to document Irish immigrants among the early converts. The records of Mormon congregations can be important as they sometimes tell a person's birthplace. See the Church Records section of chapter two.

Sources

REFERENCES AND FURTHER READING

Gandy, Michael. *Catholic Missions and Registers, 1700–1880, Volume 3, Wales and the West of England.* London: Michael Gandy, 1993.

———. *Catholic Family History: A Bibliography for Wales.* London: the author, 1996.

Guide to the Department of Manuscripts and Records. Aberystwyth, Wales: National Library of Wales, 1996.

Hickey, John Vincent. *Urban Catholics: Urban Catholicism in England and Wales From 1829 to the Present Day.* London: Geoffery Chapman, 1967.

Ifans, Dafydd. *Cofrestri anghydffurfiol Cymru/Nonconformist Registers of Wales.* Aberystwyth, Wales: National Library of Wales, 1994.

Jones, Ievan Gwynedd and David Williams, eds. *The Religious Census of*

1851: A Calendar of the Returns Relating to Wales. Cardiff: University of Wales Press, 1976.

Price, R.T. *Little Ireland: Aspects of the Irish and Greenhill, Swansea.* Swansea, Wales: City of Swansea Archives Publication, 1992.

Rowlands, John and Sheila Rowlands, eds. *Welsh Family History: A Guide to Research.* 2d ed. Baltimore: Genealogical Publishing Co., 1999.

———. *Second Stages in Researching Welsh Ancestry. . . .* Baltimore: Genealogical Publishing Co., 1999.

Rawlins, Bert and Dwight A. Radford. "The Irish in Industrial South Wales." *The Irish At Home and Abroad* 1 (4) (Spring 1994): 10–15.

Steel, D.J. *National Index of Parish Registers, II: Sources for Nonconformist Genealogy and Family History.* London: Society of Genealogists, 1978.

Addresses

Association of Family History Societies of Wales
Peacehaven, Badgers Meadow, Pwllmeyric, Chepstow
Monmouth NP16 6UE, Wales
Internet: http://www.rootsweb.com/~wlsafhs/

Glamorgan Family History Society
The Orchard, Penmark, Barry, Vale of Glamorgan CFG2 3BN, Wales
Internet: http://website.lineone.net/~glamfhsoc/

Glamorgan Record Office
County Hall, Cathays Park, Cardiff CF1 3NE, Wales
phone: (0222) 780282

Gwent County Record Office
County Hall, Cwmbran, Gwent NP44 2XH, Wales
phone: (0633) 838828

Merthyr-Tydfil Central Library
High Street, Merthyr-Tydfil, Mid Glamorgan CF47 8AF, Wales
phone: (0685) 723057

National Library of Wales
Department of Manuscripts and Records
Aberystwyth, Ceredigion SY23 3BM, Wales
phone: (01970) 632880   *fax:* (01970) 632883
Internet: http://www.llgc.org.uk/index.htm

West Glamorgan Record Office
County Archive Service, County Hall, Swansea SA1 3SN, Wales
phone: (0792) 471589   *fax:* (0792) 471340

SEVEN

The British West Indies

Tip

The British West Indies refers to the many islands in the Caribbean that were colonies of Great Britain for centuries. While some of the islands are today independent nations, others are still colonies. Not all the islands will be discussed, but the major ones in the Leeward Islands, Bermuda, Barbados, and Jamaica are included because they had the bulk of early Irish immigration, especially in the seventeenth century. By Leeward Islands, we mean Antigua, St. Kitts (St. Christopher), Nevis, and Montserrat.

Understanding this part of Irish immigrant history is vital to documenting later Irish immigration, especially northward into the mainland of America. **If you have ancestors who went to the mainland America colonies in the 1600s or early 1700s, there is a good chance they came by way of these islands, rather than straight from Ireland.** You just might find where your ancestor was from in Ireland by using the records of the islands, rather than trying to jump directly into what remains of Irish records for the seventeenth century.

We'll focus on the earlier records of these islands and some important historical information, which makes this a fascinating yet unsettling and tragic part of Irish immigrant history. In this search, you might find that your Irish ancestor was an indentured servant bound to work for a given number of years, a poor undesirable, political prisoner, or a white slave. For a detailed discussion of what all this means, see page 139. On top of this mixed lot of Irish were also the Irish gentry, who often ran the sugar plantations. The Irish were also educated merchants and Anglican ministers. They must have been a mix of folks unlike any other!

Records

This chapter will not provide a comprehensive listing of all island sources. It will, however, concentrate on records through about the year 1800 as most Irish immigration had taken place by that point anyway.

The major records for all the islands are Anglican (Church of England)

For More Info

WHITE SERVITUDE (INDENTURED AND SLAVE)

The Irish presence in the Caribbean came through several means. Among these were: (1) indentured servants, (2) forced banishment, (3) white slavery rings, and (4) those deemed socially undesirable. The idea of white servants was, of course, not limited to the Caribbean Islands, as it also took hold in the American colonies. One important historical factor of white servitude that directly affects genealogical research is that servants commonly migrated from island to island, as well as to other places such as the American colonies. Thus it is possible for an American family to trace back to a white ancestor who arrived in bondage in the Caribbean. This includes no small number of people. The 1678 Census of the Leeward Islands (St. Kitts, Nevis, Montserrat, and Antigua) showed the total population stood at 18,928, of which 3,466 were Irish, a full 18 percent. This number is augmented by 8,510 black slaves (many of whom would have had an Irish parent or grandparent), an astounding 45 percent of the population. Thus, between the Irish and the black slaves, as many as 63 percent of the population might have been in some kind of bondage—and this isn't even counting the indentured servants from England and Scotland.

As a whole, the lot of the Irish servant class would have been only slightly better off than that of African slaves. This led the indentured servants to display resistence in ways similar to those of the African slaves. The planter class often feared the Irish would assist in a slave revolt and that Irish servants would ally themselves with French Catholics. These fears were realized on Montserrat. By 1701 "Protestant Bills" were passed on the islands, limiting the civil rights of Irish Catholics and officially reducing them to an underclass. By the 1720s the number of Irish had dropped by half with widespread immigration to Jamaica and the mainland American colonies.

1. The indentured servants were men and women who signed willingly at ports in Ireland and England. These servants understood that they were to work for a set number of years in exchange for transport to the Caribbean and would then be released from their obligations. Upon freedom from bondage, these indentured servants were entitled to a small sum of money or a small parcel of land. In the islands they worked for the planter class, often in the sugar cane industry. Both Catholics and Protestants could sign up as indentured servants; the majority of the Irish who signed, however, would have been Catholic.

   The large number of Irish Catholic servants demonstrates the planter class's lack of control over the servant trade. Merchants who recruited these servants believed that the poor Irish were more willing to be workers in the West Indies than the English, Scottish, or Welsh. Also in the seventeenth century there were food shortages, unemployment, and war in

continued on page 140

Ireland, which led to a ready supply of Irish servants seeking a better life elsewhere. The island of destination was often a choice allowed in the contract between the merchants and the indentured servants.

The Irish who had been indentured servants found themselves with few opportunities for social or material advancement upon release. Being Catholic, they were feared by their overlords. These tensions and hostilities often threatened the stability of the entire white community. The planters who were at the top of island society felt the need to control indentured servants and those released from bondage.

2. The idea of forced bondage is simple: England used the islands as a dumping ground for political prisoners. A large wave of Irish arrived through forced banishment during the Cromwellian wars in Ireland. With the ensuing Protestant victory at Drogheda in 1649, many political prisoners were transported to the islands, with St. Kitts and Barbados being the favorite destinations.

3. One class of white servants, not often thought about in history, is the "white slave." White slavery rings abounded in the seventeenth century. Under this system, people (often children) were kidnapped and sold to traders, who in turn sold them to plantation owners. This happened in the coastal areas of Ireland and in England. The English government was so concerned that it called for the registration at ports such as Bristol of persons bound to the colonies for work to make sure they were indentured servants by choice and not by capture.

4. Another lesser-known historical avenue whereby planters gained workers was through England's practice of shipping "undesirables" to the West Indies. By the 1650s in Ireland governors in several counties had been ordered to arrest poor and itinerant men and women, children in hospitals and workhouses, and prisoners. The island governors did not want these involuntary servants and urged for this human trade to stop, especially since the class of people involved was not well suited to militia duty or plantation labor, nor were they generally helpful to the Protestant cause in the islands.

records. This source is the best for locating all classes of people, and since this was the state religion, you will find persons of all faiths in these records. Another early source is the census enumerations, which will often tell if a family is Irish.

Keep in mind that the written word and tombstones on these islands have suffered over the centuries. Because of hurricanes, volcanoes, the usual rain, fungus growth, earthquakes, insects, and humidity, documented history suffers. So where possible, we'll provide multiple versions of the same source (e.g. a printed version and a microfilm of the original). Always consult more than one version if possible. We are fortunate in that some researchers in the nineteenth and early twentieth centuries took an interest in these islands, and thus preserved many sources no longer with us in the original form. Also, much is on microfilm at the FHL. An excellent guide to records of the Leeward Islands is E.C. Baker's *A Guide to Records in the Leeward Islands,* which inventories sources and tells if they are on microfilm at the University of the West Indies.

There are several important sources we want to call your attention to. The first is the five-volume work by Vere Langford Oliver, *Caribbeana.* Because this source was compiled between 1910 and 1919, it is a treasure for many early records. In chapter fourteen we detail many of the sources from the seventeenth and eighteenth centuries that you can use to document some of the Irish as they left for the colonies. Both resources apply to all the islands.

More well-to-do families on the islands would have left wills and estates. Often these were probated in the English courts where copies have survived and are usually at the FHL. Indexes to these are in *Caribbeana.* Each island government also probated estates. Do not assume that an ancestor who lived in the Caribbean was "poor Irish." Quite the contrary, your ancestor might have been a wealthy planter and slaveholder.

REFERENCES AND FURTHER READING

Sources

Baker, E.C. *A Guide to Records in the Leeward Islands.* Oxford: Basil Blackwell, 1965.

Beckles, Hilary McD. "A 'Riotous and Unruly Lot': Irish Indentured Servants and Freemen in the English West Indies, 1644–1713." *The William and Mary Quarterly: A Magazine of Early American History and Culture.* 3d Series 47 (4) (October 1990): 503–522.

Bridenbaugh, Carl and Roberta Bridenbaugh. *No Peace Beyond the Line: The English in the Caribbean, 1624–1690.* Oxford: Oxford University Press, 1972.

Dunn, Richard S. *Sugar and Slaves: The Rise of the Planter Class in the English West Indies, 1624–1713.* Chapel Hill, N.C.: University of North Carolina Press, 1972.

Grannum, Guy. *Tracing Your West Indian Ancestors, Sources in the Public Record Office (PRO Readers' Guide No 11).* London: PRO Publications, 1995.

Lawrence-Archer, J.H. *Monumental Inscriptions of the British West Indies From the Earliest Date, With Genealogical and Historical Annotations, From the Original, Local, and Other Sources.* London: Chatto and Windus, 1875.

Oliver, Vere Langford. *Caribbeana: Being Miscellaneous Papers Relating to the History, Genealogy, Topography and Antiquities of the British West Indies.* 5 vols. London: Mitchell Hughes and Clarke, 1910–1919.

———. *More Monumental Inscriptions: Tombstones of the British West Indies.* San Bernardino, Calif.: Borgo Press, 1993.

Addresses

University of the West Indies
  Mona Campus, Kingston 7, Jamaica
  phone: (876) 935-8294 through 6   *fax:* (876) 927-1926
  Internet: http://isis.uwimona.edu.jm/

ANTIGUA

The English colonized Antigua in 1632. By 1674 the first large sugar estate was established on the island. As more forests were cleared for plantations, the owners sought African slaves to work them. Antigua became important in the British Empire due to its natural harbors, which allowed ships to be refitted safe from hurricanes and attacks. The 1678 census showed there were 610 Irish (13.6 percent of the population) out of a total island population of 4,480. The rest of the population consisted of 1,600 English, 98 Scots, and 2,172 Blacks.

The Irish came to Antigua as indentured servants. There were few opportunities for indentured servitude on the island, as African slaves were brought in to work in the growing sugar industry. After their release from bondage it was common for former indentured servants to leave for larger islands or for the mainland American colonies. The lack of available land (tied up in large estates) and the influx of African slaves caused the European population to drop; even the children of established planters commonly emigrated elsewhere.

There was a direct link between merchant families in County Galway and Antigua. One early wealthy Irish Catholic planter and merchant family was the Bodkin family from County Galway. The original immigrant was Dominick Bodkin, and in his will dated 9 October 1674, he left monies and items to various Catholic orders including the Benedictines, "Augustines of Gallaway," the Franciscans, and Dominicans. He even mentioned his relatives still living in "Gallaway." Remember that although this family was Roman Catholic, all family baptisms, marriages, and burials were recorded in the Anglican registers. In this case, the family for several generations mainly attended the Anglican parish of St. Paul [Oliver's *The History of the Island of Antigua,* vol. 1, pp. 64–65].

Another County Galway family was the Lynch family, who were merchants in Antigua. Ambrose Lynch was born in County Galway on 4 December 1683 and settled in Antigua. He was the son of Bartholomew Lynch, a merchant from Galway, and Mary Blake, who was the daughter of Thomas Blake of Mullaghmore, County Galway. There were also inter-island connections here, since the Blake family had connections with Montserrat [Oliver's *The History of the Island of Antigua,* vol. 3, p. 437].

Records

The island of Antigua was divided in 1681 into the Anglican parishes of St. George, St. John, St. Mary, St. Paul, St. Peter, and St. Phillip. The names of these parishes are in the civil records as well as the Anglican records. For many resources, the Web site for Antigua and Barbuda is helpful: <http://www.rootsw eb.com/~atgwgw/>.

One major work for the island is Vere Lanford Oliver's three-volume *The History of the Island of Antigua* (1894), which extracts church records, tombstones, censuses, genealogies, and civil records. This book is a major resource and is on microfilm at the FHL. The planter class genealogies recorded in Oliver's history are exceptional, as they trace families back to Ireland.

Many records are at the Antigua National Archives. One important collection is the Record of Enrollment (ROE) Books, which include deeds, wills, and other types of estate documents, account books, mortgages, powers of attorney, and miscellaneous documents filed with the Court of Common Pleas from 1676 to 1907. This collection is at the FHL.

Cemetery Records

Many of the early tombstones on Antigua were transcribed between 1894 and 1899 and published in Oliver's *The History of the Island of Antigua* (vol. 3, pp. 373–398). You can find tombstones from the parish of St. John in that work as well as in Oliver's *More Monumental Inscriptions: Tombstones of the British West Indies* and J.H. Lawrence-Archer's *Monumental Inscriptions of the British West Indies*.

Census Records

1677–1678: Lists names of persons by division and how many whites and blacks in the household (PRO CO 1/42 ff 229–241) and extracted in Oliver's *The History of the Island of Antigua* (vol. 1, p. lviii).

1753: List of inhabitants taken by order of His Excellency George Thomas, Esq. Published in Oliver's *The History of the Island of Antigua* (vol. 1, pp. cix–cxv).

Church Records

Transcripts of the early Antigua Anglican records are in several places, such as Oliver's *The History of the Island of Antigua* and *Caribbeana*, which transcribes baptisms, marriages, and burials. Transcripts of the early Anglican records were sent to London, where they are preserved in the Public Record Office in England and microfilmed by the FHL. The Society of Genealogists in London also has a collection. We suggest you search all these collections in case they differ from each other.

REFERENCES AND FURTHER READING

Gasper, David Barry. *Bondmen and Rebels: A Study of Master-Slave Relations in Antigua.* Durham, N.C.: Duke University Press, 1993.

Oliver, Vere Langford. *The History of the Island of Antigua.* 3 vols. London: Mitchell and Hughes, 1894–1899.

Sources

Addresses

Antigua National Archives
Rappaport Centre, Victoria Park, St. John's, Antigua, West Indies

BARBADOS

A handful of English citizens and African slaves arrived in Barbados in 1627. Due to the slave trade, the sugar industry, and the presence of the British Army, Barbados drew many cultures, including Irish. The island was a gateway to America (especially into North Carolina, South Carolina, and Virginia), Surinam, Jamaica, and much of the Caribbean Islands. Thus Barbados is of no small importance when it comes to the Irish presence throughout this region. Barbadian emigration to South Carolina from 1670 to about 1700 accounted for about half the settler population in the South Carolina colony.

Records

In 1629, Barbados was divided into six Anglican parishes, although more parishes were formed later. The parish names are used in wills, church records, and government records. You can generally find Barbados records at the Department of Archives in Barbados with microfilm copies of major collections at the FHL. Over the years early Barbados records, such as wills and Anglican records, have been published. Major published works have recently been placed on the CD-ROM *English Settlers in Barbados, 1637–1880* published by Genealogical Publishing Co. The title of the CD-ROM is unfortunate since it is full of Irish names. James C. Brandow's *Genealogies of Barbados Families* indexes previously published genealogies from *Caribbeana* and *The Journal of the Barbados Museum and Historical Society* and includes several families with Irish connections. You can find more details about sources for Barbados research in Radford and White's article "The Irish in Barbados" in *The Irish At Home and Abroad*. There are also good Web sites including BajanGenWeb at <http://www.rootsweb.com/~brbwgw/> and the Barbados Web page, which you can access from the Antigua Web site at <http://www.rootsweb.com/~atgwgw/resources/bsource.html>.

Cemetery Records

Vere Langford Oliver's *The Monumental Inscriptions in the Churches and Churchyards of the Island of Barbados, British West Indies* (1915) consists of transcriptions mostly from the Anglican churches and churchyards. The "dissenting chapels" and "modern cemeteries" were not transcribed in this work. Roman Catholics were buried in St. Patrick's Graveyard next to St. Patrick's Roman Catholic Cathedral as early as 1848. Those tombstones have not been transcribed. Catholics were also buried at the Garrison cemetery, at St. Mathias Anglican church, and at St. Mary Anglican church. An example of a few interesting tombstones, all taken from St. Michael's Cathedral, show the following

Sacred/to the Memory of Mrs. Mary O'Brien/Daughter of Mr. John O'Brien late of /Hallifax Nova Scotia who departed this/Life 11th Day of December 1810 Aged 27 Years

I.H.S./Sacred/To the memory of James Coulsten Esqr/Born at Drogheda in Ireland who/departed this life on the 5th day of May/1822 aged 48 years

Beneath this Stone/deposited the Remains/of/Theophilus D'Olier Esq./Merchant/of the/City of Dublin in Ireland who departed/this Life on the 22nd Novr 1809

Erected/By/George Montgomery of Belfast/Merchant/In memory of his beloved son/George/Who died at Barbadoes/on the 13th October 1839/Aged 23 Years

Census Records

1638: List of inhabitants possessing over ten acres.

1679–1680: Names of landowners at the PRO (CO 1/44, no 47, i–xxii), the Guildhall Library in London (no. 2202/1-2) and on microfilm at the FHL. It was published in David L. Kent's *Barbados and America*.

1715: Census of some parishes of all white inhabitants and their ages, held at the PRO (CO 28/16, no 2). The parishes of St. Michael, Christchurch, and St. George are printed in the *Journal of the Barbados Museum and Historical Society* volumes 4 to 9 and in Kent's *Barbados and America*. The original census is on microfilm at the FHL.

Church Records

Although the Anglican Church is the oldest of all denominations in Barbados, on the island there have historically also been Irish who were Roman Catholics, Moravians (United Brethren), Quakers (Society of Friends), and Methodists. Among the Quakers who went to Barbados were families with connections to the monthly meetings in Mountmellick (County Leix) and Wicklow (County Wicklow).

Parochial registers beginning in 1637 and including major denominations are at the Barbados Department of Archives and on microfilm up to at least 1900 at the FHL. Copies of non-Anglican registers were kept in separate books until 1884. The Garrison Chapel of St. Ann's includes families of all denominations. There are many Irish in the garrison church records, with an almost equal number of Irish Catholics and Irish Protestants. Early Anglican baptismal and marriage registers were published from their beginnings to 1800 in Joanne McRee Sanders's *Barbados Records*.

The Catholic parish of St. Patrick, located in the Barbados parish of St. Michael, has records from only 1839. Through 1900 there were four Moravian congregations on the island. The oldest, at Sharon in St. Thomas Parish, has records from 1769 and served as an African mission.

Sources

REFERENCES AND FURTHER READING

Alleyne, Warren and Henry Fraser. *The Barbados-Carolina Connection.* London: Macmillan Publishers, 1988.

Baldwin, Agnes Leland. *First Settlers of South Carolina, 1670–1700.* Easley, S.C.: Southern Historical Press, 1985.

Beckles, Hilary McDonald. *A History of Barbados: From Amerindian Settlement to Nation-State.* Cambridge, England: Cambridge University Press, 1990.

Brandow, James C. *Genealogies of Barbados Families: From Caribbeana and the Journal of the Barbados Museum and Historical Society.* Baltimore: Genealogical Publishing Co., 1983.

———. *Omitted Chapters From Hotten's Original Lists of Persons of Quality and Others Who Went From Great Britain to the American Plantations, 1600–1700.* Baltimore: Genealogical Publishing Co., 1982.

Chandler, M.J. *A Guide to Records in Barbados.* Oxford: University of the West Indies, 1965.

Kent, David L. *Barbados and America.* Arlington, Va.: the author, 1980.

Oliver, Vere Langford. *The Monumental Inscriptions in the Churches and Churchyards of the Island of Barbados, British West Indies.* 1915. Reprint, San Bernardino, Calif.: The Borgo Press, 1986.

Radford, Dwight A. and Arden C. White. "The Irish in Barbados." *The Irish At Home and Abroad* 2 (3) (1994–1995): 92–97.

Sanders, JoAnne McRee. *Barbados Records: Baptisms, 1637–1800.* Baltimore: Genealogical Publishing Co., 1984.

———. *Barbados Records: Marriages, 1643–1800.* 2 vols. Houston, Tex.: Sanders Historical Publications, 1982.

———. *Barbados Records: Wills and Administrations.* 3 vols. Houston, Tex.: Sanders Historical Publications, 1979–1981.

Addresses

Department of Archives
Black Rock, St. Michael, Barbados
phone: (809) 425-1380

BERMUDA

Bermuda was first settled in 1609 by a group of shipwrecked colonists who were sailing for the Jamestown settlement in Virginia. Many Irish prisoners were transported to the Bermudas during the mid seventeenth century. However, six months after a thwarted revolt in 1658, a resolution was passed making it illegal "to buy or purchase any more of the Irish nation upon any pretense whatsoever." In 1684 the islands officially became a British colony; and in 1767 they became a base for the British Caribbean fleet and home for traveling British militia and its accompanying artisans. In the seventeenth century close connections existed between Bermuda and the colonies of Virginia, South Carolina, North Carolina, and Georgia. Some families in these colonies were related to or descended from early Bermuda settlers. During the American Revolution, the Bermuda Islands became a place of refuge for many Tories (people loyal to the British King) who fled from the soon-to-be United States. Many of these people remained in the Bermudas and other Caribbean Islands because their mainland property had been seized during the war. If an ancestor disappeared about the time of the American Revolution, you may want to check Bermuda's records.

Records

The majority of Bermuda's records are at the Bermuda Archives in Hamilton with microfilm copies of many collections at the FHL. Copies of pedigrees and notes about particular families are available at the Bermuda Archives. For a detailed outline of Bermuda records, see Helen Rowe's *A Guide to the Records of Bermuda* and Arden C. White's article "The Irish in Bermuda" in *The Irish At Home and Abroad*. The Web site Bermudian Genealogy and History at <http://www.rootsweb.com/~bmuwgw/bermuda.htm> is an excellent source to get information on the island.

Cemeteries

Cemeteries adjoin each Anglican parish church in Bermuda, and persons of all faiths were buried there. It wasn't until the mid-1800s that Catholics and other denominations began using their own cemeteries. Catholic cemeteries date from 1846.

Census Records

The earliest known census, taken in 1699, is held at the PRO (CO 37/2:194) with copies at the Bermuda Archives. Other name lists similar to censuses are in *A Guide to the Records of Bermuda*. There are several petitions and assessments that serve as census substitutes, including petitions of 1645, 1708, and 1800; and the assessments of 1727 and 1789. An excellent historical summary of each and a list of signers in these census substitutes are in Clara Hollis Hallett's *Early Bermuda Records 1619–1826*.

Church Records

The parishes of the Anglican Church were officially established by 1622. Unfortunately, only a few of the earliest parish registers have survived, and later registers have gaps. The early Anglican records are indexed in *Early Bermuda Records 1619–1826*. The Roman Catholic parishes of St. Theresa in Hamilton and St. Anthony in Warwick have records from 1850 and 1858, respectively. These are still with the parishes.

Convict Records

Records of Irish who were sent to the penal colonies show when and where in Ireland the person was convicted, and where in Bermuda the prisoner was received. Records also provide the names and addresses of friends or relatives, religion, and age of the prisoner. Transportation registers from 1849 to 1851 of prisoners to the penal colonies are at the National Library of Ireland (Ms 3016).

The convict establishment kept convicts, who were used for labor in the dockyard and aboard ships, at anchor in the bay off Boaz Island. The establishment closed in 1865. The Bermuda legislature voted never to allow convicts who had served their time to be released in Bermuda. The released men were taken back to England or carried to Australia on "tickets of leave." Records documenting the lives of convicts are in the Assignment Lists and Quarterly Returns of the Hulk Establishment (Series HO and HO11) at the PRO.

REFERENCES AND FURTHER READING

Sources

Hollis Hallett, Clara. *Early Bermuda Records 1619–1826: A Guide to the Parish and Clergy Registers With Some Assessment Lists and Petitions.* Pembroke, Bermuda: Juniperhill Press, 1991.

———. *Bermuda Index 1784–1914: An Index of Births, Marriages, and Deaths as Recorded in Bermuda Newspapers.* Bermuda: Juniperhill Press, 1989.

McCarthy, Father J.M. *Bermuda's Priests. The History of the Establishment and Growth of the Catholic Church in Bermuda.* Quebec: P. Larose, 1954.

Mercer, Julia E. *Bermuda Settlers of the 17th Century: Genealogical Notes From Bermuda.* Baltimore: Genealogical Publishing Co., 1982.

Rowe, Helen. *A Guide to the Records of Bermuda.* Hamilton, Bermuda: The Bermuda Archives, 1980.

White, Arden C. "The Irish in Bermuda." *The Irish At Home and Abroad* 3 (3) (1995–1996): 111–115.

Wilkinson, Henry C. *Bermuda in the Old Empire: A History of the Island from the Dissolution of the Somers Island Company Until the End of the American Revolutionary War: 1684–1784.* London: Oxford University Press.

———. *Bermuda From Sail to Steam: The History of the Island From 1784–1901.* London: Oxford University Press, 1973.

Addresses

Bermuda Archives
Government Administration Bldg., 30 Parliament St.,
Hamilton HM12, Bermuda
phone: (441) 295-5151 *fax:* (441) 292-2349

Bermuda Library
Par-la-ville, 13 Queen St., Hamilton HM11, Bermuda
phone: (441) 295-3104 *fax:* (441) 292-8443

JAMAICA

The island of Jamaica has a long history of Irish immigration through the 1840s. Not only did the Irish emigrate straight from Ireland to Jamaica but they also emigrated from other Caribbean Islands. The island was in Spanish hands from 1494 to 1655. The English invaded Jamaica in 1655, and it gained its independence in 1962. In 1664, some four hundred planters came to Jamaica from Barbados. Jamaica originally had a large number of European indentured servants to work for these planters but later shifted to the massive import of African slaves. The large plantations brought unimaginable wealth not only to Jamaica but also indirectly to port cities such as Liverpool and Bristol. By 1785, the population of Jamaica stood at 30,000 whites, 10,000 free colored, and 250,000 slaves.

By the end of the eighteenth century, the sugar industry had declined. The slaves were emancipated in 1834, starting a paying system for the plantation workers. With this came the advent of new schemes that enticed workers to Jamaica, including Africans (who were never slaves), Chinese, Indians, and of course the Irish. Hamilton Brown of Jamaica brought several hundred families from Ireland during this time period. One group of 121 people was from Ballymoney Parish, County Antrim, arriving in 1835 on the ship *James Ray* and settling in St. Ann Parish. In 1836 Brown brought 185 additional Irish to St. Ann. Another migration occurred in January 1840, when 136 traveled on the *New Phoenix* from the Clarendon Estate in County Kildare to settle at Boroughbridge and Rosetta, also in St. Ann Parish. The foundation for the cessation of recruitment of European workers for settlement was laid in 1841, when 127 Irish immigrants who came on the *Robert Kerr* turned out to be the wrong class of person, leading to disaster.

Records

Jamaica was divided into parishes containing Anglican churches. The earliest parishes were St. Andrew, St. Ann, St. Catherine, Clarendon, St. David, St. Elizabeth, St. George, St. James, St. John, St. Mary, and St. Thomas. Other parishes were later added: St. Thomas in the Vale (1675), St. Dorothy (1675), Kingston (1693), Westmoreland (1703), Hanover (1723), Portland (1723), Trelawny (1770), Manchester (1814), and Metcalfe (1841). Many parishes were eventually absorbed into other parishes.

There are two guides to Jamaican research. One is Madeleine E. Mitchell's *Jamaican Ancestry: How to Find Out More*. This work treats all the major sources and will tell if they are on microfilm at the FHL. The second guide is Stephen D. Porter's *Jamaican Records: A Research Manual*. Several important sources are also on the Internet site Genealogy in Jamaica <http://www.rootsweb.com/~jamwgw/index.htm> and the site Jamaican Families: Genealogy, Property Owners, and Research <http://maxpages.com/jamaicanfamily>. The latter site has an extraction of more than seven thousand proprietors of properties from the 1840 *Jamaica Almanac*. You can also find a listing of seamen and sailors extracted from Jamaican Anglican registers.

Cemetery Records

Thankfully, many destroyed gravestones were transcribed in 1875 in J.H. Lawrence-Archer's work *Monumental Inscriptions of the British West Indies*. Several published works exist that transcribe the early tombstones on the island. Philip

Wright's *Monumental Inscriptions of Jamaica* (1966) includes virtually all the pre-1880 tombstones in the principal churches and churchyards, and a large portion of those found elsewhere. His work includes all denominations with the exception of Jewish cemeteries. Wright notes that about half the tombstones originally transcribed by Lawrence-Archer are now gone. Although Wright reproduces transcripts that were originally published in other sources, he does not reproduce Lawrence-Archer's work. Thus, between what Wright and Lawrence-Archer produced, an excellent (and indexed) collection emerges. Two examples from Montego Bay Anglican Church in St. James Parish are

> Placed by John Nowlan Esq., of the 84th Regt. [to the memory of] his wife Catherine, daughter of the late Savage Hall, of Narrow Water, Esq., Co. Down, Ireland; she d. 21 Mar. 1833 in her 36th year

> Elizabeth Gemmill, of Belfast, who left Ireland in health, to accompany a sick brother to Madeira, but was brought to this island by the Captain of the ship, and died of fever 15 Apr. 1822 aged 37

Census Records

1680: Inhabitants of Port Royal and St. Johns. The originals are at the PRO (CO 1/45, ff 96–109).

1717: Census of Spanish Town, which includes the nationality of the person. The originals are at the PRO (CO 152/12, no 67 (vi)).

1754: A census of St. Andrew parish. The originals are at the PRO (CO 137/28, pp. 191–196).

1754: List of landholders with number of acres, taken from the Quit Rent Books. Originals are at the PRO (CO 142/31).

Church Records

After the English took over the island in 1655, the Anglican (Church of England) faith became the established church. Anglican records are deposited at the Registrar General's Office in Spanish Town and on microfilm at the FHL. There was a Quaker (Society of Friends) presence on the island from 1679; however, by 1749 most had left Jamaica for Philadelphia, Pennsylvania. One of the best ways to trace Jamaica Quakers is to find them in Philadelphia meeting records transferring into the local monthly meeting. These records have been published or are on microfilm at the FHL. Roman Catholic records begin in 1795.

Research Tip

For Anglican registers, you need to know the parish of origin since there is no comprehensive index to all the Anglican records. We are fortunate that each parish has its own index up to 1872. Some parish registers have been microfilmed; transcripts of some early ones are deposited at the PRO or the British Museum; some have been published in *Caribbeana*; and there are second copies known as "Bishop's Transcripts." Whenever possible, if you are using a Bishop's Transcript or a published version, make sure to check the accuracy by looking at the original register as well. These are also on microfilm at the FHL.

Sources

REFERENCES AND FURTHER READING

Black, Clinton V. *History of Jamaica*. 2d ed. Essex: Longman Group, 1988.

Brathwaite, Edward. *The Development of Creole Society in Jamaica, 1770–1820*. Oxford, England: Oxford University Press, 1971.

Campbell, Mavis C. *The Dynamics of Change in a Slave Society: A Sociopolitical History of the Free Coloreds of Jamaica, 1800–1865*. London: Associated University Presses, 1976.

Higman, B.W. *Slave Population and Economy in Jamaica, 1807–1834*. Reprint, Cambridge: Cambridge University Press, 1976.

Mitchell, Madeleine E. *Jamaican Ancestry: How to Find Out More*. Bowie, Md.: Heritage Books, 1998.

Osborne, Francis J. *History of the Catholic Church in Jamaica*. Chicago, Ill: Loyola University Press, 1988.

Porter, Stephen D. *Jamaican Records: A Research Manual*. London: the author, 1999.

Wright, Philip. *Monumental Inscriptions of Jamaica*. London: Society of Genealogists, 1966.

Addresses

National Library of Jamaica

    12 East St., Kingston, Jamaica, West Indies

    Internet: http://www.nlj.org.jm/

Jamaica Archives

    Spanish Town, Jamaica,West Indies

National Library of Jamaica Collection

    12 East St., Kingston, Jamaica, West Indies

    phone: (876) 967-1526, 967-2516, 967-2494, 967-2496

    Internet: http://www.nlj.org.jm/docs/collection.html

Montserrat

The island of Montserrat has a long and sometimes terrible history involving the Irish. On this small island (eleven miles by seven miles), the English first established a colony in 1632. The earliest settlers were mostly English and Irish Catholics, indentured servants who had been transferred from their base on the island of St. Kitts. Montserrat, in essence, became the only Catholic colony in the Caribbean, although its rulers were Protestants. The second wave of Catholics came in 1634 as refugees fleeing persecution in the Virginia colony.

From 1636 to 1637 the governor of Montserrat, Anthony Brisket, a native of England who had Irish connections, set up a recruiting scheme whereby Irish would be brought to the island to grow tobacco and other crops to export back to Ireland. Brisket's recruiting was successful. Another wave of settlers arrived in the period from 1641 to 1645 as the term for many white indentured servants expired in St. Kitts and Barbados. There was no land available on those islands to settle, so they went to Montserrat. By 1648 there were about one thousand

Irish families on the island, most living on small farms. Following the Cromwellian victory in Ireland in 1649, Cromwell shipped Irish political prisoners to the island, thus effectively using it as a dumping ground.

By 1666 the population stood at 3,250, including 600 English, 2,000 Irish and 650 African slaves. In 1667 a massive exodus from Montserrat occurred during the war between France and England, during which the Irish Catholics sided with the French. The Irish settlers were sent to the island of Nevis and Montserrat lay in ruins. By 1678 the island was being rebuilt with an economy based on a few large plantations. The 1678 census showed the population at 2,682 whites and 992 slaves. More than two thirds of the whites were Irish subsistence farmers; the big sugar planters were English. From this point onward the white population decreased and the slave population increased.

As the wars between England and France continued to spill over into the Caribbean, the period from 1689 to 1714 saw many of the Irish farmers abandon their holdings to the large landholders and leave the island. An Irish Catholic underclass stayed to work with the slave population; the upper class viewed this as a threat and enacted laws forbidding cooperation or gatherings between "Christians and negros." Still, by 1721 about two-thirds of the white population was Catholic. The 1756 census showed a population of 10,283, of whom 1,430 were white and 8,853 were black.

The history of Montserrat has recently been altered due to the eruption of Mount Chance. The volcano began erupting in 1995 with massive eruptions into 1997, during which the capitol, Plymouth, was burned. The majority of the population has been relocated to Antigua and elsewhere in the Caribbean, with some going to the United Kingdom. At this writing, the United Kingdom has committed funds to help rebuild the nation rather than enact a complete evacuation.

Records

The eruption of Mount Chance destroyed many valuable historical places and records. Others have been moved off the island. For the up-to-date situation of records addressed in this section, contact the Montserrat National Trust, which still operates on the island. There are two Web sites that concern Montserrat: CaribbeanGenWeb at <http://britishislesgenweb.org/caribbean/montserrat/> and a well-done history page with the article "A Condensed History of Montserrat" by William G. Innanen, at <http://innanen.com/montserrat/history/index.s html>. Fortunately some record collections, mainly deed books, have been microfilmed and are at the University of the West Indies. We would like to point out that even without the eruption of Mount Chance, the survival of early Montserrat records would be poor. In fact, no records survived on the island prior to 1712, as they were burnt in the French invasion. So it is early records kept elsewhere that are most important in researching the seventeenth and early eighteenth centuries.

We also want to draw your attention to the book *If the Irish Ran the World: Montserrat, 1630–1730* by Donald Harman Akenson, which discusses how the Irish ran this colony and compares it to how the English ran their colonies. He found through records such as the ones mentioned in this section that Irish imperialism was not much different from English imperialism.

In the seventeenth century the island was divided into four parishes for administrative purposes: St. Peter (north), St. Anthony (central), St. Patrick (south), and St. George (east). The parish names follow that of the Anglican Church. A newer parish of St. John's was created to bring the number to five, all with Anglican churches.

Cemetery Records

The volcanic eruption destroyed many major cemeteries in the southern part of the island and forced others to be abandoned. Fortunately, select cemeteries on the island were studied, and the tombstones transcribed in 1913 to 1914. You can find these valuable transcriptions in Vere Langford Oliver's *More Monumental Inscriptions: Tombstones of the British West Indies*. Early Montserrat residents of all denominations would have been buried in the Anglican Parish cemetery. The Anglican graveyard in St. Patrick's parish was transcribed in Oliver's work. The major Catholic graveyard in St. Patrick's Parish was destroyed, and no transcript is known to have been made.

Census Records

1677–1678: Indicates name of person and division of the island where living (PRO CO 1/42, ff 218–228). Also extracted in *Caribbeana* 2, p. 316–320.

1729: EXT 1/258 at the PRO (extracted from PRO CO 152/18). Also published in *Caribbeana*, p. 302.

Church Records

The records of the Anglican Church are the primary source for documenting births/baptisms, marriages, and burials on the island for the eighteenth century. There are no surviving registers for the seventeenth century. The small yet vital collection of these early records for the first few decades of the eighteenth century are available at the PRO and extracted in *Caribbeana*.

The earliest Roman Catholic records for the island date from 1771 to 1838 and include baptisms, marriages, and burials. These are on microfilm at the University of the West Indies.

REFERENCES AND FURTHER READING

Akenson, Donald Harman. *If the Irish Ran the World: Montserrat, 1630–1730*. Montreal and Kingston, Canada: McGill-Queen's University Press, 1997.

Berleant-Schiller, Riva. "Free Labor and the Economy in Seventeenth-Century Montserrat." *The William and Mary Quarterly: A Magazine of Early American History and Culture*. 3d Series 46 (3) (July 1989): 539–564.

Fergus, Howard A. *Montserrat: History of a Caribbean Colony*. Basingstoke, Hampshire, England: MacMillan Press, Ltd., 1994.

Sources

McGinn, Brian. "How Irish is Montserrat?" *Irish Roots* 1994 (1): 20–23; 1994 (2): 15–17.

Wheeler, Marion M. *Montserrat West Indies: A Chronological History.* Montserrat, West Indies: The Montserrat National Trust, 1988.

Addresses

The Montserrat National Trust
P.O. Box 393, Olveston, Montserrat, West Indies
phone: (664) 491 3086   *fax:* (664) 491-3046
Internet: http://www.montserrat-natltrust.com

Montserrat Tourist Board
P.O. Box 7, Montserrat, West Indies
phone: (664) 491-2230, 8730   *fax:* (664) 491-7430
Internet: http://www.visitmontserrat.com
e-mail: mrattouristboard@candw.ag

NEVIS AND ST. KITTS (ST. CHRISTOPHER)

The two islands of Nevis and St. Kitts (also called St. Christopher) are important to Irish research in the 1600s. Many of the earliest settlers of Montserrat came from Nevis and St. Kitts. The islands of Nevis and St. Kitts are neighboring. St. Kitts became the first English settlement in the West Indies in 1623, and it soon became an important colony for its sugar industry. The French also settled on St. Kitts in 1627, and thus began a one hundred year Anglo-French rivalry. The French gave up the island in 1713 by the Peace of Utrecht, and it became a British colony in 1783. The 1678 census showed that there were 187 Irish on St. Kitts, all men, out of a population of 3,343, which also included 1,322 English, 379 French, 19 Dutch, and 1,436 black slaves. Nevis had a much larger Irish population: In 1678 the population stood at 7,381, comprised of 800 Irish (450 men, 120 women, and 230 children), 2,670 English, 51 Scots, and 3,860 Black slaves. So 10 percent of Nevis's population was Irish in this year.

Records

The islands are divided into parishes based on the Anglican parish system:

St. Kitts (St. Christopher)
The nine parishes of this island are St. Paul (Capesterre), St. Anne (Sandy Point), St. John (Capesterre), St. Thomas (Middle Island), Christ Church (Nichola Town), Trinity (Palmetto Point), St. Mary (Cayon), St. George (Basseterre), and St. Peter (Basseterre).

Nevis
Its five parishes are St. Paul (Charlestown), St. John (Figtree), St. George (Gingerland), St. James (Windward), and St. Thomas (Lowland).

The Web site St. Kitts-Nevis Genealogy is an excellent tool that includes both history and extracted records: <http://www.tc.umn.edu/~terre011/genhome.html>. This site also lists what is available for St. Kitts and Nevis at the FHL and the British Library in London.

Two books that detail Nevis families are Byron Evalie's *More Nevis Families* and *Some More Nevis Families*.

The public records of Nevis for the period prior to 1706 were destroyed in the French invasion of that year. The courthouse on St. Kitts was destroyed by fire in the 1980s. Although this complicates research in these two islands, enough early records have been published and are already on microfilm that the loss can to some degree be circumvented. Records such as some deeds, wills, church records, and some genealogies are housed at the Nevis Historical and Conservation Society. The St. Christopher Heritage Society, although not a genealogical archive, does house a library, maps, and various documents and reports detailing the culture of St. Kitts.

Cemetery Records

Selected tombstones from St. Kitts graveyards were published in James Henry Lawrence-Archers's 1875 work *Monumental Inscriptions of the British West Indies* (pp. 418–420). However, these are just a few of the older ones, and the record is by no means complete. More cemeteries are transcribed in Oliver's *More Monumental Inscriptions: Tombstones of the British West Indies* (pp. 67–198) and *Caribbeana* [vols. 1 (1910) and 2 (1912)]. **Remember, in the early days people of all denominations were buried in the Anglican graveyards.** A few examples from St. Kitts read

Reminder

> Here Lies the Body of Jn. Beavor Esqr of Kingfale in the Kingdom of Ireland late of the ifland of Tortola who departed this Life the 31st July 1768 in the 58th year of his Age Also in this is Interred the Body of Mrs. Honour Beavor of the Ifland of Montserat [Anglican graveyard, Trinity Parish, Palmetto Point, St. Kitts]

> Sacred to the Memory of Ulick Burke Esqr Planter of this Island Born in the County of Galway in Ireland who died on the 17th of May, 1808 in the 69th Year of Age [Anglican Church, St. Peter's Parish, Basseterre, St. Kitts]

> Here lies the body of Mary-Anne Blake, alias Bohun, the wife of Patrick Blake Fitz-Peter, of Cummer, in the county of Galway, in Ireland, who departed this life the 18th day of February, 1720, in the 38th year of her age. Here also lies the body of the above-mentioned Patrick Blake Fitz-Peter, of Cummer, in the county of Galway, in the Kingdom of Ireland, late of this island, departed this life the 7th day of March 1744, aged 68 years [Anglican church, St. Anne's Parish, Sandy Point, St. Kitts]

Census Records

The Irish can be documented by name in several early enumerations of the population. They have been published.

St. Kitts (St. Christopher)
1677–1678: PRO CO 1/42, ff 195–200; also printed in *Caribbeana* 2 (1912): 68–77

1707: PRO CO 152/7, f 47; also printed in *Caribbeana* 3 (1914): 132–139

1711: PRO CO 152/9, ff 305–315

1776–1780: Population and Taxes of French Possessions in the West Indies (PRO Add. MS. 38346 ff. 76, 76V, 77V).

Nevis
1677–1678: PRO CO 1/42, ff 201–217; also printed in *Caribbeana* 3 (1914): 27–35

1707: PRO CO 152/7 f 47; also printed in *Caribbeana* 3 (1914): 173–179

Church Records

The church records for the two islands are available in several places. Fortunately some have been published in *Caribbeana*, others microfilmed, and transcripts of others sent to London. The PRO, British Library and the Society of Genealogists both have collections. The Nevis Historical and Conservation Society and the FHL also have some collections. There are no surviving Catholic registers in St. Kitts prior to 1865. However, saying this, there is an odd collection of indexes from 1682 for Catholics on St. Kitts, which are part of the records of St. Barthélemy on the island of Guadeloupe (a French possession). Although not registers, these indexes are at least one more key into the lives of early Catholics on St. Kitts.

REFERENCES AND FURTHER READING

Sources

Evalie, Byron. *More Nevis Families*. Basseterre, St. Kitts: Offset Commercial Printers Ltd., 1981.

———. *Some More Nevis Families*. Basseterre, St. Kitts: Offset Commercial Printers Ltd., 1979.

Hubbard, Vincent. *Swords, Ships and Sugar: A History of Nevis to 1900*. Placentia, Calif.: Premiere Editions, 1993.

Inniss, Sir Probyn. *Whither Bound St. Kitts-Nevis?* Antigua, W.I.: Antigua Printing and Publishing, 1983.

Oliver, Vere Langford. *The Registers of St. Thomas, Middle Island, St. Kitts, 1729–1832*. London: Mitchell Hughes and Clark, 1915 (FHL #1162487 item 3).

Sharon, Frank and Emilia Stone. *Discover St. Kitts: Columbus' Favourite Island*. St. Kitts, W.I.: Creole Publishing, 1987.

Addresses

Nevis Historical and Conservation Society
Nelson Museum, Belle Vue, Charlestown, Nevis
(*Mailing*) NHCS Archives, P.O. Box 563, Charlestown, Nevis

phone: (869) 469-0408   *fax:* (869) 469-0274

Internet: http://www.nevis-nhcs.org/

National Archives

Govt. Headquarters, P.O. Box 186, Basseterre, St. Kitts

phone: (869) 465-2521   *fax:* (869) 465-1001

St. Christopher Heritage Society

(*Location*) Corner of Bank and West Square streets

(*Mailing*) P.O. Box 888, Basseterre, St. Kitts

phone/fax: (869) 465-5584

Internet: http://www.islandimage.com/schs/home.htm

EIGHT

An Introduction to Irish Research

WHAT TO EXPECT AND JUDGING RESULTS

Many who begin Irish genealogical research have a goal to find out where in Ireland the immigrant ancestor came from. Usually a budding genealogist will soon discover that his or her approach to research needs to be tailored to the social status of the ancestor and the time period of immigration. Tracing the impoverished ancestor, or the ancestor who immigrated in the 1600s or 1700s, might be difficult or even impossible. If you use effective strategies, however, you can often find the origin of your ancestor in Ireland.

Whether you are conducting research yourself or hiring a professional to do it, remember that there are limitations to just how far back an Irish family can be traced. Success in Irish research has to be judged by different standards from, for example, Scandanavian, English, or Scottish research.

Most Irish Catholic and Presbyterian church records simply do not begin until about the 1820s. Consequently, the average Catholic or Presbyterian lineage can be traced back only to the late eighteenth century. The Church of Ireland was the established church. Although the Church of Ireland registers often commenced earlier, remember that more than half of these registers were destroyed in 1922.

Although you might not be able to trace your ancestors into antiquity, Irish research holds the possibility of being able to visit the exact home site where your ancestors lived and even their house itself. There are not many places where you can actually walk through the same doorway or over the same pasture that your ancestor did.

Not all Irish lineages come to a halt in the late 1700s. In the case of gentry or the upper class, there are frequently extensive pedigrees that can take a family back hundreds of years. Although very few such pedigrees exist for the common family, don't assume your ancestors were peasants simply because they left Ireland.

Important

WHAT DOES THE WORD "IRISH" MEAN?

We need to define the word "Irish." We realize that this can be an emotional topic. We have found that many Americans have the perception that "Irish" means both Gaelic and Catholic, thus eliminating anyone who doesn't fit into those categories. Our Canadian, Australian, and New Zealander friends know better. When we visit Irish festivals and genealogy gatherings around the United States, we find that at least half of the people have ancestors from Ireland who were Protestants rather than Catholics. We also find that many Irish Catholics and their children left the church in America. Does that mean are they no longer Irish?

Many thousands of Presbyterians from the lowlands of Scotland settled in Ulster (the northern province of Ireland) in the 1600s, and their descendants came in great numbers to America starting in 1718. There were both "Old English" (Normans who were Catholics) and "New English" (Protestants who came after the Reformation) families who settled in Ireland as well. Irish residents of English origin were often called the Anglo-Irish. The more prominent Anglo-Irish residents comprised the Protestant Ascendancy, which ruled Ireland for several centuries.

We can't use religion as a guideline to what "Irish" means, because religion is so intermixed among families in Ireland. Mixed marriages are more common than anyone wants to talk about. For example, in the North of Ireland you will find numerous Roman Catholic Campbells whose ancestors were originally Presbyterians from Scotland. **For our purposes, "Irish" means simply "from the island of Ireland."**

\di'fin\ *vb*

Definitions

THE REPUBLIC OF IRELAND AND NORTHERN IRELAND

The island of Ireland is politically divided. In 1921 twenty-six counties separated from Great Britain to form the Irish Free State, which eventually became the Republic of Ireland. The six remaining counties (Antrim, Armagh, Down, Fermanagh, Londonderry, and Tyrone) voted to remain in the United Kingdom with Great Britain. Many records from the Republic counties are centralized in Dublin, while Belfast has its own repositories covering Northern Ireland (see the Appendix).

DIFFERENCES BETWEEN IRISH CATHOLIC AND IRISH PROTESTANT RESEARCH

There are some sources that we generally look at sooner if we are tracing a Protestant family. Take freeholders lists, for example (chapter nineteen). You won't find Catholics in them before 1793, but you will find many Protestants listed in them. Other sources high on the list for tracing Protestants would be the Registry of Deeds (chapter nineteen), and Wills and Administrations (chapter twenty-four). Of course, you won't find all Protestants listed in these sources, since there were poor Protestants as well as wealthy ones. A rule of thumb: the more wealthy, educated, and prominent a family, the more you will be able to find about them.

Not all Catholic families in Ireland were poor or landless, although a large share was. There are generally fewer surviving records of Catholics than Protestants. You might have to look to the records of your Catholic ancestor's Protestant landlord to find documentation of your tenant family in the landlord's estate papers (chapter fifteen).

HARDSHIPS OF RESEARCH IN IRISH RECORDS

You might hear someone say Irish research is impossible because "all the Irish records were destroyed." This is a common oversimplification of what has happened to Irish records. Actually, there are many Irish records to use.

Having said that, it is true that some significant Irish records have been destroyed. During the 1922 Irish Civil War, the Public Record Office of Ireland at Four Courts in Dublin was destroyed by fire, and a great variety of Irish records was lost. As terrible as this event was, we need to ask just what was destroyed and how this affects our research of the average Irish ancestor. You will see that the loss, while significant, was not as catastrophic as people sometimes make it out to be. The office housed a number of key genealogical records that were destroyed:

- Pre-1858 wills and administrations
- 1821 to 1851 census records
- Over half of the Church of Ireland parish registers

The destruction of the Public Record Office of Ireland forever impacted the course of research for the Irish genealogist. However, this is by no means a reason to avoid using Irish records. It was only one national repository. Looking at the above list, remember that most Irish people didn't have wills or administrations, and the Church of Ireland included only about 10 percent of the population. The major loss for the average family history is thus the 1821 to 1851 census records. Still remaining are all of the records not deposited in the Public Record Office of Ireland in 1922. The Registry of Deeds, General Register Office material, Genealogical Office collections, Valuation Office material, newspapers, Freemason records, school registers, estate records of landlords, and of course the vast collections at the Public Records Office in England. The Roman Catholic, Presbyterian, Methodist, Quaker, and the other half of the Church of Ireland registers could also be added to this list. This book will attest to the wide variety of sources available for your research.

Reminder

Accessing Irish Records

There are some Irish records you can search in repositories outside Ireland, and some that are only available in Ireland. The following chapter describes these two cases. At some point, you may want to have the exciting experience of going to Ireland to do research. But don't go to Ireland unprepared. Do what work is possible in your home country before going to research in Ireland. The addresses and contact information for Irish record repositories in Ireland and worldwide are in the Appendix.

LIBRARIES AND ARCHIVES IN IRELAND

Why go to Dublin or Belfast for your Irish research? Isn't everything available through the Mormons' Family History Library (FHL) in Salt Lake City anyway, you might ask? The truth is that many Irish genealogy sources *are* available through the FHL in Salt Lake City, but on the other hand, many original records of our Irish ancestors are only available in Ireland. A large number of these records are in central repositories in Dublin and Belfast. Some main Dublin repositories include the National Archives of Ireland (NAI), the National Library of Ireland (NLI) and the Representative Church Body Library (RCBL), while the largest archives in Belfast is the Public Record Office of Northern Ireland (PRONI). The individual chapters of this book explain where records are located and whether copies are available outside of Ireland.

Remember that the island of Ireland is politically divided. Belfast has its own repositories covering Northern Ireland. There are also libraries and archives in other locations, such as the county libraries and the Cork Archives Institute in the city of Cork. *Directory of Irish Archives*, edited by Helferty and Refaussé, is a good guide to libraries and archives throughout the island.

Remember that even if the records you want are not available outside Ireland, you might be able to find inventories or catalogs of Irish records that will help you in planning how to find records in Ireland. Many such inventories and catalogs are on the Internet, at the FHL, and at the library of the Irish Genealogical Society International in Saint Paul, Minnesota.

Research Tip

How can you access records in Dublin or Belfast if you can't go there yourself, or your tour of Ireland doesn't allow you the time to stop at these archives? In many cases, you will need to hire a professional researcher to do some work for you. The archives staff usually will not do research for you. You can find contact information for genealogists in Ireland and around the world who do Irish research on the What's What in Irish Genealogy Web site at <http://indigo .ie/~gorry/research.html>.

FROM OUTSIDE IRELAND
Irish Resources at the Family History Library

Many records from Ireland are available to people in their home countries around the world. In most places you have access to many Irish records in your own town (or close by) just by ordering them on microfilm from the FHL in Salt Lake City. The library, which houses the largest collection of Irish records outside of Ireland itself, is operated by the Church of Jesus Christ of Latter-day Saints (the Mormons). The church's Genealogical Society of Utah has microfilmed records from repositories in Ireland and collected books and periodicals about Irish genealogy. The Mormons also have satellite centers called Family History Centers in many of their churches around the world, where you can order the microfilm held at the FHL for the cost of the postage. Find addresses of Family History Centers worldwide on the Family Search Web site: <http://www.familysearch.org>.

Tip

From one perspective, doing Irish research is easier in Salt Lake City than it is in Ireland itself. That is because the FHL has microfilm from multiple repositories in Ireland: the Genealogical Office, the General Register Office, the NAI, the NLI, and the Registry of Deeds, all in Dublin; the PRONI in Belfast; Irish county libraries, and other repositories. Many records of Irish people held at the PRO at Kew, Surrey, England are also on microfilm at the FHL. At the FHL, all of the microfilm is on one floor of one building, whereas in Dublin, you might have to visit five or more repositories to get a similar range of records. By the way, the FHL and its collections are open to the public free of charge, six days a week, regardless of a researcher's religious background (no questions are ever asked). Family History Centers have more limited hours, and we advise you to call ahead for their schedules.

Just to give you an idea of some of the major collections of Irish records at the FHL, here is a short list:

Cemetery records: Many published volumes of tombstone transcripts. Microfilm of registers of the major Protestant cemetery, Mount Jerome in Dublin City.

Censuses and census substitutes: The 1901 and 1911 censuses of Ireland. Census fragments from the nineteenth century. Many census substitutes from the 1600s to the 1800s.

Church records: Microfilm of church registers from about one-third of the Catholic parishes in Ireland; Quaker registers of births, marriages, and deaths for all of Ireland; a few transcripts of Church of Ireland and Presbyterian registers.

Civil registration: Microfilm copies of indexes to Irish civil registration from 1845 through 1958. Copies of many of the original registers of birth, marriage, and death, although there are gaps in the collection.

Directories: Countrywide and local town directories as books or on microfilm, including a significant series of directories for Belfast and Dublin.

Estate records: Relatively few are available, but some major collections have been filmed at the PRONI.

Genealogies: Most of the manuscripts of the Genealogical Office, Dublin, are on microfilm.

Inventories and catalogs: Descriptive catalogs of the PRONI. Kew Lists for the Public Record Office in England. Many genealogical guides and inventories.

Land records: Records of the Registry of Deeds from 1708 to 1929, along with indexes by the name of the grantor and by the locality (such as townland).

Military records: Many British Army, Irish militia, and yeomanry records microfilmed at the Public Record Office in England.

Occupational records: Guild records for Dublin City and other cities. Royal Irish Constabulary records and indexes.

Reference material: Most Irish genealogy reference works and Irish county genealogy guides.

Taxation records: Tithe Applotment Books (1823 to 1837). Griffith's Primary Valuation (1847 to 1864). Griffith's Revision Lists for Republic of Ireland counties.

Wills and administrations: Indexes to pre-1858 records by diocese. Records and indexes by probate registry for post-1858 period.

For More Info

GENEALOGICAL OFFICE COLLECTION

The collections at the Genealogical Office (GO) mainly concern the gentry and nobility, whether Catholic or Protestant. Many of these genealogies are extended into Scotland and England. The GO collections are particularly valuable since some are based on research done in records that were destroyed in the 1922 Four Courts fire. The compiled pedigrees may be the only "proof" left of a lineage after the original sources were destroyed in the fire. While these pedigrees concern the upper classes, remember that most upper class families had younger sons and daughters, the descendants of whom may have ended up common farmers just like everybody else. So don't assume you'll never connect into a GO pedigree just because your ancestors were tenant farmers or immigrants in the nineteenth century. The GO collections also include abstracts of records such as censuses and freeholders lists. John Grenham wrote a chapter in *The Genealogical Office Dublin* (Dublin: Irish Manuscripts Commission, 1998) that inventories the collections of the GO by manuscript number. Many of the vast collections of the GO are indexed in Virginia Wade McAnlis's *The Consolidated Index to the Records of the Genealogical Office, Dublin, Ireland* (4 vols. Issaquah and Port Angeles, Washington: the author, 1994–1997). This monumental work not only provides easy access to the pedigrees but also lists the accompanying FHL microfilm numbers where they apply. Another inventory of these genealogies is in Richard Hayes's *Manuscript Sources for the History of Irish Civilisation* (11 vols. Boston: G.K. and Co., 1965).

Other Repositories Outside Ireland

In the United States, there are other libraries with large Irish record collections that you can use for your research, such as the Allen County Public Library in Fort Wayne, Indiana, and the New England Historic Genealogical Society in Boston, Massachusetts. The library of the Irish Genealogical Society International in St. Paul, Minnesota, is especially worth mentioning because it collects a large number of books and journals from Ireland, including many that are out of print or of limited circulation. The Emigration Library of the Irish Cultural and Heritage Center of Wisconsin in Milwaukee holds an increasing number of Irish records in book and microfilm form.

Library/Archive Source

The Society of Genealogists in London is a major repository of Irish records, including many periodicals and some manuscripts. For details, see Anthony J. Camp's *Sources for Irish Genealogy in the Library of the Society of Genealogists,* which organizes the holdings by source type and Irish county. The Irish

Genealogical Research Society, also in London, holds special collections of Irish records and indexes. Much manuscript material relating to Irish people is held at the PRO at Kew, Surrey, England, and a guide to sources is Alice Prochaska's *Irish History from 1700: A Guide to Sources in the Public Record Office.*

Sources

REFERENCES AND FURTHER READING

Camp, Anthony J. *Sources for Irish Genealogy in the Library of the Society of Genealogists.* 2d ed. London: Society of Genealogists, 1998.

Helferty, S. and R. Refaussé, eds. *Directory of Irish Archives.* 3d ed. Dublin: Irish Academic Press, 1999.

Prochaska, Alice. *Irish History from 1700: A Guide to Sources in the Public Record Office.* British Records Association, 1986.

NINE

Administrative Divisions and Place Names: The Key to Irish Research

Important

T he subject of how the land in Ireland has been subdivided can be one of the most complex subjects in the study of Irish family history. **Understanding of land and its divisions is literally the key to successful research.** You will find that the subject of land division also spills over into your immigrant research, since Irish place names find their way into records the world over.

Ireland is divided into provinces, which in turn are divided into counties, which in turn are divided into civil parishes (not the same thing as church parishes, mind you). Civil parishes are divided into townlands, each of which is a surveyed area of land with a certain acreage and set of boundaries. Townlands also have localized place names within them. As if this were not enough, Irish records are also arranged by poor law unions, superintendent registrar's districts, and baronies that were all created to meet the government's needs to serve its growing population.

These administrative units often overlap one another, which means you must think in a more abstract way than you would in other types of genealogical research. Following is more detail about what each administrative division really means and why it is important for your Irish and Irish immigrant research. You will find maps of some administrative divisions in Brian Mitchell's *A New Genealogical Atlas of Ireland*.

Provinces and nations: Ireland has historically been divided into the provinces of Connaught, Leinster, Munster, and Ulster. There are several counties in each of these historical provinces. Present-day Northern Ireland encompasses all of Ulster except for the three counties of Cavan, Donegal, and Monaghan, which belong to the Republic of Ireland. Northern Ireland is part of the United Kingdom of Great Britain and Northern Ireland, while the Republic of Ireland is a separate country.

Counties: The island was historically comprised of thirty-two counties. A county is a political unit made up of a number of civil parishes. Be aware that in the course of Ireland's political history, Queen's County became County Leix (or Laois) and King's County became County Offaly after the island was divided in 1921. Also, different people use the names Derry and Londonderry, but they mean the same thing; these are two names for the same county.

Civil parishes: The government's parishes were called civil parishes. The civil parish is an important administrative unit for land and taxation purposes. When you start using Irish records, you will notice that it is also the division used to catalog many Irish records at several repositories, including the FHL. You can find maps of the civil parish boundaries of all counties published in Brian Mitchell's book.

Reminder

Church (or ecclesiastical) parishes: Church parishes are not the same as civil parishes in Ireland. The Church of Ireland and the Roman Catholic Church have separate parish systems. Following the Reformation, the Church of Ireland took over the medieval Catholic church parishes and their buildings. The Church of Ireland parishes historically had the same boundaries as the civil parishes. However, the uneven distribution of Church of Ireland parishioners in the eighteenth and nineteenth centuries caused Church of Ireland parishes to be subdivided and combined. This means the Church of Ireland parish boundaries are not necessarily the same as the civil parish's boundaries.

With the reorganization of the Roman Catholic church in the later eighteenth century, the number of Catholic parishes increased. A civil parish may have parts of one or more Catholic parishes within its boundaries. You can find approximate Catholic parish boundaries in each county in John Grenham's book. Brian Mitchell's *A Guide to Irish Parish Registers* lists the names of Catholic parishes within each civil parish. Find out what Catholic and Protestant congregations existed in each civil parish in 1837 by consulting Samuel Lewis's *Topographical Dictionary of Ireland*.

Dioceses: Church of Ireland and Catholic parishes are grouped into dioceses. The two churches have distinct diocesan systems. Prior to 1858, wills, administrations, and marriage licenses were under the jurisdiction of Church of Ireland dioceses, regardless of the person's religion. Roman Catholic records on microfilm at the NLI are filed by diocese.

Baronies: A discussion of baronies is nothing other than odd. A barony is comprised of several civil parishes or parts of civil parishes. Barony boundaries cross county and civil parish boundaries. The reason we're even talking about them is that baronies were widely used in land and tax records. For example, the Registry of Deeds arranged some deed indexes by barony. You can find the barony for the town, townland, or parish of your ancestors' residence by consulting the 1851, 1871, or 1901 *General Alphabetical Index to the Townlands and Towns*. . . . Barony maps are included in Brian Mitchell's book.

Poor Law Unions: Under the Poor Law Act of 1838, Ireland was divided into unions of townlands whose inhabitants were responsible for the care of the poor among them. The name of a union was derived from the town at its center, where the workhouse for the poor was located. The union boundaries crossed civil parish boundaries. A Poor Law Union was divided into electoral divisions (see page 167).

Superintendent Registrar's Districts: Civil registration of births, marriages, and deaths in Ireland was compiled by the Superintendent Registrar's District (also called the registration district). The Superintendent Registrar's Districts in the nineteenth century had the same names and boundaries as the Poor Law Unions. A Superintendent Registrar's District was divided into local Registrar's Districts.

Electoral divisions: An electoral division is a number of townlands joined together as a unit for the purpose of electing its representative to the Poor Law Union Board of Guardians. In essence, it is a neighborhood. Electoral divisions are important because they were used in arranging Griffith's Valuation revision books (see chapter twenty-three). Determine the electoral division in which a townland is located from the 1871 and 1901 *General Alphabetical Index to the Townlands and Towns. . . .* Note that the 1851 version of the index does not list the electoral division. Major changes in the boundaries of electoral divisions occurred after Ireland was partitioned in 1921. Most of the changes occurred in Northern Ireland, which then started publishing its own townland indexes reflecting the changes. View these indexes at the PRONI, the OSNI, and the FHL.

Cities and towns: In Ireland towns are not townlands, but you can locate towns or villages within one or more townlands. An example is the town of Draperstown in County Londonderry, which lies in the three adjoining townlands of Cahore, Moykeeran, and Moyheeland. You can be in the middle of the street in Draperstown and literally stand in three townlands at once. Since 1921 some changes have occurred in city and town names. Some you should be aware of include: Queenstown, County Cork became Cobh; Kingstown, County Dublin became Dun Laoghaire; and Parsonstown, Kings County became Birr, County Offaly. Remember to use the old name of the town when looking at pre-1921 records.

Townlands: The townland is the smallest official geographical unit in Ireland. A townland is not a town, nor does it have its own government. It is a surveyed piece of ground that might not even have people living within its boundaries. The bottom line is that a townland might be a cow pasture, a bog, or a mountaintop. Usually, but not always, townlands have Gaelic names. The size of townlands varies greatly, from a few acres to several thousand acres. It's inaccurate to equate a townland in Ireland to a United States or Canadian township, but this is the closest we can come to a comparison.

The borders of Ireland's townlands were not officially surveyed until the Ordnance Survey in the 1830s. Many changes in the names and boundaries of townlands had occurred prior to this time. Due to their small size, townlands do not usually appear on standard road maps. However, the Ordnance Survey of Ireland and the OSNI have published modern maps of Ireland, called the "Discovery Series" in the Republic and the "Discoverer Series" in the North; these maps list the names of townlands but do not show their boundaries.

Townland sub-denominations: Within the official townlands, there might be smaller subdivisions such as field and farm names. You might also find small communities within townlands that have unique names even though they might

\di'fin\ *vb*

Definitions

include only a few houses. These sub-denominations within a townland are not listed in the *General Alphabetical Index to the Townlands and Towns.* . . . You can find sub-denominations, however, in official records such as civil registration or on the Ordnance Survey maps of Ireland. An example is the place "Cherry Grove," which is located in Croom civil parish, County Limerick. At one time it might have literally been a cherry grove, but by the time of the Ordnance Survey a cluster of families had taken this as the place name where they lived.

Sources

SOURCES FOR FINDING PLACE NAMES

If you have an Irish place name and you're not sure what it is or where it is located, we suggest the following sources:

1. *Topographical Dictionary of Ireland*: This book by Samuel Lewis, first published in 1837, gives sketches of each civil parish, town, barony, and county in Ireland. It is on Family Tree Maker's CD #270.

2. *The Parliamentary Gazetteer of Ireland*: This ten-volume gazetteer, published in 1844, is similar in its content to Samuel Lewis's work.

3. Townland Indexes: Use the 1851, 1871, and 1901 *General Alphabetical Index to the Townlands and Towns, Parishes and Baronies of Ireland* to find the official spelling and the location of each townland in Ireland. The 1871 and 1901 indexes are available on microfilm. The 1851 edition has been reprinted by Genealogical Publishing Co.

4. Ordnance Survey Maps: If a parish or townland is known, check the 6″-to-the-mile Ordnance Survey maps, which date from 1833 to 1846. These maps are detailed and often identify localized place names. You can find the correct map by locating the townland of interest or a nearby townland or town in the 1851, 1871, or 1901 townland index. The column "No. of Sheet of the Ordnance Survey Maps" in these indexes tells the map number(s) to locate the town or townland. If you know only a civil parish, use the section in the back of the book to determine the correct map number(s). More sub-denominations appeared on later editions of the 6″-to-the-mile maps than on the original edition.

5. Ordnance Survey Map Place Name Indexes: The Ordnance Survey compiled a manuscript index to all place names listed on the original 6″-to-the-mile Ordnance Survey maps, titled "Manuscript Index to the Original 6″ to the Mile Ordnance Survey Maps." This source alphabetically indexes the places within townlands or sub-denominations. You can search this index on microfilm at the NLI in Dublin (p. 4621–4625) and at the Irish Cultural and Heritage Center of Wisconsin in Milwaukee. For each place name, the civil parish and barony of location are given.

6. Northern Ireland Place-Name Project: This project of the Celtic Department of Queen's University in Belfast has compiled a computer database with names from the Ordnance Survey Place Name Books for the six counties of Northern Ireland. If you cannot find a place name in the six

counties, the Place-Name Project might be of some assistance. The project is publishing a series of books called *Place-Names of Northern Ireland*.

7. Ordnance Survey (John O'Donovan) Place Name Books: The books show the different names that were used for the same townland as well as spelling variations in townland names prior to standardization in the 1830s. The manuscript *Name Books* for all counties are available on microfilm at the NLI. There are also typed transcripts of *Name Books* for many counties at the NLI (reference number IR 9294203). The books are divided by county and alphabetically by civil parish. Microfilm copies for Ulster are at Queen's University in Belfast (Mic. A/1-13).

REFERENCES AND FURTHER READING

Sources

Andrews, J. H. *History in the Ordnance Map: An Introduction for Irish Readers*. Kerry, Wales: David Archer, 1993.

General Alphabetical Index to the Townlands and Towns, Parishes and Baronies of Ireland. Based on the Census of Ireland for the Year 1851. 1861. Reprint, Baltimore: Genealogical Publishing Co., 1984.

Lewis, Samuel. *Topographical Dictionary of Ireland: Comprising the Several Counties, Cities, Boroughs, Corporate, Market and Post Towns, Parishes and Villages with Historical and Statistical Descriptions*. London: S. Lewis, 1837.

Mitchell, Brian. *A Guide to Irish Parish Registers*. Baltimore: Genealogical Publishing Co., 1988.

———. *A New Genealogical Atlas of Ireland*. Baltimore: Genealogical Publishing Co., 1986.

The Parliamentary Gazetteer of Ireland. 10 vols. Dublin: A. Fullarton, 1844.

Radford, Dwight A. and Kyle J. Betit. "Irish Place Names and the Immigrant." *The Irish At Home and Abroad* 5 (1) (1st Quarter 1998): 7–14.

Stockman, Gerard, gen. ed. *Place-Names of Northern Ireland*. 7 vols. Belfast: The Northern Ireland Place-Name Project, Department of Celtic, The Queen's University of Belfast, 1992–1998.

Addresses

Northern Ireland Place-Name Project
Department of Celtic
School of Modern and Medieval Languages
Queen's University of Belfast
7 University Sq., Belfast BT7 1NN, Northern Ireland
phone: (01232) 273689   *fax:* (01232) 324549

TEN

Cemetery Records

Technique

W alking through an Irish cemetery, you would be struck by the number of tombstones that tell you where people settled abroad. This makes a trip to an Irish cemetery a unique and exciting experience to say the least.

If you find a tombstone for your ancestor in Ireland, the inscription might preserve important information such as birth and death dates or townlands of origin. Relationships between family members might also be given. However, you must remember that the stark reality of the situation is that most of the population in Ireland never had tombstones.

If you don't find a tombstone for your ancestor, don't give up on the cemetery by any means! **Notice where people from the area went abroad, and notice the other people with your ancestor's surname or from your ancestor's townland who were buried there.** These might end up being important details later on in your research. Tombstones can help determine who did not emigrate by showing who was buried in Ireland. In other words, which Patrick Kelly is not yours? If the ancestor emigrated, you can eliminate those candidates buried in Ireland.

Other than what is recorded on tombstones, most Irish cemeteries did not have written records. However, the associated church might have kept burial registers, particularly Church of Ireland parishes. Town or city cemeteries can be an exception; sexton's records of the burials in the cemetery might have been kept. Search Church of Ireland cemeteries and burial registers for persons of all denominations because the Church of Ireland was the state church, and people of all faiths had a right to be buried in the parish cemetery.

INDEXES AND TRANSCRIPTS

Many groups have published tombstone transcripts in books and periodicals. Some unpublished transcripts are available in repositories such as county librar- ies. Tombstone inscriptions from many Irish cemeteries are indexed by heritage centres in Ireland, which will search their records for a fee.

For More Info

EMIGRATION DETAILS ON TOMBSTONES

In some cases information about emigrants is included on Irish tombstones. Many tombstones were erected by immigrant children living throughout the world who sent money back home to put up stones in memory of family and relatives. Stones commonly indicate where the immigrant was living.

Another type of tombstone, erected by an immigrant's parents or siblings who remained in Ireland, listed where the immigrant siblings went worldwide. These can help you in reconstructing a family history of who went where and what happened to each relative. Use the listings of children as a substitute for destroyed parish registers or for time periods before parish registers start. The following few examples should illustrate our point vividly:

Erected by Luke Carson of Savannah, Georgia, United States of America to the Memory of his beloved Father and Mother. Luke Carson of Drumreagh died October 1833 aged 63 years. And his wife Jane Carson died November 1838 aged 52 years. And their daughter Margaret died February 1870 aged 52 years (Kilcarn Graveyard, Killinchy Parish, *Gravestone Inscriptions, County Down*, vol. 5, p. 90).

John Marshall of Crossgaren in memory of his beloved wife Mary who died 5 January 1885 aged 70 years also their daughter Margaret who died 25 September 1863 aged 17 years—Buried in Paisly Cemetery also their son Thomas who died 28 December 1874 aged 38 years at sea also their son William John who died in Australia on the 18th October 1895 age 57 years—The above John Marshall died 4 November 1897 aged 86 years (Macosquin Presbyterian church graveyard, Macosquin Parish, County Londonderry).

Erected by S.J. Reynolds in Loving Memory of Her Mother Sarah McAlevy Who Died at Scarva 11th May 1875 and of Her Father Francis McAlevy, Who Died At Scarva 25th November 1879 and of Her Brother Robert Peel McAlevy Staff Assistant Surgeon Who Died at Meean Meer, Punjaub, India 12th October 1872 and George Washington McAlevy Sixth Son of Francis and Sara McAlevy Who Died at Cebu, Philippine Island 22nd of July 1900 Sarah Jane Raynolds Died 1st December 1914 Mary McAlevy Died 8th December 1918 Aged 68 Years (Roman Catholic church cemetery, Aghaderg, County Down).

In Memory of John Lowry who died 28 May 1887 His Wife Elizabeth Sarah died 16 May 1912 His Sons Hamilton Lowry Rector of Pelham, Lincolnshire Who Died 25 February 1862, Robert Keachey Died at Buenos Aires 21 October 1893, James Atkinson died at Mexico 29 October 1895, William Ainsworth died at Kobe 10 May 1905 His Daughter Alicia Matilda Lowry died 4 August 1925 (Downpatrick Church of Ireland Cathedral cemetery, County Down).

Don't assume your work is done if you find a tombstone transcript. The transcribers might not have listed all the data given on every stone. For this reason it is important to either visit an Irish cemetery yourself or make sure that a complete transcription has been made.

Library/Archive Source

The following are some of the most useful sources and repositories to consult for lists of published tombstone transcripts:

1. Lists of published transcripts are included in the works of John Grenham, James G. Ryan, and Donal Begley.

2. Allen County Public Library in Fort Wayne, Indiana, publishes *Periodical Source Index (PERSI)*, the Irish section of which includes a cemetery category that lists published tombstone transcripts. All journals indexed in *PERSI* are available at the Allen County Public Library. *PERSI* is available on CD-ROM or for a fee at <http://www.ancestry.com>.

3. The Society of Genealogists in London, England, has collected numerous tombstone transcripts of Irish cemeteries. Many of the transcripts are from published works such as genealogical journals and parish histories; other transcripts are in manuscript form. An inventory is *Monumental Inscriptions in the Library of the Society of Genealogists, Part II: Northern England, Wales, Scotland, Ireland, and Overseas,* edited by Lydia Collins and Mabel Morton.

4. At the FHL, *Smith's Inventory of Genealogical Sources: Ireland* series is a crucial research tool and includes a section on tombstone inscriptions for each county (see chapter seventeen). This section lists tombstone transcripts from journals, books, and manuscripts available at the FHL. In addition, cemetery records can be found in the FHL Place Search Catalog under the county, parish, or town.

Although *Smith's Inventory* lists Irish cemetery transcripts available at the Society of Genealogists in London, it does not indicate the original sources of those copies. Here's a suggestion if you find a *Smith's Inventory* reference to a transcript at the Society: Consult *Monumental Inscriptions in the Library of the Society of Genealogists* to find the original source. Frequently the FHL and other libraries have copies of the journal, book, or manuscript that is the original source. For example, *Smith's Inventory* lists transcripts for Camus Juxta Bann (Macosquin) cemetery (County Londonderry) at the Society of Genealogists. *Monumental Inscriptions . . .* shows that the original source is the journal *Scottish Genealogist* 11 (2) (1964): 6–28. You might think from looking at *Smith's Inventory* that the transcript was only available at the society, but it is at the FHL and other libraries as well.

SOME MAJOR TOMBSTONE TRANSCRIPT COLLECTIONS

Genealogical Office manuscripts: The GO in Dublin has some tombstone transcripts, a noteworthy example being the collection of M.R. Lascelles-Kelly (formerly Silles-Kelly) (GO manuscript 564 or 682) available on microfilm through the FHL. About 140 cemeteries from all over Ireland are included. In some cases the collection appears to have only partial cemetary transcripts. A two-part index to names of persons and cemeteries is also included in this collection (GO manuscript 565, mislabeled on FHL microfilm as manuscript 562).

Irish Genealogical Research Society collection: The IGRS in London has compiled a collection of Irish cemetery transcripts, copies of which are available at the IGRS and the GO. You can find a list of the cemeteries included in the collection in John Grenham's book.

"Memorials of the Dead" series: A series of memorial inscriptions from Irish churches, churchyards, and graveyards was published beginning in 1888. The title of the series changed over time, finally becoming the *Journal of the Irish Memorials Association.* Sometimes only selected inscriptions from a particular cemetery were included; other times, the entire graveyard was transcribed. Volumes 1 through 13, no. 1, are available on microfilm through the FHL. The first seven volumes are indexed in *Journal of the Association for the Preservation of the Memorials of the Dead, Ireland. Consolidated Index of Surnames and Place-Names to Volume I to VII (1888–1909)*, by Vigors and Mahony, available on microfilm through the FHL. Some volumes are individually indexed by personal name and place name.

STRATEGIES FOR FINDING GRAVESTONES IN IRELAND

Technique

The search for family gravestones should start with the nearest Catholic or Protestant church graveyard. Many graveyards are attached to the churches themselves. Most Catholic chapels are relatively new buildings dating from the 1850s to the early 1900s. There might be an older cemetery where the original chapel was located, and when the "new" chapel was built, a new cemetery was started. Some parishes have several graveyards, which might be at some distance from the church.

As mentioned, persons of all faiths could be buried in Church of Ireland cemeteries, since the Church of Ireland was the state religion. Besides the family's own denomination, consider graves in Church of Ireland cemeteries. Some Church of Ireland cemeteries had separate Catholic sections.

Other cemeteries in Ireland are not associated with a particular church or congregation's building. You will often find church ruins throughout Ireland filled with tombstones of both Catholics and Protestants. Cemeteries can also be located in fields on their own. In some communities, residents of different denominations might be buried together in such cemeteries.

Local people often know where cemeteries in the area are located. A local undertaker, sexton, or postal official would be a good source of information. If you know a specific townland, a visit on-site can be helpful in identifying relevant cemeteries. Be aware that a person may have gone to church or been buried outside the geographical parish where he or she lived. If a townland was easily accessible to three Catholic chapels, all three parishes' graveyards need to be examined.

Figure 10-1
''Old Church'' Cemetery, Cobh, County Cork, Ireland. Photo used with the permission of Mr. Luke Cassidy, Great Island Historical Society, Cobh, County Cork.

Here are some geographical sources for pinpointing the locations of cemeteries in the area you are researching:

Mitchell's guide: Brian Mitchell's *A Guide to Irish Churches and Graveyards* locates cemeteries by county, civil parish, and townland. Do not, however, assume that all cemeteries in Ireland are listed in this work. It is based on the churches and graveyards listed in Richard Griffith's *General Valuation of Rateable Property in Ireland* (commonly called Griffith's Primary Valuation and dating 1847 to 1864). This book is widely available and is probably the place most people start.

Discovery/Discoverer map series: You can use the modern Discovery Series maps for the Republic and Discoverer Series maps for Northern Ireland. These are modern road maps that show the names of the townlands (not their boundaries) and the locations of cemeteries and other historical and geographical features. If you know your townland, look at all of the cemeteries nearby. You can buy these maps at book stores and even news agents in Ireland, as well as at the Ordnance Survey in Dublin and the Ordnance Survey of Northern Ireland in Belfast. The Irish Genealogical Society International in Saint Paul, Minnesota, has many Discovery/Discoverer Map Series for sale as well.

Original Ordnance Survey Maps: The original 6″-to-the-mile Ordnance Survey maps (dating from the 1830s and 1840s) show the locations of all cemeteries existing at that time. The situation may have changed considerably in the last 150 years. If the cemeteries from the 1830s and 1840s still exist, they should be on the Discovery/Discoverer Series Maps. If an old cemetery hasn't survived to this day, you might be able to find a tombstone transcription of the cemetery in a published or manuscript work. The original Ordnance Survey maps are available on microfiche at a number of libraries in Ireland and abroad.

REFERENCES AND FURTHER READING

Collins, Lydia and Mabel Morton, eds. *Monumental Inscriptions in the Library of the Society of Genealogists, Part II: Northern England, Wales, Scotland, Ireland, and Overseas.* London: Society of Genealogists, 1987.

Langtry, Joe. "Mount Jerome: A Victorian Cemetery." *The Irish At Home and Abroad* 4 (2) (1997): 72–75.

Mitchell, Brian. *A Guide to Irish Churches and Graveyards.* Baltimore: Genealogical Publishing Co., 1990.

Vigors, Miss and Mrs. Peirce G. Mahony. *Journal of the Association for the Preservation of the Memorials of the Dead, Ireland. Consolidated Index of Surnames and Place-Names to Volume I to VII (1888–1909).* Dublin: Ponsonby and Gibbs, 1914.

Sources

ELEVEN

Censuses and Name Lists

\di'fin\ *vb*

Definitions

T he earliest surviving census for Ireland is 1901. Nearly all Irish census returns for 1821, 1831, 1841, and 1851 were destroyed in the Dublin Four Courts fire of 1922. The census returns for 1861, 1871, 1881, and 1891 were pulped after the statistical information was compiled. In addition to the 1901 census, the 1911 census has been released to the public and microfilmed. There are few fragments of earlier censuses in existence.

Because of this destruction, researchers commonly speak in terms of using "census substitutes." **These substitutes are actually partial name lists recorded for a variety of reasons, such as taxation or voter registration.** When used with a realistic sense of their limitations, census substitutes can be helpful in your research.

CENSUS FRAGMENTS

Some fragments of government censuses survive for particular localities. The most important surviving fragments are transcripts of the 1831 census of County Londonderry and much of the 1821 census of County Cavan, both on microfilm at the FHL. Therefore, if you know your county of origin in Ireland, a relevant census fragment might help to determine the origin within the county. The 1831 Census of Londonderry lists head of household and statistics and has been indexed. The 1821 Census of County Cavan listed the name of each member of the family. It was microfilmed twice; use the later microfilming because it is easier to read.

1901 AND 1911 CENSUSES

The 1901 and 1911 censuses for all of Ireland are at the NAI, with microfilm copies at the FHL. Some Irish county libraries have copies of the 1901 census. In order to use the 1901 and 1911 censuses at the FHL, look up the 1901 census reference number for your townland in the 1901 index to townlands in Ireland, which is available at the FHL. Then consult the FHL Place Search Catalog under *Ireland, County, Civil Parish–Censuses* and choose the film with your reference number on it. The censuses of some counties have been indexed and others are being indexed.

If you are researching in one of Ireland's cities, *Ireland 1901 Census Street Index,* compiled by the FHL, lists FHL microfilm numbers for the 1901 census of Ireland, arranged alphabetically by street name within each city. The street index is available on microfiche from the FHL.

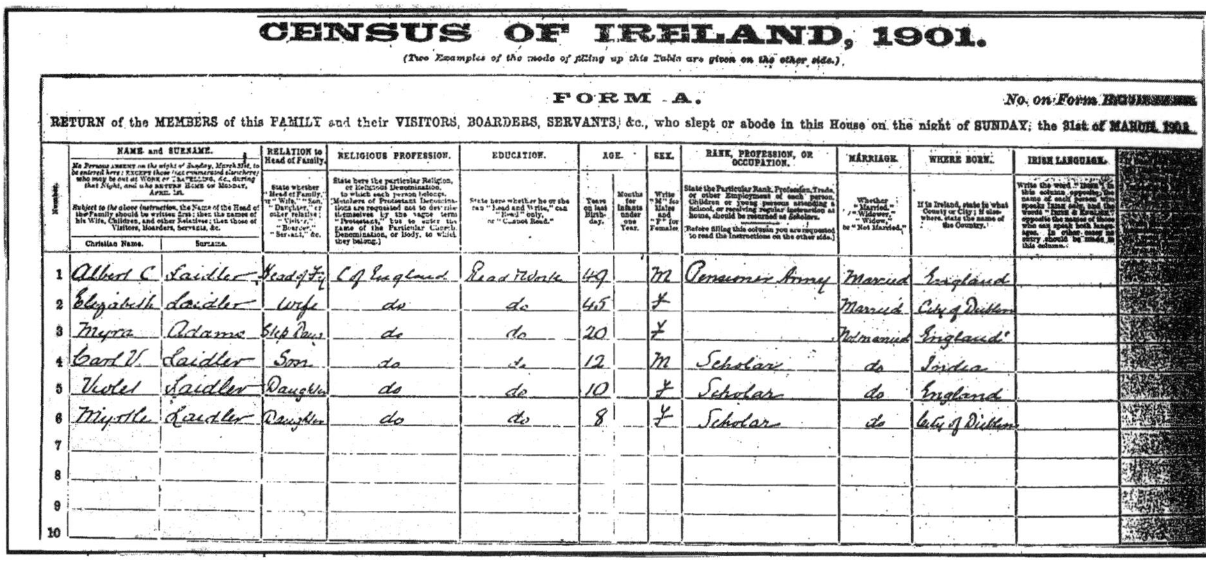

CENSUS OF IRELAND, 1901.

(Two Examples of the mode of filling up this Table are given on the other side.)

FORM A.

No. on Form

RETURN of the MEMBERS of this FAMILY and their VISITORS, BOARDERS, SERVANTS, &c., who slept or abode in this House on the night of SUNDAY, the 31st of MARCH, 1901.

Number	Christian Name	Surname	Relation to Head of Family	Religious Profession	Education	Age: Years on last Birthday	Age: Months for Infants under one Year	Sex	Rank, Profession, or Occupation	Marriage	Where Born	Irish Language
1	Albert C	Laidler	Head of Fy	C of England	Read & Write	49		M	Pensioner Army	Married	England	
2	Elizabeth	Laidler	Wife	do	do	45		F		Married	City of Dublin	
3	Myra	Adams	Step Daur	do	do	20		F		Not married	England	
4	Carl V.	Laidler	Son	do	do	12		M	Scholar	do	India	
5	Violet	Laidler	Daughter	do	do	10		F	Scholar	do	England	
6	Myrtle	Laidler	Daughter	do	do	8		F	Scholar	do	City of Dublin	
7												
8												
9												
10												

Figure 11-1
1901 Census, St. Andrew's Parish, Dublin City. Original at National Archives of Ireland, Dublin. Used with permission of the NAI.

INVENTORIES

Fortunately, many authors have put together lists of what they consider useful census fragments and name lists. We recommend you check each one, since the lists differ. You can find them in all the popular books such as Ryan's, Grenham's, and Mac Conghail and Gorry's. Two other lists are noteworthy. The FHL's list of its holdings in the guide *Register of Irish Census and Census Substitutes*, and the "County Focus" articles published in *The Irish At Home and Abroad* journal.

RELIGIOUS CENSUSES

You can find some censuses in parish registers. For example, a list of Catholic householders in the parish of Killalaghten, County Galway, from 1806 to 1810 is included in Catholic parish registers, which are available on microfilm at the NLI (p. 2431). You can find parish censuses in church records for many denominations, but there has not been a composite listing of them.

Other religious censuses covered a much wider geographical area than just one parish. Two of those, taken in 1740 and 1766, were nearly all destroyed in the 1922 Four Courts fire, but many extracts had been made prior to the fire. The Church of Ireland conducted these censuses at the direction of the Irish Parliament. The 1740 census included Protestant households in some areas of Ulster, and the 1766 census included members of all faiths countrywide. You can find surviving abstracts of the 1740 and 1766 censuses in private collections at the GO, the RCBL, and the NAI. Many are available on microfilm from the FHL, while others have been published in various Irish periodicals.

The 1766 census generally states the name of the head of the family, residence (townland, parish, and county or diocese), and religion. Some returns give the number of family members; other returns are more statistical in nature. Australia's Immigration and Family History Centre is producing *1766 Irish Religious Census—Part 1*. The first volume contains eleven thousand names from selected parts of Ireland taken from two sources: the Tenison Groves Manuscripts (GO Ms. 536–537) and the transcript "Tuam Wills" by Philip Crossle. Both are on microfilm at the FHL.

SOME CENSUS SUBSTITUTES (NAME LISTS)

Notes

1796 spinning wheel survey: In 1796 the Irish Parliament began distributing spinning wheels and reels to people growing specified quantities of flax for the linen trade. A list of recipients was compiled by parish and county. This survey is an important source if you have ancestors from a county like Tyrone, where there was a linen trade and many people qualified for the wheels and reels. Because the average Presbyterian or Catholic church register does not begin until the 1820s or 1830s, the Spinning Wheel Survey is one of the few sources for the eighteenth century in which to trace the common Irish family.

The original survey is available on microfilm from the FHL. The lists for counties Dublin and Wicklow apparently have not survived; County Longford listings are by barony rather than by parish. Brøderbund produced a CD-ROM Index, "International Land Records: Irish Flax Growers, 1796" (CD#271).

Census searches for old age pension applications: There is a lot of potential in this set of records. Old age pensions were introduced in Ireland in 1908. To prove how old they were, people seventy and over could request a search of the then-surviving 1841 and 1851 censuses.

Applicants could send their requests directly to the PRO in Dublin where the staff extracted the information from the censuses. Abstracts of the census entries showing the applicants were noted on census search forms between 1910 and 1922. The "Census Search Forms" are now arranged at the NAI by county, barony, civil parish, and townland.

Alternatively, you could also make a request to the PRO by a local pension office for a search of the 1841 and 1851 censuses. The resulting "Form 37s" survive for large areas of Ulster and are held at the PRONI, with microfilm copies at the FHL. Josephine Masterson produced two volumes indexing Form

37s from the PRONI, one for Northern Ireland counties and another for Republic of Ireland counties.

Census Search Forms and Form 37s might include extracts of the entire household in the 1841 and 1851 censuses. So, even if an applicant was not your ancestor, you might get information not only on the person who applied for the search, but also on brothers, sisters and parents—who might include your ancestor.

Freeholders lists: A freeholder either owned land outright or held land for the term of his life or a "lease of lives." Freeholders with land of a qualifying value held the right to vote. Many lists of freeholders were printed or survive as abstracts (see chapter nineteen).

Catholic qualification rolls: Beginning in 1774, Catholics could take an oath of allegiance to the Crown. A transcript of the oaths from 1775 to 1776, giving names, occupations, and addresses, was made by Ignatius Jennings and published as Appendix III (pp. 50–84) in the *59th Report of the Deputy Keeper of the Records* (1961). The *59th Report* is available at the NLI. Starting in 1778, taking the oath gave Catholics certain rights, so many more people are recorded taking the oath from this year onward. There is an index to Catholic Qualification Rolls from 1778 to 1790 at the NAI with a microfilm copy at the FHL. For further details about the qualification rolls and their background, see Kyle J. Betit's article "Catholic Qualification Rolls, 1775–1801" in *The Irish At Home and Abroad.*

REFERENCES AND FURTHER READING

Sources

Betit, Kyle J. "Catholic Qualification Rolls, 1775–1801." *The Irish At Home and Abroad* 6 (4) (4th Quarter 1999): 165–167.

"Irish Manuscript Ecclesiastical Census Returns: A Survey With an Example From Clogherny Parish, Co. Tyrone 1851–1852." *Local Population Studies* 29 (Autumn 1982): 35–49.

Mannion, Marie. "The 1908 Old Age Pension Claims." *Galway Roots (Clanna na Gaillimhe): Journal of the Galway Family History Society West* IV (1996–97): 157–160.

Masterson, Josephine. *Ireland: 1841/1851 Census Abstracts (Northern Ireland).* Baltimore: Genealogical Publishing Co., 1999.

———. *Ireland: 1841/1851 Census Abstracts (Republic of Ireland)* Baltimore: Genealogical Publishing Co., 1999.

Reakes, Janet and Eileen Johnson. *1766 Irish Religious Census—Part 1.* Microfiche. Queensland, Australia: Australia's Immigration and Family History Centre, 1995.

Reilly, James R. "The Old Age Pension, an Unfamiliar Source." *Newsletter of The Irish Family History Forum, Inc.* 3 (Oct. 1993): 1–2.

Addresses

Australia's Immigration and Family History Centre
P.O. Box 937, Hervey Bay, Queensland 4655, Australia
phone/fax: (071) 28 4458

Church Records

hatever your Irish ancestors' denomination, the church was part of their lives. This means that some of your ancestors' records were probably kept by their church. These usually included records such as birth or baptism, marriage, and death or burial. Church records might not begin early in Ireland, but hopefully they precede the Irish government's keeping of civil registration.

Roman Catholics make up the majority of Ireland's population. The second largest denomination is the Church of Ireland, followed by Presbyterianism. Methodists are the fourth-largest community. Minority faiths of historical significance include the Baptists, Congregationalists, Huguenots (French Calvinists), Jews, Moravians (United Brethren), Mormons, and Quakers (Society of Friends). John Calvin (1509–1564) was born in France and was a leader in the sixteenth-century Protestant Reformation. He laid a theological foundation upon which Presbyterianism, Congregationalism, and the Huguenot churches developed. The standard text on Irish church records is *Irish Church Records*, edited by James G. Ryan. This book is an advanced text that discusses the records of most faiths represented in Ireland, but it excludes Congregationalists, Moravians, Mormons, and some other denominations.

Regardless of an ancestor's faith, do not overlook the records of the Church of Ireland. Roman Catholics and non-conformists were commonly buried in Church of Ireland cemeteries. If a Catholic or Presbyterian family had real estate, members of the family might have had a Church of Ireland marriage ceremony to make the union legal and preserve their property rights. In the eighteenth century, you will find baptisms of non-conformists (e.g., Presbyterians, and Methodists) in Church of Ireland registers.

Omissions and errors are found in parish registers. For example, Riobard O'Dwyer, who compiled a series of books regarding the genealogy of families of the Beara Peninsula of County Cork, found 350 errors in the first thirty-two

Membership in Irish Churches According to the 1861 Census	
Total Population	5,794,864
Roman Catholic	4,505,265
Church of Ireland	693,357
Presbyterian	523,291
Methodist	45,399
Independent	4,532
Baptist	4,237
Quaker	3,695
Jew	393
Other	14,695

Note: The category "other" may include Christian, Congregationalist, Lutheran, Moravian, and different sects of Presbyterianism.

years of the Eyeries Catholic parish registers. In the same parish he found that two hundred people were never entered in the Eyeries baptismal records.

Step By Step

STEP-BY-STEP: SEARCHING PARISH REGISTERS

1. If you know the county your ancestors lived in, you can contact the appropriate heritage centre that has indexed the church records for that county (see chapter sixteen).

2. Whether or not the heritage centre helps you find records of your family, you will want to consult the original church records for more information and to check the accuracy of the indexes. The heritage centres have not indexed all church records, and there are inevitably errors and omissions.

3. If you know a specific town or townland where your ancestors lived, you can find out what churches of your ancestor's denomination served that place. One easy way to do this is to use the *Irish Times* Irish Ancestors Web site, <http://www.ireland.com/ancestor>, which charges a fee. Alternatively, look up the availability of church records in several sources, among them Brian Mitchell's *A Guide to Irish Parish Registers*, which lists church registers for selected denominations according to the civil parish and the year registers began. For Ulster, see the PRONI's *An Irish Genealogical Source: Guide to Church Records*, which details records held in Belfast repositories and local churches. Books and articles published about particular counties frequently include information about church registers.

Technique

EMIGRATION STRATEGIES

1. You might find details of your ancestor's emigration in an Irish church record. This varies by denomination, if not by congregation. Some churches gave transfer certificates or letters to emigrating members to be presented to their new congregations in their new homes. Transfer records were common among the Quakers, the Moravians, and the Presbyterians.

2. Sometimes when a heritage centre finds records of a family in a parish

register, there is no indication of where the family lived in the parish (e.g., the townland). In cases like this, church records can be used along with other sources to pinpoint a townland of residence. You can look in tax records such as Griffith's Valuation or the Tithe Applotment Books to see where parents, witnesses at marriages, and godparents may have been living. The names of witnesses and godparents should be provided by the heritage centre.

3. The name of a minister associated with your immigrant ancestor could be important. Your ancestor might have left Ireland with a minister who took his congregation to settle elsewhere. If you can trace the minister's origin in Ireland, you have indirectly traced your own ancestor's origin.

4. A date of birth or baptism in an Irish church register can differ from the date expected from immigrant records. It would not be unusual to see a variation of up to ten years when the actual baptismal record is found.

For More Info

CELTIC CHRISTIANITY

Celtic Christianity, symbolized by the Celtic Cross, was a fusion of native belief with Christian doctrine. The Celtic Cross combines the Cross of Christ with a circle representing the old, pre-Christian beliefs. Also symbolic of Celtic Christianity are illuminated manuscripts designed by Irish monks, which interweave animals with Christian symbols. Christian saints replaced older Celtic figures in the consciousness of Irish people. The fusion of native and Christian beliefs dates back to the fourth century and Saint Patrick, who is credited with converting the Irish people. The early missionaries in Ireland incorporated native symbols and beliefs into Christianity rather than eradicating them. Even today, you see an emphasis on nature in Irish spirituality: holy wells, sacred mountains, pilgrimage places, islands with spiritual significance, sacred rocks. Both the Roman Catholic Church in Ireland and the Church of Ireland see their roots in Celtic Christianity of the early centuries.

CHURCH OF IRELAND

The Church of Ireland is a catholic, reformed church and is part of the worldwide Anglican Communion of churches. Historically, the term "Protestant" was used in Ireland in its most narrow sense to refer strictly to members of the Church of Ireland. It was the Established Church, or official religion of the government of Ireland, from 1536 to 1871. Other churches were termed "nonconformist" because they did not conform to the official religion.

Church of Ireland parishes are grouped into dioceses; a diocese is led by a bishop. Records of genealogical value are mainly found on the parish level. However, Church of Ireland dioceses were responsible for recording wills, administrations, and marriage licenses until 1858. The Church of Ireland Who

Figure 12-1
Donaghadee Church of Ireland, County Down. Photograph by Todd Madsen Frazier.

We Are Web site <http://www.ireland.anglican.org/geninfo/whoweare.html> provides good background.

Church of Ireland registers were official government documents. Many Church of Ireland registers had been deposited at the Public Record Office of Ireland prior to 1922, when the office was burned during the Irish Civil War. All but four of the 1,006 deposited registers were lost, but some of the burned registers had been copied or published prior to the fire. The most common Church of Ireland records are of baptism, marriage, and burial. Because the Church of Ireland churchyard was a public burying place, its burial records are particularly important. Some of these churchyards even had separate Catholic sections.

Church of Ireland records are held in various locations. Some are being indexed by heritage centres throughout Ireland, and this might be your first place to start your search. The PRONI holds microfilm copies of most of the Church of Ireland registers for Northern Ireland and for counties Cavan, Donegal, Leitrim, Louth, and Monaghan. Many registers for the Republic of Ireland are deposited in the NAI and the RCBL. One surprising repository of registers is the Maritime History Archive at the Memorial University of Newfoundland, which has microfilm for many parishes in counties Cork, Tipperary, and Waterford. Kyle J. Betit's article "Memorial University of Newfoundland" in *The Irish At Home and Abroad*, provides an inventory of church registers at this repository. Some registers from the Republic are still in local custody. To locate the addresses of local parishes, consult a current Church of Ireland directory.

There are three excellent inventories of records and their locations. These are (1) Noel Reid's *A Table of Church of Ireland Parochial Records and Copies;* (2) for Ulster parishes, *An Irish Genealogical Source: Guide to Irish Church Records;* and (3) for registers at the RCBL, Raymond Refaussé's *A Handlist of Church of Ireland Parish Registers in the Representative Church Body Library, Dublin.*

Aside from the typical birth/baptism, marriage, and burial records, you will want to consult some of the following records:

Vestry Minutes: Don't limit your search to the baptism, marriage, and burial records. You can find important details about your ancestor's life and circumstances in vestry minutes. You will find signatures of the vestry members, who conduct the affairs of the parish; sometimes parish censuses; and lists of poor parishioners. Vestry minutes are not limited to members of the Church of Ireland. If the church registers have been destroyed, vestry minutes can serve as a substitute source of information about your ancestor. Most vestry minutes are held in local custody, although some have been deposited at the RCBL and the PRONI. See Raymond Refaussé's *A Handlist of Church of Ireland Vestry Minute Books in the Representative Church Body Library, Dublin.*

Parish Search Forms: Another source for reconstructing lost parish registers is the Parish Search Forms. Prior to the 1922 destruction of the Public Record Office, the office made abstracts of baptismal registers at the request of individuals for proof of age and other purposes. These Parish Search Forms, now available at the NAI, are listed in the "Parish Registers and Related Material" catalog in alphabetical order by parish.

Church of Ireland Ministers: If your ancestor was a Church of Ireland minister, detailed information about him might be available. Many of the ministers attended Trinity College Dublin, and their biographical information is preserved in the college's records. See *Alumni Dublinenses,* edited by Burtchaell and Sadleir. Trinity College Dublin (the University of Dublin) was established in 1592 for the education of prominent Protestants, including Church of Ireland ministers. Its students were exclusively Protestant until 1793.

"Biographical succession lists" describe the clergy on a diocesan basis. Some succession lists have been published, while others remain in unpublished form at the RCBL. The RCBL has a four-volume unpublished index of ministers listed in the biographical succession lists. Among the data you can find in the lists is the names of the minister's parents, wife, and children, where the minister was educated, and the places where he served.

To identify the diocese or urban parish to which a clergyman was attached, consult commercial directories or clergy directories. For example, J. Pigot's 1824 *City of Dublin and Hibernian Provincial Directory* has a composite alphabetical index of the nobility, gentry, and clergy listed under each town in Ireland. Beginning in 1814 with Samuel Percy Lea's *Ecclesiastical Registry,* separate directories of ministers were occasionally published. Beginning in 1862 the *Irish Church Directory* was published every year and listed the ministers serving in each diocese with an overall index of ministers.

BAPTISTS

Followers of Cromwell established several Baptist congregations in Ireland beginning in 1651, but many disappeared with the restoration of the monarchy in 1660. Baptist churches were established again beginning in the early nineteenth century. Baptists were a small religious denomination in Ireland and are named for their practice of baptizing believers upon a confession of faith, not at infancy. You can find notations of baptisms in the congregation's minutes. Membership lists can give you information about emigration, transfers between congregations, marriages, and deaths. Nearly all Baptist registers are in local congregational hands; some, however, are available at the PRONI or the Irish Baptist Historical Society. The society has published *Irish Baptist Historical Society Journal* since 1968. Contact the society for information about particular congregations and the whereabouts of their records. A few records extend back to the seventeenth and eighteenth centuries.

CONGREGATIONALISTS

The Congregational Church was present in Ireland in the latter half of the seventeenth century and from the 1790s, when Congregational churches were established in Dublin. Congregational churches were founded in Ulster in the first half of the nineteenth century. The Congregational Church has been a small denomination in Ireland. Many records from County Dublin and other locations are held at the PRONI, while others are in local custody. Congregationalists kept membership lists in which you can find details about members emigrating or transferring to other congregations. The records also include baptismal and marriage registers.

HUGUENOTS

French Huguenots were Calvinist Protestants who settled in Ireland between the late 1500s and mid-1700s. They fled Catholic France due to religious persecution and founded settlements throughout Ireland. If your Irish ancestor's surname appears to be French, it might be that the name went to Ireland with a French Huguenot refugee.

\di'fin\ *vb*

Definitions

There were "French churches" in Ireland that operated as part of the Church of Ireland (known as "conformist") and other French churches that operated independently (known as "non-conformist"). Where there were no separate French churches, the registers of the local Church of Ireland parishes are often a primary source for documenting Huguenot families. Over time the descendants of the Huguenot refugees joined or married into the Church of Ireland and other denominations in Ireland.

There are not many Irish Huguenot church records that survive. The surviving ones were published in volumes 7, 14, and 19 of *Publications of the Huguenot Society of London*. The Irish Section of the Huguenot Society of Great Britain and Ireland has an archive in the RCBL. Its collections include family papers, church registers, and other Huguenot material. Archbishop Marsh's Library in Dublin holds the Huguenot Charitable Fund papers that contain transcripts of many Dublin Huguenot records.

JEWS

There were few Jews in Ireland until the late nineteenth century. Some did, however, live in Ireland beginning in the eighteenth century, the earliest communities being in the cities of Dublin and Cork. **In the late nineteenth and early twentieth centuries, several thousand Jews went to Ireland from Eastern Europe, particularly Russia.** The 1911 census showed that there were 5,148 Jews in Ireland. The Irish Jewish Museum in Dublin holds the Registry Book of the Dublin congregation that is published in Louis Hyman's *A History of the Jews in Ireland*. In Ireland there was a high rate of intermarriage between Jews and Christians, and as a result many Jews in Ireland converted to Christianity or raised children as Christians.

METHODISTS

Methodist societies began forming in England in the early 1730s under Rev. John Wesley (1703–1791) as a movement within the Church of England. John Wesley visited Ireland many times, and Methodist societies soon spread among members of the Church of Ireland. At first, members of Methodist societies remained part of the Church of Ireland or Presbyterian churches. In the 1780s some emigrant members of Irish Methodist societies formed the first Methodist churches in the United States. Thus, the first independent Methodist churches formed by the Irish were in America, not Ireland.

It was not until about 1818 that a group of Methodists in Ireland separated from the Church of Ireland and formed the Irish Wesleyan Methodist Church with its own ministers and its own records. Methodists who continued to belong to the Church of Ireland were known as Primitive Wesleyan Methodists. In 1878 the two groups united to form the Methodist Church in Ireland.

Methodist records useful to your genealogical research include class lists (lists of members of each class in the society), baptismal registers, and marriage registers. Baptismal registers are nearly all arranged on a circuit basis while marriage registers are on a congregational basis. The congregations that comprised a circuit changed often, which can complicate the search for the relevant circuit register. Methodist records generally remain in the custody of the society or circuit. Some have also been indexed by heritage centres. The PRONI holds a microfilm copy of the central register of baptisms in the Irish Wesleyan Methodist Church.

A history that can shed light on individual Methodist ancestors is C.H. Crookshank's three-volume *History of Methodism in Ireland*. This work includes information about preachers and prominent members of the Methodist societies from 1747 to 1859. Crookshank's history is indexed by people and places. An excellent guide to Methodist research from a genealogical perspective is Steven C. ffeary-Smyrl's *Irish Methodists—Where Do I Start?*

Aside from the registers themselves, there are a few things you will need to know while researching an Irish Methodist family. These are the German Palatines and Methodist Ministers.

Irish Palatines: The Palatine families who settled in Ireland in the early 1700s were Protestant refugees from the Palatinate Rhineland (now Germany). They generally attended Church of Ireland worship when they first arrived, then many became Methodists. Although they were settled by the British government in a number of places in Ireland, the largest group was settled in County Limerick near the town of Rathkeale on the Southwell estate, where they maintained culturally distinct communities. A significant group of the Irish Methodist Palatines emigrated to what is now the province of Ontario in Canada in the 1820s.

\di'fin\ *vb*

Definitions

Henry Z Jones's book *The Palatine Families of Ireland* has a genealogical focus and is organized by surname. It traces each Palatine family through several generations, beginning with its origins in the Palatinate. Several excellent histories have been written of the Palatine migrations and settlements, including Patrick J. O'Connor's *People Make Places: The Story of the Irish Palatines* and Carolyn A. Heald's *The Irish Palatines in Ontario: Religion, Ethnicity and Rural Migration.* For a genealogical experience, see Carolyn A. Heald's article "Researching Irish Palatines in Ireland and Ontario" published in *The Irish At Home and Abroad.*

Methodist Ministers: If your ancestor served as a Methodist minister in Ireland, there might be detailed information available about him and his family. In her monumental work, *Irish and Scotch-Irish Ancestral Research*, Margaret Dickson Falley reproduced two lists from *Thom's* 1847 directory: one an alphabetical list of Wesleyan Methodist ministers, showing the year each minister began to travel and the name of his circuit; and the other an alphabetical list of Primitive Wesleyan Methodist ministers showing the name of each minister's circuit. An extensive database of Methodist ministers is being compiled by Rev. Robin Roddie [Epworth, 16 Brooklands Road, Newtownards, County Down BT23 4TL, Northern Ireland; e-mail: robin_roddie@msn.com].

MORAVIANS (UNITED BRETHREN)

The first Moravian associations were established in Bohemia in 1458. The Moravian Church was founded in Ireland in 1746 by missionaries from England. There were three types of Moravian organizations in Ireland: the society, the congregation, and the settlement. A society had its own minister and a building. Congregations were smaller and scattered throughout rural parts of Ireland. A settlement was a community where members lived together and were economically self-sufficient. There were Moravian congregations in Ballinderry, Belfast, and Gracehill in County Antrim; Cootehill in County Cavan; Corofin in County Clare; Kilkeel and Kilwarlin in County Down; Dublin City; and Gracefield in County Londonderry.

The number of Moravians in Ireland during the eighteenth and nineteenth centuries is uncertain, but J. Taylor Hamilton in *A History of The Church Known as the Moravian Church* estimates the number at five thousand in 1834.

The strength of the Irish Moravian church has always been in the northern province of Ulster.

The Moravians kept records of baptisms and marriages. Burial records were also kept if there was a specifically Moravian burial ground. Moravian records might include a list of members and their families, details on movements and emigration of church members, information about services held, and absences of members, as well as arrivals, departures and deaths of members. Ministers' diaries often provide a biographical sketch of a member who has died. All Irish Moravian records have been microfilmed and are at the PRONI.

MORMONS (LATTER-DAY SAINTS)

The Church of Jesus Christ of Latter-day Saints (Mormons or LDS Church) was founded in 1830 in New York state by Joseph Smith (1805 to 1844), who proclaimed a restored Christian religion with new scriptures. It is neither Catholic nor Protestant. You might find that one of your ancestor's brothers or sisters joined the Mormon church and left behind a family historical record with details about your ancestors in Ireland. If you find an entry for your family on one of the LDS computer databases, such as the Ancestral File, it may be your first clue that there is a Mormon branch in your family. The records of the LDS Church should never be overlooked because its members kept detailed family history records often dating back generations before the church was even founded.

The first LDS missionaries went to Ireland in 1840 with most activity confined to Ulster, although there was a presence in Dublin, Athlone, Carrickmacross, Rathkeale, and near Tullamore. Official church policy encouraged converts to settle in Mormon colonies in the western United States. As a result, the church did not acquire a more stable membership in Ireland until the 1880s. Interesting enough, many more Irish converted to the faith while living in England, Wales, and Scotland. LDS records for Great Britain, Ireland, and the United States are on microfilm at the FHL (see chapter two).

PRESBYTERIANS

Scottish lowlanders who were settled in Ulster during the seventeenth century Plantation of Ulster brought their Presbyterian religion with them. The majority of the Presbyterian churches in Ireland are located in the northern counties of Ireland with others scattered throughout the island. There was a high rate of emigration of Presbyterians from Ulster. It was these Presbyterian immigrants who became known in American history as the Scotch-Irish or Scots-Irish. Some scholars also use the term Ulster Scots. **(See pages 43 to 46.)**

See Also

For the history of individual Irish Presbyterian congregations, see the Presbyterian Historical Society of Ireland's *A History of Congregations in the Presbyterian Church in Ireland, 1610–1982*. It includes a brief history of each congregation with the succession of ministers, date the congregation began, and whether it merged or closed. It does not include the status of records. The society published a supplement and index to this work in 1996. You can also find a detailed study of the Presbyterian faith in Margaret D. Falley's chapter, "Presbyterian Records" in *Irish and Scotch-Irish Ancestral Research*.

The Presbyterian faith was divided into rival branches, such as non-subscribing, succeeder, or covenantor, during the eighteenth and nineteenth centuries. One town could have several Presbyterian churches, one for each of the divisions. If you can find surviving records in a community for more than one Presbyterian denomination, you would be wise to search all of them.

The two main Presbyterian denominations (Session Synod and Synod of Ulster) united in 1840, but the Reformed Presbyterians have remained separate to this day. During the twentieth century, many smaller congregations have united, so the combined congregation might have all the earlier records.

Don't look for most Presbyterian records to begin until the early 1800s. Although many of the original registers are still with the local churches, the PRONI has an extensive collection of microfilm copies. The Presbyterian Historical Society in Belfast has some registers not in the PRONI collection, including many of the earliest surviving records dating from the 1700s.

You will often find records of Presbyterians in Church of Ireland parish registers and vestry minutes. A family might commonly have some children baptized

For More Info

PRESBYTERIAN MINISTERS

Irish Presbyterian ministers are important figures for genealogy, since some brought their congregations abroad, and others' names can be in family records. Thus, tracing the minister's origins in Ireland indirectly traces your own origins. To document a minister, look in the following "Fasti" books (list books), which contain brief biographical sketches about where the minister trained, where he was stationed, and often his birth, death, and emigration information:

- Loughridge, Adam. *Fasti of the Reformed Presbyterian Church of Ireland.* [S.I.]: Reformed Presbyterian Synod of Ireland and Presbyterian Historical Society, 1970.

- McConnell, James and Samuel G. McConnell. *Fasti of the Irish Presbyterian Church, 1613–1840.* Belfast: Presbyterian Historical Society, 1951.

- Barkley, John M. *Fasti of the General Assembly of the Presbyterian Church in Ireland, 1840–1910.* (3 parts in 1). Belfast: Presbyterian Historical Society, 1986–1987.

There are also almanacs that list where Presbyterian ministers were serving. Simm and McIntyre's *Belfast Almanack*, published in 1837, lists ministers and their addresses in the Presbyterian Synod of Ulster. William McComb's 1857 *Presbyterian Almanack* alphabetically lists the ministers of the General Assembly of the Presbyterian Church, indicating their congregation and post town. Copies of these almanacs are at the PHS or NLI.

in the Presbyterian church and others baptized in the Church of Ireland. You might even find some of the children baptized in the Methodist church!

Another important source that is often overlooked is the session minutes of the congregation. These minutes concern the daily affairs of the congregation and often predate the registers of births and marriages by as much as a century. In the body of the minutes, you might find lurid details about your ancestor's life. Session minutes sometimes contain references to vital events such as marriage.

RELIGIOUS SOCIETY OF FRIENDS (QUAKERS)

The Religious Society of Friends, or Quakers, originated in England under the leadership of George Fox, and the society went to Ireland in the 1650s. Several Quaker Meetings did not survive into the nineteenth century. There were about three thousand members in Ireland in 1845. The large number of Quaker immigrants to America in the seventeenth and eighteenth centuries makes Irish Quaker records especially important in these centuries.

The Friends gathered in "meetings," which were grouped into "monthly meetings." Monthly meetings were in turn organized into provincial meetings. The Irish Provincial Meetings belonged to the Dublin Yearly (or National) Meeting. A Quaker family might have belonged to a Monthly Meeting centered in a county neighboring the county where it actually lived.

You can find a "List of Chief Irish Quaker Surnames," in Appendix 2.1 in Richard Harrison's chapter "Irish Quaker Records" in *Irish Church Records*, edited by James G. Ryan. A more extensive list, "Surnames Occurring in Irish Quaker Registers," is in Olive C. Goodbody's *Guide to Irish Quaker Records 1654–1860*.

The "Jones Index" at the DFHL is an excellent detailed research tool that shows which monthly meetings each surname was associated with. The "Jones Index" is computerized and is also available on microfilm at the FHL.

You can find Quaker records at the PRONI, the Society of Friends Library, in Belfast, the DFHL and other repositories. Goodbody's book *Guide to Irish Quaker Records, 1654–1860* discusses the records available in Irish repositories. In her work you can find information not only about the records of particular meetings but also about family collections, diaries, will abstracts, and other genealogical material.

Quaker records of births, marriages, and burials extend back into the mid-1600s. Records called "abstract registers" were created from the original records, and you can access these at the DFHL or on microfilm through the FHL.

Abstracts from the records of the Quaker Monthly Meetings at Bandon, Cork, and Youghal, County Cork, are in volume 11 of Albert E. Casey's *O'Kief, Coshe Mang, Slieve Lougher and Upper Blackwater in Ireland*.

Monthly meetings had books of removals recording emigration abroad and migration within Ireland. Minute books record certificates of emigration. Some of the original certificates of removal survive. For example, the DFHL holds certificates of removal for the Dublin Monthly Meeting dating back to 1682.

For More Info

THE REFORMATION AND THE PENAL LAWS

In 1536, the Irish Parliament adopted the Act of Supremacy, making King Henry VIII supreme head of the Church of Ireland and denying the authority of the pope. In the centuries to come, Irish subjects of the British monarchy resisted this denial of the pope's authority. James II, a Roman Catholic, ascended the throne of England and Ireland in 1685. But the parliament did not want a Catholic king, so it invited the Protestant William, Prince of Orange and son-in-law of James II, to invade England by force. In 1690 at the Battle of the Boyne in Ireland, William defeated James II. James fled to the European continent, and the Treaty of Limerick terminated the war. William and his wife, Mary, succeeded to the throne of England and Ireland.

Following the Battle of the Boyne, the Church of Ireland minority held power over the Catholic majority and the non-conformists. The wholly Protestant Irish parliament passed anti-Catholic legislation in Ireland beginning in 1695, and the 1704 Act To Prevent the Further Growth of Popery placed many restrictions on Catholics. They were forbidden to observe Catholic holy days, to make pilgrimages, or to use the old monasteries for burying their dead. Priests who were members of religious orders (such as Franciscans and Jesuits) and Catholic bishops were exiled, but many remained in Ireland and were tolerated by the government. The penal laws lasted until they were repealed between 1772 and 1829. Some of the penal laws, such as those governing property, were carefully followed. Many of the laws, however, were largely ignored or circumvented. Many landholding and prominent Catholic families converted to the Church of Ireland to retain their rights.

ROMAN CATHOLICS

Celtic Christianity differed significantly from the practices of Rome for centuries. This might be one explanation for why parish registers begin comparatively late in Ireland. The starting dates of Catholic parish registers vary widely depending on the county and the parish. Some registers from cities such as Cork and Dublin begin in the early or middle eighteenth century. In contrast, registers for many parishes in County Donegal do not commence until after the 1850s. Maps showing the dates of first surviving church registers are in Kevin Whelan's article "The Regional Impact of Irish Catholicism 1700–1850" in *Common Ground: Essays on the Historical Geography of Ireland*.

Historically, Catholicism in Ireland cannot be judged by today's standards of Catholic practice. The Catholic Church was weakened by the religious struggles of the sixteenth and seventeenth centuries; it was only in the late nineteenth century that the Catholic Church became a dominant feature of life for Irish Catholics. You might think your eighteenth-century Irish Catholic ancestor went to Mass every week, but in fact he or she might have seen a priest only rarely. The local unit of the Catholic Church is the parish. Catholic parishes are grouped into dioceses; a diocese is governed by a bishop. Records of genealogical value are kept mainly on a parish level. One reason for the scarcity of priests and disorganization of parishes was the set of Penal Laws that restricted Catholic clergy in the eighteenth century.

You can find microfilm copies of nearly all Catholic parish records, including those in Northern Ireland, up to 1880 at the NLI. Some of these microfilm copies are at the FHL. The FHL has also independently microfilmed some registers into the early twentieth century. The PRONI has microfilm copies of the pre-1880 registers for Ulster province.

Important

As of this writing, you have to get written permission from the bishop of the diocese in order to examine the registers from the dioceses of Kerry and Limerick at the NLI:

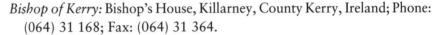

> *Bishop of Kerry:* Bishop's House, Killarney, County Kerry, Ireland; Phone: (064) 31 168; Fax: (064) 31 364.
>
> *Bishop of Limerick:* Kilmoyle, North Circular Road, Limerick, Ireland; Phone: (061) 451 433; Fax: (061) 310 186.

Permission is usually granted for family historians researching their own ancestors. If you know only that your ancestor came from either County Kerry or County Limerick, your best strategy might be to contact the relevant heritage centre to search its indexes. Even though the Diocese of Kerry registers are closed to the public, you can get information from them without writing the bishop for permission. The Killarney Genealogical Centre is indexing records of Kerry parishes; the Maritime History Archive has microfilm copies of some Kerry Catholic registers, and other registers have been abstracted in Albert E. Casey's *O'Kief, Coshe Mang, Slieve Lougher, and Upper Blackwater in Ireland* (indexed in the Mormon IGI computer database, available on the Internet, <http://www.familysearch.org>).

The Archbishop of Cashel and Emly does not presently grant permission for registers from his diocese to be examined at the NLI. All researchers are referred to the Tipperary Heritage Unit to access information from parishes in this diocese. See chapter sixteen.

The Maritime History Archive of the Memorial University of Newfoundland has Roman Catholic registers on microfilm for counties Donegal, Kerry, Kilkenny, Waterford, and Wexford. The Archive collected these records because many of the settlers of Newfoundland came from these areas of Ireland and were involved in the maritime industry.

You might find that one Catholic parish used several names. Sometimes the parish was known by the name of the town or townland where it was located, and other times the ancient medieval parish name was used. The NLI usually lists these names at the beginning of the microfilm copy of the parish records. Beware that some parishes do cross county boundaries. Sketched maps of Catholic parishes within each county are in John Grenham's *Tracing Your Irish Ancestors: The Complete Guide*. Samuel Lewis's 1837 *Topographical Dictionary of Ireland* lists under each civil parish the Catholic parishes and chapels within its boundaries.

If you're looking for your family's origins in Ireland, the quickest way to find out might be to trace the life of the family member who became a priest or joined a religious order. This is because good records were kept on these people, records that might indicate where the family originated in Ireland and the parents' names. Religious orders such as the Dominicans and Franciscans include both priests and brothers. Other priests who do not belong to an order are attached to a diocese and its bishop. *The Irish Catholic Directory, Almanac and Registry,* published annually since 1836, includes for each diocese an alphabetical list of parish priests with their curates (assistants), giving the names of their parishes and the location of chapels with their post towns. There is also information on deceased priests.

The main places you can find records of diocesan priests are diocesan archives and seminary archives. For priests, brothers, and sisters belonging to religious orders, the main repository of records is the archives of the order. The addresses of Catholic dioceses, seminaries, and religious orders are in the current edition of *The Irish Catholic Directory.* The Catholic Central Library in Dublin holds copies of *The Irish Catholic Directory* from 1836 to the present. The library also has collections of books and periodicals relating to church history and to the history of religious orders in Ireland.

St. Patrick's College, Maynooth was established in 1795 by act of Parliament for the training of Catholic priests. Since Maynooth was founded, more than ten thousand Catholic priests have studied there. Prior to its establishment, many priests studied in continental colleges in Spain, France, Italy, and elsewhere. Although Maynooth's *Matriculation Register* was destroyed in a fire in 1940, Patrick J. Hamell's *Maynooth Students and Ordinations Index 1795–1895* gives the name of the student, his diocese, date of matriculation, class, and ordination date.

Other colleges for training priests were established in Ireland beginning in 1793 with St. Patrick's in Carlow. All Hallows College was established to train priests for missions abroad. Extensive information about the students, including their parents' names and addresses, is in Kevin Condon's *The Missionary College of All Hallows 1842–1891.*

The nineteenth century saw a dramatic increase in the number of women's religious orders in Ireland. In 1801 there were six orders of nuns (Benedictines, Carmelites, Dominicans, Poor Clares, Presentation Sisters, and Ursulines) living in eleven convents. One hundred years later, there were thirty-five religious orders and 368 convents in Ireland. Kyle J. Betit's article "Priests, Nuns and Brothers in Ireland" in *The Irish At Home and Abroad* discusses the records of priests and religious orders and how to get them.

REFERENCES AND FURTHER READING
General

Betit, Kyle J. "Memorial University of Newfoundland." *The Irish At Home and Abroad* 3 (1995/96): 78–81.

Burtchell, G.D. and T.U. Sadleir, eds. *Alumni Dublinenses: a Register of the*

Figure 12-2
From Kevin Condon's *The Missionary College of All Hallows 1842–1891* (Dublin: All Hallows College, 1986). Used with permission of the college.

Matricula: 1842-'91

1. Bernard Coyle, Oct.17, 1842, from St Kieran's Kilkenny; aged 32. Of Peter and Mary Finlay, Killann, Kilmore. For British Guiana. Left in March 1844. 'Ordained priest in America.'

2. Patrick O'Leary, Nov. 9, 1842. Of Daniel and Ellen Collins, Kinnagh, Cork; aged 29. For British Guiana. 'Went home,' Feb. 1844.

3. John O'Malley, Nov. 13, 1842, from St Jarlath's (and St Mary's, Youghal.) Of Edmund and Henrietta, Kilgeever, Tuam; aged 28. Ord. for British Guiana, 5.1.1843. 'Died in his mission after two months.'

4. Patrick McGowan, Nov. 13, 1842, from St Mary's, Youghal. Of Cormac and Eleanor Connolly, Rossinver, Kilmore; aged 22. For Sydney.'Went home.'

5. Thomas Mannion, Nov. 14, 1842. Parish of Roscommon, diocese of Elphin. Left in Oct. 1843.

6. Patrick Henaghan, Nov. 14, 1842. Of Anthony and Nora Haydon, Termonbarry, Elphin; For Sydney; aged 27. 'Went home sick, July 1843.' In Philadelphia seminary in 1845.

7. Timothy Rooney, Nov. 18, 1842. Of Cormac and Mary Foley, Killasnet, Kilmore diocese; aged 24. For Sydney. Went home, 23.10.1843.

8. Daniel Doherty, Nov. 26, 1842, from St Malachy's, Belfast. Of John and Mary Gibney, Ballykindlar, Down and Connor; aged 21. Ord. for Madras. 15.5.1847. Died of tuberculosis while serving at Madras Cathedral, 24.7.1857. (1858 Report, p. 72.)

9. Daniel Lordan, Dec. 10, 1842. Of Timothy and Margaret Cummins, Kinneagh, Cork; aged 27. Ord. subd. by Archb. Murray, 19.7.1845. Served under Bishop Hynes in Demerara (New Amsterdam) until latter's resignation in 1858. Came to Bishop Goold of Melbourne. Taught for a while at St Patrick's College. St Francis, Melbourne, '59; Beechworth, '59; Yarraville and Ballarat, '60; St Francis again 1861-. Confessor in three languages. Shunned public life. Died, 25.12.1879.

10. Philip McBreen, Dec. 14, 1842. From Knockbride, Kilmore; aged 32. 'Went home, 14.2.1843.'

11. Patrick Canavan,Dec.18, 1842. Of Parick and Sarah Connolly, Killyman, Armagh; aged 24. For Demerara. Went home.

12. Daniel Molony, Jan. 1843. Of Michael and Judith Delany, Mountrath, Leighlin; aged 34. Left for the diocese of Vincennes on Apr. 10,1845.Ord. subd. for Vincennes, Ind., 8.3.45. Served at Scipio, 1845-52 and 59-63; Indianapolis, 1853-57; also Lafayette.For a while in Milwaukee dioc. and in Dubuque. Returned to Jennings Co., Ind. in 1871 and died, 26.6.'74. Buried outside Scipio church. (Msgr. John Doyle.)

12a Michael O'Flanagan.Of John and Bridget Considine, Cratloe, Limerick; aged 22. Sailed for Vincennes, Ind., 13.7.1846. Lagro in 1848. Cf. Purcell, no. 103.

13. Henry Turpin, Feb. 1843. St Francis parish, Dublin aged 17. For Cape Province. Went home,14.7.1844. (Later Birmingham.)

14. John Ryan, Jan. 1843. Of John and Mary, Pallasgreen, Cashel; aged 31. Left for Vincennes, Ind., 15.4.'45. Richmond, Ind., 1845-; Lagro, Ind., 1848-; Canton, Ill., 1864; Kewanee, Ill., 1870; Macomb, Ill., 1881-91. Builder of many parishes and churches. Died, Galesburg, Ill., 26.4.1894. (Msgr. John Doyle.)

15. Michael Prendergast, Feb. 1843. Of James and Margaret Hoyne, Mayo parish, Tuam; aged 21. Went home sick, 10.6.1844. Philadelphia seminary in 1845; Westchester, Pa., in 1852.

16. Thomas Fitzsimons, Feb. 1843. From Granard, Ardagh; aged 19. For Madras. subdeaconate from Archb. Murray, 4.6.1846. To his mission, Aug. 1847. Died at Burrisaul, East Bengal, 10.6.1854.

17. George Carroll, Mar. 1843. Of William and Catherine Gibson, St Mary's, Dublin; aged 21. For Madras. Went home sick, Feb. 1844.

18. Michael Gough, Mar.1843. Of Matthew and Catherine Cox,Collinstown, Meath; aged 23. Ord. for Madras by Abp Murray, 18.5.1847. Royapuram, 1854-; Kitchery, 1857-; Pallavaram, 1859. To Maitland, N.S.W. in 1868. Tamworth from about 1869. Died, 20.7.1880. (1848 R., 32f; 1851, 17f; 1855, 74f.) Buried at Petersham.

19. Bernard Cox, Mar. 1843. Of James and Winifred Fallon, Aughrim, Elphin; aged 23. For Madras. Went to America, March 1845. (New York?)

20. Henry Lennon, Apr. 1843. Of Francis and Rose McArdle, Upper Creggan, Crossmaglen, Armagh; aged 23. Ord. for Boston, Mass., by Archb. Murray, 18.5.1847. Appointed at first to St. Alban's Vt. On Christmas Eve, 1848 became lifelong pastor of Newburyport, (with missions at Groveland, Georgetown, and Ipswich.) Died, much loved and respected, 13.7.1871. (Purcell, no. 21)

21. Nathanael O'Donnell, Apr. 1843. Of Matthew and Anne Porter, Carndonagh, Derry; aged 18. Ord. in Derry for Madras by Bishop McGinn, 15.9.1848. Served in the Vicariate house in Madras. Died, 4.12.1852. (1851 Report, 11-15; 1853, 7f.)

22. John Prendergast, Apr. 1843, from Tubridge, Clogheen, Waterford; aged 26. To his mission, St. John's College, Calcutta, in Apr. 1844. Died, ca. 1859.

23. Hugh McMahon, Apr. 1843. Of Hugh and Bridget Donnelly, Ballintacken, Armagh; aged 19. Went home, 23.10.1843.

24. Patrick Murphy, Apr. 1843, from St Mary's, Youghal. Of John and Bridget Ryan, Kilteely, Cashel; aged 21. To Vincennes, Ind., July 1846. Pastor of St Mary's (including Bloomington. He became a trustee of the University in 1858, and received an honorary degree in 1865.) In Chicago dioc. from 1858; Mendota- Rock Island - Chaplain to 58th Infantry - St James, Carville - St James, Chicago. Killed when boarding a train at Vincennes Junction, 10.9.1869. (Msgr John Doyle).

25. Terence Scollon, May 1843. Of Andrew and Catherine Maguire, Clones, Clogher; aged 24. Ord. for New York by Archb. Murray, 18.5.1847. Pastor, Wappingers Falls, 1850; Haverstraw, 1852-57. Left to teach at St Bonaventure's, Allegany. Later to Grand Rapids, Michigan. Died, chaplain to the convent at Morris, Minn. 23.2.1889.

26. Thomas Fogarty, May 1843, from St Mary's, Youghal. Of Thomas and Mary Hayes, Kilteely, Cashel; aged 20. Ord. for W.D. of Scotland by Archb. Murray, 16.5.1845. Died of tuberculosis at Taunton, 3.11.1850. (Canning, 107.)

27. James Danagher, May 1843, St Mary's, Youghal. Cf. no. 365. Of John and Bridget Lee, Croom, Limerick, aged 21. Ord. for W.D. of Scotland, 16.5.1845 by Archb. Murray. PP, St Mary's, Greenock, 1845-52; St Joseph's, Glasgow, 1852-59; St Mary's, Hamilton, 1859-86. Canon in 1884. Died, Nov. 13, 1886. Buried, Dalbeth. (Canning, p.71.)

28. James Tracy, May 1843. Of James and Mary Jennings,

Students, Graduates, Professors and Provosts of Trinity College. Dublin, 1935.

Casey, Albert E. and Eugene P. Thomas. *O'Kief, Coshe Mang, Slieve Lougher and Upper Blackwater in Ireland*. 15 vols. Birmingham, Ala.: Amite and Knockagree Historical Fund, 1952–1971.

Herlihy, Kevin. *The Religion of Irish Dissent, 1650–1800*. Blackrock, Co. Dublin: Four Courts Press, 1996.

An Irish Genealogical Source: Guide to Church Records. Belfast: Public

For More Info

CATHOLIC RELIGIOUS ORDERS IN IRELAND

You may find the abbreviation for a relative's religious order in an obituary, a family history, a parish history, or other record. Knowing the name of the order to which your relative belonged is the key to accessing biographical records from the order.

Abbreviation for Selected Religious Orders of

Men Active in Ireland Prior to 1920

CFC	Congregation of Christian Brothers (of Ireland)
CM	Congregation of the Mission (Vincentians)
CP	Congregation of the Passion (Passionists)
C.S.Sp	Holy Spirit (Holy Ghost) Congregation
C.SS.R	Congregation of the Most Holy Redeemer (Redemptorists)
FPM	Presentation Brothers
FSC	Brothers of the Christian Schools (De La Salle Brothers)
FSP	Congregation of the Brothers of St. Patrick (Patrician Brothers)
IC (prev. OC)	Institute of Charity (Rosminians) (prev. Order of Charity)
O.Carm (prev. OCC)	Order of Carmelites (of the Ancient Observance, prev. Calced Carmelites)
OCD	Order of Discalced Carmelites
OCSO (prev. Cist.)	Cistercian Order of the Strict Observance (Trappists)
OFM (OSF until 1897)	Order of Friars Minor (Franciscans)
OFM.Cap (prev. OSFC)	Capuchin Friars
OFM.Conv	Conventual Franciscans
OH	Hospitaller Brothers of the Order of St. John of God (St. John of God Brothers)
OMI	Oblates of Mary Immaculate
OP	Order of Preachers (Dominicans)
OSA	Order of St. Augustine (Augustinians)
OSB	Order of St. Benedict (Benedictine Monks)
OSF	Brothers of the Third Order Regular of St. Francis (Franciscan Brothers)
SJ	Society of Jesus (Jesuits)
SM	Society of Mary (Marists)
SMA (prev. AM)	Society of African Missions

Abbreviation for Selected Religious Orders of

Women Active in Ireland Prior to 1920

CHF	Holy Faith Sisters
CSB	Congregation of St. Brigid (Brigidine Sisters)

DC	Daughters (Sisters) of Charity of St. Vincent de Paul
IBVM	Institute of the Blessed Virgin Mary (Loreto Sisters)
OCD	Order of Discalced Carmelite Nuns
OP	Nuns of the Order of Preachers (Dominican Sisters)
OSB	Sisters of the Order of St. Benedict (Benedictine Nuns)
OSU	Order of St. Ursuline (Ursuline Nuns)
PBVM	Sisters of the Presentation of the Blessed Virgin Mary (Presentation Sisters)
PCC or OSC	Poor Clares
RSC	Religious Sisters of Charity (Irish Sisters of Charity)
RSM	Religious Sisters of Mercy
RGS or CGS	Good Shepherd Sisters

Sources: 1998 and 1920 issues of *Irish Catholic Directory.* "Prev." refers to the abbreviation used in 1920 if different from the current usage.

Record Office of Northern Ireland and the Ulster Historical Foundation, 1994.

Lewis, Samuel. *Topographical Dictionary of Ireland.* London: S. Lewis, 1837. This work describes parishes and towns in Ireland as they were in 1837.

Mitchell, Brian. *A Guide to Irish Parish Registers.* Baltimore: Genealogical Publishing Co., 1988.

Radford, Dwight A. "Irish Immigrants Among Three American Minority Religions." *The Irish At Home and Abroad* 5 (2) (2d Quarter 1998): 77–83.

Ryan, James G., ed. *Irish Church Records: Their History, Availability, and Use in Family History Research.* Dublin: Flyleaf Press, 1992.

Church of Ireland

Ford, Alan, James McGuire and Kenneth Milne, eds. *As by Law Established: The Church of Ireland Since the Reformation.* Dublin: The Lilliput Press, 1995.

Milne, Kenneth. *The Church of Ireland: A History.* Rathmines, Dublin: Church of Ireland House, 1994.

Refaussé, Raymond. "The Representative Church Body Library and the Records of the Church of Ireland." *Archivium Hibernicum* 49 (1995): 115–124.

Reid, Noel. *A Table of Church of Ireland Parochial Records and Copies.* Naas, Co. Kildare: Irish Family History Society, 1994.

Baptists

Herlihy, Kevin. " 'The Faithful Remnant': Irish Baptists, 1650–1750." In *The Irish Dissenting Tradition 1650–1750,* edited by Kevin Herlihy, 65–80. Blackrock, Co. Dublin: Four Courts Press, 1995.

Thompson, Joshua. *Century of Grace: Baptist Union of Ireland, 1895–1995, A Short History*. Belfast: Baptist Union of Ireland, 1995.

Congregationalists

Archibald, James E. *A Century of Congregationalism: The Story of Donegall Street Church, Belfast (1801–1901)*. Belfast: William Cleland Ltd., [1901?].

Coles, Malcolm. *I Will Build My Church: The Story of the Congregational Union of Ireland, Written to Mark the Terjubilee, 1829–1979*. [Lisburn, County Antrim: Congregational Union of Ireland, 1979].

Huguenots

Forrest, G. Andrew. "Religious Controversy Within the French Protestant Community in Dublin, 1692–1716: An Historiographical Critique." *The Irish Dissenting Tradition 1650–1750*, edited by Kevin Herlihy, 96-110. Blackrock, Co. Dublin: Four Courts Press, 1995.

"The Huguenot Society of Great Britain and Ireland." *Irish Roots* (2) (1996): 6–7.

St. Leger, Alicia. *Silver, Sails, and Silk: Huguenots in Cork, 1685–1850*. Cork: Cork Civil Trust Ltd., 1991.

Jews

Hyman, Louis. *A History of the Jews in Ireland*. London/Jerusalem, 1972.

Methodists

Cole, R. Lee. *One Methodist Church History of Methodism in Ireland, (Volume IV)*. Belfast: The Irish Methodist Publishing Co. Ltd., 1960.

Crookshank, C.H. *History of Methodism in Ireland*. 3 vols. Belfast: R.S. Allen and London, T. Woolmer, 1885–1888.

ffeary-Smyrl, Steven C. *Irish Methodists—Where Do I Start?* Dublin: Council of Irish Genealogical Organisations, 2000.

Heald, Carolyn A. "Researching Irish Palatines in Ireland and Ontario." *The Irish At Home and Abroad* 4 (2) (1997): 64–71.

Jones, Henry Z. *The Palatine Families of Ireland*. 2nd ed. Camden, Maine: Picton Press, 1990.

O'Connor, Patrick J. *People Make Places: The Story of the Irish Palatines*. Newcastle West, Co. Limerick, Ireland: Oireacht na Mumhan Books, 1989, 1996.

Taggart, Norman W. *The Irish in World Methodism 1760–1900*. London: Epworth Press, 1986.

Moravians

Hamilton, J. Taylor. *A History of The Church Known as the Moravian Church, or The Unitas Fratrum, or The Unity of the Brethren, During the Eighteenth and Nineteenth Centuries*. Bethlehem, Pa.: Times Publishing Company, 1900.

Mormons (Latter-day Saints)

Barlow, Brent A. *History of the Church of Jesus Christ of Latter-day Saints in Ireland Since 1840*. Thesis Paper presented to the Department of Graduate Studies in Religious Instruction, Brigham Young University, 1968.

Daughters of the Utah Pioneers. "The Mormons from Ireland." *Our Pioneer Heritage* 13 (1970): 313–372.

Presbyterians

Holmes, Finlay. *The Presbyterian Church in Ireland: A Popular History*. Blackrock, Co. Dublin: The Columba Press, 2000.

Presbyterian Historical Society of Ireland. *A History of Congregations in the Presbyterian Church in Ireland, 1610–1982*. Belfast: Presbyterian Historical Society, 1982.

Presbyterian Historical Society of Ireland. *A History of Congregations in the Presbyterian Church in Ireland, 1610–1982. A Supplement of Additions, Emendations and Corrections With an Index*. Belfast: Presbyterian Historical Society, 1996.

Religious Society of Friends (Quakers)

Eustace, P. Beryl and Olive C. Goodbody. *Quaker Records, Dublin: Abstracts of Wills*. Dublin: Stationery Office, 1957.

Goodbody, Olive C. *Guide to Irish Quaker Records, 1654–1860*. Dublin: Stationery Office for Irish Manuscript Commission, 1967.

Wigham, Maurice J. *The Irish Quakers: A Short History of the Religious Society of Friends in Ireland*. Dublin: Historical Committee of the Religious Society of Friends in Ireland, 1992.

Roman Catholics

Betit, Kyle J. "Priests, Nuns and Brothers in Ireland." *The Irish At Home and Abroad* 5 (2) (2d Quarter 1998): 70–76.

Clear, Caitríona. *Nuns in Nineteenth-Century Ireland*. Dublin: Gill and Macmillan, 1987.

Condon, Kevin. *The Missionary College of All Hallows 1842–1891*. Dublin: All Hallows College, 1986.

Cosgrave, Marianne. "An Introduction to the Archives of Roman Catholic Congregations of Women Religious in Ireland, With Particular Reference to Genealogical Research." *Irish Archives* (Journal of the Irish Society for Archives) 4 (2) (Autumn 1997): 5–12.

Hamell, Patrick J. *Maynooth Students and Ordinations Index 1795–1895*. Maynooth, Ireland: St. Patrick's College, 1982.

Whelan, Kevin. "The Regional Impact of Irish Catholicism 1700–1850." In *Common Ground: Essays on the Historical Geography of Ireland*, 253–277. Cork, Ireland: Cork University Press, 1988.

THIRTEEN

Civil Registration

One thing you might notice is that government registration of births, marriages, and deaths in Ireland began much later than in other countries. Registration of non-Catholic marriages began in April 1845. The recording of births, deaths, and all marriages began in January 1864. Registrars customarily sent copies of civil registration entries to Dublin, where they were indexed on a countrywide basis. It's relatively easy to find an Irish civil registration entry if one was recorded for your ancestor. That's because there are yearly indexes for 1845 to 1877 and quarterly indexes starting in 1878 that cover the whole island. Mind you, there are some limitations; for example, the birth indexes don't give parents' names. The Republic of Ireland and Northern Ireland have kept separate civil registrations since 1921.

RECORD AVAILABILITY AND CONTENT

The original records of 1845 to 1921 for all of Ireland are at the General Register Office at Joyce House in Dublin. Those from 1921 to the present for the Republic of Ireland are at Joyce House, and those for Northern Ireland are at the General Register Office at Oxford House in Belfast. The indexes at Joyce House are open to the public. You can search them in person or through the mail for a fee.

You can get microfilm copies of the indexes to civil registration from 1845 through 1958 from the FHL. The FHL also holds microfilm copies of many of the original registers, but beware, there are some odd gaps in its collection (see page 200).

Irish civil registration contains the following information:

Births: Name of child, date and place of birth, parents' names (including mother's maiden name) and residence, father's occupation, and name and address of informant.

Marriages: Date and place (including name of church or registrar's office) of

Microfilm Source

Civil Registration at the Family History Library	
Ireland (Pre-1922)	
Indexes	Births, Marriages, and Deaths 1864–1921
Indexes	Protestant Marriages 1845–1921
Registers	Births 1864—March 1881; 1900–1913
	Marriages 1845–1870
	Deaths 1864–1870
Foreign Registers	Births, Marriages, and Deaths 1864–1923
Marine Registers	Births and Deaths 1864–1884
Republic of Ireland	
Indexes	Births, Marriages, and Deaths 1922–1958
Registers	Births 1930–1955
	Marriages—None
	Deaths—None
Northern Ireland	
Indexes	Births, Marriages, and Deaths 1922–1959
Registers	Births 1922–1959
	Marriages 1922–1959
	Deaths 1922–1959
Army Registers	Births, Marriages, and Deaths 1923–1953
Marine Registers	Births and Deaths 1922–1953
	Deaths On-board H.M. Ships 1922–1954
Foreign Registers	Births, Marriages, and Deaths 1923–1952

marriage; name, age, and residence of bride and groom; names and occupation of bride's father and groom's father; names of witnesses. You will usually find the age listed as "minor" or "of full age," but in some cases ages are given in years.

Deaths: Name of deceased person, date and place of death, age, occupation, cause of death, name and address of informant, and sometimes the relationship to the deceased of the informant.

ADMINISTRATIVE DIVISIONS

On the top of each civil registration page, you will find the Superintendent Registrar's District and the registrar's district for entries on that page. Registrar's districts were subdivisions of the Superintendent Registrar's Districts. The national indexes list the Superintendent Registrar's District (which was also called the *registration* district) for each entry.

You need to identify which Superintendent Registrar's Districts covered the area you are interested in. The names and boundaries of Superintendent Registrar's Districts and of poor law unions are the same. As a side note, the 1851 and 1871 townland indexes identify the poor law union in which each town and townland was located.

If you already know a county of origin, you can determine the Superintendent Registrar's Districts covering that county (see page 201). Look at all entries for a particular surname, district, and time period to find records of your family.

The townland or street address, and sometimes the parish, is given in civil

Research Tip

Superintendent Registrar's Districts in Ireland

The following is a list showing each county and the superintendent registrar's districts located within the county. Districts often crossed county boundaries.

County	District
Antrim	Antrim, Ballycastle, Ballymena, Ballymoney, Belfast, Coleraine, Larne, Lisburn, Lurgan
Armagh	Armagh, Banbridge, Castleblayney, Dundalk, Lurgan, Newry
Carlow	Baltinglass, Carlow, Enniscorthy, New Ross, Shillelagh
Cavan	Ballieborough, Bawnboy, Cavan, Cootehill, Enniskillen, Granard, Kells, Oldcastle
Clare	Ballyvaghan, Corrofin, Ennis, Ennistimon, Gort, Killadysert, Kilrush, Limerick, Scarriff, Tulla
Cork	Bandon, Bantry, Castletown, Clonakilty, Cork, Dunmanway, Fermoy, Kanturk, Kilmallock, Kinsale, Lismore, Macroom, Mallow, Middleton, Millstreet, Mitchelstown, Skibbereen, Skull, Youghal
Donegal	Ballyshannon, Donegal, Dunfanaghy, Glenties, Inishowen, Letterkenny, Londonderry, Millford, Strabane, Stranorlar
Down	Banbridge, Belfast, Downpatrick, Kilkeel, Lisburn, Lurgan, Newry, Newtownards
Dublin	Balrothery, Celbridge, Dublin North, Dublin South, Dunshaughlin, Naas, Rathdown
Fermanagh	Ballyshannon, Clones, Enniskillen, Irvinestown, Lisnaskea
Galway	Ballinasloe, Ballinrobe, Clifden, Galway, Glennamaddy, Gort, Loughrea, Mount Bellew, Oughterard, Portumna, Roscommon, Scarriff, Tuam
Kerry	Cahersiveen, Dingle, Glin, Kenmare, Killarney, Listowel, Tralee
Kildare	Athy, Baltinglass, Carlow, Celbridge, Edenderry, Naas
Kilkenny	Callan, Carrick-On-Suir, Castlecomer, Kilkenny, New Ross, Thomastown, Urlingford, Waterford
Leitrim	Bawnboy, Ballyshannon, Carrick-On-Shannon, Manorhamilton, Mohill
Leix (Queens)	Abbeyleix, Athy, Carlow, Donaghmore, Mountmellick, Roscrea
Limerick	Croom, Glin, Kanturk, Kilmallock, Limerick, Mitchelstown, Newcastle, Rathkeale, Tipperary
Londonderry (Derry)	Ballymoney, Coleraine, Londonderry, Magherafelt, Newtownlimavady
Longford	Ballymahon, Granard, Longford
Louth	Ardee, Drogheda, Dundalk
Mayo	Ballina, Ballinrobe, Belmullet, Castlebar, Castlereagh, Claremorris, Clifden, Killala, Newport, Oughterard, Swineford, Westport
Meath	Ardee, Celbridge, Delvin, Drogheda, Dunshaughlin, Edenderry, Kells, Navan, Oldcastle, Trim
Monaghan	Carickmacross, Castleblayney, Clogher, Clones, Cootehill, Dundalk, Monaghan
Offaly (Kings)	Edenderry, Mountmellick, Parsonstown, Roscrea, Tullamore
Roscommon	Athlone, Ballinasloe, Boyle, Carrick-On-Shannon, Castlereagh, Glennemaddy, Roscommon, Strokestown, Swineford
Sligo	Sligo, Ballina, Boyle, Dromore West, Tobercurry
Tipperary	Borrisokane, Callan, Carrick-On-Suir, Cashel, Clogheen, Clonmel, Nenagh, Parsonstown, Roscrea, Thurles, Tipperary, Urlingford
Tyrone	Armagh, Castlederg, Clogher, Cookstown, Dungannon, Enniskillen, Gortin, Irvinestown, Omagh, Strabane
Waterford	Carrick-On-Suir, Clogheen, Clonmel, Dungarvan, Kilmacthomas, Lismore, Waterford, Youghal
Westmeath	Athlone, Ballymahon, Delvin, Granard, Mullingar, Tullamore
Wexford	Enniscorthy, Gorey, New Ross, Shillelagh, Wexford
Wicklow	Baltinglass, Naas, Rathdown, Rathdrum, Shillelagh

registration. The registrars were supposed to use the official standardized town-land names, but we have found that sometimes they weren't careful and recorded a non-standardized local name. Once, we found an 1869 marriage record for Martin Naughton and Kate Mulkerins that stated they were married in the Roman Catholic chapel of Killeen (County Galway) and that she was a resident of "Derreenglass." Derreenglass is not a townland name in this area, and we knew from other records that the Mulkerins lived in the townland of Lettermore. So we were a bit puzzled until we went to Lettermore and met an older resident, who pointed out a desolate, rocky spot on the shore where small boats used to land, and stated that this had been called Derreenglass.

Even if the registrar got the right name, it could have been misspelled. The same 1869 certificate listed Martin Naughton's residence as "Innistraver" or "Innistrawer," depending on how you read it. Well, we couldn't find that place anywhere either. We contacted the Galway Family History Society West heritage centre, and its research showed that "Innistrawer" was an island today called *Inis Treabhair* off the coast of Lettermore. The island is its own townland with the English transliteration Inishtravin. In other words, Martin got in his little boat on the island of Inishtravin, sailed to Derrenglass and was in Lettermore townland, where he and his future wife would court.

It's also not uncommon for the address given in civil registration to be different from that given in church registers. It's possible that one place name was the official townland name while the other was an unofficial local place name.

LDS INDEXES TO CIVIL REGISTRATION

International Genealogical Index (IGI): The FHL has incorporated some of the earliest birth and marriage entries from Irish civil registration into the IGI database, which is available on computer or microfiche at family history centres or on the Internet <http://www.familysearch.org>. The extracted information includes the date and parents' names for births or the name of the spouse for marriages. **Beware, though, the IGI does *not* show the townland, but rather the registrar's district, county, and page number.** With the computer version of the IGI, you will find the microfilm number on which the entry is given.

Warning

You can use the IGI to find out what births or marriages occurred for people of a certain surname during a given time period. Use the computer to narrow the search further to include events in a particular county or to list births to a particular couple. Remember that the IGI is only an index; use it to go to the original source.

Vital Records Index British Isles CD-ROM: An abbreviated version of civil registration extracts not yet part of the IGI has been released in a CD set titled "Vital Records Index British Isles." This CD indexes some marriages from the years 1847 to 1850 and 1863 to 1864 and births from 1864 to 1874. Beware that the CD is not complete for some of these years. What is on the IGI is not duplicated on this CD. You can access the information for the births in various search formats including a parent search. The CD is available for purchase from the LDS Church at <http://www.familysearch.org>. It is important to realize this is an incomplete extraction, so if you don't find an entry you're looking for on the CD or on the IGI, be sure to look at the original civil registration indexes.

POTENTIAL PITFALLS

We'd like to share with you some pointers so you can avoid some of the frustrations we have encountered in using civil registration.

Warning

Birth dates: The plain truth is that Irish immigrants often did not know their own birth dates. When you find an immigrant's christening or birth record in Ireland, the year can vary as much as ten years from what you expected from another document or a tombstone. In some cases you might find that the date of christening in church records precedes the date of birth in Irish civil records. Of course, no one can be christened before birth, so somebody was wrong. Was the family fudging on civil registration to avoid paying a late fine, or was the priest or minister careless? It might not be possible to know which date is correct.

Spelling of names: An ancestor can even be listed in the civil registers under a different name from what you expect. Consider all possible spelling variations of your surname (such as O'Reilly, O'Riley, Reily, Riley, etc.). Don't fall into the trap of saying, "My name is spelled *this* way." After all, how does an illiterate or semi-literate person spell his or her name? Also consider given name variations and nicknames (for example, you may find Biddy or Delia listed instead of Bridget).

Missing entries: Although civil registration was mandatory, many people were not registered during the first decades. One possible reason for not finding your ancestor's birth record is that the child's first name was not recorded in the entry, so check the index for "male" or "female" under your surname. Late registrations of births are listed at the back of the birth indexes. If you do not find the birth record of an ancestor in civil registration, search for the birth record of a sibling. This will tell where the parents were living and indirectly lead you to your ancestor.

Illegible townland names: It is fairly common in civil registration documents to find indecipherable townland names due to the handwriting of the registrar. To determine the correct townland name spelling, compare the written name to one of the 1851, 1871, or 1901 townland indexes.

Another option is to use *Registration of Births, Deaths and Marriages, Ireland. List of Townlands in Each Poor Law Union (or Superintendent Registrar's District), and Registrar's District*, published in 1891. Since you will know the name of the union (or superintendent registrar's district) and the registrar's district from the civil registration certificate, you can scan the list of townlands under the appropriate district to see if one closely matches the handwritten townland name. A copy of the 1891 list is available on microfilm through the FHL. The list was reprinted in George B. Handran's *Townlands in Poor Law Unions*.

Sources

REFERENCES AND FURTHER READING

Betit, Kyle J. and Dwight A. Radford. "Irish Civil Registration." *The Septs* (Irish Genealogical Society International) 18 (1) (January 1997): 1, 5–6.

Blossom, Catherine. "Civil Registration of Births, Deaths, and Marriages in Ireland: A Practical Approach." *Familia: Ulster Genealogical Review* 12 (1996): 33–51.

Civil Registration Districts of Ireland. Salt Lake City, Utah: Genealogical Library, The Church of Jesus Christ of Latter-day Saints, 1983.

Handran, George B. *Townlands in Poor Law Unions: A Reprint of Poor Law Union Pamphlets of the General Registrar's Office.* Salem, Mass.: Higginson Book Co., 1997.

Registration of Births, Deaths and Marriages, Ireland. List of Townlands in Each Poor Law Union (or Superintendent Registrar's District), and Registrar's District. Dublin: Printed for Her Majesty's Stationery Office, by Alex. Thom and Co., 1891.

FOURTEEN

Emigration Lists

T he primary ports of departure from Ireland were Queenstown (Cobh), Belfast, Londonderry (Derry), and Dublin, although smaller numbers of emigrants left from many other ports. In this chapter we discuss sources you can use to document emigrants leaving Ireland. Be warned, however, that none of these sources is complete. The reality is that only scattered passenger lists going out of Ireland prior to 1890 survive. You have a better chance of finding a document of arrival in the new country.

One noteworthy database that draws from many different sources is the Ulster American Folk Park's Emigration Database. Search it at the Research Library of the Ulster American Folk Park in Omagh, County Tyrone; and at the Northern Ireland Education and Library Boards in Armagh, Ballymena, Ballynahinch, Belfast, Enniskillen, Londonderry, and Omagh.

The following are some of the Irish departure lists we have found useful, arranged chronologically. The books compiled by Brian Mitchell, mentioned in this chapter, are published on the Family Tree Maker CD #257, *Irish Immigrants to North America, 1803–1871.*

1600s: Three works by Peter Wilson Coldham list many emigrants who went to the American colonies and West Indies in the 1600s. These are important books for this time period. Don't be fooled because they look like sources for English emigrants; many people went from Ireland to England to catch ships bound for the New World. **Coldham's works have all been placed on Family Tree Maker CD #350.**

CD Source

> Coldham, Peter Wilson. *The Bristol Registers of Servants Sent to Foreign Plantations, 1654–1686.* Baltimore: Genealogical Publishing Co., 1988.
>
> Lists of indentured servants bound for "foreign plantations" are in this book, including the names of all servants embarking from the port of Bristol, England, taken from the records of the Corporation of the City of Bristol. Among these were many Irish, and the records sometimes tell

where in Ireland they originated. These registers were intended to help document willing servants (including children) as opposed to the white slave trade, which was going on in the same time period.

Coldham, Peter Wilson. *The Complete Book of Emigrants in Bondage, 1614–1775*. Baltimore: Genealogical Publishing Co., 1988.

This work details those who were sent as prisoners mainly to America, with a few of the prison ships bound for Barbados and the West Indies. Although the people listed were deported from England, there were many Irish among them. Some Irish were in England, where they were convicted and transported.

Coldham, Peter Wilson. *The Complete Book of Emigrants, 1607–1660*. Baltimore: Genealogical Publishing Co., 1987.

This work indexes many sources from English public records that detail those going to the colonies for political, religious, and economic reasons. Many Irish are included in lists of deported persons such as vagrants, nonconformists, and those sold into labor. Many of those listed (including the Irish) were deported because they were considered undesirable. Numerous ships included in this work were bound for the West Indies.

1700s: During the 1700s passengers on a ship from Ulster would customarily sign a "letter of thanks" to the ship's captain for a good trip. These letters with the names of the passengers were published in Ulster newspapers to encourage others to sign up for passage with the captain—in other words, free advertising. Not every ship did this, so you're just getting a selection of the ships leaving Ireland in the 1700s.

Between 1737 and 1772 the major newspaper in Ulster was the *Belfast Newsletter*, which published notices regarding ships (including the "letters of thanks") from ports throughout the north of Ireland. Fortunately, there is a detailed index to this paper, called the *Belfast Newsletter Index, 1737–1800*. Compiled by John Greene, it is a five-part microfiche index to surnames, places, ships, general topics, and advertisements. This index is also on the Internet at <http://www.ucs.usl.edu/bnl/>. The Linen Hall Library in Belfast has a copy of the microfiche index as well as microfilm copies of the *Belfast Newsletter*.

You can find the same type of emigration material in the *Londonderry Journal*, which began publication in 1772. This material and other items dating from 1772 to 1784 were abstracted in Donald M. Schlegel's *Irish Genealogical Abstracts From the Londonderry Journal*. This book has an every-name index. Copies of the *Londonderry Journal* are available at the NLI and various libraries in Ulster.

1735–1743: If your ancestor went to the American colonies in the seventeenth or eighteenth century, he or she could have been transported there as a felon or political dissident. For a small time period there is published data about transported Irish felons. In the 1740s the Irish government conducted an investigation of the system of transporting felons to the colonies. The information presented by the investigating committee contained data about men and women transported to America between 1735 and 1743. This "Report of the

Irish House of Commons Into Enforced Emigration to America" was transcribed in Frances McDonnell's *Emigrants from Ireland to America, 1735–1743: A Transcription of the Report of the Irish House of Commons Into Enforced Emigration to America.*

1788–1868: Convict transportation registers from Ireland to Australia are held at the NAI, and the information in them may be accessed online at the NAI Web site, <http://www.nationalarchives.ie/search01.html> (see chapter four).

1803–1806: An interesting source was generated between March 1803 and March 1806. During this three-year period, masters of ships were required by law to provide a register of their passengers as they left Irish ports. The law was intended to help keep skilled laborers from leaving the country, so don't necessarily rely on the occupation listed since people fudged to avoid the law. These lists are called the Hardwicke Papers. They give each passenger's name, age, occupation, and residence. Brian Mitchell extracted and indexed these records in *Irish Passenger Lists, 1803–1806: Lists of Passengers Sailing from Ireland to America Extracted from the Hardwicke Papers.*

1817–1831: There are some surviving lists of Irish immigrants to Canada who were sent in subsidized British immigration schemes. In these cases, groups of immigrants went to Canada to settle land with the help of the government. The surviving lists of immigrants are in the Colonial Office series at the PRO (Colonial Office 384). Microfilm copies of CO 384 lists dating between the years 1817 and 1831 are available at the National Archives of Canada (NAC), with an index (NAC Manuscript Group 11, on NAC microfilm reel C-4252). The lists themselves provide names, former residences, occupations, and dates of entry.

Some of the lists are actually returns of families *preparing* to emigrate. For example, a pair of November 1817 lists includes Catholics and Protestants, primarily from Counties Carlow and Wexford (but also including families from Counties Kilkenny and Wicklow). This pair of lists was published as an appendix to Bruce S. Elliott's article, "Immigration from South Leinster to Eastern Upper Canada."

1833–1839: In the 1830s the Ordnance Survey (which mapped the country) planned to make a parish by parish listing of emigrants. It only completed lists for County Londonderry and County Antrim before giving up that part of the project. Brian Mitchell published the lists for these two counties in *Irish Emigration Lists, 1833–1839: Lists of Emigrants Extracted from the Ordnance Survey Memoirs for Counties Londonderry and Antrim,* arranged by parish with a general index to all names. The records give name, age, year emigrated, townland of residence, destination, and religion. The original manuscripts are deposited at the Royal Irish Academy in Dublin with photocopies at the PRONI.

1847–1871: There are surviving records kept by two shipping line companies that took passengers from the port of Londonderry to Canada and the United States, available at the PRONI: J & J Cooke Line (microfilm MIC13) and William McCorkell & Co. (microfilm MIC14). These lists are indexed in Brian Mitchell's *Irish Passenger Lists 1847–1871: Lists of Passengers Sailing from Londonderry to America on Ships of the J. & J. Cooke Line and the McCorkell Line.* Of course, Londonderry was not the only port of departure from the north of Ireland at this time, so you are only getting a portion of the emigrants who left in this period.

1849–1851: Transportation registers of prisoners who were sent from Ireland to the penal colonies at Van Diemen's Land (Tasmania), Gibraltar, and Bermuda are held at the NLI (Ms. 3016) for these three years. We should note that the convicts who went to Tasmania generally stayed there; those who went to Gibraltar returned; and those who went to Bermuda either died there or were shipped elsewhere, since they were not allowed to stay in Bermuda.

1890–1960: Only starting in 1890 do we actually have surviving continuous lists of outward-bound passengers from Ireland. The lists are in the Board of Trade records (BT 27) at the PRO. But there is no index to these lists, so you have to know an approximate date and port of departure to use them. As a side note, there are also lists of inbound passengers beginning in 1878 (BT 26). There is a fifty-one-year restriction on access to BT 26 and BT 27 records. The FHL has a microfilm copy of the Board of Trade passenger list inventory, which provides the PRO reference numbers you would need to call up the records in London. This inventory is also available on the Internet at the PRO Web site, <http://www.open.gov.uk/pro/prohome.htm>.

REFERENCES AND FURTHER READING

Sources

Begley, Donal F. "Emigrant Passenger Lists to America." In *Handbook on Irish Genealogy: How to Trace Your Ancestors and Relatives to Ireland*, edited by Donal F. Begley, 99–128. 6th ed. Dublin: Genealogy Bookshop, 1984.

Elliott, Bruce S. "Immigration from South Leinster to Eastern Upper Canada." *Wexford: History and Society*, edited by Kevin Whelan. Dublin: Geography Publications, 1987.

Greene, John, comp. *Belfast Newsletter Index, 1737–1800*. Ann Arbor, Mich.: UMI, 1993.

McDonnell, Frances. *Emigrants from Ireland to America, 1735–1743: A Transcription of the Report of the Irish House of Commons into Enforced Emigration to America*. Baltimore: Genealogical Publishing Co., 1992.

Mitchell, Brian. "Irish Emigrant Passenger Lists." *The Irish At Home and Abroad* 4 (3) (3d Quarter 1997): 118–120.

———, ed. *Irish Emigration Lists, 1833–1839: Lists of Emigrants Extracted from the Ordnance Survey Memoirs for Counties Londonderry and Antrim*. Baltimore: Genealogical Publishing Co., 1989.

———, ed. *Irish Passenger Lists, 1803–1806: Lists of Passengers Sailing from Ireland to America Extracted from the Hardwicke Papers*. Baltimore: Genealogical Publishing Co., 1995.

———, ed. *Irish Passenger Lists 1847–1871: Lists of Passengers Sailing from Londonderry to America on Ships of the J. & J. Cooke Line and the McCorkell Line*. Baltimore: Genealogical Publishing Co., 1988.

———. "The Ordnance Survey Memoirs: A Source for Emigration in the 1830s." *History Ireland* 4 (4) (Winter 1996): 13–17.

Schlegel, Donald M. *Irish Genealogical Abstracts From the Londonderry Journal, 1772–1784*. Baltimore: Clearfield Co., 1990.

FIFTEEN

Estate Records

E state records are the private papers of the landlords of Ireland, those who held tracts of land and leased or rented property to the occupiers of that land. Only a few people in Ireland actually owned land outright. The vast majority of inhabitants prior to the twentieth century leased or rented their holdings. Your ancestor could have been a landlord or someone renting from a landlord. In either case, estate records are relevant.

Why are estate papers relevant to the common tenant? **Because the landlords often kept detailed records, such as rent rolls and leases, of the people living on their estates.** In fact, before church records begin, estate papers could be among the only sources available for tracing the common classes.

Many estate landowners were members of the nobility, landed gentry, or Church of Ireland clergy. Land was also held by the Crown (the reigning monarch), the Church of Ireland, London guilds (similar to modern-day trade unions), and various companies. This means that a large majority of landholders after the Reformation were Protestants.

Let's dispel one myth right here. You might have heard that after the Reformation all the landlords in Ireland were Protestant, and that all Catholics were stripped of their land. Well, the situation is more complicated. In reality, a significant group of Irish Catholic landowners retained their lands from the Protestant Reformation in the sixteenth century all the way until Catholic Emancipation in 1829. There was no law against Catholics owning land. There *were* penal laws enacted against Catholics purchasing land, inheriting land from a Protestant, and passing on their land to only one child if there were several children in the family.

Many gentry families converted to the Church of Ireland in name only to protect their property, and then went about promoting and protecting Catholic interests in Ireland. Some family situations were even more complicated: Each eldest son would "conform" to the Church of Ireland while all the other children

Reminder

remained Catholic, or a landowning family would raise its sons Protestant and daughters Catholic.

How does all of this affect the landlord-tenant relationship? You might find in your research that your Protestant tenant ancestor was leasing from a Roman Catholic landowner. If you have gentry ancestors, you might find that your supposedly Protestant family or Catholic family was much more a mixture of both than you thought, since within the gentry class there was a great deal of intermarriage and conversion both ways (the population in Wexford City is a classic example). For an excellent discussion on this, we recommend Charles Chenevix Trench's *Grace's Card: Irish Catholic Landlords 1690–1800*. In engaging language, he sifts through the often contradictory and ugly history of landlordism in this time period. Another helpful resource is W.E. Vaughan's *Landlords and Tenants in Mid-Victorian Ireland*.

TYPES OF RECORDS AND INFORMATION

You can find a wide variety of records and information in estate papers. Two of the most frequent types are rent rolls and leases. A leaseholder held a written agreement for the term that the property would be held, while a renter could rent from year to year. Other records in estate papers can include estate maps, emigration lists, petitions to the landowner, wills and deeds, freeholders and poll lists, mortgages, and eviction records. Estate record collections range from meticulous to sloppy. Remember, these are private family papers with no rules for their content or even their survival.

Estate papers can indicate relationships and death dates of tenants. For example, it was common for land to be occupied under a "lease of lives" in which the tenant held the lease as long as three people named in the lease were living. The people named were often relatives, particularly children, of the lessee. The ages and relationships of the "lives" at the time the lease was written as well as their dates of death might be stated in the estate papers.

GENERAL STRATEGY FOR ACCESSING ESTATE PAPERS

Step By Step

Large numbers of Irish estate papers have survived, but the major obstacle in using this record source is that they are in numerous repositories in Ireland, Great Britain and elsewhere. **Use the following steps to locate estate papers that pertain to the place where your ancestor lived:**

1. Determine the townland (preferably) or parish where your ancestor lived.
2. Identify the landowner's full name and title. By title, we mean that many of the landlords were earls, marquises, dukes, and other nobles. So the MacDonnell family of Antrim were the Earls of Antrim.
3. Determine where the landowner's estate papers are deposited.
4. Search the estate papers looking for records covering the appropriate time period and townland/parish of interest. You would be surprised what you can find out about your ancestor's life. But don't assume that all of a landowner's estate papers are in one repository.

SOURCES FOR IDENTIFYING THE LANDOWNER

You can use the following sources to identify the landowner of the property that your ancestor occupied in a particular time period. Our point is not to use these records to look for your ancestor's name, but rather to look at these records to find out who the landowner was where your ancestor lived. You will need the landowner's name to access estate papers. Land did change hands due to confiscations, sales, bankruptcies, and inheritances, so over time you might need to pay attention to more than one landowner's name.

Sources

Landowner Sources

Time Period	Source
1708–present	*Registry of Deeds* records are available through the FHL and at the Registry of Deeds in Dublin. Access deeds by townland or town name using the Lands Indexes. By examination of the deeds registered for a particular place, you can ascertain a chronology of land ownership and registered leases (See chapter nineteen).
1823–1837	*Tithe Composition Applotment Books* sometimes indicate the landowner (chapter twenty-three).
1830s	*Ordnance Survey (John O'Donovan) Place Name Books* are available at the NLI and the Northern Ireland Place Name Project, and some county libraries have copies of the books for their own county. These books often identify the landowner of a townland in the time period before many estates went bankrupt later in the century (See chapter nine).
1847–recent	*Griffith's Valuation* of 1847 to 1864 and subsequent revision books include an "Immediate Lessor" column indicating the landlord of each occupier. A landlord may in turn be leasing from another person. Landowners in this source can often be identified by the term "in fee" in the Immediate Lessor column or by titles such as baronet ("bt." or "bart."), esquire, earl, or lord used with their names (see chapter twenty-three).

SOURCES FOR LOCATING ESTATE PAPERS

Major repositories of estate papers include the NLI, NAI, PRONI, Trinity College, and county and university libraries in Ireland and Great Britain. The FHL has microfilm copies of some estate papers. Estate papers might not have been deposited in the county where the estate was located or even in Ireland. Landowners often had land in several Irish counties and might have lived outside of Ireland altogether (called "absentee landlords").

The following is a list of reference works for locating estate papers:

Sources

* Richard J. Hayes's *Manuscript Sources for the History of Irish Civilisation* catalogs estate papers (1) under the name of county, then "estates," for example: "Galway, County: Estates"; (2) under the name of the estate (as in a town or castle name); and (3) under the name or title of the estate owner (see chapter nineteen).
* "County Source Lists" in John Grenham's book, the "Census and Census Substitutes" listings for each county in James G. Ryan's work.
* *National Inventory of Documentary Sources in the United Kingdom*

(NIDS), published by Chadwyck-Healy, includes Trinity College, University College Dublin, University College Galway, university archives, and county record offices in England, Wales, and Scotland. The index to NIDS is available on CD-ROM with capability for keyword searches.

- The National Register of Archives produced by the Royal Commission on Historical Manuscripts inventories manuscript collections repositories in the United Kingdom and the Republic of Ireland. A subject index to the NRA may be searched online: http://www.hmc.gov.uk/nra/nra2.htm.

- *Estate Records of the Irish Famine: A Second Guide to Famine Archives, 1840–1855*, by Andrés Eiríksson and Cormac O Gráda, lists collections at the National Archives, the NLI, the PRONI, and county, university and other libraries in Ireland. The book is arranged alphabetically by county and name of proprietor.

- Estate record inventories of papers in the NLI and the NAI were published in a joint project of the Irish Genealogical Society International and the GO. At this writing, inventories have been published for counties Armagh, Cavan, Cork, Donegal, Fermanagh, Galway, Kerry, Leitrim, Mayo, Monaghan, Roscommon, Sligo, Tyrone, and Waterford, as well as for the Lismore Papers.

- The PRONI's *Guide to Landed Estate Records* inventories records in the six Northern Ireland counties held at the PRONI.

- Estate paper collections at Trinity College were described in "Byways, A Look at Lesser Used Sources," *Irish Roots* 2 (1996): 8–9 and in M.D. Evans's chapter "Manuscripts of Genealogical Interest in Trinity College, Dublin," published in *Aspects of Irish Genealogy II*.

- *Records in Private Keeping:* The NLI has "reports" that inventory Irish estate papers in private keeping. Lists of the NLI reports were printed in *Analecta Hibernica* nos. 15, 20, 23, 25, and 32.

INCUMBERED ESTATES RECORDS

The Incumbered Estates Act of 1849 created a court to sell debt-ridden estates. More than three thousand estates were processed by the court between 1849 and 1857. The court continued to sell estates through the 1880s. Printed sales brochures for estates sold by the court are available at the NAI, NLI, PRONI, and FHL. They usually include a map of the estate and a listing by townland or street of the tenants, their yearly rents, and the types of agreement by which they occupied their land. If the land was leased, the brochure lists the number of years or names of lives involved, sometimes going back into the 1700s.

The NAI has a finding aid, arranged by townland, to the Incumbered Estates records (called LEC or Landed Estate Court rentals), and the NLI has a finding aid arranged alphabetically by owners' names. You can also call up the sales brochures in volumes by date at the NLI. The FHL has microfilmed eighty-three volumes of printed sales brochures, but there is no index.

A CASE STUDY IN LOCATING THE HOME SITE BY USING ESTATE PAPERS

Church records pinpointed the residence of Matthew Devine in Clooncumber townland, Cloone civil parish, County Leitrim. However, by the time of the printing of Griffith's Primary Valuation of this townland in 1857, Matthew Devine had immigrated to Scotland, so we could not use Griffith's to find out the exact plot of land Matthew lived on. Still, Griffith's Primary Valuation did show us that the landowner in Clooncumber townland was the Earl of Leitrim, so we turned to a search of his estate papers. We discovered from the inventories compiled by the IGSI and the GO that estate papers of the Earl of Leitrim are held at the NLI. In an 1842 to 1854 rental book of the Earl's estate, Matthew Devine was listed as a tenant "at will" on six acres, sixteen perches of land, and his name was crossed out. He was given a "notice to quit" in September 1842; by December 1844 the property was in the Earl's immediate possession, and in September 1845 it was given to Thomas Thompson. The key here is that Thompson does appear in Griffith's Primary Valuation of Clooncumber townland with several plots of land including plot #36 (six acres, seventeen perches); although the house on #36 was gone. The acreage of plot #36 almost exactly matched that given for Matthew Devine's plot in the Earl of Leitrim's papers. This allowed us to determine the exact plot of land in Clooncumber townland on which Matthew Devine was living in the early 1840s prior to his immigration to Scotland, even though he had left prior to Griffith's Primary Valuation.

REFERENCES AND FURTHER READING

De Burgh, U.H. Hussey. *The Landowners of Ireland. An Alphabetical List of Owners of Estates of 500 Acres or £500 Valuation and Upwards.* Dublin: Hodges, Foster and Figgis, 1878.

Eiríksson, Andrés and Cormac O Gráda. *Estate Records of the Irish Famine: A Second Guide to Famine Archives, 1840–1855.* Dublin: Irish Famine Network, 1995.

Evans, M.D. "Manuscripts of Genealogical Interest in Trinity College, Dublin." In *Aspects of Irish Genealogy II*, edited by M.D. Evans, 61–82. Dublin: Irish Genealogical Congress Committee, 1996.

Guide to Landed Estate Records. Belfast: Public Record Office of Northern Ireland, 1994.

Landowners in Ireland. Return of Owners of Land of One Acres and Upwards. 1876. Reprint, Baltimore: Genealogical Publishing Co. 1988.

Trench, Charles Chenevix. *Grace's Card: Irish Catholic Landlords 1690–1800.* Cork: Mercier Press, 1997.

Vaughan, W.E. *Landlords and Tenants in Mid-Victorian Ireland.* Oxford: Clarendon Press, 1994.

SIXTEEN

Heritage Centres

O ne of the most important resources you can use in your Irish research, especially if you only know a county of origin, is a heritage centre. The Irish heritage centres are county-based and have indexed parish registers and other records for their respective counties. Centres will search their databases for you for a fee to find information about your ancestors. Fees vary according to the individual centre and are often listed on their Internet sites. Sometimes you can pay in your local currency or in U.S. dollars. At the end of this chapter is a detailed list of the heritage centres with their contact information.

The types of records indexed and the services offered vary among the heritage centres, and may we add, so does the quality and completeness of the indexing. Each centre has indexed at least some church records, while some have gone as far as to index tombstone inscriptions, tax records, civil registration, census records, newspapers, passenger lists, and other types of records.

USING A HERITAGE CENTRE

It's been our experience that it's usually not as simple as writing a letter and receiving the response you want. If it were only that simple! **There are, however, many ways to effectively use a heritage centre, and we would like to offer some avenues drawn from our experience.**

Tip

Finding a more specific residence: If you know an ancestor's county of origin, a heritage centre can help you pinpoint where in the county your ancestor lived. Having a heritage centre's database searched can save you a great deal of time spent searching the records parish by parish.

Accessing church register data: If church registers are available only at the local church, accessing the information through the heritage centre's indexes can be easier than visiting or contacting the church itself.

In some cases the information in church registers is only available through the heritage centre. Such is the case for the Roman Catholic Archdiocese of Cashel and Emly (parts of counties Limerick and Tipperary). You must obtain information from the registers of this Catholic diocese from the Tipperary Heritage Unit.

Some heritage centres have indexed Catholic registers that were not microfilmed by the NLI. Thus, a heritage centre might have more information from earlier Catholic parish registers than those available on microfilm at the NLI, the PRONI, or the FHL. For example, you will find no pre-1880 registers for Kilcommon Catholic parish (Erris barony, County Mayo) at the NLI. The Mayo North Heritage Centre, however, has information from registers of this parish dating back to 1843. In another example, the NLI missed filming the earliest register, dating 1831 to 1855, of Moyvane Catholic parish in County Kerry; this register has been indexed by the Killarney Genealogical Centre.

Surname	Firstname	Date of Death	Graveyard	PlotNumber
BOYLE	MARGARET	18940128	IMMACULATE CONCEPTION RC	2838-B018
BOYLE	FRANK	19620101	IMMACULATE CONCEPTION RC	2838-C006
BOYLE	BRIGID	19630501	IMMACULATE CONCEPTION RC	2838-C006
BOYLE	JOSEPH	19640401	IMMACULATE CONCEPTION RC	2838-C006
BOYLE	M. PHILOMENA	19560513	CONVENT OF MERCY	2824-B013
BOYLE	MARY T	0	CHAPEL HILL RC COOKSTOWN	2817-D089
BOYLE	TARENCE	17590901	OLD DRUMGLASS R.C.	2824-A004
BOYLE	ELENAR	17830107	OLD DRUMGLASS R.C.	2824-A004
BOYLE	CORNELIUS	17610627	OLD DRUMGLASS R.C.	2824-B011
BOYLE	CHERALS	17810421	OLD DRUMGLASS R.C.	2824-B011

Figure 16-1
Burial Report from Heritage World Database for Cos. Fermanagh and Tyrone

Second opinion on deteriorated records: You can use a heritage centre to get a "second opinion" about the information contained in deteriorated parish registers. The staff of the heritage centre generally has become familiar with the writing and style of the register and even local names and how they are spelled. They can confirm or correct your reading of an entry in a damaged, faded, or otherwise difficult-to-read parish register. When you contact them, tell them this is exactly what you want them to do.

Formatting your request: It is vital that you be concise but specific when requesting a search. Indicate the full name of the emigrant and a year when the emigrant left Ireland; include the names of parents and siblings, if known. Be specific about the information you are seeking, but don't drone on with unnecessary data irrelevant to the search. Request that the heritage centre include townlands of residence as well as the names of witnesses at marriages and godparents (sponsors) at a baptism. State what records you have already searched and tell them you don't need them searched again if that is really the case. Remember, the centres are there to help you, and they need to know what you already know before they begin.

A heritage centre might require you to complete a standard form. Forms for some centres are on the Internet (see the Irish Family History Foundation's Internet Web site at <http://www.irishroots.net>).

Limitations of services: We need to point out that heritage centres have definite limitations and that they will not always be able to find what you want. The information you want from a heritage centre might be something they could not provide even if they wanted to, so it is essential to determine in advance exactly what services and indexes the centre offers and what the cost of searches will be. There is significant variability among centres in the completeness of the service provided. Some centres have indexed nearly all of the surviving church records in the county, while others have only indexed a portion of them.

Check the original source: No index is perfect. Inaccuracies and omissions occur. Some of the heritage centres' indexes were compiled by trainees who were not experienced in genealogy and old records.

An index might not include all the information in the original source. Do not use the information available from a heritage centre as a substitute for original records except when unavoidable. You should follow up with research in the original records to confirm the information provided by the heritage centre and to determine whether more information is available in the original or microfilm copies of the records.

Research in the original records can identify siblings not in the heritage centre's index. For example, a mother's given name listed for her children's baptisms in parish registers can vary, causing some siblings to be omitted from a family unit reported by a heritage centre.

Multiple centres: Because some counties are served by more than one heritage centre, you might have to have more than one index searched. The southern part of County Tipperary, for example, is serviced by the Brú Ború Heritage Centre, and the northern area by the Tipperary North Family History Foundation. However, the Catholic register indexes of the Archdiocese of Cashel and Emly, which includes much of the county, are available only at a third heritage centre, the Tipperary Heritage Unit.

Using and Interpreting a Centre's Report

Now that you have a report in your hands, what do you do with it? What does it really mean? **Where do you go from here?**

Getting complete information: A successful report will usually identify the parish or congregation in which church records of the family were found. Two important sets of details often mentioned in parish registers are the townlands of residence and the names of witnesses and godparents (sponsors). You might need to write the centre again to obtain the "rest of the story," if the report fails to include this material. If the centre found an ancestor's baptism, make sure it provides you with the baptismal information for all the siblings.

Extending the pedigree further: Some centres provide information on only one generation of your pedigree at a time. Depending on how early parish registers start for the area in question, you may need to write back to the centre

Step By Step

to see if it can take the lineage back another generation in its records.

All entries for your surname: You may wish to obtain all the information the centre has in its indexes on individuals of the surname in a particular area. Some centres will provide this information; others refuse to. It can help you if you're not sure the person from the centre's database is actually your ancestor. For example, you can look for relatives from Ireland going to the place where your ancestor settled.

Pinpointing townland of origin: If the report fails to identify a townland, it might still contain clues for you to figure it out with further research. You can take the names of the godparents or marriage witnesses and compare them to the occupiers of the area listed in Griffith's Primary Valuation (see chapter twenty-three). You might find a pattern emerges and all of these people lived in the same townland. We recommend Griffith's, but it's certainly not the only source you could use in this fashion.

Converting catholic parish to civil parish: A successful report on Catholic ancestors will identify the Catholic parish where your family's baptisms and marriages occurred. Remember that the Catholic parish is not the same as the civil parish, and the heritage centre will often not provide you with the civil parish. To continue using many kinds of local records, you will need to identify what civil parish(es) correspond to the Catholic parish (see chapter nine).

When your ancestor was born earlier than the start of registers: If the registers for your ancestral parish begin too late to include the baptism of the ancestor you are looking for, you might still be able to use the heritage centre's report to pinpoint the ancestral family's origins. For example, baptisms of younger siblings might identify what townland your family was from.

Interpreting Negative Results

The heritage centre might write back to you saying it could not find anything relating to your request. Don't be too upset. **There are some legitimate reasons your ancestor could not be found.** Possible explanations for a negative report include:

Notes

- Often records do not go back far enough to include the christening or marriage you are searching for. Many of the Church of Ireland registers were destroyed in the 1922 Four Courts fire. Some Catholic registers start as late as the 1860s or 1870s.
- Your ancestor's christening or marriage might not have been recorded in the registers. To help circumvent this problem, furnish the centre with a listing of all the known brothers and sisters of your ancestor. If they find one of the family members, chances are you have still found out where your ancestor is from.
- Your family might have lived near the border between two counties, with records of the family located in the adjoining county and covered by a different heritage centre. This happens more often than you might think, and it means you might need to write to more than one centre.
- Name variations can cause difficulties in an index search. An Irish surname such as MacGlashan may have been used in some of the records and its

English equivalent Green in others. A *Mc* or *O* prefix might be added or dropped, such as Sullivan/O'Sullivan, or there might be other spelling variations such as Holland, Hawney, Mulholland, and Wholiham. The given name you provide to the centre might be different from the name recorded in your ancestor's christening record. A nickname could have been used, such as Nancy for Agnes or Delia for Bridget. The Latin equivalent of the given name recorded in a register might have several possible English translations; for example, both Jacob and James are Jacobus in Latin.

REFERENCES AND FURTHER READING

Sources

Directory of Irish Parish Registers Indexed. 3d ed. Naas, Co. Kildare, Ireland: Irish Family History Society, 1997.

Heritage and Research Centers in Ireland. St. Paul, Minn.: Irish Genealogical Society International, 1997.

O'Neill, Robert K. *Ulster Libraries, Archives, Museums & Ancestral Heritage Centres.* Belfast: Ulster Historical Foundation, 1997.

HERITAGE CENTRES IN IRELAND

Most of the heritage centres in Ireland belong to the Irish Family History Foundation. You can access current information about them through the IFHF Internet site: <http://www.irishroots.net>. The information includes county history, what records are indexed, and what publications are available. Some heritage centres have their own Internet sites and e-mail addresses; these are listed below. The following list of heritage centres is divided by county. The area of the county covered by each centre is given in parentheses, unless the centre covers the entire county.

* = Centre is not a part of IFHF.

Antrim

Ulster Historical Foundation
   Balmoral Buildings, 12 College Sq. East, Belfast BT1 6DD, Northern Ireland
   phone: (028 90) 332288   *fax:* (028 90) 239885
   Internet: http://www.ancestryireland.com   *e-mail:* enquiry@uhf.dnet.co.uk

Armagh

Armagh Ancestry
   42 English St., Armagh BT61 7BA, Northern Ireland
   phone: (028 37) 521802   *fax:* (028 37) 510033
   Internet: http://www.armagh.gov.uk/   *e-mail:* ancestry@acdc.btinternet.com

Carlow

Carlow Genealogy Project
   The Old School, College St., Carlow, Ireland
   phone/fax: (0503) 30850

Cavan

Cavan Genealogy Research Centre
   Cana House, Farnham St., Cavan, County Cavan, Ireland
   phone: (049) 61094   *fax:* (049) 31494   *e-mail:* canahous@iol.ie

Clare

Clare Heritage and Genealogical Centre
   Church St., Corofin, County Clare, Ireland
   phone: (065) 6837955   *fax:* (065) 6837540
   Internet: http://clare.irishroots.net/   *e-mail:* clareheritage@eircom.net

Cork

Cork City Ancestral Project
   ‰ County Library, Farranlea Rd., Cork City, Ireland
   phone: (021) 546499   *fax:* (021) 343254 (Cork City Area)
Mallow Heritage Centre
   27/28 Bank Pl., Mallow, County Cork, Ireland
   phone/fax: (022) 21778 (County Cork outside Cork City)

Killarney Genealogical Centre
  Cathedral Walk, Killarney, County Kerry, Ireland
  phone: (064) 35946
  (Catholic Diocese of Kerry)

Donegal
Donegal Ancestry
  Old Meeting House, Back Ln., Ramelton, County Donegal, Ireland
  phone/fax: (074) 51266
  Internet: http://indigo.ie/~donances/   *e-mail:* donances@indigo.ie

Down
Ulster Historical Foundation
  Balmoral Bldgs., 12 College Sq. East, Belfast BT1 6DD, Northern Ireland
  phone: (028 90) 332288   *fax:* (028 90) 239885
  Internet: http://www.ancestryireland.com   *e-mail:* enquiry@uhf.dnet.co.uk

Dublin
*Dublin Heritage Group
  ℅ Dublin Public Libraries, 2d Floor
  Cumberland House, Fenian St., Dublin 2, Ireland
  phone: (01) 6269324 (Ballyfermot Library)
  (01) 6619000 (Dublin Public Libraries)   *fax:* (01) 6761628
  Internet: http://www.dublincorp.ie/hermain.htm   *e-mail:* dubcilib@iol.ie
  (Dublin City)
Fingal Heritage Group
  Carnegie Library, North St., Swords, County Dublin, Ireland
  phone: (01) 8403629
  (North County Dublin)
Dun Laoghaire Rathdown Heritage Society
  Moran Park House, Dun Laoghaire, County Dublin, Ireland
  phone: (01) 2806961 ext. 238   *fax:* (01) 2806969
  (South County Dublin)

Fermanagh
Heritage World
  The Heritage Centre, 26 Market Sq.
  Dungannon, County Tyrone BT70 1AB, Northern Ireland
  phone: (028 87) 724187   *fax:* (028 87) 752141
  Internet: http://www.heritagewld.com/   *e-mail:* info@heritagewld.com

Galway
Galway Family History Society West Ltd
  Research Unit, Venture Centre, Liosbaun Estate, Tuam Rd.
  Galway City, Ireland
  phone/fax: (091) 756737

East Galway Family History Society
   Woodford, Loughrea, County Galway, Ireland
   phone/fax: (0509) 49309   *e-mail:* eastgalwayfhs@tinet.ie

Kerry
Killarney Genealogical Centre
   Cathedral Walk, Killarney, County Kerry, Ireland
   phone: (064) 35946

Kildare
Kildare Heritage and Genealogy Society
   ℅ Kildare County Library, Newbridge, County Kildare, Ireland
   phone: (045) 433602   *fax:* (045) 432490
   Internet: http://kildare.ie/library/kildareheritage/index.html
   e-mail: capinfo@iol.ie

Kilkenny
Kilkenny Archaeological Society
   Rothe House, 16 Parliament St., Kilkenny City, Ireland
   phone: (056) 22893

Laois (Leix, Queens)
Laois & Offaly Family History Research Centre
   Bury Quay, Tullamore, County Offaly, Ireland
   phone/fax: (0506) 21421
   Internet: http://www.iol.ie/~ohas/   *e-mail:* ohas@iol.ie

Leitrim
Leitrim Genealogy Centre
   County Library, Ballinamore, County Leitrim, Ireland
   phone: (078) 44012   *fax:* (078) 44425
   e-mail: leitrimgenealogy@tinet.ie

Limerick
Limerick Ancestry
   The Granary, Michael St., Limerick, Ireland
   phone: (061) 415 125   *fax:* (061) 312 985
   Internet: http://www.irishwebsites.com/limarchives/
*Tipperary Heritage Unit
   The Bridewell, St. Michael St., Tipperary, County Tipperary, Ireland
   phone/fax: (062) 52725
   Internet: http://www.tipp.ie/tipphu.htm
   e-mail: thu@iol.ie
   (Catholic Archdiocese of Cashel & Emly)

Londonderry (Derry)

County Derry Genealogy Centre

Heritage Library, 14 Bishop St., Derry City, County Londonderry
BT48 6PW, Northern Ireland
phone: (028 71) 269792/361661   *fax:* (028 71) 360921
e-mail: ancestors@irelandmail.com

Ulster Historical Foundation

Balmoral Bldgs., 12 College Sq. East, Belfast BT1 6DD, Northern Ireland
phone: (028 87) 332288   *fax:* (028 87) 239885
Internet: http://www.ancestryireland.com   *e-mail:* enquiry@uhf.dnet.co.uk
(Catholic Diocese of Connor)

Longford

Longford Research Centre

Longford Roots, 1 Church St., Longford, County Longford, Ireland
phone: (043) 41235
e-mail: longroot@iol.ie

Louth

Meath-Louth Family Research Centre

Mill St., Trim, County Meath, Ireland
phone: (046) 36633   *fax:* (046) 37502
e-mail: meathhc@icl.ie

Louth County Library

Roden Pl., Dundalk, County Louth, Ireland
phone: (042) 35457   *fax:* (042) 34549
(Catholic Archdiocese of Armagh)

Mayo

South Mayo Family Research Centre

Main St., Ballinrobe, County Mayo, Ireland
phone/fax: (092) 41214   *e-mail:* soumayo@iol.ie

North Mayo Family Research Centre

Enniscoe, Castlehill (near Crossmolina), Ballina, County Mayo, Ireland
phone: (096) 31809   *fax:* (096) 31885
e-mail: normayo@iol.ie

Meath

Meath-Louth Family Research Centre

Mill St., Trim, County Meath, Ireland
phone: (046) 36633   *fax:* (046) 37502
e-mail: meathhc@iol.ie

Monaghan

Monaghan Ancestry

6 Tully, Monaghan, County Monaghan, Ireland
phone/fax: (047) 82304
e-mail: theo@tinet.ie

Offaly (Kings)
Laois & Offaly Family History Research Centre
    Bury Quay, Tullamore, County Offaly, Ireland
    phone/fax: (0506) 21421
    Internet: http://www.iol.ie/~ohas/   *e-mail:* ohas@iol.ie

Roscommon
Co. Roscommon Heritage & Genealogy Centre
    Church St., Strokestown, County Roscommon, Ireland
    phone: (078) 33380
*Athlone Public Library
    Athlone, County Westmeath, Ireland
    phone: (0902) 92166
    (Athlone Town Area Only)

Sligo
County Sligo Heritage & Genealogy Centre
    Aras Reddan, Temple St., Sligo, County Sligo, Ireland
    phone: (071) 43728
    e-mail: heritagesligo@tinet.ie

Tipperary
Brú Ború Heritage Centre
    Rock of Cashel, County Tipperary, Ireland
    phone: (062) 61122   *fax:* (062) 62700
    e-mail: bruboru@comhaltas.com
    (South County Tipperary)
Tipperary North Family Research Centre
    The Gatehouse, Kickham St., Nenagh, County Tipperary, Ireland
    phone: (067) 33850   *fax:* (067) 33586
    e-mail: relaybooks@tinet.ie
    (North County Tipperary)
*Tipperary Heritage Unit
    The Bridewell, St. Michael St., Tipperary, County Tipperary, Ireland
    phone/fax: (062) 52725
    Internet: http://www.tipp.ie/tipphu.htm
    e-mail: thu@iol.ie
    (Catholic Archdiocese of Cashel & Emly)
Waterford Heritage Centre
    St. Patrick's Church, Jenkin's Ln., Waterford City, Ireland
    phone: (051) 876123   *fax:* (051) 850645
    Internet: http://www.iol.ie/~mnoc   *e-mail:* mnoc@iol.ie
    (Catholic Diocese of Waterford & Lismore)

Tyrone

Heritage World

   The Heritage Centre, 26 Market Sq.

   Dungannon, County Tyrone

   BT70 1AB, Northern Ireland

   phone: (028 87) 724187   *fax:* (028 87) 752141

   Internet: http://www.heritagewld.com/   *e-mail:* info@heritagewld.com

Waterford

Waterford Heritage Genealogy Centre

   St. Patrick's Church, Jenkin's Ln., Waterford City, Ireland

   phone: (051) 876123   *fax:* (051) 850645

   Internet: http://www.iol.ie/~mnoc   *e-mail:* mnoc@iol.ie

Westmeath

Dun na Si Heritage Centre

   Knockdanney, Moate, County Westmeath, Ireland

   phone: (0902) 81183   *fax:* (0902) 81661

   e-mail: dunnasimoate@tinet.ie

*Athlone Public Library

   Athlone, County Westmeath, Ireland

   phone: (0902) 92166

   (Athlone Town Area Only)

Wexford

Wexford Genealogy Centre

   Yola Farmstead, Tagoat, County Wexford, Ireland

   phone/fax: (053) 31177

Wicklow

*Wicklow Family History Centre

   Court House, Wicklow, County Wicklow, Ireland

   phone: (0404) 67324   *fax:* (0404) 67464

   Internet: http://www.wicklow.ie/heritage/wh_proj.html

   e-mail: wfh@tinet.ie

*Cualann Historical Society

   128 Newcourt Rd., Bray, County Wicklow, Ireland

   phone: (01) 2863119

   (Town of Bray)

SEVENTEEN

Internet Resources

J ust about every day more useful material for Irish genealogy becomes available on the Internet. You can find extracted records, indexes, reference material, addresses, repository descriptions, and a wide variety of other material useful to your research. Our following description can only include some of the more important sites and some examples of what you can find. You will have the pleasure of exploring the Internet to see what current offerings there are. Be aware that Web site addresses change frequently. For Web sites of repositories, see the Appendix.

GENERAL IRISH GENEALOGY SITES
Listed here are some of the more important Web sites for accessing Irish genealogical material and for keeping current about information available on the Internet. **These sites are excellent starting points for your Irish research.**

What's What in Irish Genealogy
http://indigo.ie/~gorry

This is one of the best sites for keeping up to date and finding information about what's current in Irish genealogy. It contains the following sections: Research Services (including researchers in Ireland and abroad; heritage centres); Research Tours; Record Repositories; Publications; Events and Courses; Societies to Join; Online Information.

Cyndi's List of Genealogy Sites on the Internet: Ireland and Northern Ireland
http://www.CyndisList.com/ireland.htm

Cyndi's List contains the most links to genealogy sites of any site on the Internet. The Ireland and Northern Ireland page is an extensive catalog of Irish genealogy and related Internet sites, some with brief descriptions. Categories are General Resource Sites, History and Culture, How To, Heritage Centres,

Internet Source

Libraries and Archives, Mailing Lists and Newsgroups, Maps and Gazetteers, Newspapers, People and Families, Research Services, Publications, Queries and Surname Lists, Records, and Societies and Groups.

Irish Ancestors on the Irish Times Web Site

http://www.ireland.com/ancestor/

John Grenham maintains extensive reference material for Irish genealogy, including featured periodicals with free articles. Place names are searchable countrywide, or by city or county. The "Browse" section gives a general overview of some of the records relevant to Irish family history research. You can get a personalized report for a fee.

Ireland World Gen Web Project

http://www.rootsweb.com/~irlwgw

You can post queries here under the Irish counties. In the section labeled Ireland Specific Lookups, volunteers will look up information for you from published works, records, and the Ireland phone book. There are ads for professional research, surname links, and resource lists for each Irish county.

The Irish Ancestral Research Association

http://tiara.ie

This site includes the following link pages to Irish Library Catalogs, Book Stores and Publishers, Online Newspapers, Periodicals and Journals, Emigration and Passenger Lists, Family and Clan Associations, Databases and Search Engines, Professional Researchers, and Commercial Services.

Irish Genealogical Society, International

http://www.rootsweb.com/~irish/

This site contains links to Irish surnames, townlands and counties, and many genealogy resources. There are also pages about getting started in Irish genealogy. Articles from *The Septs*, IGSI's journal, have been uploaded, and there is an index to genealogical articles in Irish periodicals.

UK + Ireland Genealogy (GENUKI)

http://www.genuki.org/uk

This site has regional sections on England, Ireland, Scotland, Wales, Channel Islands, and Isle of Man; subject sections relating to all the British Isles; and information on archives and libraries.

The Fianna: Irish Ancestry & Historical Research

http://www.geocities.com/Heartland/Meadows/4404/

This site aims to be a "comprehensive online guide to Irish genealogy links, history, and more" with links pages to Irish County Web sites, Irish Immigration and Ship sites, Irish Land, Geography and Map sites, and Searchable Irish Genealogy sites. Extensive links to databases are included.

SEARCHABLE DATABASES

In some cases you can actually search records on the Internet relating to Irish people. Here are a couple of examples:

Ireland to Australia Transportation Records Database
http://www.nationalarchives.ie/search01.html

The NAI holds a wide range of records relating to transportation of convicts from Ireland to Australia from 1788 to 1868. A computerized index to the records is available here for online searches.

Commonwealth War Graves Commission Debt of Honour Register (WWI and WWII)
http://www.cwgc.org

This site hosts a database register of 1.7 million members of the armed forces in British Commonwealth countries (including the United Kingdom, Canada, Australia, and New Zealand) who died in World War I and II. Details generally include date and place of death, age, rank, parents' names, hometown, and place of burial.

COUNTY AND LOCAL GENEALOGY WEB SITES

A growing number of local sites relating to genealogy in specific parts of Ireland is available, including the following examples:

County Kilkenny Genealogy and History
http://www.rootsweb.com/~irlkik/

This page is part of the Ireland World Gen Web site. It includes maps of civil parishes, Roman Catholic parishes, baronies, poor law unions, and towns in County Kilkenny; and detailed listings of available record sources including the FHL microfilm numbers for Catholic parish registers.

Wicklow United Irishmen Database 1797–1804
http://www.pcug.org.au/~ppmay/wicklow.htm

This database of 995 records gives name and native place.

Newport (Co. Mayo) Historical Society
http://www.geocities.com/Heartland/Park/7461/histsochome.html

The society's page contains historical details of Newport and the parish of Burrishoole in County Mayo, together with lists of contents of the society's journal *Back the Road*. The site includes a map of the parish showing town-lands, a townland index, a list of surnames in the parish, and links to Newport and Mayo sites and Irish genealogy sites. There is also information about ancestors from this area, including a link to a sister site used for storing family genealogies of people with connections to the parish of Burrishoole.

Tip

IRISH GENEALOGY MAILING LISTS

There are numerous genealogy mailing lists available on the Internet for the exchange of information about topics such as Irish research, the Scots-Irish, or Canadian Orangemen. For Ireland you can find mailing lists for particular counties, such as Antrim and Wexford. A list of available Ireland mailing lists is at John Fuller's Web site, Genealogy Resources on the Internet: <http://www.roots web.com~jfuller/gen_mail.html>. A list and description of the Roots Web genealogy mailing lists for countries around the world is at <http://www.rootsweb .com/~maillist/>.

In these mailing lists you can find queries about ancestors or groups; history of surnames; information and questions about record sources; religious, historical, and cultural background; and news relating to genealogy. You can make a search by keyword of past messages from Roots Web Mailing Lists at this Web site: <http://searches.rootsweb.com/cgi-bin/listsearch.pl>.

EIGHTEEN

Inventories and Catalogs

S ometimes the record you need is published in a journal or book. But how do you find it? We often use the many published and compiled inventories available in Ireland and abroad to locate a record, a published work, a genealogy, or a pedigree. For example, you know the exact cemetery you want, but have its tombstone inscriptions been published? The following are some of the best places to look in our experience. **If you know the name of your townland, run it through these inventories** (especially the CD or Internet versions) to see what pops up.

Timesaver

PUBLISHED INDEXES AND INVENTORIES

PERSI: The Periodical Source Index (PERSI) was created by the Allen County Public Library in Fort Wayne, Indiana. This library collects periodicals from all over the world, and each year it publishes an index of articles in its periodicals and journals. You can search PERSI by places, research methodology, family names, and keyword. Many libraries have PERSI in book form or CD-ROM. Access the index online at the Ancestry HomeTown Web site <http://www.ances try.com> for a fee. Copies of the articles indexed are available from the Allen County Public Library. Remember, PERSI is not an index to everything in the articles, but rather an index to the article titles.

Smith's Inventory: FHL staff and volunteers compiled an inventory of material in periodicals, books, and microfilm held in its British Isles collections. This inventory is separate from the main FHL Catalog. The series, titled *Smith's Inventory of Genealogical Sources: Ireland*, includes a general section and one for each county. The inventory is most useful for accessing estate papers, freemen and freeholders records, genealogies, and tombstone inscriptions, but it includes other subjects as well. *Smith's Inventory* is available on microfiche.

Hayes's *Manuscript Sources* and periodical sources: Richard Hayes's fourteen-volume series *Manuscript Sources for the History of Irish Civilisation* (hereafter called *Manuscript Sources*) inventories manuscripts in Irish repositories, in private collections, and in Britain and Europe. Many of these inventoried manuscripts are at or microfilmed by the NLI. *Manuscript Sources* acts as a catalog of the NLI for materials collected through 1976. *Manuscript Sources* is available on microfilm from the FHL.

Hayes also edited a nine-volume *Sources for the History of Irish Civilisation: Articles in Irish Periodicals.* This series was published in 1970 and inventories published articles concerning genealogy, history, and other subjects. A list of the periodicals inventoried is on pages v–vii of volume one.

NIDS: *The National Inventory of Documentary Sources in the United Kingdom and Ireland* (NIDS) inventories sources in repositories in Great Britain and Ireland. Many records relating to the Irish are in Great Britain. The NIDS microfiche is arranged by repository and includes extensive details of each repository's collections. A subject index to the NIDS series, including U.S. repositories as well as Irish and British, is available on CD-ROM at the FHL. Search the CD-ROM by keyword for material in all of the repositories included in NIDS. Also search the CD-ROM Index by repository.

National Register of Archives: The Royal Commission on Historical Manuscripts (see the Appendix) produces the National Register of Archives (NRA) series. Each item in the series is an inventory of manuscript collections at a repository in the United Kingdom or Republic of Ireland. You can search a subject index to the NRA online: <http://www.hmc.gov.uk/nra/abtnra.htm>.

KEW Lists: KEW Lists is a seventeen-volume set of microfiche that inventories the holdings of the PRO at Kew, Surrey, England. The PRO has many sources concerning the Irish both in Ireland and throughout the world. Some are available on microfilm from the FHL. *KEW Lists* has a subject index to the appropriate PRO reference codes. Use these codes to access the seventeen-volume inventory. A PRO code has two parts: a letter code indicating a governmental department or institution such as the War Office (WO); and a number code such as ninety-seven, indicating a record group generated by that department. The PRO catalog is now online (see the Appendix). Specifically Irish material at the PRO is in Alice Prochaska's guide, *Irish History from 1700: A Guide to Sources in the Public Record Office.*

REFERENCES AND FURTHER READING

Hayes, Richard J., ed. *Manuscript Sources for the History of Irish Civilisation.* 11 vols., Boston: G.K. Hall and Co., 1965.

———, ed. *Sources for the History of Irish Civilisation: Articles in Irish Periodicals.* Boston: G.K. Hall and Co., 1970.

Prochaska, Alice. *Irish History from 1700: A Guide to Sources in the Public Record Office.* London: British Records Association, 1986.

Smith, Frank. *Smith's Inventory of Genealogical Sources: Ireland.* Salt Lake City, Utah: Corporation of the President, Church of Jesus Christ of Latter-day Saints, 1994.

Sources

NINETEEN

Land Records

LANDHOLDING IN IRELAND

Many of our Irish ancestors were tenant farmers who leased or rented their land directly from a landowner or indirectly from a middleman. Only a small percentage of people in Ireland owned their land outright, called "in fee." There could be several layers of subleasing between the actual landowner and your ancestor. Changes over time in the nature of tenants' arrangements with landlords were vitally important in the lives of Irish tenant farmers. Landholding arrangements affected economic well being, farming, inheritance, and emigration patterns. One common type of lease with great potential for genealogical information was the "lease for lives." **A lease for lives is in effect as long as the person(s) named in the lease are still living.** As soon as all of the "lives" named in the lease have died, the lease ceases to be in effect. Alternatively, a lease could be granted for a set number of years, or a tenant could rent from year to year without holding a lease of any kind. A tenant could occupy land completely at the landlord's discretion, called "at will."

\di'fin\ *vb*

Definitions

REGISTRY OF DEEDS

Beginning in 1708, land transactions in Ireland were registered with the Registry of Deeds in Dublin, although registration was not mandatory. In the Registry of Deeds you can find deeds of sale, lease agreements, marriage settlements, and wills. When a deed was registered in the Registry of Deeds, it was not filed there; rather, it was returned to the party who delivered it for registration. A "memorial" or synopsis of the deed was filed in the Registry of Deeds.

Don't assume that just because your ancestor was not rich and prominent, you won't find information about him or her in the Registry of Deeds. One of the most valuable finds you can make is a deed with a list of the tenants on the land. It's just unfortunate that there aren't more such deeds.

Notes

From 1708 until the relaxing of the penal laws in 1778, few deeds of Catholics were registered. Only beginning in 1782 could Catholics purchase land outright. This means that the Registry of Deeds is mainly a Protestant source for the eighteenth century. However, there were some Catholics who converted, either actually or for convenience, to Protestantism and might be in the deed books. Indeed, the penal laws did not prevent Catholics from retaining land they already owned, so some Catholics owned land throughout the period of the eighteenth-century Penal Laws.

By the nineteenth century, with religious freedom guaranteed in Ireland, these are records of persons of all religions as lessors and owners. But let's look at this realistically. Even with emancipation, **the majority of the population, Catholic and Protestant, was still landless.** They were still renting or leasing. That was all to change by the turn of the twentieth century, when the government helped many tenant farmers purchase their farms from their landlords. The Land Purchase Acts set up a Land Commission to carry out this transfer.

There are actually two useful indexes to the Registry of Deeds, but they are only in manuscript form. Understanding these indexes is your key to this valuable set of records.

Surname Index: This index is a personal name index to the sellers (grantors) of land. This index does not list the buyers (grantees) or identify the county or townland where the property was located until after 1833.

Lands Index: The other index, called the Lands Index or County Index, is arranged geographically and lists streets within towns and cities. This index is divided by county or city and time period, and groups townland names by first letter. After 1828 the County Index divides entries by the barony within the county. The Lands Index is an important source because you can access all registered transactions for a particular townland. If you really want to get a full picture of what was going on in your ancestral townland, we recommend extracting all deeds for a townland from 1708 forward. Many times the townland names are spelled phonetically, and a number of different spellings for the same townland are in the records. For an example see page 233.

The huge collection of records of the Registry of Deeds from 1708 to 1929, and the corresponding Surname Index and Lands (or County) Index, are available on microfilm from the FHL. The Registry of Deeds on Henrietta Street in Dublin has books of memorials dating 1708 to the present and microfilm copies dating 1930 to present.

If your ancestor was a landowner or had a registered lease, the Registry of Deeds might provide a wealth of information. You can find information about deaths, inheritances, and the relationships of family members in the text of the deeds. Some wills were registered in the Registry of Deeds, primarily for prominent families. Wills dating 1708 to 1832 in the Registry of Deeds have been extracted and published with a place name index as follows:

- Beryl P. Eustace. *Registry of Deeds, Dublin, Abstract of Wills.* Volume 1

THE CALLAGHY DEED SAGA

Contributed by Professor Thomas Callaghy, University of Pennsylvania

From Whence the Ancestral Callaghys in County Galway?

My great-grandfather, Thomas Callaghy, married Ellen Mary Mahoney. I don't know when or where they were married, but Ellen was from Athenry town, County Galway. This couple, along with some of the Mahoneys from Athenry, immigrated to Northbridge, Massachusetts.

Callaghy [Callagy] is a rare Irish name found mostly in County Galway. I did not find any record of my Callagys in the parts of Galway where the name is usually found. After much work, I unearthed an 1878 death certificate for a James Callagy in Athenry, County Galway, which lies north of normal Callagy terrain. Although I found my great-grandmother's family [Mahoneys] in both the Catholic parish register and civil registration records for Athenry, I could find no other evidence of Callagys in Athenry civil parish except for three references to Callaghy godparents in the parish register.

Callagys in Athenry Civil Parish in 1821

I remembered, however, that one of the few remaining fragments of the 1821 census covers Athenry civil parish. In it I found the Patrick Callagy family, consisting of nine people with first names that are common in my family, including a six-year-old James, who I think is my great-great-grandfather and the man who died in Athenry in 1878. The family lived on three acres in a huge townland called Castle and Spiddle Gate, which covers about fifteen surveyed townlands in modern-day Ireland. Now my research problem was: Where were the Callagys living in 1821 in terms of the modern townlands? Using notations in the 1821 census margins and matching surnames against Griffith's Primary Valuation, I did manage to narrow it down to three possible current townlands: Castle Turvin, Clamper Park, and Turloughalanger.

Trying the Registry of Deeds

I turned to deeds as a possible way to determine where the Callagys were in 1821. I hoped that I might find in the deeds a list of tenants including my ancestors, although this happens only rarely. The deeds are hard to read at first because of all the legal language, but you quickly learn to spot names and places. The Registry of Deeds indexes and memorials I used were all on microfilm at the Family History Library in Salt Lake City.

I started using the Lands Index, which lists deeds by county, barony, and townland. I first worked backward from 1821 to 1708. Castle Turvin occurred infrequently and only after about 1790, but in the few deeds where it was listed, I came across other names for it, such as "Maugheranure and Monroe called

Castle Turvin." Looking under Maugheranure and Monroe and other newly discovered townland names in the Lands Index, I discovered a number of deeds that were not listed under Castle Turvin.

I also used the Surname Index to the Registry of Deeds, looking up the surnames of Turvin and other major landowners I had identified from the 1821 census. This Surname Index search yielded many of the same deeds, some referring to Castle Turvin and/or Maugheranure and Monroe. Turloughalanger shows up by itself in the indexes first in 1820, and Clamper Park not until 1867.

Diligent Searching Pays Off

None of these deeds, however, contained any reference to tenants. Hence, with hope in my heart, I started working in the time period after 1821, using all the new townland names that had emerged from the land indexes before 1821. I looked at all of these deeds on the rolls of microfilm at my local family history center as they came in from Salt Lake City, covering the period 1820 to 1880. Finally, I struck gold with a short 1840 deed of lease between a Mark Browne, Esquire of Rockville (Rockfield) and a John Burke, farmer, "regarding that part of the lands of Turloughalanger lately in the possession of himself and that part held lately by Patrick Callagy containing fifteen acres." The deed includes the usual covenants between landlord and tenant and also a covenant against subletting. I interpret this deed to mean that Patrick Callagy had left the land by 1840. Samuel Lewis's *Topographical Dictionary of Ireland* (1837) lists, under Craughwell town, several gentlemen seats in the neighborhood among which is "Rockfield, of Mark Browne, Esq."

There it was; I had just moved the Callagys from 1821 to 1840 and shown their residence in Turloughalanger townland, Athenry civil parish. Of course, this still only brings the Callagys up to 1840, with the big gap until the 1878 death certificate remaining unfilled, so I have more work to do.

(1708–1745), Volume 2 (1746–1788). Dublin: Stationery Office for the Irish Manuscript Commission, 1954–1956.
- Eilish Ellis and P. Beryl Eustace. *Registry of Deeds, Dublin, Abstract of Wills*. Volume 3 (1785–1832). Dublin: Stationery Office for the Irish Manuscript Commission, 1984.

PRE–1708 DEEDS

The NAI has acquired manuscript copies of a number of pre-1708 Irish deeds from private collections. These are deeds from before the time of the Registry of Deeds. The NAI also has a card index to the deposited pre-1708 deeds arranged alphabetically by surname, and another index arranged geographically.

FREEHOLDERS RECORDS

A freeholder was a man who held his property either "in fee," which, as mentioned, means outright ownership, or by a lease for one or more lives (such as the term of his life or the term of three lives named in the lease). A tenant who held land for a definite period such as thirty-one years or one hundred years did not qualify as a freeholder. A person with a freehold of sufficient value, depending on the law at the time, could register to vote. The records are called freeholders registers. **A freeholders register may list some or all of the following information:**

1. The name of the freeholder
2. The residence of the freeholder
3. The location of the freehold
4. The value of the freehold
5. The lives named in the lease or other tenure
6. The date and place the freeholder registered
7. The name of landlord
8. The occupation of tenant

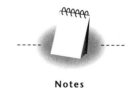

Notes

A freeholders register can help pinpoint where your ancestor was living within a county, particularly helpful if the relevant church records were destroyed. The lives named in leases were often related to the leaseholder, so the freeholders list can suggest family relationships. With the name of a landlord, you can turn to estate papers (see chapter fifteen).

Unfortunately, many original manuscript freeholders registers were destroyed in the Public Record Office fire of 1922. However, not all is lost. Some freeholders registers were published in places such as newspapers prior to the fire. Copies of the destroyed records do exist in some cases. In other cases, freeholders registers were kept by private individuals, such as landowners who wanted to know what voting freeholders lived on their estates. The NAI, the NLI, and the PRONI each have significant collections of freeholders records they have built over the years from the surviving material.

Kyle J. Betit's article "Freeholders, Freemen and Voting Registers" in *The Irish At Home and Abroad* lists known surviving freeholders records for every county in Ireland. Other freeholders records not listed in this article are in some other inventories, such as John Grenham's book, James G. Ryan's work, and the card catalogue in the Manuscript Reading Room of the NLI, which lists the library's latest manuscript acquisitions.

LAND COMMISSION

If you want to find out how property in Ireland came into the ownership of a family member, you will often need to consult records of the Land Commission. The Land Commission made loans from public funds to tenants so they could buy their farms from their landlords. The commission operated from 1881 to 1923 according to the Land Purchase Acts. If you see "LAP" in the Griffith's Valuation revision lists (see chapter twenty-three) for your townland, it refers

Barony of Bunratty.

No	Name of Freeholder.	Place of Abode.	Situation of Freehold.	Name of Landlord.	Val.	Names of Lives or other Tenure	Date of Registry.
	Connor Clune	Ballymaclune	Ballymaclune	Thos. Browne, Esq.	40s	Mathew and Connor Clune	June 14, 1824
	Patrick Connellan	Ballinruan	Ballinruan	Rt. Hon. J. FitzGerald	40s	Maurice O'Connor, and Michael Clarke	June 25, 1824
	Wm. Clarke	Clounamony	Clounamony	same	40s	same	Do.
	Charles Clarke	same	same	same	40s	same	Do.
	Patrick Carney	Gurtnemerican West	Gurtnemerican West	same	40s	same	Do.
	John Carney	same	same	same	40s	Peter Regan Junior	Do.
	Edmond Carmody	Callura East	Callura East	same	40s	same	Do.
	Michael Conway	same	same	same	40s	same	Do.
	Michael Carney	same	same	same	40s	same	Do.
	Patrick Clohessy	same	same	same	40s	Lott Cunneen	Do.
	Martin Cunneen	Crusheenbeg	Crusheenbeg	same	40s	Patrick Corry	Do.
51	Patrick Curry	Clounmony	Clonmony	same	40s	Patrick M'Namara	Do.
52	John Conney	Callura West	Callura West	same	40s	William Carroll	Do.
53	Michael Carrol	Nutfield	Clouncashin	R. C. Fleming, Esq.	40s	Pat. Hinchy	Do.
64	Michael Cunnigham	Dromanin	Dromanin	Mr. Hugh Carrigg	40s	Patrick Hussett	Do.
65	Michael Collins	Ballyvanna	Ballyvanna	same	40s	Patrick Hinchy	Do.
66	John Casack	Dromanin	Dromanin	Rt. Hon. J. FitzGerald	40s	Hugh O'Loghlen and John Silver	June 28, 1824
67	Stephen Casey	Clonmony	Clonmony	John Colpoys, Esq.	40s	Robert Creagh, Esq	Do.
68	Patrick Cunneen	Brickhill	Brickhill	same	40s	same	Do.
69	William Collins	same	same	same	40s	same	Do.
70	Michael Corry	same	same	same	40s	same	Do.
71	Thomas Carmody	Ballinvonte	Do. & Ballinvonte	same	40s	same	Do.
72	Michael Carmody	same	same	same	40s	William Cross	Do.
73	William Cross	Granahan	Granahan	William Scott, Esq.	40s	Bridget M'Mahon	Do.
74	Patrick Callahan	Pouligill	Pouligill	Augustine Butler, Esq	10s	John Clune	July 14, 1824.
75	Michael Conway	Gortafuka	Gortofika	same	10s	same	Do.
76	Connor Conway	same	same	same	40s	same	Do.
77	John Conway	same	same	same	10s	same	Do.
78	Michael Clune	same	same	same	40s	same	Do.
79	Thomas Conway	same	same	same	40s	John M'Mahon	Do.
80	Patrick Cullinan	Shranagalloon	Shranagalloon	same	40s	John Carroll	Do.
81	James Carroll	same	same	same	40s	Batt Conway	Do.
82	Batt Conway	Cullinagh	Cullinagh	same	40s	John Markum	Do.
83	John Cunningham	Clonneen	Clonneen	E. S. Hickman, Esq.	40s	Rt. Hon. J. Fitzgerald and Mathias M'Mahon	July 31, 1824
84	Michael Connors	Gaurus	same	same	40s	same	Do.
85	Patrick Connors	same	Knockanoura	same	40s	Michael and Mathew Clune	Do.
86	Michael Clune	Knockanoura	Crevagh	John Scott, Esq.	40s	Patrick Slattery	Do.
87	Thomas Carmody	Creevagh	Knockangon	same	40s	James, John, and Michael Coffee	Do.
88	Patrick Coffee	Knocknagon	Carowhill	Rob. Kean Chas. Esq.	40s	Michael Conway	August 27, 1824
89	Thomas Cusack	Carrowhill	same	same	40s	same	Do.
90	Michael Conway	same	same	same	40s	same	Do.
91	Richard Curran	same	Ballybrehane	Chas. Stuidert, Esq.	40s	Michal M'Namara, Pat M'Inerheny & Jn. Torpy	Do.
92	Thomas Clune	Ballybrehane	Maghery	Michael Foster, Esq.	40s	William Dillon	Do.
93	James Corbett	Maghery	same	Hor. Stapleton, Esq.	40s	James Corbett and John M'Mahon	Sept. 3, 1824
94	Edmond Corbett	same	same	Thomas Spaight, Esq.	40s	James Corbett	Do.
95	James Corbett	Cappamore	Cappamore	Jas. B. Butler, Esq	40s	Patrick Coffy	October 11, 1824
96	Patrick Coffy	Quin	Quin	Rev. P. M'Mahon	40s	Thomas Collins	Oct. 21, 1824
97	Thomas Collins	Knockaughrim	Knockaughrim	C. O'Callaghan	40s	John Kerin and John Keane	October 28, 1824
98	Thomas Clohessy	same	same	same	40s	John Kerin, John Keane, and John Clohessy	Do.
99	John Clobessy	Gurteen	Gurteen	Stamers Minors	40s	Michael, John, Daniel and Tim Clune	Oct. 29, 1824
100	John Clune	same	same	same	40s	same	Do.
101	Daniel Clune	same	same	same	10s	same	Do.
102	Timothy Clune	Doramore	Knockogan	same	10s	Michael, John, and Mathew M'Inerheny	Do.
103	James Connell	Crogane	Crogane	same	10s	John Burns and Pat Nihill	Do.
104	James Clune	Croagh	Crevagh	John Scott, Esq	10s	Patrick Slattery	Do.
105	Patrick Carmody	Newmarket	Newmarket	Ths. M'Mahon, Esq	10s	Martin Lewis and Thomas Carroll	Nov. 6, 1824
106	Thomas Carrol	Knockanean	Cappa	Rich. Gregg, Esq	40s	John, Denis and Wm. Considine	Do.
107	Michael Considine	Moohane	Moohane	Sir E. O'Brien, Bart	40s	James Clancy	Nov. 11, 1824
108	Denis Cunneen	same	same	same	40s	same	Do.
109	John Clancy	same	same	same	40s	same	Do.
110	Patrick Clancy	Loungah	Loungah	same	40s	James Cunneen	Do.
111	Patrick Cunneen	Rathfoland	Rathfoland	same	40s	John Woods	Do.
112	Cornelius Conry	Carnakelly	Carnakelly	same	40s	John Cullinan	Do.
113	John Cullinan	same	same	same	40s	Patrick Cahill	Do.
114	Patrick Cahill	Castlekeal	Ballinacraggy	same	20s		Dec. 7, 1824
115	Michael Connell	Moohane	Moohane	same	40s	James Clancy	Do.
116	John Cullinan	Portrine	Portrine	Dunat O'Brien, Esq	40s	Owen Cain	Do.
117	Michael Cain	same	same	same	40s	same	Do.
118	Patrick Cleary	Derryealliff East	Derryealliff East	Henry Butler, Esq.	40s	P. Halloransen, P. Halloran jun. & Jn. Hencher	Dec. 15, 1824
119	Daniel Considine	same	same	same	40s	same	Do.
120	Patrick Connors	same	same	same	40s	same	Do.
121	Thomas Clancy	Derryealliff West	Derryealliff West	same	40s	same	Do.
122	Thomas Connell	same	same	same	40s	same	Do.
123	Michael Culligan	Commeen	Commeen	same	40s	same	Do.
124	Michael Considine	same	same	same	40s	same	Do.
125	Timothy Considine	Knockareddane	Knockeredane	same	40s	same	Do.
126	John Cummane	same	same	same	40s	same	Do.
127	Denis Cummane	Derryhuma	Derryhuma	same	40s	same	Do.
128	Edmond Cusack			same	10s	same	Do.

D.

No	Name of Freeholder.	Place of Abode.	Situation of Freehold.	Name of Landlord.	Val.	Names of Lives or other Tenure	Date of Registry.
1	James Doherty	Oilacotty	Oilacotty	Sir Ed. O'Brien, Bart.	40s	Laurence Boughly and John Liddy Jones	Feb. 3, 1824
2	John Doherty	same	same	same	40s	same	Do.
3	John Doherty	same	same	same	40s	Pat. Mitchell, Jas. Doherty, & Margt. Sheehan	Feb. 13, 1824
4	James Doherty	same	same	same	40s	same	Do.
5	John Doyle	Newmarket	Newmarket	same	40s	John Doyle	Do.
6	Samuel Doyle	same	same	same	40s	Samuel Doyle	Do.
7	George Darcy	same	same	same	40s	George Darcy	Do.
8	Andrew Deloughery	Moohane	Moohane	same	40s	Edmond Doloughery	Feb. 20, 1824
9	James Daveen	Kilkeran	Kilkeran	same	40s	James Davern	June 7, 1824
10	John Dolan	Granahan	Granahan	John Colpoys, Esq	40s	Thomas Donohoe	June 10, 1824
11	John Dolan jun.	Atish	Atish	Rt. Hn. J. Fitzgerald	40s	Maurice O'Connor, and Michael Clarke	June 25, 1824
12	Patrick Dolan	Caluragh East	Calluragh West	same	40s	Daniel Dally	Do.
13	Thomas Donnellan	Gurtnemerican West	Gurtnemerican West.	same	40s	John Halloran	Do.
14	John Dally	Stonepark	Stonepark	Robt. C. Fleming, Esq	40s	Maurice O'Connor, and Michael Clarke	Do.

Figure 19-1
County Clare Voters 1824, Barony of Bunratty (back of first page, surnames C and D), from the Co. Clare Crown and Peace Office. Material now at the National Archives of Ireland, Dublin (1D/40/37).

to the transfer of ownership to the tenant by "Land Purchase Act."

The NLI holds two card indexes to the Land Commission records, a Topographical Index arranged by county, barony, and landowner; and a Names Index arranged alphabetically by landowner. Each card in the Names Index gives the baronies in which the estate was located and the estate number. Using the estate number, you can consult bound volumes that give a summary description of the estate's documents. These bound volumes were prepared by Edward Keane in his survey of the Land Commission records.

The Land Commission is located in the same building as the NAI and has the records for the counties that are now in the Republic of Ireland. Its holdings are vast but difficult to access because you must call ahead for permission. In preparation for land transfers to tenants, the commission created documents listing the tenants and their acreage and prepared maps showing the boundaries of farms in each townland in the estate. Once the Land Commission had processed the land, the tenant's deed and subsequent transactions relating to the property became the concern of the Land Registry.

The Land Commission records for the Northern Ireland counties were sent to the PRONI after the political division of Ireland. You can access Land Commission records at the PRONI by using the Land Registry Archive inventory in the PRONI's guide, *Guide to Landed Estate Records*. Consult Ian Maxwell's book for further details about the PRONI's Land Registry Archive.

LAND REGISTRY

The Land Registry was established in 1892 to provide a system of compulsory registration of land titles. When a title is registered in the Land Registry, the deeds are filed there, and all relevant information concerning the property and its ownership are entered on registers called, which are folios maintained in the Land Registry. Once under the jurisdiction of the Land Registry, records of a plot of land are no longer found in the Registry of Deeds. A folio is a document describing the registered property and the registered owner and refers to a plan on the Registry maps that go with the folios. The Registration of Title Act of 1891 made registration of title compulsory for all land bought under the Land Purchase Acts. This meant that all subsequent transactions affecting the land would have to be registered. **The Land Registry is split into several offices, each covering certain counties:**

Cavan, Louth, Monaghan, Donegal, Leitrim, Meath & Westmeath: Central Office, Chancery Street, Dublin 7, Ireland; Phone: (01) 6707500.

Cork, Kerry, Limerick, Waterford, Carlow, Kilkenny, Wexford & Laois: New Government Buildings, Cork Road, Waterford City, Ireland; Phone: (051) 303001.

Dublin & Counties West of the Shannon: Setanta House, Nassau Street, Dublin 2, Ireland; Phone: (01) 6707500.

Kildare & Wicklow: Block 1, Irish Life Centre, Lower Abbey Street, Dublin 1, Ireland; Phone: (01) 6707500.

Notes

Land Registry Internet Site
http://www.irlgov.ie/landreg/land_registry_services.htm

REFERENCES AND FURTHER READING

Sources

Agnew, Jean. "How to Use the Registry of Deeds of Ireland, Dublin." *Familia: Ulster Genealogical Review* 2 (1990): 78–84.

Betit, Kyle J. "Freeholders, Freemen and Voting Registers." *The Irish At Home and Abroad* 6 (4) (4th Quarter 1999): 146–164.

Collins, Peter. "Eighteenth-Century Records." *Pathways to Ulster's Past: Sources and Resources for Local Studies*, 21–23. Belfast: The Institute of Irish Studies, The Queen's University of Belfast, 1998.

TWENTY

Military Records

T he Irish made up a large percentage of the British Army. Not only were well-educated young men attracted to the British Army, but many poor young men also would use Army enlistment to improve their status in life. The Army was often a family tradition. Use the records generated about these men and their families in your genealogical research to reconstruct what your ancestor did with his life. If you're looking for your Army ancestor's birthplace, his military records might reveal it.

Exploring the topic of British military records is literally a journey through the history of one of the greatest (for good and bad) empires in world history. The expression "The sun never set on the British Empire" is literally true. Within this vast empire, Irish men and their families found themselves far from home in places such as the Ionian Islands in Greece, British India, the Caribbean Islands, the Pacific, and Africa. Wherever the English went, the Irish were present also. This military sojourn around the globe was accompanied by Irish merchants, civil servants, and politicians. It also led to the Irish intermarrying into most cultures wherever the military went, bringing Irish culture worldwide.

The chances of finding your Irish ancestor or a relative somehow involved with the British Army is good. This chapter will relate some of the major sources for using British Army records as well as related organizations, such as the local Irish militias and Irish yeomanry (cavalry) that supplemented the regular British Army. We will also discuss some sources up through World War I.

RESEARCH GUIDES

We recommend a couple of research guides to consult in beginning to use Army records: Michael J. Watts and Christopher T. Watts's *My Ancestor Was in the British Army: How Can I Find Out More About Him?* and Simon Fowler's *Army Records for Family Historians.*

Most British military records are at the PRO at Kew, with large collections

Printed Source

on microfilm at the FHL. The PRO classifies military records under the War Office (WO) series. With the British Army, your problem might not be a scarcity of records, but rather so many different types of records that you don't know where to start! Because of this, the WO reference number for a set of records is particularly important.

IDENTIFYING A REGIMENT

Research Tip

One difficulty in using military records is that you must determine the ancestor's regiment, since most records are arranged and accessible by the regiment. Fortunately, some computer databases are making this job easier. A prime source for identifying your soldier ancestor's regiment is the PRO's computerized index of the Soldiers' Documents (WO 97), 1760 to 1854. You can search it by name, regiment, and county or country of birth. If you can't get to the PRO yourself, you will have to have an agent search this index. This index can be a quick fix, but remember: Not all soldiers received a pension, and some soldiers took land in lieu of a pension. Only pensioners are indexed.

Family sources and other records that can help identify the name or number of a British Army regiment include:

Family pictures: If you have a photograph of your ancestor in a uniform, this can be an essential clue to get you off the ground. Books that describe uniforms and contain pictures are Robert Wilkinson-Lathams' *Infantry Uniforms*; W.Y. Carman's *Richard Simkins Uniforms of the British Army*; Ronald H. Montague's *Dress and Insignia of the British Army in Australia and New Zealand, 1770–1870*. Compare your picture with those in these books.

Badges and medals: A military item such as a sword, badge, or some type of medal might have been passed down as a family heirloom. You might also notice such items in a photograph of your soldier ancestor. Sources recording servicemen who received medals are at the PRO with microfilm copies at the FHL.

Names of battles and places of service: A legend in your family that your ancestor fought in a particular battle or that he was stationed at a certain place might be an important clue for determining his Army regiment. Arthur Swinson's *A Register of the Regiments and Corps of the British Army* provides a chronology of where each regiment served as well as the various names by which it was known. John M. Kitzmiller's *In Search of the "Forlorn Hope": A Comprehensive Guide to Locating British Regiments and Their Records (1640–WWI)* lists not only where regiments were stationed but also from where they were originally recruited. Note that in Kitzmiller's work, a regiment listed as originally recruited in England does not preclude the presence of Irish soldiers in the regiment.

Local sources: By "local sources," we mean sources in whichever country the soldier lived or was stationed. Local sources include censuses, birth, death and marriage registers, obituaries, tombstones, cemetery records, hospital records, land records, and church records.

Civil registration: Irish civil registration beginning in 1879 registered marriages and deaths of Irish personnel serving in the British Army abroad along with the births of their children. Beginning in 1882 (for marriages) and 1886 (for births and deaths), the indexes to the Army registers are at the end of the country-wide civil registration indexes (see chapter thirteen).

ARMY SOURCES FOR ENLISTED MEN

Regimental registers (1761–1924): These contain births/baptisms, marriages, and burials of soldiers and their families compiled by each regiment. There is a composite index of births/baptisms but not of marriages or deaths. The birth records identify the regiment in which the father was serving. To access the marriages and deaths, you must know a regiment. If you suspect that a soldier was in a specific regiment because he was stationed in a certain place, regimental registers might confirm this theory. The records and the index to births are at the Family Records Centre in London.

Chaplains' returns (1796–1880): These contain records of baptisms, marriages, and burials kept by military chaplains at stations abroad but do not include Ireland. The indexed records are at the Family Records Centre in London and identify the soldier's regiment. The microfiched index is widely available.

District pensions (WO 22): Pensioned soldiers were paid by district offices throughout the Empire between 1842 and 1862, with records in some areas of the world continuing longer. You can trace a soldier geographically through pension records even though his regiment is unknown. When a pensioned soldier changed his residence or emigrated, his pension was transferred to a new district office. If you know a residence, you can examine the district pensions for that place in the appropriate time period to identify his regiment. For further information, including a list of districts in Ireland and worldwide with PRO reference numbers, see Dwight A. Radford's article "District Pension Records of the British Army" in *The Irish At Home and Abroad*.

Chelsea and Kilmainham hospitals: Pension applicants were processed through the Chelsea Hospital in London and the Royal Hospital Kilmainham in Dublin. Records of both hospitals are at the PRO with many on microfilm at the FHL. At these hospitals, applicants for pension were examined, statements were taken, and the soldiers were either discharged to pension or refused pension. The most important feature about these hospital records is that they provide the birthplace of the soldier, his age, and where he enlisted and was discharged. Following are descriptions of some of the Chelsea and Kilmainham records in the War Office series.

- Chelsea Regimental Registers (WO 120): These are lists of soldiers discharged to pension. From about 1750 to 1843, they provide biographical information. From 1843 to 1857, biographical information was not given, but the registers do name the district pay office where the pension was paid (see WO 22). The registers are arranged by regiment and date of discharge and are at the PRO. A partial index to registers from 1806 to

1836 is in *Index, "Chelsea Out Pensioners From 1806–1836, (Source WO 120/20–33 at KEW)."* Norman K. Crowder's *British Army Pensioners Abroad* serves as an index to veterans who settled abroad with an army pension who are included in WO 120.

- Soldiers' Documents (1760–1913) (WO 97): Soldiers' Documents concern soldiers discharged on pension through Chelsea. The documents survive only for soldiers who received a pension. There is a wealth of information in the records including age, regiment, birthplace, and place stationed. Soldiers' Documents are filed by regiment and alphabetically by surname. They are at the PRO with microfilm copies at the FHL. Just as a reminder, the PRO has a computerized index of the Soldiers' Documents (WO 97), from 1760 to 1854. This is a prime source for locating birthplaces and regiments.

  A major difficulty with the Chelsea records is that many soldiers have the same name. For this reason, even with a complete index to the Chelsea records, you will often need to know more than just the name of the soldier ancestor to identify the correct individual. Vital information such as where stationed, where born, when born, or the regiment will assist in this search.

- Kilmainham Admission Books (1704–1922) (WO 118): These are arranged in chronological order, and those dating 1759 to 1822 are indexed. Up to 1822, they generally give the soldier's age and a record of his service and pension. From 1822 on, they usually give other details such as birthplace and occupation. The Kilmainham Admission Books from 1759 to 1863 are on microfilm at the FHL. Gregory O'Connnor's article "Records of the Royal Hospital, Kilmainham (RHK)" in *Gateway to the Past* discusses the records of this hospital.

Regimental description and succession books (1756–1878) (WO 25): These books give brief biographical information such as birthplace for each enlisted man in the regiment. Unfortunately, many of these books have not survived. A regiment must be identified before using these records. A number of the books are on microfilm at the FHL.

Pay lists and muster books: These records show the service of officers and enlisted men in a regiment over a specific time period such as three months or a year. Use these volumes to determine where a soldier and his regiment were stationed throughout his career. They will tell you if a soldier was on detachment, which means he served in a location separate from the main body of the regiment. When a soldier joined a regiment, his age and physical description might be given. When a soldier left a regiment, the books tell if he was discharged or to what regiment he was transferred. You must know a regiment to use pay lists and muster books.

BRITISH ARMY OFFICERS

Within the ranks of the officers, you will find members of well-educated and affluent families. They were mainly Protestants, including many Irish. During

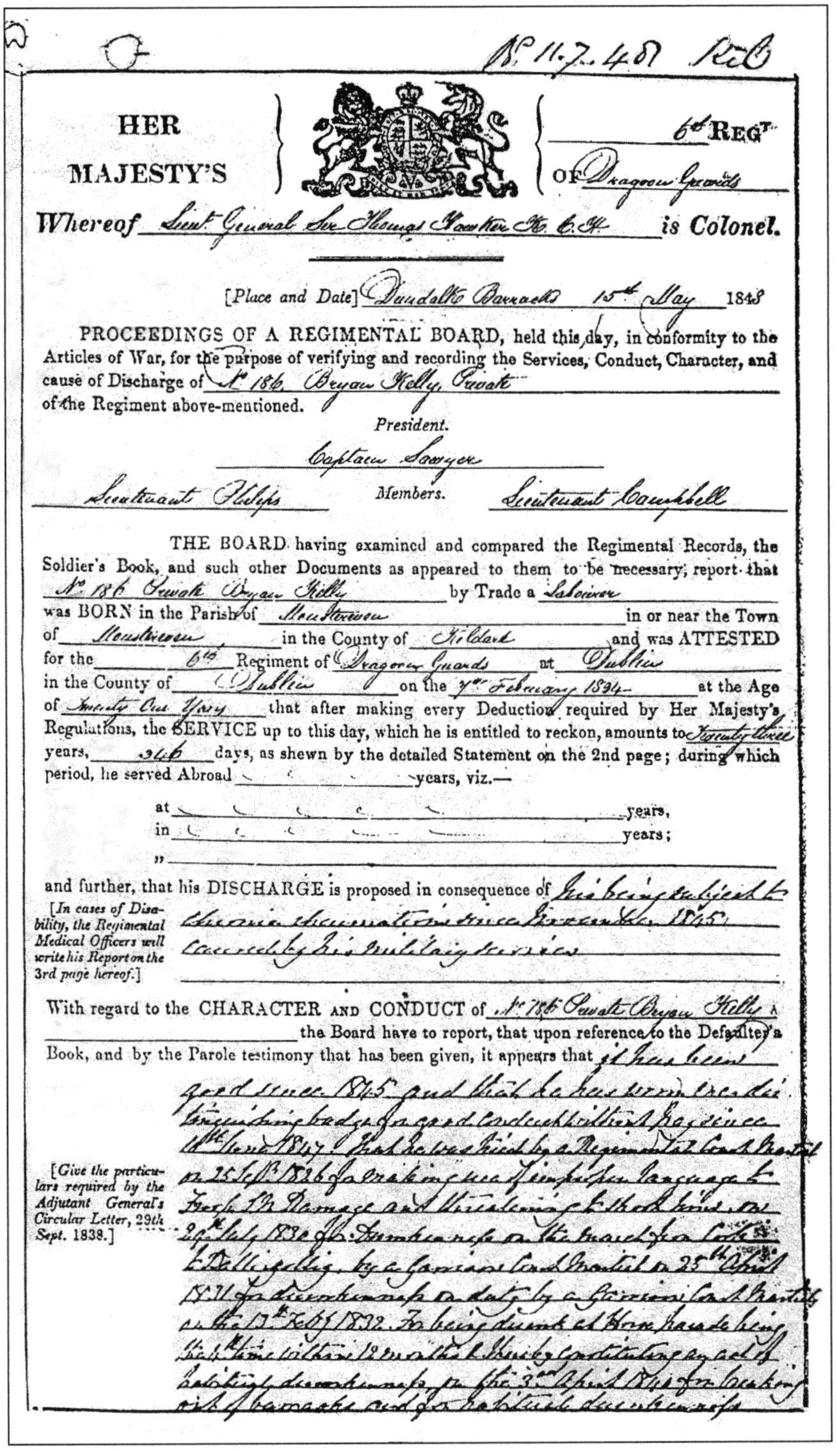
HER MAJESTY'S 6th REGT. OF Dragoon Guards

Whereof Lieut. General Sir Thomas Hawker K. C. H. is Colonel.

[Place and Date] Dundalk Barracks 15th May 1848

PROCEEDINGS OF A REGIMENTAL BOARD, held this day, in conformity to the Articles of War, for the purpose of verifying and recording the Services, Conduct, Character, and cause of Discharge of No. 186 Bryan Kelly, Private of the Regiment above-mentioned.

President.

Captain Sawyer

Lieutenant Philips *Members.* Lieutenant Campbell

THE BOARD having examined and compared the Regimental Records, the Soldier's Book, and such other Documents as appeared to them to be necessary, report that No. 186 Private Bryan Kelly by Trade a Labourer was BORN in the Parish of Monasterevan in or near the Town of Monasterevan in the County of Kildare and was ATTESTED for the 6th Regiment of Dragoon Guards at Dublin in the County of Dublin on the 7th February 1834 at the Age of Twenty One Years that after making every Deduction required by Her Majesty's Regulations, the SERVICE up to this day, which he is entitled to reckon, amounts to Twenty three years, 346 days, as shewn by the detailed Statement on the 2nd page; during which period, he served Abroad years, viz.—

at years,
in years;
"

and further, that his DISCHARGE is proposed in consequence of his being subject to chronic rheumatism since November 1845 caused by his military services

[*In cases of Disability, the Regimental Medical Officers will write his Report on the 3rd page hereof.*]

With regard to the CHARACTER AND CONDUCT of No. 186 Private Bryan Kelly the Board have to report, that upon reference to the Defaulter's Book, and by the Parole testimony that has been given, it appears that it has been good since 1845 and that he has worn one distinguishing badge of good conduct without pay since ... 1847 ...

[*Give the particulars required by the Adjutant General's Circular Letter, 29th Sept. 1838.*]

Figure 20-1
Sample from British Army Soldier's Documents, WO97/76. Original at the Public Record Office, Kew, Surrey, England (Crown copyright).

the early days of the British Army, Catholics were prohibited from being officers. Records you can use to identify an officer's regiment and other information about an officer include:

Lists of officers (WO 65): These annual lists provide the regiment. The officers' names were published in *Army List* (London: several publishers,

1754–present). Editions of *Army List* from 1754 to 1915 are on microfilm at the FHL. The lists are indexed beginning in 1765; however, the half-pay (semi-retired) officers were not included in the earlier indexes.

1828 and 1829 Return of Officer's Service (WO 25/780–805): All officers (retired or active) living in 1828 and 1829 were required to fill out forms showing their military history as well as their family history. The return was transcribed as *Children of Officers on Fullpay, 1829* and *Children of Officers on Full or Halfpay, 1828*. These records can act as an index to the Return of Officer's Service for 1828 and 1829.

Applications for pensions for widows and children (WO 42): These records are arranged alphabetically. The applications for the period of 1755 to 1908 are on microfilm at the FHL.

Records of Officers' Service (WO 76): These documents, filed by regiment, cover the period 1771 to 1919 and give birthplaces. They are on microfilm at the FHL.

WORLD WAR I

It is an unfortunate fact of history that many of the service records of the World War I soldiers in the British Army were destroyed during World War II, and most of the surviving World War I records are badly damaged. The surviving records are called the "Burnt Collection" and pertain to about 25 to 30 percent of the approximately three million men who served in the British Army during World War I. The records are at the Ministry of Defence at Hayes, Middlesex, England. The staff will conduct a search for a fee. The PRO has microfilmed the Burnt Collection (WO 363).

The so-called "Unburnt Collection" of WWI service records was compiled from duplicate records of the Ministry of Pensions. These records cover about 10 percent of those who served. They are available at the PRO (WO 364) and on microfilm from the FHL.

Sources

Information about soldiers and officers who died in WWI are in the following sources:

- The Commonwealth War Graves Commission Debt of Honour Register (WWI and WWII) at <http://www.cwgc.org> site hosts a database register of 1.7 million members of the armed forces in British Commonwealth countries, including the United Kingdom, Canada, Australia, and New Zealand, who died in WWI and WWII. Details generally include date and place of death, age, rank, parents' names, hometown, and place of burial.
- The CD-ROM *Soldiers Died in the Great War 1914–19* is a complete database of all officers and soldiers in the British Army who died in WWI. This CD is produced by The Naval and Military Press Ltd. (Version 1.1 published in 1998) <http://www.naval-military-press.co.uk>. There are about 635,000 soldiers and 37,000 officers included.
- *Officers Died in the Great War 1914–1919.* London: H.M.S.O., 1919. New enlarged ed., Polstead, Suffolk: J.B. Hayward and Sons, 1988.

- *Soldiers Died in the Great War, 1914–19.* 80 parts. London: H.M.S.O., 1920–1921. Reprint, Colchester: J.B. Hayward and Sons, 1988.
- *The Bond of Sacrifice: A Biographical Record of All the British Officers Who Fell in the Great War.* 2 vols. Anglo-African Publishing Contractors, 1916.

IRISH MILITIA

The term militia refers to a body of infantry men enrolled for emergency military service on a local basis. Local cavalry forces were called "yeomanry." The Irish militia and yeomanry supplemented the regular British Army forces during certain periods. Irish militia and yeomanry records are largely kept at the PRO in the WO class just like the Army records are. Other militia and yeomanry documents are found at the PRONI in Belfast and the FHL. For historical background about the militia and yeomanry, see G.A. Hayes-McCoy's *Irish Battles: A Military History of Ireland.* For genealogical perspectives, we recommend Gibson and Medlycott's *Militia Lists and Musters 1757–1876: A Directory of Holdings in the British Isles* and Kyle J. Betit's article "Irish Militia and Yeomanry Records" in *The Irish At Home and Abroad.*

Militia Records of the Seventeenth Century

In the early 1600s Ulster was "planted" with Protestant settlers from Scotland and England. The "undertakers" who were granted land in the Plantation were required to muster their Protestant tenants for inspection by the Muster Master General, who recorded the names and ages of the tenants and the types of arms they had. All Protestant males between the ages of sixteen and sixty were liable to service in the militia. Copies of some seventeenth century Ulster militia records survive and are detailed on the PRONI Web site at <http://proni.nics.gov.uk/records/militia.htm>. The seventeenth century Ulster militia records list the undertakers and sometimes divide the lists of tenants by parish or by barony.

Militia Records 1793–1925

The Irish militia was reestablished in 1793 with thirty-seven county or city battalions and regiments. Under the 1793 Militia Bill, the militia was drawn by lot from the able-bodied male population aged eighteen to forty-five, without respect to religion; men served four-year enlistments in Ireland outside their home counties. During the period 1793 to 1816 the Irish militia was quite active. Militia units moved around Ireland, to England and other localities but not overseas. Records include

- Militia records of the Irish county and city militia, 1793 to 1909 (WO 68). These are on microfilm at the FHL. They include "Enrollment and Description Books" for soldiers and "Record of Officers Services" books for officers.
- Militia muster books and pay lists (WO 13).

- Militia Attestation Papers, 1806 to 1915 (WO 96), were filed at recruitment but also in most cases give the date of discharge. The attestation papers give date and place of birth.
- Militia soldier's documents, 1760 to 1872 (WO 97, vol. 1091–1112). These concern soldiers discharged to pension. They are arranged in surname alphabetical order regardless of unit and give birthplace, age at enlistment, and service data. The militia soldier's documents are available on microfilm from the FHL.

IRISH YEOMANRY CORPS, 1796–1834

The Irish yeomanry corps originated in 1796 as a civilian volunteer defense force to augment the regular army and militia. The yeomen were primarily Protestant, although there were Catholic members. The yeomanry could be called out to suppress public disorders and assist the regular army in case of invasion or insurrection. The yeomanry was officially disbanded in 1834.

There are quarterly muster returns of yeomanry companies in Ireland from 1823 to 1834 (WO 13). You can find collections of records of local yeomanry corps in other repositories such the NAI and Armagh County Museum.

The Armagh County Museum also has typescript copies of lists of officers of the yeomanry in Ireland for 1797, 1804, 1820, and 1825. The officers' dates of commission are given. The 1797 list is indexed while the later three are not. You can find these lists on microfilm at the FHL.

REFERENCES AND FURTHER READING

Sources

Bartlett, Thomas and Keith Jeffery, eds. *A Military History of Ireland.* Cambridge, England: Cambridge University Press, 1996.

Betit, Kyle J. "Irish Militia and Yeomanry Records." *The Irish At Home and Abroad* 6 (3) (3d Quarter 1999): 102–108.

Blackstock. Allan. *An Ascendancy Army: The Irish Yeomanry 1796–1834.* Dublin: Four Courts Press, 1998.

Carman, W.Y. *Richard Simkin's Uniforms of the British Army: Infantry, Royal Artillery, Royal Engineers and Other Corps.* Exeter, England: Webb and Bower, 1985.

Colwell, Stella. "Records of the Irish in the British Army." *Aspects of Irish Genealogy: Proceedings of the 1st Irish Genealogical Congress,* edited by M.D. Evans and Eileen Ó Dúill, 54–74. [Dublin]: 1st Irish Genealogical Congress Committee, 1993.

Crowder, Norman K. *British Army Pensioners Abroad, 1772–1899.* Baltimore: Genealogical Publishing Co., 1995.

Fowler, Simon. *Army Records for Family Historians.* London: Public Record Office Publications, 1992.

Gibson, Jeremy and Mervyn Medlycott. *Militia Lists and Musters 1757–1876: A Directory of Holdings in the British Isles.* 3d ed. Birmingham, England: Federation of Family History Societies, 1994.

Hayes-McCoy, G.A. *Irish Battles: A Military History of Ireland.* 1969. 2d ed. Belfast: The Appletree Press Ltd., 1989.

Holding, Norman. *World War I Army Ancestry.* 3d ed. Birmingham, England: Federal of Family History Societies, 1997.

Kitzmiller, John M. II. *In Search of the "Forlorn Hope": A Comprehensive Guide to Locating British Regiments and Their Records (1640–WWI).* 2 vols. Salt Lake City, Utah: Manuscript Publishing Foundation, 1988.

Montague, Ronald. *Dress and Insignia of the British Army in Australia and New Zealand, 1770–1870.* Sydney: Library of Australian Genealogists, 1981.

O'Connor, Gregory. "Records of the Royal Hospital, Kilmainham (RHK)." *Gateway to the Past* (Ballinteer Branch, Irish Family History Society) 2 (3) (March 1998): 157–159.

Oliver, Rosemary M. "War Office District Pension Returns, 1842–62." *Genealogists' Magazine: Journal of the Society of Genealogists* 21 (June 1984): 196–199.

Radford, Dwight A. "District Pension Records of the British Army." *The Irish At Home and Abroad* 4 (1) (1st Quarter 1997): 11–17.

Schaefer, Christina K. *The Great War: A Guide to the Service Records of All the World's Fighting Men and Volunteers.* Baltimore: Genealogical Publishing Co., 1998.

Spencer, William. *Records of Militia and Voluntary Forces, 1758–1945.* London: PRO Publications, 1997.

Swinnerton, Iain. *An Introduction to The British Army: Its History, Tradition and Records.* Birmingham, England: Federation of Family History Societies, 1996.

Swinson, Arthur. *A Register of the Regiments and Corps of the British Army: the Ancestry of the Regimented Corps of the Regular Establishment.* London: The Archive Press, 1972.

Thomas, Garth. *Records of the Militia from 1757: Including Records of the Volunteers, Rifle Volunteers, Yeomanry, Fencibles, Territorials and the Home Guard* (Public Record Office Readers' Guide No. 3). London: PRO Publications, 1993.

Watts, Michael J. and Christopher T. Watts. *My Ancestor Was in the British Army: How Can I Find Out More About Him?* London: Society of Genealogists, 1992.

Wilkinson-Latham, Robert [and Christopher]. *Infantry Uniforms: Including Artillery and Other Supporting Troops of Britain and the Commonwealth 1742–1855 in Colour.* London: Blandford, 1969.

TWENTY-ONE

Research Guides and Reference Material

We would like to describe for you some of the important Irish genealogy, local history, and archives guides that are available. Some of these focus on Ireland as a whole, or on Northern Ireland or Ulster. Others focus on a particular county or town in Ireland. Guides aimed at local historians can often be useful for you as a family historian as well. We also list a number of the most useful Irish genealogical journals available in Ireland and around the world. At the end of the chapter, we provide a listing of places worldwide and on the Internet where you can purchase Irish genealogy reference material.

IRISH GENEALOGY AND ARCHIVES GUIDES (GENERAL)

Printed Source

- Begley, Donal F., ed. *Irish Genealogy: A Record Finder* (Dublin: Heraldic Artists, Ltd., 1987). This work, originally published in 1981, covers a number of topics in depth, including chapters about censuses, deeds, directories, newspapers, and wills and administrations. A reprint of the classic "Report on Surnames in Ireland," by R.E. Matheson, is included.
- Falley, Margaret Dickson. *Irish and Scotch-Irish Ancestral Research: A Guide to the Genealogical Records, Methods and Sources in Ireland* (1962. Reprint, Baltimore: Genealogical Publishing Co., 1981). This work, although dated, has been the "encyclopedia" of Irish research for several decades. There is detailed treatment of source material and the history behind some of the sources. Chapters concern the Registry of Deeds, the Genealogical Office, church records, plantation and settlement records, estate records, tax records, and military records.
- Grenham, John. *Tracing Your Irish Ancestors: The Complete Guide* (2d ed. Dublin: Gill and Macmillan, Ltd., 1999). This book contains an overview of the major record sources in Ireland. Chapter twelve lists Catholic registers found at the NLI, PRONI, FHL, and heritage centres (with reference numbers), as well as those registers that are published. There are

accompanying county maps showing Catholic parish boundaries and the diocese to which each parish belongs. A county-by-county section details sources and periodicals available for each Irish county.

- Helferty, Seamus and Raymond Refaussé. *Directory of Irish Archives* (3d ed. Dublin: Irish Academic Press, 1999). The holdings of various repositories are outlined in this work. Its focus is not specifically genealogy, but you can use it effectively.

- *Ireland Research Outline* (Salt Lake City, Utah: Corp. of the President of the Church of Jesus Christ of Latter-day Saints, 1997). This outlines the Family History Library's collection of Irish records and is available on the Internet site <http://www.familysearch.org>.

- Irvine, Sherry and Nora M. Hickey. *Going to Ireland: A Genealogical Researcher's Guide* (Victoria, BC: Ancestry Ireland, 1997). This guide contains advice about preparing for research, with chapters about research in Dublin and Belfast repositories and "Research at the County Level."

- Mac Conghail, Máire and Paul Gorry. *Tracing Irish Ancestors* (Glasgow: Harper Collins, 1997). This book concentrates on record sources and techniques. The coverage of church records and trades and professions is particularly good. Most chapters include a "Practicing Research Techniques" section in which the material is applied to case studies followed throughout the book.

- Maxwell, Ian. *Tracing Your Ancestors in Northern Ireland: A Guide to Ancestry Research in the Public Record Office of Northern Ireland* (Edinburgh: The Stationery Office, 1997). This guide includes an extensive series of topics including Crown and peace records, electoral records, militia and yeomanry, Ordnance Survey memoirs, encumbered estates, Poor Law records, valuation records, Land Purchase Commission, and land registry.

- McCarthy, Tony. *The Irish Roots Guide* (Dublin: The Lilliput Press, Ltd., 1991). This book concentrates on tracing the Catholic tenantry of Ireland. However, it discusses record sources relevant to all social groups. These include chapters on Land Commission records, valuation and poor law records, the Religious Census of 1766, and graveyard records.

- Ryan, James G. *Irish Records: Sources for Family & Local History* (rev. ed. Salt Lake City, Utah: Ancestry, 1997). This book is arranged by county, showing a wide variety of sources. The listings of Church of Ireland and Roman Catholic parish records detail records in local custody; also noted are Church of Ireland records destroyed in 1922.

IRISH LOCAL HISTORY GUIDES

- Collins, Peter. *Pathways to Ulster's Past: Sources and Resources for Local Studies* (Belfast: The Institute of Irish Studies, The Queen's University of Belfast, 1998). This book explains the historical units of administration in Ireland and includes a survey of record sources arranged by century of documentary and other sources. The sections on sixteenth- and seventeenth-century sources are particularly useful for researchers trying to access material in that time period.

- Crawford, W.H. and R.H. Foy. *Townlands in Ulster: Local History Studies* (Belfast: Ulster Historical Foundation, 1998). The eight remarkable chapters in this book are local history studies, but the sources and methods the authors used can be useful for the genealogist seeking to build the history of a family. Extracts and copies of various records such as tax, census, and estate records are included. The bibliographies of published and manuscript material are valuable resources for the family historian.

- Gillespie, Raymond and Myrtle Hill, eds. *Doing Irish Local History: Pursuit and Practice* (Belfast: The Institute of Irish Studies, The Queen's University of Belfast, 1998). The chapter in this book on the history of Armagh town is a good example of the sources available for studying towns and their inhabitants in the eighteenth century. The chapter "The Study of Townlands in Ulster" includes both sources and methodology for documenting residents of a particular townland.

- Nolan, William and Anngret Simms, eds. *Irish Towns: A Guide to Sources* (Dublin: Geography Publications, 1998). This work includes an impressive range of sources for researching the history of towns in Ireland, with chapters about maps, taxation, census and other government records, estate records, church records, newspapers, directories, and gazetteers. An extensive bibliography lists published works relating to many of the towns in Ireland. The book is beautifully illustrated with maps, documents, and photographs.

IRISH RESEARCH GUIDES (COUNTY AND LOCAL)

Books and articles concerning specific counties give a local perspective on the holdings of the county libraries and other local sources.

Printed Source

Antrim

Agnew, Jean. "Sources for the History of Belfast in the Seventeenth and Early Eighteenth Centuries." *Familia: Ulster Genealogical Review* 2 (1992): 150–158.

Betit, Kyle J. and Dwight A. Radford. "County Antrim." *The Irish At Home and Abroad* 5 (4) (4th Quarter 1998): 186–194.

———. "Belfast City," *The Irish At Home and Abroad* 6 (3) (3d Quarter 1999): 127–135.

Armagh

Guide to County Sources: Armagh. Belfast: Public Record Office of Northern Ireland, 1996.

Handran, George B. "County Armagh." *The Irish At Home and Abroad* 4 (2) (1997): 76–82.

Carlow

Betit, Kyle J. "County Carlow." *The Irish At Home and Abroad* 5 (3) (3d Quarter 1998): 121–127.

Cavan

Cullen, Sara. *Sources for Cavan Local History*. Monaghan, Ireland: R&S Printers, no date.

Farrell, Noel. *Cavan Town Family Roots Book*. Longford: Noel Farrell, 1992.

Radford, Dwight A. "County Cavan." *The Irish At Home and Abroad* 2 (1994/95): 60–64.

Clare

Betit, Kyle J. and Dwight A. Radford. "County Clare." *The Irish At Home and Abroad* 5 (2) (2d Quarter 1998): 84–90.

Morris, Andrew J. *Genealogical Guide to County Clare Ireland*. Book-on-disk. Farmington, Mich.: the author, 1995.

Cork

Betit, Kyle J. "County Cork." *The Irish At Home and Abroad* 2 (4) (1995/96): 113–121.

Hickey, Nora M. "Trace Your Ancestors in County Cork." *Irish Family History: Journal of the Irish Family History Society* 7 (1991): 11–20.

McCarthy, Tony and Tim Cadogan. *A Guide to Tracing Your Cork Ancestors*. Glenageary, Co. Dublin: Flyleaf Press, 1998.

Donegal

Duffy, Godfrey F. *A Guide to Tracing Your Donegal Ancestors*. Glenageary, Co. Dublin: Flyleaf Press, 1995.

Farrell, Noel. *Exploring Family Origins in Ballybofey/Stranorlar and Killygordon*. Longford: Noel Farrell, 1996.

———. *Exploring Family Origins in Ballyshannon*. Longford: Noel Farrell, 1996.

———. *Exploring Family Origins in Letterkenny*. Longford: Noel Farrell, 1996.

———. *Exploring Family Origins in Mountcharles, Inver & Donegal Town*. Longford: Noel Farrell, 1997.

O Ronain, Liam. "Tracing Donegal Ancestors." *Donegal Annual* 44 (1992): 118–123.

Dublin

Ryan, James G. and Brian Smith. *A Guide to Tracing Your Dublin Ancestors*. 2d ed. Glenageary, Co. Dublin: Flyleaf Press, 1998.

Fermanagh

Guide to County Sources: Fermanagh. Belfast: Public Record Office of Northern Ireland, 1994.

Galway

Farrell, Noel. *Exploring Family Origins in Ballinasloe Town.* Longford: Noel Farrell, 1998.

Mannion, Marie. "Research in Galway." Lecture at the Third Irish Genealogical Congress, September 1997, Maynooth, Co. Kildare, Ireland. (Audio tape available from Repeat Performance, 2911 Crabapple Ln., Hobart, IN 46342; Internet: http://www.repeatperformance.com).

Kerry

O'Connor, Michael H. *A Guide to Tracing Your Kerry Ancestors.* 2d ed. Glenageary, Co. Dublin: Flyleaf Press, 1994.

Betit, Kyle J. and Dwight A. Radford. "County Kerry." *The Irish At Home and Abroad* 4 (4) (4th Quarter 1997): 168–175.

Kildare

Kiely, Karel, Mary Newman, and Jacinta Ruddy. *Tracing Your Ancestors in Co. Kildare.* Naas, Co. Kildare: Kildare County Library, 1992.

Radford, Dwight A. "County Kildare." *The Irish At Home and Abroad* 3 (1) (1995/96): 33–37.

Kilkenny

Handran, George B. "County Kilkenny." *The Irish At Home and Abroad* 4 (3) (3d Quarter 1997): 126–132.

Nolan, Pat. *A Guide to Genealogical Sources in and for Kilkenny City and County.* Kilkenny, Ireland, 1997.

Laois/Leix (Queens)

Morris, Andrew J. "Genealogical Research in County Laois." *Heritage Quest* 27 (1990): 33–37.

Leitrim

Betit, Kyle J. and Dwight A. Radford. "County Leitrim." *The Irish At Home and Abroad* 5 (1) (1st Quarter 1998): 39–45.

Farrell, Noel. *South Leitrim Roots Book: Exploring Family Origins and Old Carrick-on-Shannon.* Longford: Longford Leader, 1994.

O Suilleabháin, Séan. "Tracing Your Leitrim Ancestors." *Familia: Ulster Genealogical Review* 2 (1992): 78–86.

Londonderry (Derry)

Mitchell, Brian. *County Londonderry: Sources for Family History.* Derry, Ireland: Genealogy Centre, 1992.

Radford, Dwight A. and Kyle J. Betit. "County Londonderry." *The Irish At Home and Abroad* 3 (3) (1995/96): 116–123.

Longford

Farrell, Harry. *Exploring Family Origins and Old Longford Town.* Longford: The Longford Leader, 1990.

Louth

Comerford, Hugh. "Sources for Local History in Drogheda Public Library." *Journal of the Old Drogheda Society* 7 (1990): 17–21.

Mayo

Smith, Brian. *A Guide to Tracing Your Mayo Ancestors.* Glenageary, Co. Dublin, Ireland: Flyleaf Press, 1997.

Meath

Farrell, Noel. *Exploring Family Origins in Navan Town.* Longford: Noel Farrell, 1998.

French, Noel E. *Meath Ancestors: A Guide to Sources for Tracing Your Ancestors in Co. Meath.* Trim, Co. Meath: Trymme Press, 1993.

Monaghan

Collins, Peter. *County Monaghan Sources in the Public Record Office of Northern Ireland.* Belfast: Public Record Office of Northern Ireland, 1998.

Farrell, Noel. *Exploring Family Origins in Monagham Town.* Longford: Noel Farrell, 1998.

MacMahon, Theo. "Research in Monaghan." Lecture at the Third Irish Genealogical Congress, September 1997, Maynooth, Co. Kildare, Ireland. (Audio tape available from Repeat Performance, 2911 Crabapple Ln., Hobart, IN 46342; Internet: http://www.repeatperformance.com).

Offaly (Kings)

Byrne, Michael. *Sources For Offaly History.* Tullamore, Co. Offaly: Offaly Research Library, 1978.

Farrell, Noel. *Exploring Family Origins in Birr.* Longford: Noel Farrell, 2000.

———. *Exploring Family Origins in Tullamore.* Longford: Noel Farrell, 1999.

Roscommon

Betit, Kyle J. "County Roscommon." *The Irish At Home and Abroad* 3 (2) (1995/96): 58–64.

Farrell, Noel. *Exploring Family Origins in Old Roscommon Town.* Longford: Noel Farrell, 1998.

Sligo

Handran, George B. "County Sligo." *The Irish At Home and Abroad* 4 (1) (1997): 28–33.

McTernan, John C. *Sligo Sources of Local History: A Catalogue of The Local History Collection, With an Introduction and Guide to Sources.* Rev. ed. Sligo, Ireland: Sligo County Library, 1995.

Tipperary

Betit, Kyle J. "County Tipperary." *The Irish At Home and Abroad* 3 (4) (1995/96): 163–170.

Higgins, Noreen. "Genealogical Sources for Co. Tipperary." *Tipperary Historical Journal* 1991: 181–189.

Murphy, Nancy. *Tracing North West Tipperary Roots: Genealogical Sources for the Barony of Upper Ormond, Lower Ormond, Owney and Arra*. Nenagh, County Tipperary, Ireland: Relay, 1982.

St. Ailbe's Heritage: A Guide to the History, Genealogy & Towns of the Archdiocese of Cashel & Emly. Tipperary, Ireland: Tipperary Heritage Unit, n.d.

Tyrone

Campbell, Tim and Ian Rice. *Guide to County Sources: Tyrone*. Belfast: PRONI, 1998.

Waterford

Waterford Heritage Genealogical Centre. *A Guide to Tracing Your Ancestors*. Waterford: the centre, n.d.

Westmeath

Keaney, Marian. *Westmeath Local Studies: A Guide to Sources*. Mullingar, Co. Westmeath, Ireland: Longford-Westmeath Joint Library Committee, 1982.

Wexford

Farrell, Noel. *Exploring Family Origins in Enniscorthy*. Longford, Ireland: Noel Farrell, 1998.

———. *Exploring Family Origins in New Ross*. Longford, Ireland: Noel Farrell, 1999.

Goodall, Sir David. "The Historian's Microscope: Genealogy and Social History in the County of Wexford." *The Irish Genealogist* 9 (3) (1996): 297–304.

Radford, Dwight A. "County Wexford." *The Irish At Home and Abroad* 6 (2) (2d Quarter 1999): 74–90.

Wicklow

Farrel, Noel. *Exploring Family Origins in Arklow Town*. Longford, Ireland: Noel Farrell, 1998.

IRISH GENEALOGICAL PERIODICALS

We refer you to articles from a variety of periodicals throughout this book. Many of these journals are available at the FHL, the NLI, and the Allen County Public Library (Ft. Wayne, Indiana). The Allen County Public Library specializes in collecting genealogical periodicals (see chapter eighteen for the library's PERSI index). The following are publishers and addresses of some current periodicals:

Anglo-Celtic Roots
> published by the British Isles Family History Society of Greater Ottawa
> P.O. Box 38026, Ottawa, ON K2C 1N0, Canada
> *phone:* (613) 224-9868   *Internet:* http://www.cyberus.ca/~bifhsgo

British Isles Family History Society—U.S.A. Journal
> published by the Society, 2531 Sawtelle Blvd. #134
> Los Angeles, CA 90064-3163
> *Internet:* http://www.rootsweb.com/~bifhsusa/

Familia: Ulster Genealogical Review
> published by Ulster Historical and Genealogical Guild, Ulster Historical
> Foundation, 12 College Sq. East, Belfast BT1 6DD, Northern Ireland
> *Internet:* http://www.uhf.org.uk

The Irish At Home and Abroad: A Journal of Irish Genealogy and Heritage
> published by The Irish At Home and Abroad (1993–1999).
> Available at many libraries in the United States, Canada, Australia, New
> Zealand, and Ireland

Irish Family History
> published by Irish Family History Society, P.O. Box 36, Naas, County
> Kildare, Ireland
> *Internet:* http://www.mayo-ireland.ie/geneal/ifhissoc.htm

The Irish Genealogical Quarterly
> published by the Irish Genealogical Society of Wisconsin
> P.O. Box 13766, Wauwatosa, WI 53213-0766
> *Internet:* http://www.execpc.com/~igsw/

The Irish Genealogist
> published by the Irish Genealogical Research Society
> 82 Eaton Sq., London SW1W 9AJ, England

Irish Roots
> published by Belgrave Publications
> Belgrave Ave., Cork, Ireland
> *Internet:* http://www.iol.ie/~irishrts/

Journal of the Genealogical Society of Ireland
> (formerly *Cumann Geinealais Dhun Laoghaire*, 1992–1999)
> published by the Genealogical Society of Ireland (formerly Dun Laoghaire
> Genealogical Society)
> 14 Rochestown Park, Dun Laoghaire, Co. Dublin, Ireland
> *Internet:* http://www.dun-laoghaire.com/genealogy/main.html

North Irish Roots
> published by North of Ireland Family History Society
> c/o Queen's University School of Education
> 69 University St., Belfast BT7 1HL, Northern Ireland
> *Internet:* http://www.mni.co.uk/nifhs

The Septs
> published by the Irish Genealogical Society International
> P.O. Box 16585, St. Paul, MN 55116
> *Internet:* http://www.rootsweb.com/~irish/

Sources

PURCHASING IRISH BOOKS

You can purchase books and CD-ROMs for Irish research from distributors in Ireland and worldwide. Some of the major distributors include

Ireland

Eason Hanna's Bookstore
    1 Dawson St., Dublin 2, Ireland
    phone: (01) 677 1255   *fax:* (01) 671 4330
    Internet: http://www.hannas.ie/

Heraldic Artists
    3 Nassau St., Dublin 2, Ireland
    phone: (01) 679 7020
    Internet: http://www.heraldicartists.com

Heritage World On-Line Shop
    The Heritage Centre, 26 Market Sq., Dungannon
    County Tyrone BT70 1AB, Northern Ireland
    phone: (028 87) 724187   *fax:* (028 87) 752141
    Internet: http://www.heritagewld.com/choose.htm

Kenny's Bookshop & Art Galleries
    High St., Galway City, Ireland
    Internet: http://cgi-bin.iol.ie/resource/kennys/

Australia

Society of Australian Genealogists Bookstore
    Richmond Villa, 120 Kent St., Sydney NSW 2000, Australia
    Internet: http://www.sag.org.au/bookshop.htm

Canada

Global Genealogical Supply
    158 Laurier Ave., Milton, ON L9T 4S2, Canada
    phone: (800) 361-5168   *fax:* (905) 875-2176
    Internet: http://globalgenealogy.com/

Interlink Bookshop
    3040A Cadboro Bay Rd., Victoria, BC V8N 4G2, Canada
    phone: (250) 477-2708   *fax:* (250) 595-2495

SEL Enterprises
    Box 92, Thornhill, ON L3T 3N1, Canada
    phone: (905) 889-0498   *fax:* (905) 889-3845

New Zealand

Beehive Books
    P.O. Box 25-025, St Heliers, Auckland, New Zealand
    phone/fax: (09) 521-1518

United States

Family Tree Imports

2420 Newport Dr., Lansing, MI 48906-3541

Frontier Press

Genealogical and Historical Books, 21 Railroad Ave.

P.O. Box 126, Cooperstown, NY 13326

phone: (800) 772-7559   *fax:* (607) 547-9415

Internet: http://www.frontierpress.com

Genealogical Publishing Company

1001 North Calvert St., Baltimore, MD 21202

phone: (800) 296-6687   *fax:* (410) 752-8492

Internet: http://www.genealogybookshop.com

Irish Books and Graphics

580 Broadway, Room 1103, New York, NY 10012

phone: (212) 274-1923   *fax:* (212) 431-5413

Irish Books and Media, Inc.

1433 E. Franklin Ave., Minneapolis, MN 55404-2135

phone: (612) 871-3505   *fax:* (612) 871-3358

New England Historic Genealogical Society Sales

160 North Washington St., Boston, MA 02114

phone: (888) 296-3447   *fax:* (617) 624-0325

Internet: http://www.newenglandancestors.org

TWENTY-TWO

Society Records

Notes

I t was popular to belong to societies in the eighteenth and especially the nineteenth centuries. These societies included many "brotherhoods" of men in fraternal organizations such as the Freemasons and Orange Lodges, where they would make and maintain social, political, and business contacts. The United Irishmen and the Fenian Brotherhood are two prime examples of societies organized around political reasons. These were not, however, the only societies operating in Ireland in this time period. **We briefly discuss the history and records available for these four societies to give you an idea of what you can gain from using society records in Ireland.** Society records can be relevant to your research whether your ancestor was Protestant or Catholic. The Fenians were strictly Catholic, and the Orange Lodges were entirely Protestant. The Freemasons (especially prior to the 1830s) and the United Irishmen drew from both the Catholic and Protestant populations. Most of the people who belonged to organized societies were from the middle and upper classes.

FREEMASONS

The Masonic Lodge has existed in Ireland since 1732, when the first lodge was given a warrant to operate in Dublin. Membership records, however, generally begin in the 1760s. More complete membership records begin in the 1780s and continue to the present. In Ireland it is an all-male organization. The Grand Lodge of Ireland had lodges throughout the island and even administered overseas lodges, especially in countries of the British Empire.

The Masonic tradition is a fraternal organization open to people regardless of religious affiliation. It surprises many people to know that the Masonic Lodge in Ireland prior to 1826 had a mixture of Catholic and Protestant members. In fact, some of the earliest Grand Masters in Ireland were Roman Catholics. Catholic membership drastically fell off in the 1820s after Papal Bulls (official pronounce-ments by the pope) were published condemning Freemasonry. Although the Papal Bulls were published in Ireland in 1826, in some areas they were ignored and Catholic members continued their Lodge activities. For example, in Ennis, County Clare, the local lodge remained mixed as late as the 1860s.

Material about the history of Freemasonry in Ireland is in a pair of journals: *Transactions of the Lodge of Research #200 of the Grand Lodge of Ireland* and *Transactions of the Quatuor Coronati Lodge #2076, England.*

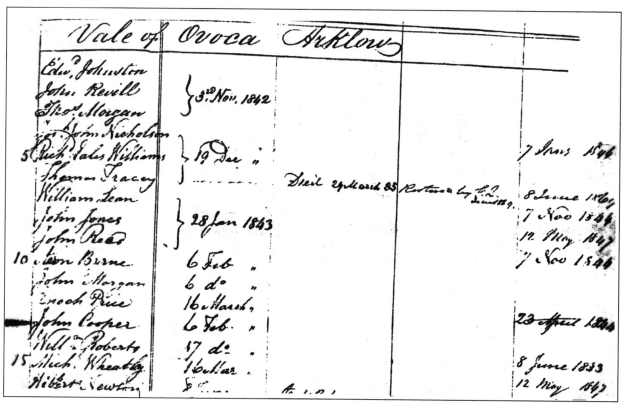

Figure 22-1
Membership Record, Lodge #207, Vale of Avoca, County Wicklow. Used with permission of the Grand Lodge of Ireland.

Masonic Records

The Grand Lodge of Ireland has a library open to the public, although its book collection is limited in genealogical value. Its archives houses the membership records and other manuscripts. The staff welcomes researchers, but an appoint-ment is necessary. You may request searches through correspondence, but be brief and provide a specific time frame and locality for your ancestor. It is also appropriate to give a donation to the Lodge for any search requested. There are a variety of records at the Grand Lodge of Ireland, but for genealogical purposes the two most helpful types we can steer you to are

Membership records: Each subordinate (local) lodge submitted to the Grand Lodge copies of its membership records. It is still uncertain how many of the original subordinate lodge records have survived in local custody, so we recommend that you use the collection at the Grand Lodge. The early membership records act as a locator by placing a man in a locality at a specific time. They usually do not provide birth information, ages, or parents' names. Because membership records are filed by lodge number, it is necessary to know the lodges that existed in a given geographic area. The membership records of Cork City and Dublin City through 1860 are indexed. There is an alphabetical index of all new members since 1875.

Deputy Grand Secretary correspondence files (1820–1880): These records, filed by the lodge number, are the correspondence of the individual lodge with the Grand Lodge. Typical correspondence concerns minutes, officers' business, and charity petitions. The emigration of individual members might be noted.

To find out what lodges existed in an area you are researching, consult Dwight A. Radford's article "Irish Masonic Records: A Catholic and Protestant Source" in *The Irish At Home and Abroad*, which includes an extensive chart arranged by civil parish of where lodges in Ireland were located based upon the Grand Lodge's 1804 records. If you know a civil parish, this is a quick reference. If you're interested in a period after 1804, see *Irish Masonic Records*, by Philip Crossle, which lists Irish lodges through 1973; however, Crossle's work does not tell the years for which records survive or in what parish a lodge was located. The journal *The Irish At Home and Abroad*, in cooperation with the Grand Lodge of Ireland, published lists of surviving pre-1900 lodge records for counties Carlow, Clare, Kerry, Kildare, Leitrim, Roscommon, Sligo, Tipperary, and Wexford.

SOCIETY OF UNITED IRISHMEN

The goal of the United Irishmen was to unite Catholics and Protestants in seeking the repeal of penal laws limiting Catholics. The society was founded in Belfast in 1791 and spread throughout Ulster and Leinster. The minutes of the Dublin society from 1791 to 1794, including lists of members, are in the Rebellion Papers (Reference 620/19–21) at the NAI and were published in R.B. McDowell's *Proceedings of the Dublin Society of United Irishmen*. The NAI holds a United Irishman Index with the name of the member and the document in which his name is found. Deirdre Lindsay's article "The Rebellion Papers" in *Ulster Local Studies* provides an inventory of the Rebellion Papers in the National Archives.

In 1794, the government declared the United Irishmen an illegal organization, but the membership reorganized into a secret society seeking to separate Ireland from the British Empire. When the United Irishmen rebellion of 1798 failed, members fled to the United States and elsewhere. Many United Irishmen were transported to New South Wales (Australia) in the 1790s and early 1800s (see Anne-Maree Whitaker's *Unfinished Revolution*).

FENIAN BROTHERHOOD

The Fenian Brotherhood was founded in New York City and in Dublin in 1858. This organization is the forerunner of the modern Irish Republican Army (IRA).

The goal of this secret society was the overthrow of British rule in Ireland. American monies and manpower were used for this goal.

A number of Fenians who returned to Ireland from America were imprisoned for their political activities. The NAI has a "Fenian Suspect File" that might tell where in Ireland and America these men were from. The Fenian Papers (1857 to 1883), housed at the NAI, are part of the Police and Crime Archives. In these papers are some photographs of Fenians and consular dispatches from America. The most useful method of locating Fenian material at the NAI is using the index to the Irish Crimes Records at the NAI.

LOYAL ORANGE LODGES

The Orange Lodge is a Protestant fraternal organization established in 1795 on the basis of loyalty to Crown, Country, and Protestantism. The word "Orange" is in honor of William, Prince of Orange in the Netherlands. The Protestant William defeated the Catholic King James II at the Battle of the Boyne in 1690; William and his wife, Mary, ascended the English throne.

In the beginning, membership was drawn from the laboring and artisan classes of the Church of Ireland. Orangeism quickly spread via British military soldiers and immigrants to America, Canada, England, and Scotland. Later it was established in Australia, India, New Zealand, and South Africa.

Many immigrants who had belonged to Orange lodges in Ireland had transfer certificates used to join new lodges in their countries of settlement. Such Irish transfer certificates are in the immigrant countries; the certificates indicate a lodge to which the member had belonged in Ireland.

The Orange lodges in Ireland are organized under the Grand Orange Lodge of Ireland, within which each county has a Grand Lodge and its subordinate lodges. **There are surviving nineteenth-century directories of Orange lodges in Ireland available at the Grand Orange Lodge of Ireland:**

Printed Source

- The 1856 directory gives lodge number, county, district, place the lodge met, post town, master's name, and observations.
- The 1875 directory lists lodge number, master's name, county, district, sometimes place of meeting and post town, and observations.

Also use the "First and Second Reports from the Select Committee on Orange Lodges in Ireland with Minutes of Evidence and Appendices 1835," which were presented to the British Parliament and include a listing of lodges in Ireland with their locations.

Orange Lodge records are not centralized in an archives; many are still with the local lodges. Contact the Grand Orange Lodge of Ireland, which can research lodge numbers and forward requests to local lodges for information from their records. The Grand Orange Lodge does not hold records of individual lodges.

REFERENCES AND FURTHER READING

Sources

Freemasons

Crossle, Philip. *Irish Masonic Records*. Dublin: Grand Lodge of Ireland, 1973.

Lepper, John Heron and Philip Crossle. *History of the Grand Lodge of Free and Accepted Masons of Ireland*, vol. 1. Dublin: Lodge of Research, 1925.

List of Lodges of the Most Ancient & Honorable Fraternity of Free and Accepted Masons Held Under the Sanction of the Right Worshipful Grand Lodge of Ireland . . . Dublin: Brother C. Downes, 1804.

Parkinson, R.E. *History of the Grand Lodge of Free and Accepted Masons of Ireland*, vol. 2. Dublin: Lodge of Research, 1957.

Radford, Dwight A. "Irish Masonic Records: A Protestant and Catholic Source." *The Irish At Home and Abroad* 3 (4) (1995/96): 140–149.

Society of United Irishmen

Lindsay, Deirdre. "The Rebellion Papers: An Introduction to the Rebellion Papers Collection in the National Archives, Bishop Street, Dublin." *Ulster Local Studies* (Journal of the Federation for Ulster Local Studies Limited) 18 (2) (Spring 1997): 28–42.

McDowell, R.B. *Proceedings of the Dublin Society of United Irishmen* (Dublin: Irish Manuscripts Commission, 1998.) (Originally published in the journal *Analecta Hibernica* 17 (1949).

Musgrave, Sir Richard. *Memoirs of the Different Rebellions in Ireland, From the Arrival of the English: Also, A Particular Detail of That Which Broke Out the 23d of May, 1798; With the History of the Conspiracy Which Preceded It*, edited by Steven W. Myers and Delores E. McKnight. 3d ed., 1802. 4th ed., Fort Wayne, Ind.: Round Tower Books, 1995.

Whitaker, Anne-Maree. *Unfinished Revolution: United Irishmen in New South Wales, 1800–1810*. Sydney, NSW, Australia: Crossing Press, 1994.

Fenian Brotherhood

Quinlivan, Patrick J. "Hunting the Fenians: Problems in the Historiography of a Secret Organization." *The Creative Migrant*, edited by Patrick O'Sullivan, 133–153. Leicester, London, New York: Leicester University Press, 1994.

Orangeism

Dewar, M.W., John Brown and S.E. Long. *Orangeism: A New Historical Appreciation*. 2d ed. Belfast: Grand Orange Lodge of Ireland, 1969.

"First and Second Reports from the Select Committee on Orange Lodges in Ireland With Minutes of Evidence and Appendices 1835." Irish University Press Series of British Parliamentary Papers, *Civil Disorder 5*. Shannon, Ireland: Irish University Press, 1970.

Senior, Hereward. *Orangeism in Ireland and Britain*. London: Routledge and Kegan Paul Ltd., 1966.

Addresses

Grand Lodge of Ireland
    Freemasons' Hall, 17 Molesworth St., Dublin 2, Ireland
    phone: (01) 6761337   *fax:* (01) 6625101
    e-mail: glfi@iol.ie
Grand Orange Lodge of Ireland
    65 Dublin Rd., Belfast BT2 7HE, Northern Ireland
    phone: (02890) 322801   *fax:* (02890) 332912
    Internet: http://www.grandorange.org.uk/   *e-mail:* info@goli.demon.co.uk

TWENTY-THREE

Taxation Records

Important

In tracing just about any ancestor in the nineteenth or twentieth century in Ireland, you will find tax records to be an indispensable resource. The major tax sources most people use in their research are the Tithe Applotment Composition Books (1823 to 1837) and Griffith's Valuation of Ireland (1847 to 1864). The tax records are particularly important because the nineteenth-century censuses were destroyed. One point not to be missed is that these tax records don't only record landowners; they list renters and leaseholders as well, and sometimes even squatters. You can use the records to as a locator.

TITHE APPLOTMENT COMPOSITION BOOKS

The tithe was a tax based on how much land a person occupied, and it was paid by rural inhabitants to support clergy of the Church of Ireland. Persons of all denominations were required to pay the tithe because the Church of Ireland was the Established Church until 1871. The Tithe Applotment Books were arranged by Church of Ireland parish and were compiled between 1823 and 1837.

The tithe was not limited to this period of time in Ireland. The Church of Ireland as the state religion had levied a yearly "cess," or tax, since the 1600s. The reason the Tithe Applotment Books were compiled is that the Tithe Composition Act of 1823 allowed this tax to be paid in cash rather than "in kind" (by giving a portion of your crops or herds). The Tithe Applotment Books record how much each tithe-payer (taxpayer) was liable to pay to the Church of Ireland parish.

The Tithe Applotment Books are readily available in Ireland and elsewhere. The books for counties in the Republic of Ireland are at the NAI. For counties now in Northern Ireland, the books are at the PRONI. Microfilm copies of all counties are available at the FHL.

Strategies for Using Tithe Books
The following points are helpful in using the Tithe Books:

- Not every land occupier was included in the Tithe Applotment, only those people who were responsible for paying the tithe. Some classes of occupiers, such as cottiers (occupiers who paid rent in labor) and farm servants, were not listed. You also might see an entry such as "John Lynch & Co.," which means that John Lynch was the designated tithe-payer and there were other people (the "Co.") living in the townland not named in the records.

- James R. Reilly published a study about what percentage of a given population may not appear in the Tithe Applotment Books in his article "The Sacred Tenth: The Tithe Applotment Book as a Genealogical Resource" in *The Irish At Home and Abroad*. In his study of Ballymacue parish, County Cavan, which had a surviving 1821 Census as well as Tithe Books dating from 1824, he found that slightly above 35 percent of the population was listed in the Tithe Books.

- Although the Tithe Applotment is not a complete listing of households, you can use indexes to the Tithe Applotment Books to examine the distribution of a surname in Ireland or in a particular county. This is especially useful because it is a pre-Famine source dating prior to the massive exodus from Ireland beginning in the late 1840s.

- Tithe Books do not exist for some parishes. In other cases, one parish is included in the Tithe Book for another parish. A list of parishes having no Tithe Book or those included in another parish is contained in Appendix A of the Irish Research Group (Ottawa Branch, Ontario Genealogical Society) work, *Basic Irish Genealogical Sources: Description and Evaluation* (pp. 56–58).

- Place names of townlands in the Tithe Applotment Books will often differ from those in Griffith's Primary Valuation. The Ordnance Survey in Dublin officially set the boundaries and standardized the townland names during the 1830s, after the Tithe Books were compiled in some civil parishes. Some place names in the Tithe Books simply disappeared, and some townlands were subsequently subdivided. Occasionally the Tithe Books have townland maps accompanying them.

- The Irish plantation acre was larger than the English statute acre, and some of the Tithe Books list measurements in Irish plantation acres. The later Griffith's Primary Valuation used the English statute acre.

Technique

Here is an example of a situation where the information from the Tithe was not straightforward and we had to continue research in other sources. We were looking for an Edward Tracy and found more than one in Aglish Parish, County Mayo. The Tithe Applotment showed an E. Tracy and an Edward Tracy in Aglish Parish, which is where the town of Castlebar is. The Tithe was taken in the spring of 1835.

The E. Tracy was from Creaghadwa, and the Tithe showed "E. Tracy & Co." as the only person in the townland. By the time the Ordnance Survey went

Case Study

through this area of Ireland standardizing townland boundaries and spellings, Creaghadwa had ceased to exist. So to get a handle on who this E. Tracy was, and if he was our Edward Tracy, we had to first figure out what happened to Creaghadwa. We found in the John O'Donovan Name Books, compiled by the Ordnance Survey name teams, that in the surveyed townland of Knockaphunta was a place called Creaghadua and sometimes Creaghdhu. By looking at a modern "Discovery Series" road map for this area, we found that this place was about one mile from the center of Castlebar.

This ties into the other Edward Tracy listed in the Tithe of Castlebar (on Westport Road). Was he the same as the E. Tracy in Knockaphunta? An important question in our search for the right Edward Tracy. Castlebar town actually occupies part of the townland of Knockaphunta. The Castlebar Catholic records are so sketchy that we found no Edward having children christened.

The date on the Tithe of 1835 proved to be important. In the Catholic registers of Castlebar was the marriage of an Edward Tracy to Margaret McGuire on 4 October 1825. This Edward could not have been the E. Tracy or the Edward Tracy in the Tithe because on 10 February 1834, in Castlebar, Margaret "Tracy or McGuire" remarried to a Thomas Moran. This means that the Edward who married in 1825 must have died. So this at least proved that there were two Edward Tracy's in Aglish Parish with the possibility of a third.

Although not a conclusive search, these types of little tidbits help when you have sketchy church records and discontinued place names. In our case, by the time Griffith's came around, Edward Tracy was long gone. So use the Tithe to develop hypotheses even when the information is not straightforward, and then go to other sources to try to prove or disprove your hypotheses. This is what we are going to do with the Tracys now that we know some townlands; we are going to see if anyone from these areas (based on Griffith's Primary Valuation) immigrated abroad with the correct Tracy family. If so, this would tie us back into the Castlebar area and provide evidence that we are dealing with the right Edward Tracy.

Indexes to the Tithe Applotment Books
- Some heritage centres in Ireland have indexed the Tithe Applotment Books of their counties. The centre will examine these indexes for a fee.
- *An Index of Surnames of Householders in Griffith's Primary Valuation and Tithe Applotment Books* (commonly called *Householders Index*) is a surname index by county, barony, and civil parish for all thirty-two counties.
- *Tithe Applotment Index for Northern Ireland Counties* compiled by the PRONI includes counties Antrim, Armagh, Down, Fermanagh, Londonderry, and Tyrone. This full-name card index lists the townland, county, and sometimes the parish where the property was located, with the year of the Tithe in that place and the corresponding PRONI reference number for the original document. This index is available on microfilm at the FHL.

- *International Land Records: Tithe Applotment Books, 1823–1838*, Family Tree Maker's Family Archives CD#262, produced by Brøderbund in collaboration with Heritage World and the Genealogical Publishing Company, includes Counties Antrim, Armagh, Derry, Down, Fermanagh, and Tyrone. It states tithe payer's name, location, and year.

TITHE DEFAULTERS LISTS (1831)

As you can imagine, not everyone was happy paying tithes to a church they did not belong to. A rebellion against tithes began in 1830 when many tithe payers refused to pay their tithes. As a result the British Parliament set up a Clergy Relief Fund in 1832 to assist Church of Ireland clergy who had suffered because of non-payment of tithes due them in 1831. Now, in order to receive relief, the clergyman had to submit an application listing the names of the defaulting tithe-payers in his parish, their places of residence, and the amount of tithe owed by each for 1831. Many of the clergy included the occupation of tithe defaulters. Compare the Tithe Applotment Book and the 1831 Tithe Defaulters List for the same parish to find what changes in land occupation might have occurred in the interim period. Why use the Tithe Defaulters Lists?

- You may find your ancestor's occupation.
- The Tithe Defaulters List and Tithe Book for your parish might have been compiled in different years, so you might find different people listed.

These lists are contained in the "OPMA" (Official Papers: Miscellaneous and Assorted) boxes at the NAI. Lists survive for some parishes in the counties of Carlow, Cork, Kerry, Kilkenny, Laois (Queens), Limerick, Louth, Meath, Offaly (Kings), Tipperary, Waterford, and Wexford. The number of surviving lists varies; the largest number are from counties Kilkenny and Tipperary. Abstracts of the lists were made by Stephen McCormac, and a copy is at the NAI. McCormac's abstracts have been published on microfiche by Data Tree Publishing.

The standard article from a genealogical perspective on the Tithe Defaulters Lists is Suzanne C. Hartwick's article "Schedules of the Clergy Relief Fund, 1831: Tithe-Defaulters and Their Occupations" published in *The Irish Genealogist* (Irish Genealogical Research Society, London). Hartwick's article includes an extract of the schedule for Grangesilvia parish, County Kilkenny (as an example), and a list of all of the surviving schedules (arranged by county) with their "OPMA" reference numbers.

GRIFFITH'S PRIMARY VALUATION

The printed version of Griffith's Valuation of Rateable Property (commonly called "Griffith's Primary Valuation") was published between 1847 and 1864. See page 268 for the dates in individual counties and cities. Griffith's was a valuation of land and building holdings arranged by poor law union, barony,

PUBLICATION DATES OF GRIFFITH'S PRIMARY VALUATION

County or City	Dates Published
Antrim	1859–1862
Armagh	1854, 1863–1864
Belfast City	1861
Carlow	1852
Cavan	1854–1857
Clare	1852, 1855
Cork	1850–1853
Donegal	1857–1858
Down	1860–1864
Dublin City	1847–1854
Dublin County	1847–1852
Fermanagh	1862
Galway	1855–1857
Kerry	1851–1853
Kildare	1850–1853
Kilkenny	1849–1851
Kings (Offaly)	1851–1854
Leitrim	1856–1857
Limerick	1850–1852
Londonderry	1858–1859
Longford	1854
Louth	1851, 1854
Mayo	1855–1857
Meath	1851, 1854
Monaghan	1854, 1858–1861
Queens (Leix)	1850–1851
Roscommon	1855–1858
Sligo	1856–1858
Tipperary	1848–1852
Tyrone	1858–1860
Waterford	1848–1851
Westmeath	1854
Wexford	1853
Wicklow	1852–1854

Source of dates: James R. Reilly. *An Inventory of the Books of Sir Richard Griffith's General Valuation of Rateable Property in Ireland.* Salt Lake City: Redmond Press, 1998.

civil parish, and townland. **Griffith's is an important source because it lists a greater percentage of the occupiers of the land than the Tithe Applotment Books.** It includes landowners, landlords, tenants with leases, and renters. If your ancestors were in Ireland in this time period, it is common to find them listed in Griffith's Primary Valuation.

If you didn't find an ancestor in Griffith's when the family is supposed to have been in Ireland, there could be several logical explanations. Perhaps several families resided in a single house, but only one occupier is listed in Griffith's. Another reason might be that an ancestor's home was owned by a large corporation, such as a mining company; the company will be named rather than the occupants. For this reason, mining areas such as those in County Wicklow will not have as complete a listing as a farming area.

Collections of Griffith's Primary Valuation are available on microfilm, microfiche, and CD-ROM. However, no repository has a complete set covering all of Ireland. Appendix 9 of James R. Reilly's *Richard Griffith and His Valuations of Ireland* lists the volumes of Griffith's Primary Valuation at the major Irish repositories, in Irish county libraries, in the Irish Microforms microfiche set, and at the FHL.

For further detail and historical background regarding Griffith's Primary Valuation and the associated manuscript materials, see Reilly's book based on his earlier path-breaking article "Richard Griffith and His Valuations of Ireland" in *The Irish At Home and Abroad*. Reilly's book explains how the surveys were conducted, what to expect in their content, how the valuators assigned the value of property, how the information was publicized, and the relationship of the valuations to the Irish poor laws. Aside from history, he delves into the intricacies of the valuations, showing how an understanding can help researchers access other Irish records.

Indexes to Griffith's Primary Valuation

- *Index to Griffith's Valuation of Ireland, 1848–1864* was published jointly on CD-ROM by Brøderbund, Heritage World, and Genealogical Publishing Company. This is an alphabetical index of occupiers' names throughout Ireland giving the county, civil parish, and residence.
- *An Index of Surnames of Householders in Griffith's Primary Valuation and Tithe Applotment Books* (commonly called *Householders Index*). The city of Belfast is not listed in the *Householders Index* but is covered in other indexes.
- All-Ireland Heritage compiled full-name indexes to Griffith's Primary Valuation for counties Carlow, Cork, Fermanagh, Limerick, Longford, Monaghan, Tipperary, and Waterford; there are separate indexes for the cities of Belfast, Cork, and Dublin.
- Some heritage centres in Northern Ireland and the Republic of Ireland have compiled their own county indexes to the Tithe Applotment Books and Griffith's Primary Valuation. These indexes can be searched by the centre's staff for a fee.
- Other county indexes include full name indexes to Griffith's for County

PRIMARY VALUATION OF TENEMENTS.

PARISH OF FINUGE.

57

No. and Letters of Reference to Map.		Names.		Description of Tenement.	Area.			Net Annual Value.								
		Townlands and Occupiers.	Immediate Lessors.					Land.			Buildings.			Total.		
					A.	R.	P.	£	s.	d.	£	s.	d.	£	s.	d.
		BALLINRUDDERY. (Ord. S. 11.)														
1	a	Knight of Kerry,	In fee,	House, offices, and land (part plantation),	267	1	2	174	5	0	23	10	0	197	15	0
				River,	16	3	2	—			—					
–	b	Mary M'Coy,	Knight of Kerry,	House, office, & garden,	0	0	35	0	2	0	0	6	0	0	8	0
	c	John Connor,	Same,	House and garden,	0	0	32	0	2	0	0	7	0	0	9	0
2		Patrick Dwyer,	Same,	Land,	4	0	25	2	0	0	—			2	0	0
3	a	Daniel Wilmott,	Same,	House, offices, and land,	14	3	31	10	10	0	1	0	0	11	10	0
–	b	Mary Wilmott,	Same,	House and garden,	0	1	14	0	4	0	0	7	0	0	11	0
4	a	Jeremiah Doolan,	Same,	House and land,	5	3	15	2	10	0	0	10	0	3	0	0
..	b	Margaret Pembroke,	Same,	House and garden,	0	1	7	0	2	0	0	6	0	0	8	0
5 A		Patrick M'Elligott,	Same,	Land	5	3	31	2	5	0	—			3	10	0
– B					4	0	15	1	5	0						
6 A		James Latch,	Same,	House, office, & land,	0	3	26	0	10	0	0	10	0	2	5	0
– B					5	1	9	1	5	0						
7		Thomas Archer,	Same,	House, offices, and land,	6	0	32	2	0	0	0	10	0	2	10	0
8 A		Ellen Fealy,	Same,	House and land,	4	1	16	1	10	0	0	10	0	2	10	0
– B					2	0	27	0	10	0						
9		Timothy Doolan,	Same,	House and land,	2	3	0	0	11	0	0	6	0	0	17	0
10		John Doolan,	Same,	House, office, and land,	8	2	0	3	5	0	0	10	0	3	15	0
11 A		Peter Doolan, sen.	Same,	House, offices, & land,	5	3	21	3	0	0	—			10	5	0
– B					9	1	24	6	5	0	1	0	0			
12	a	Garrett Callaghan,	Same,	House, offices, and land,	20	3	33	14	10	0	4	10	0	19	0	0
–	b	Patrick Dwyer,	Same,	House, office, & garden,	0	1	23	0	5	0	1	0	0	1	5	0
13		John Donegan,	Same,	House, offices, and land,	26	3	7	16	15	0	1	0	0	17	15	0
14		Peter Doolan, jun.	Same,	House and land,	4	1	16	2	15	0	0	10	0	3	5	0
				Total,	418	0	3	246	6	0	36	12	0	282	18	0
		BALLYGRENANE. (Ord. Ss. 10, 11, 16, & 17.)														
1	a	Samuel Shewell,	Earl of Listowel,	House, offices, and land,	68	2	29	34	10	0	7	15	0	42	5	0
				River,	3	0	33	—			—					
..	b	Sylvester Foran,	Samuel Shewell,	House, office, & garden,	0	1	5	0	3	0	0	8	0	0	11	0
–	c	Catherine Buckley,	Same,	House and gardens,	0	0	13	0	1	0	0	6	0	0	7	0
–	d	Nicholas Quill,	Same,	House and garden,	0	0	13	0	1	0	0	6	0	0	7	0
–	e	Michael Shanaghan,	Same,	House, offices, & sm. gar.	—			—			0	7	0	0	7	0
2		Samuel Shewell,	William Sandes, Esq.	Land,	1	1	15	1	5	0	—			1	5	0
3		William Sandes, Esq.	Earl of Listowel,	Land,	29	3	25	29	15	0	—			29	15	0
				River,	5	1	8	—			—					
–	a	John Connor,	Same,	House and garden,	0	2	4	0	8	0	0	7	0	0	15	0
4	a	Edward Kennely,	Same,	House, offices, and land,	47	2	14	26	5	0	5	0	0	31	5	0
..	b	Vacant,	Edward Kennely	House,							0	10	0	0	10	0
–	c	Maurice Barry,	Same,	House,				—			0	6	0	0	6	0
–	d	Joseph Heffernan,	Same,	House,				—			0	5	0	0	5	0
5	a	Timothy M'Namara,	Same,	House, offices, and land,	18	1	4	8	0	0	0	15	0	8	15	0
–	b	Daniel Lyons,	Same,	House and garden,	0	0	19	0	1	0	0	7	0	0	8	0
6		Mary Henigan,	Same,	Land,	5	3	34	3	5	0	—			3	5	0
7	a	Mary Henigan,	Earl of Listowel,	House, offices, & land,	178	1	24	23	15	0	1	5	0	25	0	0
	b	Laurence Buckley, jun.		House, offices, & land,				23	15	0	1	15	0	25	10	0
	c	Laurence Buckley, sen.		House, offices, & land,				23	15	0	2	0	0	25	15	0
8		William Keane,	Same,	House, offices, and land,	52	2	18	26	10	0	1	10	0	28	0	0
9		John Keane (John),	Same,	House, offices, and land,	51	3	10	28	0	0	1	5	0	29	5	0
10	a	Cornelius Keane,	Same,	House, offices, and land,	44	2	1	16	0	0	1	5	0	17	5	0
–	b	Patrick Barry,	Cornelius Keane,	House,				—			0	6	0	0	6	0
11		John Keane (Con),	Earl of Listowel,	House, offices, and land,	38	3	27	15	5	0	1	0	0	16	5	0
				Total,	547	2	11	260	14	0	26	18	0	287	12	0
		BEALKELLY. (Ord. Ss. 16 & 10.)														
1		Rev. Maurice Hewson,	Richard S. Oliver, Esq.	House, offices, and land,	28	2	36	18	15	0	3	5	0	22	0	0
				River,	2	0	13	—			—			—		
2		William Walsh,	Rev. Maurice Hewson,	House and land,	1	3	8	1	0	0	0	7	0	1	7	0
3	a	William Horrigan,	Same,	House, offices, and land,	30	0	4	20	0	0	1	5	0	21	5	0
				River,	6	0	3	—			—					
–	b	James Dalton,	William Horrigan,	House and garden,	0	0	19	0	1	0	0	7	0	0	8	0
4	a	Martin Sheehy,	Rev. Maurice Hewson,	House, offices, and land,	8	2	3	4	0	0	0	15	0	4	15	0

[B]

Q

Figure 23-1

Richard Griffith's *General Valuation of Rateable Property in Ireland* (9 & 10 Vict., Cap. 110). County of Kerry, Barony of Clanmaurice, Parish of Finuge, p. 57. Dublin: Printed for H.M. Stationery Office, 1852. Used with the permission of the Valuation Office of Ireland.

Wicklow and County Mayo, compiled by Andrew J. Morris; and for County Wexford compiled by A.O. McGuire. David Leahy's *County Longford Survivors of the Great Famine* is an index of occupiers and immediate lessors in Griffith's Primary Valuation of County Longford.

Strategies for Using Griffith's
The following are some helpful strategies for using this source:

Avoiding assumptions: Do not assume that a person in Griffith's with your ancestor's name was indeed your ancestor. Irish names tend to be common. You must use other records in conjunction with Griffith's to prove your case.

Dates of publication: Always keep in mind the date Griffith's Primary Valuation was printed for the area in question. See if this fits the time period in which your family would have been there.

Use of agnomens: If there was more than one Eugene Callaghan or Patrick Sullivan in a townland (not hard to imagine), Griffith's distinguishes them by using an agnomen such as "Red," "Farmer," "Tim," or "Big Tim." When a man's given name was used as an agnomen, such as "Patrick Sullivan (Michael)," Michael usually refers to the name of Patrick's father.

Use with church records: Sometimes a parish priest or minister recorded a baptism, marriage, or burial in the church registers but did not record a townland of residence. Use Griffith's Primary Valuation to overcome this omission, since it lists people in each townland. Beware that the civil parish boundaries of Griffith's can differ from church (ecclesiastical) parish boundaries.

If you cannot find your ancestor in Griffith's, you might still be able to deduce a probable townland within the parish. Determine in church records the names of witnesses and godparents (sponsors) associated with your family. These individuals probably lived in the same or a neighboring townland. If the names are concentrated in the same few townlands, this suggests your family also originated there.

GRIFFITH'S TOWNLAND VALUATION AND TENEMENT VALUATION MANUSCRIPT MATERIALS

Griffith's Primary Valuation, which we have been discussing, is a printed source. There were also manuscript materials that led up to this printed record. Let us explain some history of the records compiled by Richard Griffith and his teams prior to the printing of Griffith's Primary Valuation.

Richard Griffith supervised the compilation of the Townland Valuation in Ireland beginning in 1830. In the course of their work, the valuators compiled manuscript land field books and manuscript house books. The former described the quality of land in each townland, and the latter described the physical dimensions of houses and construction material. The land books sometimes recorded names of occupiers, depending on which county and parish you are dealing with. A list of the counties and parishes that have lot occupier names in the Townland Valuation field books is given in Appendix 3 of Reilly's book *Richard Griffith and His Valuations of Ireland* (present-day Republic of Ireland counties only). House books listed the name of each person occupying any house that was measured. The manuscript land field books and house books are accessible at the NAI, Valuation Office, and PRONI.

The Tenement Valuation, also supervised by Richard Griffith, began in 1844 and used the individual person's holding as the basis for valuation. Manuscript materials (perambulation and other books) were developed in the field preliminary to the printing of the Griffith's Primary Valuation familiar to researchers. The manuscript books are available at the Valuation Office, NAI, and PRONI.

You can often find more information in the manuscript materials than in the published version of Griffith's Primary Valuation. For example, you might find information in the perambulation books about lease agreements between tenants and landlords. Sometimes there are sketch maps showing the locations of houses in small communities.

We have found that the manuscript materials of the Tenement Valuation can predate the printed Griffith's Primary Valuation by one to four years. This can be helpful if your ancestor died or emigrated in those years, thus not appearing in the printed version. An inventory of the dates when Griffith's Valuation was compiled and when it was published in localities in Northern Ireland is at the PRONI. This inventory was microfilmed and is available at the FHL.

Valuation Revision Books

The Griffith's Valuation manuscript revision books, sometimes called "canceled" books, continue what Griffith's Primary Valuation (1847 to 1864) began. The revision books record changes in the occupiers of property over the years. You can see in these records that some properties were combined, and many of the old farmhouses were torn down or used for other purposes. The revision books can be an essential tool for you to trace what happened to your ancestral home and farm over time.

The revision books usually continue the numbering of properties in each townland that is found in the printed Griffith's Primary Valuation. Exceptions include when mass evictions or mass emigration from a townland took place.

When the person occupying a piece of land changed, the year of the change might have been noted in the records. The changes through the years can suggest possible death dates, daughters' marriages, or when a family emigrated. Although the revision books usually do not provide direct proof of any of these possibilities, they provide clues for you to continue following the paper trail in other records, such as civil registration of marriages and deaths, wills, and church records.

When a book became filled with changes, a new book was started. In the earlier years, each valuation book covered only a few years. Later, you will often find several decades of changes per canceled book. The original books for the Republic of Ireland are at the Valuation Office in Dublin. With very few exceptions, microfilm copies of these are available at the FHL. The revision books for Northern Ireland are available only at the PRONI and cover the years through 1975. The counties and approximate dates of the records are shown on page 274.

Accessing the Revision Books

Within a county, the revision books were filed by poor law union (later, rural or urban district) and electoral division. **The steps to use revision books for a particular townland are**

1. Use the 1871 townland index or the 1901 townland index on microfilm at the FHL to find the electoral division in which the townland was located.
2. If you are using the FHL collection, go to the FHL Locality Catalog under the category of "Ireland, COUNTY—Land and Property" to locate the microfilm for the appropriate electoral division.
3. The "canceled books" for an electoral division are bound together, often in reverse chronological order. Page numbering starts anew with each book.
4. Again, if you are using the FHL collection, keep track of the approximate years covered in each revision book and the page numbers on which you found your ancestral townland. When you photocopy the books, always copy the cover page, immediately staple it to the appropriate pages, and write the years on the back. With so many smaller books bound into one, you must use a system to keep them in order.

GRIFFITH'S VALUATION MAPS

You can use Griffith's Valuation to find the ancestor's home or the site of a former home on a map. Each property listed in Griffith's was assigned a number. This number is called the "map reference number" and is found in the leftmost column of the record. The numbers correspond to a set of Griffith's Valuation maps where you can locate your ancestral land or home. Property valuators used the original 6″-to-the-mile Ordnance Survey maps compiled in the 1830s and 1840s to show where each holding listed in Griffith's Primary Valuation was located. There are also Ordnance Survey maps corresponding to the valuation revision books.

The Griffith's Primary Valuation maps for Republic of Ireland counties are held at the NAI with electronically scanned copies at the Valuation Office in Dublin. The maps corresponding to the revision books for Republic of Ireland counties are at the Valuation Office. The Griffith's Primary Valuation and revision maps for Northern Ireland are held at the PRONI. A word of warning is appropriate here. The Griffith's Valuation maps marked with plot numbers are *not* available outside Ireland.

EMIGRATION STRATEGIES

Tax records can be a key to locating where your emigrant ancestor originated, or to narrowing the search for a civil parish or townland. **Some strategies for using these tax records are**

Full-name indexes: If an ancestor came from a particular county but you don't know the civil parish, you can use a full-name index to determine in which civil parishes the ancestor's full name was listed. You can then look

REVISION BOOKS: NORTHERN IRELAND COLLECTION AT THE PRONI

County or City	Dates of Records
Antrim	1863–1975
Armagh	1859–1975
Belfast City	1862–1975
Down	1863–1975
Fermanagh	1864–1975
Londonderry	1860–1975
Tyrone	1860–1975

REVISION BOOKS: REPUBLIC OF IRELAND COLLECTION AT THE FHL

County or City	Date of Records
Carlow	1857–1957
Cavan	1857–1945
Clare	1855–1947
Cork	1855–1967
Donegal	1857–1962
Dublin	1855–1963
Dublin City	1855–1947
Galway	1857–1954
Kerry	1858–1952
Kildare	1858–1954
Kilkenny	1856–1969
Kings (Offaly)	1855–1955
Leitrim	1858–1952
Limerick	1857–1961
Longford	1860–1942
Louth	1856–1957
Mayo	1855–1967
Meath	1855–1966
Monaghan	1860–1966
Queens (Leix)	1855–1968
Roscommon	1855–1962
Sligo	1855–1966
Tipperary	1856–1968
Waterford	1855–1968
Westmeath	1850–1967
Wexford	1855–1962
Wicklow	1860–1960

1 = Ending dates refer to the latest records microfilmed in that county. However, ending dates for most localities are in the 1920s or 1930s.

at church records that cover those civil parishes to see if you can find your ancestor.

Surname distribution: If your surname is uncommon, the available surname indexes to tax records can help to narrow the search to the few counties where the surname appears. For example, if you find the surname in only three counties, the odds are that one of these is the county of origin. Having two surnames to use in a surname distribution search is more effective. If you know the maiden name of your emigrant ancestor's mother, you can examine the distribution of this surname with her husband's surname.

Confirming or eliminating families: If you suspect that a family living in a particular parish or townland is your family, look at the dates this family is listed in the tax records versus the date that your family was supposed to have emigrated. If they continue to appear in the tax records after your ancestors emigrated, this is not the correct family for you.

Identifying relatives left behind: The tax records can show who stayed on the family property after your ancestors left. If your ancestor emigrated prior to Griffith's Primary Valuation, you can still use it for locating the family's origins. Unless the entire family (parents, siblings, cousins, uncles, and aunts) emigrated, someone may have remained on the family property.

REFERENCES AND FURTHER READING

Hartwick, Suzanne C. "Schedules of the Clergy Relief Fund, 1831: Tithe Defaulters and Their Occupations." *Irish Genealogist* (Irish Genealogical Research Society, London) 8 (1) (1990): 82–102.

An Index of Surnames of Householders in Griffith's Primary Valuation and Tithe Applotment Books. 14 vols. Dublin: National Library of Ireland, 1970.

Irish Research Group, Ottawa Branch, Ontario Genealogical Society. *Basic Irish Genealogical Sources: Description and Evaluation.* Rev. ed. Ottawa, Ontario: Ottawa Branch, Ottawa Genealogical Society, 1993.

Leahy, David. *County Longford Survivors of the Great Famine: A Complete Index to Griffith's Primary Valuation of Co. Longford.* Raheen, Co. Limerick, Ireland: Derryvrin Press, 1996.

Reilly, James R. "Is There More in Griffith's Valuation Than Just Names?" *The Irish At Home and Abroad* 5 (2) (2d Quarter 1998): 58–68.

———. "The Sacred Tenth: The Tithe Applotment Book as a Genealogical Resource." *The Irish At Home and Abroad* 3 (1995/96): 4–9.

———. "Richard Griffith and His Valuations of Ireland." *The Irish At Home and Abroad* 4 (3) (3d Quarter 1997): 106–113.

———. *Richard Griffith and His Valuations of Ireland.* Baltimore: Clearfield Press, 2000.

Trainor, Brian. "Tithe and Valuation Records for Ulster c.1823–c.1930." Appendix in *Ulster Libraries: Archives, Museums & Ancestral Heritage Centres,* by Robert K. O'Neill. Belfast: Ulster Historical Foundation, 1997.

Sources

Addresses

Data Tree Publishing
  Suite 393, 45 Glenferrie Rd., Malvern VIC 3144, Australia
McGuire, A.O.
  54 Standard Rd., Enfield, Middlesex, London EN3 6DP, England
Morris, Andrew J.
  P.O. Box 535, Farmington, MI 48332

TWENTY-FOUR

Wills and Administrations

We can divide Irish wills and administrations into two categories: pre-1858 and post-1858. Prior to 1858, wills and administrations were under the jurisdiction of the Church of Ireland. After 1858, the jurisdiction changed to the government's district registries. A person who left a written last will and testament had his or her will probated after death by the executors. The other type of record about a person's estate left behind is the estate administration, which was for people who didn't leave a written will. **When you are searching for an Irish will or administration, remember that the majority of people in Ireland, Catholic and Protestant, were too poor to leave a will.**

Reminder

RECORD LOSS AND RECONSTRUCTION

A law of 1857 required that all wills and administrations older than twenty years be sent to the Public Record Office in Dublin, a fateful decision since most of the Irish wills and administrations were destroyed in the office during the 1922 Irish Civil War. A number of the original indexes survived, however. Also, except for the Principal Registry in Dublin, there were transcripts of the district registry wills that survived. Researchers made abstracts of a significant number of wills and administrations prior to 1922 that were donated to the Public Record Office (now the NAI) after the fire to help mitigate the loss.

In addition to will abstracts, copies of wills held by individual families and lawyers have been collected over the years and deposited in the NAI (where they are termed "testamentary documents") and the PRONI. Many testamentary documents from the NAI are on microfilm at the FHL. Accessing a document at the FHL can be difficult, however, since there is no systematic key to the film containing each document. In general, we recommend you check the FHL Catalog under *Ireland—Probate records* and *Ireland—Probate records—Inventories, registers, catalogs* to find lists of the microfilms containing particular documents.

Indexes to the will collections of both the NAI and the PRONI are at the FHL and include

National Archives: *Testamentary Documents Card Index* covers the time period of the seventeenth to the twentieth centuries:

PRONI: *Card Index to Wills (1536–1920)*

Even if the only record that survives is an index, this record is valuable. In the pre-1858 period it states the person's name, place of residence, and the year of the will or administration. After 1858, printed yearly calendars summarize the wills and administrations for the whole island, including those of the Principal Registry at Dublin.

REGISTRY OF DEEDS

Some wills were also recorded with the Registry of Deeds, and it is quite exciting to find one of these when you least expect it. Wills in the Registry of Deeds from 1708 to 1832 have been transcribed and indexed. For additional information, see chapter nineteen.

PRE-1858 WILLS AND ADMINISTRATIONS
Prerogative Court of Armagh

The Prerogative Court had jurisdiction over estates of persons who had property worth more than £5 in more than one diocese. The Prerogative Court was the responsibility of the Church of Ireland Archbishop of Armagh.

Administrations: Indexes are available at the FHL on microfilm from 1595 to 1858.

Wills: Indexes are in Sir Arthur Vicars' *Index to the Prerogative Wills of Ireland 1536–1810* and in manuscript form for 1811 to 1858. Abstracts of the wills are available on microfilm from the FHL in various collections.

Prerogative Court of Canterbury

Wealthy Irish, especially Protestant landowners with property in England and Wales, had their wills probated in the Prerogative Court of Canterbury as well as the Prerogative Court in Ireland. Between 1812 and 1857, Irish wills probated in English courts were subject to an estate duty tax. Abstracts of these wills were kept at the Estate Duty Office in London and were later moved to the PRONI in Belfast. They are on microfilm at the FHL from 1821 to 1857, with indexes from 1812.

Consistorial Courts

Wills were proved in the Consistorial Court of each Church of Ireland diocese. Its jurisdiction was over testators and their property in the diocese. The indexes for some of these Consistorial Courts are published in *Indexes to Irish Wills*, edited by Phillimore and Thrift. Other indexes are available in manuscript form and on microfilm from the FHL. The Consistorial Courts ended by 1858, when the Church of Ireland was no longer responsible for the proving of wills.

When searching the FHL microfilms for the Consistorial Courts, examine both the will index and the administration index. To access a will or administration, it is helpful to know the name of the diocese in which your ancestor lived. The listing below shows which dioceses covered which counties. For counties with more than one diocese, consult Brian Mitchell's *A New Genealogical Atlas of Ireland* to identify which civil parishes were in which dioceses.

For More Info

Church of Ireland Diocesan Jurisdictions	
County	*Consistorial Courts*
Antrim	Connor, Derry, Down, Dromore
Armagh	Armagh, Dromore
Carlow	Leighlin
Cavan	Ardagh, Kilmore, Meath
Clare	Killaloe and Kilfenora, Limerick
Cork	Ardfert and Aghadoe, Cork and Ross, Cloyne
Donegal	Clogher, Derry, Raphoe
Down	Connor, Down, Dromore, Newry and Mourne
Dublin	Dublin
Fermanagh	Clogher, Kilmore
Galway	Clonfert, Elphin, Killaloe and Kilfenora, Kilmacduagh, Tuam
Kerry	Ardfert and Aghadoe
Kildare	Dublin, Kildare, Leighlin
Kilkenny	Leighlin, Ossory
Leitrim	Ardagh, Kilmore
Leix (Queens)	Dublin, Kildare, Leighlin, Ossory
Limerick	Cashel and Emly, Killaloe and Kilfenora, Limerick
Londonderry	Armagh, Connor, Derry
Longford	Ardagh, Meath
Louth	Armagh, Clogher, Drogheda
Mayo	Killala and Achonry, Tuam
Meath	Armagh, Kildare, Kilmore, Meath
Monaghan	Clogher
Offaly (Kings)	Clonfert, Kildare, Killaloe and Kilfenora, Meath, Ossory
Roscommon	Ardagh, Clonfert, Elphin, Tuam
Sligo	Ardagh, Elphin, Killala and Achonry
Tipperary	Cashel and Emly, Killaloe and Kilfenora, Waterford and Lismore
Tyrone	Armagh, Clogher, Derry
Waterford	Waterford and Lismore
Westmeath	Ardagh, Meath
Wexford	Dublin, Ferns
Wicklow	Dublin, Ferns, Leighlin

Will and Administration Abstracts

Major collections of will and administration *abstracts* (summaries of important details from wills) include

Sources

1. Betham's Prerogative Will and Administration Abstracts (pre-1800) (indexed in Virginia Wade McAnlis's *The Consolidated Index to the Records of the Genealogical Office, Dublin, Ireland.*)
2. Sir Bernard Burke's collection of wills for forming Irish pedigrees.
3. The Crossle, Jennings, and Thrift collections of abstracts (indexed in the Eneclann CD-ROM *Indexes to Irish Wills 1484–1858* described later in this chapter).

These abstract collections are at the NAI and on microfilm at the FHL. For lists of additional abstracts and transcripts for particular surnames or dioceses, see John Grenham's *Tracing Your Irish Ancestors.*

Inland Revenue Commission

In the period from 1828 to 1879, you can find Irish will and administration registers with the Inland Revenue Commission. They contain abstracts of all Irish wills and administrations dated 1828 to 1839 and indexes of all Irish wills and administrations for 1828 to 1879. What is important about these indexes is that they list the name and address of the executor or administrator, information you don't find in the Consistorial Court indexes. The Inland Revenue material is at the NAI with microfilm copies at the FHL.

CD Source

CD-ROM Indexes to Irish Wills and Administrations

1. *Indexes to Irish Wills 1484–1858*, by Eneclann Ltd., Dublin, 1999. This CD-ROM provides an index to original records, copies, extracts, and abstracts, totaling more than seventy thousand records. This volume is only concerned with those records that survive in more than index form. Not only does this index include the Testamentary Card Catalogues, Charitable Donations and Bequests Will Extracts, Thrift, and Crossle and Jennings Abstracts but it also indexes the surviving Inland Revenue Will and Administration Registers from 1828 to 1839. The Betham Abstracts and Groves Papers are *not* included. While most of the records are wills or relate to testamentary matters (wills, probate, administrations, etc.), about 10 percent are not. Most of these additional records are marriage licences and assorted genealogical abstracts.

2. *Indexes to Irish Wills*, CD#2 by Andrew J. Morris <http://www.genealogy .org/~ajmorris>. Contains references to approximately 72,900 wills covering the period 1536 to 1858. Includes Sir Arthur Vicars's *Index to the Prerogative Wills of Ireland 1536–1810*, Dublin, 1897; also, *Indexes to Irish Wills*, 5 vols., edited by W. P. W. Phillimore.

3. *Indexes to Irish Wills*. Edited by W.P.W. Phillimore. London, 1909. 5 volumes. CD#34 from Quintin Publications, <http://www.quintinpublicat ions.com>. Contains indexes to wills probated in the following dioceses before 1800: Ossory, Leighlin, Ferns, Kildare, Cork, Ross, Cloyne, Cashel and Emily, Waterford and Lismore, Killaloe and Kilfenora, Limerick, Ardfert and Aghadoe, Dromore, Newry and Mourne, Derry and Raphoe.

A Step-By-Step Research Strategy for Locating Pre-1858 Wills and Administrations

Step By Step

You can see the following strategy applied to a particular case in the case study on page 281.

1. The first place to look is in the surviving indexes. You can use the manuscript indexes, published book indexes, or CD-ROM indexes mentioned before. Be sure to check the Eneclann CD-ROM Will Index because it indexes material not included in the consistorial and prerogative court indexes.

FINDING THE WILL OF EDWARD BIRCH OF CORVILLE, COUNTY TIPPERARY

We were in search of a will or administration for Edward Birch, not knowing if he left such a document. He died in about 1800. We used the following steps in our investigation:

1. Our first step was to look at indexes to wills and administrations for the time period around 1800. This included indexes for the Prerogative Court of Armagh, as well as consistorial courts covering County Tipperary. These are in print and on CD-ROM (see page 280). We found that Edward Birch had a will in 1801 in the Prerogative Court of Armagh, listed in Sir Arthur Vicars's *Index to the Prerogative Wills of Ireland, 1536–1810*.

2. This original 1801 will was destroyed in 1922. So our next job was to see if a second copy of the will has survived. We looked at the card index to testamentary documents that have been collected by the NAI (this index is on microfilm at the FHL and part of the Eneclann CD-ROM *Indexes to Irish Wills 1484–1858*). The index showed that the NAI indeed has collected another copy of the original will, probably from family or lawyer's papers. The NAI gave this will the reference number of T11599.

3. The FHL Catalog lists which T-numbers from the NAI are on which FHL microfilms. With this reference number of T11599, we were able to access a copy of the will on microfilm at the FHL. The will gives such details as the names of Edward's father-in-law, Thomas Walker of the City of Cork; his brother, Richard Birch of the City of Dublin; and his daughters Margaret and Jane Birch by his late wife Margaret.

2. If you find a will or administration in the indexes, examine the collections of wills gathered by the NAI and PRONI for a surviving copy.
3. If no full copy of the will survives, consult appropriate will abstract collections.
4. For the period 1828 to 1858, examine the Inland Revenue Commission will and administration registers. Throughout this period, they will add to your information the name and address of the executor or administrator. Between 1828 and 1839, abstracts of all Irish wills and administrations are in the Inland Revenue Commission registers.
5. In some cases, the index is all that survives. Even in this case, the index may provide an indication of when and where your ancestor lived and died.

POST-1858 WILLS AND ADMINISTRATIONS
District Registries

Since 1858, wills have been proved in district registries or in the Principal Registry in Dublin. All wills proved since 1904 have survived. Copies of wills proved in district registries after 1858 (with the exception of the Principal Registry in Dublin) are available at the NAI with microfilm copies at the FHL.

You can also use compiled yearly calendars of wills and administrations, formally titled "Calendars of the grants of probate and letters of administration made in the principal registry and in the several district registries." These calendars are arranged alphabetically by surname and provide an abstract of the will or administration. Those dating 1858 to 1920 are available on microfilm from the FHL. These calendars are helpful not only in finding the wills and administrations you're looking for but also in locating in which registry a person's document was filed. There is a general index to calendars for 1858 to 1877 for all of Ireland, available at the NAI or on microfilm at the FHL. Eneclann has produced a comprehensive CD-ROM Index to the yearly calendars from 1858 to 1900.

FAMILY HISTORY LIBRARY COLLECTIONS

The staff of the library has compiled a guide, *Irish Probates Register,* to its collections giving appropriate microfilm references. This guide can make the

District Registries for Each County

County	District Registry
Antrim	Belfast
Armagh	Armagh
Carlow	Kilkenny
Cavan	Cavan
Clare	Limerick
Cork	Cork
Donegal	Londonderry
Down	Belfast
Dublin	Principal Registry
Fermanagh	Armagh
Galway	Tuam
Kerry	Cork, Limerick
Kildare	Principal Registry
Kilkenny	Kilkenny
Leix (Queens)	Kilkenny
Leitrim	Ballina, Cavan
Limerick	Limerick
Londonderry	Londonderry
Longford	Cavan
Louth	Armagh
Mayo	Ballina
Meath	Principal Registry
Monaghan	Armagh
Offaly (Kings)	Mullingar, Principal Registry
Roscommon	Tuam
Sligo	Ballina
Tipperary	Limerick, Waterford
Tyrone	Armagh, Londonderry
Waterford	Waterford
Westmeath	Mullingar
Wexford	Waterford
Wicklow	Principal Registry

task of sorting through probate records easier than searching the FHL Catalog for the correct microfilm.

Another helpful source for FHL research is *Index to Irish Probate Films at the Family History Library*, compiled by Joyce Parsons and Jeanne Jensen, which includes names from wills, land and court documents, genealogies, pedigrees, and special collections at the FHL. This index includes the National Archives testamentary documents ("T-documents"), which are in the FHL microfilm collection. The index is available on microfilm and under the title "Irish Records Index, 1500–1920" on the Web site <http://www.ancestry.com> for a fee.

REFERENCES AND FURTHER READING

Sources

McAnlis, Virginia Wade. *The Consolidated Index to the Records of the Genealogical Office, Dublin, Ireland.* 4 vols. Issaquah and Port Angeles, Wash.: by author, 1994–1997.

Mitchell, Brian. *A New Genealogical Atlas of Ireland.* Baltimore: Genealogical Publishing Co., 1986.

Parsons, Joyce and Jeanne Jensen. *Index to Irish Probate Films at the Family History Library.* 2 vols. Salt Lake City, Utah: J and J Limited Company, 1998.

Phillimore, W.P.W. and Gertrude Thrift, eds. *Indexes to Irish Wills.* 5 vols. 1909–20. Reprint, Baltimore: Genealogical Publishing Co., 1970.

Vicars, Sir Arthur, ed. *Index to the Prerogative Wills of Ireland 1536–1810.* 1897. Reprint, Baltimore: Genealogical Publishing Co., 1967.

Archives and Libraries

T he following listing includes libraries and archives that house Irish records and genealogical collections. Some Irish records such as Griffith's Primary Valuation are available at many repositories worldwide. Some chapters of this book have address lists appropriate to their content.

REPUBLIC OF IRELAND

Archbishop Marsh's Library
   Cathedral Ln., Dublin 8, Ireland
Catholic Central Library
   74 Merrion Sq., Dublin 2, Ireland
   phone: (01) 6761264
Cork Archives Institute
   Christ Church, South Main St., Cork, Ireland
   phone: (021) 277809   *fax:* (021) 274668
Dublin Friends Historical Library
   Swanbrook House, Morehampton Rd., Dublin 4, Ireland
Genealogical Office
   2 Kildare St., Dublin 2, Ireland
   phone: (01) 6030200   *fax:* (01) 6621062
General Register Office
   Joyce House, 8–11 Lombard St. East, Dublin 2, Ireland
   phone: (01) 6711000   *fax:* (01) 6711243
Gilbert Library
   138/141 Pearse St., Dublin 2, Ireland
Grand Lodge of Ireland
   Freemasons' Hall, 17 Molesworth St., Dublin 2, Ireland
   phone: (01) 6761337   *fax:* (01) 6625101

Irish Jewish Museum
   Walworth Rd., Portobello, Dublin 8, Ireland
National Archives of Ireland
   Bishop St., Dublin 4, Ireland
   phone: (01) 4783711   *fax:* (01) 4783650
   Internet: http://www.nationalarchives.ie
Guide to the National Archives of Ireland (by Centre for
   Irish Genealogical & Local Studies)
   Internet: http://homepage.tinet.ie/~seanjmurphy/nai
National Library of Ireland
   Kildare St., Dublin 2, Ireland
   phone: (01) 6618811   *fax:* (01) 6766690
   Internet: http://www.heanet.ie/natlib/
Ordnance Survey of Ireland
   Phoenix Park, Dublin 8, Ireland
   phone: (01) 8206100   *fax:* (01) 8204156
Representative Church Body Library
   Braemor Park, Churchtown, Dublin 14, Ireland
   phone: (01) 4923979   *fax:* (01) 4924770
   Internet: http://www.ireland.anglican.org/library/library.html
Registry of Deeds
   Henrietta St., Dublin 1, Ireland
   phone: (01) 6707500   *fax:* (01) 8048408
   Internet: http://www.irlgov.ie/landreg/registry_of_deeds_services.htm
Royal Irish Academy
   19 Dawson St., Dublin 2, Ireland
   phone: (01) 6762570   *fax:* (01) 6762346
   Internet: http://www.ria.ie
St. Patrick's College Maynooth Library
   National University of Ireland, Maynooth, County Kildare, Ireland
   phone: (01) 708 3884   *fax:* (01) 628 6008
Trinity College Dublin Library
   College St., Dublin 2, Ireland
   phone: (01) 608 1189   *fax:* (01) 608 2690
   Internet: http://www2.tcd.ie/Library
University College Cork
   Boole Library and College Archives, Cork, Ireland
   phone: (021) 276871
University College Dublin
   Archives Department, Belfield, Dublin 4, Ireland
   phone: (01) 706 7547   *fax:* (01) 706 1146
   Internet: http://www.ucd.ie/~archives/
University College Galway
   James Hardiman Library, Galway, Ireland
   phone: (091) 524411
Valuation Office of Ireland

Irish Life Center, Abbey St. Lower, Dublin 1, Ireland
phone: (01) 817 1000   *fax:* (01) 817 1180
Internet: http://www.valoff.ie

County and city libraries:
Public Library List for the Republic of Ireland
   Internet: http://www.iol.ie/~libcounc/paddress.htm

You can also write for addresses to:
An Chomhairle Leabharlanna—The Library Council
   53–54 Upper Mount St., Dublin 2, Ireland
   phone: (01) 676 1167/676 1963   *fax:* (01) 676 6721

NORTHERN IRELAND

Armagh County Museum
   The Mall East, Armagh BT61 9BE, Northern Ireland
   phone: (028 37) 523070   *fax:* (028 37) 522631
Belfast Central Library
   Royal Ave., Belfast BT1 1EA, Northern Ireland
   phone: (028 90) 243233   *fax:* (028 90) 332819
General Register Office of Northern Ireland
   Oxford House, 49–55 Chichester St.
   Belfast BT1 4HL, Northern Ireland
   phone: (028 90) 252021/2/3/4/5   *fax:* (028 90) 252120
Irish Baptist Historical Society
   The Baptist Union of Ireland, 117 Lisburn Rd.
   Belfast BT9 7AF, Northern Ireland
   phone: (028 90) 663108   *fax:* (028 90) 663616
Linen Hall Library
   17 Donegall Sq., Belfast BT1 5GD, Northern Ireland
   phone: (028 90) 321707   *fax:* (028 90) 438586
Ordnance Survey of Northern Ireland
   Colby House, Stranmillis Ct., Belfast BT9 5BJ, Northern Ireland
   phone: (028 90) 255755   *fax:* (028 90) 255700
   Internet: http://www.doeni.gov.uk/ordnance/index.htm
Presbyterian Historical Society
   Church House, Fisherwick Pl., Belfast BT1 6DW, Northern Ireland
   phone: (028 90) 322284   *fax:* (028 90) 236609
Public Record Office of Northern Ireland
   66 Balmoral Ave., Belfast BT9 6NY, Northern Ireland
   phone: (028 90) 251318   *fax:* (028 90) 255999
   Internet: http://proni.nics.gov.uk/index.htm
Queen's University of Belfast
   Belfast BT7 1NN, Northern Ireland
   phone: (028 90) 245133

Religious Society of Friends
Ulster Quarterly Meeting, Friends Meeting House, Railway St.,
Lisburn, County Antrim, Northern Ireland
Ulster-American Folk Park
2 Mellon Rd., Castletown, Omagh, County Tyrone BT78 5QY
Northern Ireland   *phone:* (028 82) 243292   *fax:* (028 82) 242241
Internet: http://www.folkpark.com/
Ulster Historical Foundation
Balmoral Buildings, 12 College Sq. East
Belfast BT1 6DD, Northern Ireland
phone: (028 90) 332288   *fax:* (028 90) 239885
Internet: http://www.ancestryireland.com
Wesley Historical Society—Irish Branch
Aldersgate House, 9–11 University Rd.
Belfast BT7 1NA, Northern Ireland
phone: (028 91) 81559

Local education and library boards:
Public Library List for Northern Ireland
Internet: http://www.iol.ie/~libcounc/paddress.htm

ENGLAND

British Library Newspaper Library
Colindale Ave., London NW9 5HE, England
phone: (0171) 412 7353   *fax:* (0171) 412 7379
Family Records Centre
1 Myddelton St., London EC1R 1UW, England
phone: (0171) 233 9233
Friends Historical Library
Friends House, Euston Rd., London NW1 2BJ, England
phone: (0171) 387 3601
Irish Genealogical Research Society Library
82 Eaton Sq., London SW1W 9AJ, England
Ministry of Defence
CS(RM)2, Bourne Ave., Hayes, Middlesex UB3 1RF, England
Public Record Office
Ruskin Ave., Kew, Richmond, Surrey TW9 4DU, England
phone: (0181) 392 5200   *fax:* (0181) 878 8905
Internet: http://www.pro.gov.uk/
Royal Commission on Historical Manuscripts
Quality House, Quality Court, Chancery Ln.
London WC2A 1HP, England
phone: (0171) 242 1198   *fax:* (0171) 831 3550

Society of Genealogists
14 Charterhouse Buildings, Goswell Rd., London EC1M 7BA, England
phone: (0171) 2518799
Internet: http://www.sog.org.uk/

UNITED STATES

Allen County Public Library
Historical Genealogy Department, 900 Webster St., P.O. Box 2270
Fort Wayne, IN 46801-2270
phone: (219) 424-7241 Ext. 3315   *fax:* (219) 422-9688

Detroit Public Library
Burton Historical Collection, 5201 Woodward Ave., Detroit, MI 48202
phone: (313) 833-1480

Family History Library
35 North West Temple, Salt Lake City, UT 84150
phone: (801) 240-2367 (*British Isles Ref*)
Internet: http://www.familysearch.org

Irish Genealogical Society International
Minnesota Genealogical Society Library
(Location) 5768 Olson Memorial Highway, St. Louis Park, MN
(Mailing) P.O. Box 16585, St. Paul MN 55116
phone: (612) 595-9347   *Internet:* http://www.rootsweb.com/~irish

Irish Cultural and Heritage Center of Wisconsin
Emigration Library, 2133 West Wisconsin Ave.
Milwaukee, WI 53233
phone: (414) 345-8800   *fax:* (414) 345-8805

Library of Congress
Washington, DC 20540
Local History & Gen. Reading Room
(Location) Ground Floor, Jefferson Bldg.
(Mailing) Washington, DC 20540-5554
phone: (202) 707-5537   *fax:* (202) 707-1957
Geography and Map Reading Room
(Location) Basement Floor, Madison Bldg.
(Mailing) Washington, DC 20540-4760
phone: (202) 707-MAPS   *fax:* (202) 707-8531
Newspaper and Periodical Room
(Location) Madison Bldg., Room 133
(Mailing) Washington, DC 20540-5590
phone: (202) 707-5522   *fax:* (202) 707-6128
Main Reading Room
Humanities & Social Science Division
(Location) First Floor, Jefferson Bldg.
(Mailing) Washington, DC 20540
phone: (202) 707-4773

The Newberry Library
  Local and Family History Section
  60 W. Walton St., Chicago, IL 60610-3380
  phone: (312) 943-9090
New England Historic Genealogical Society
  99–101 Newbury St., Boston, MA 02116-3084
  phone: (312) 536-5740   *fax:* (617) 536-7307
  Internet: http://www.newenglandancestors.org/
New York Public Library
  Fifth Ave. and Forty-second St., New York, NY 10018
  US History, Local History, Genealogy Division
  Room 315S
  phone: (212) 930-0828   *fax:* (212) 221-3423
  Map Division
  Room 117
  phone: (212) 930-0587
  Periodicals Division
  Room 108
  phone: (212) 930-0578
  General Research Division
  Room 315
  phone: (212) 930-0830
Samford University's Harwell G. Davis Library
  Albert E. Casey Collection
  800 Lakeshore Dr., Birmingham, AL 35229-0001
  phone: (205) 870-2846   *fax:* (205) 870-2644
United Irish Cultural Center Library
  2700 Forty-fifth Ave., San Francisco, CA 94116
University of St. Thomas
  Department of Special Collections
  O'Shaughnessy-Frye Library, Mail #5004
  2115 Summit Ave., St. Paul, MN 55105-1096
  phone: (612) 962-5467   *fax:* (612) 962-5406

CANADA

Memorial University of Newfoundland
  St. John's, NF
  Maritime History Archive
  St. John's, NF A1C 5S7, Canada
  phone: (709) 737-8428   *fax:* (709) 737-3123
  Queen Elizabeth II Library
  St. John's, NF A1B 3Y1, Canada
  phone: (709) 737-7427   *fax:* (709) 737-2153

Metropolitan Toronto Reference Library
789 Yonge St., Toronto, ON M4W 2G8, Canada
fax: (416) 393-7229
Montreal Public Library
Salle Gagnon (Gagnon Collection), 1210 Sherbrook St. E.
Montreal, QC H2L 1L9, Canada
phone: (514) 872-5923
The National Archives of Canada
395 Wellington St., Ottawa, ON K1A 0N3, Canada
phone: (613) 995-5138   *fax:* (613) 943-8491
phone: (613) 996-7458 (Genealogy Desk)
Internet: http://www.archives.ca
The National Library of Canada
395 Wellington St., Ottawa, ON K1A 0N4, Canada
phone: (613) 995-9481   *fax:* (613) 943-1112
Saskatchewan Genealogical Society Library
1870 Lorne St., Regina, SK S4P 2L7, Canada
phone: (306) 780-9207   *fax:* (306) 781-6021
Internet: http://www.saskgenealogy.com

AUSTRALIA

Mitchell Library
State Library of NSW, MacQuarie St., Sydney, NSW 2000, Australia
phone: (02) 2301414
National Library of Australia
Parkes Pl., Canberra, ACT 2600, Australia
phone: (06) 2621111
Society of Australian Genealogists
Richmond Villa, 120 Kent St., Sydney, NSW 2000, Australia
phone: (02) 2473953   *fax:* (02) 2414872

NEW ZEALAND

Auckland City Library
(Location) Wellesley and Lorne streets, Auckland
(Mailing) P.O. Box 4138, Auckland, New Zealand
phone: (649) 377-0209
National Library of New Zealand
Alexander Turnbull Library
(Location) 70 Molesworth St., Wellington
(Mailing) P.O. Box 12-349, Wellington, New Zealand
phone: (644) 474-3000
New Zealand Society of Genealogists
P.O. Box 8795, Symonds Street, Auckland 1035, New Zealand
phone: (649) 525-0625   *fax:* (649) 525-0620

Index